TROUT
FAMILY HISTORY

By W. H. TROUT

Mechanical Engineer and Machinery Designer

—

MILWAUKEE, WISCONSIN

1916

Printed by
Meyer-Rotier Printing Co.
Milwaukee

William Henry Trout

In his 83d year 1916

DEDICATION

While the time and mental effort involved in the make-up of this book is virtually a gift to the whole Trout fraternity, still we particularly wish, to thankfully remember, those among them, who so kindly have gathered for us, so much of this mass of names and dates, and other helpful information, to them, we feel this volume should be, and is, most respectfully, and gratefully dedicated.

Nov 1st 1916.   W. H. Trout

TABLE OF CONTENTS.

CONTINUATION OF TABLE OF CONTENTS.

TYPOGRAPHICAL AND OTHER ERRORS IN HISTORY

Page   48—6th line from bottom "large" for *larger*.

Page   52—2d line from the top "or" for *of*.

Page   60—14 lines from the bottom "immerse" for *immense*.

Page   68—7 lines from the top "It appears on the next page" should have been scored out. The correction is near the bottom of the previous page.

Page   79—Top line "staff" should be *stuff*.

Page   90—16 lines from the bottom, in place of "stop" read *step*.

Page   195—13 lines from the top, in place of "apper" read *upper*.

Page   216—11 lines from the top, paragraph should begin with "We," with semi-colon after "dissipators."

Page   219—Near the middle, "A few after this" should be *A few years after this.*

Page   245—At the bottom there is a statement relating to patents that does not cover the whole situation.

    Patents taken out on my own account, and those assigned to the E. P. Allis Co., and the Allis-Chalmers Co., also the Allis-Chalmers Mfg. Co., number together 25. At least four of them have expired. Seven applications for the Allis-Chalmers Mfg. Co. are still pending; also two for myself. In all 34.

Page   285—At the middle, Professor "Goodwin Smith" should read *Goldwin*. This reference to the professor and Mr. Robertson should read, "Professor Goldwin Smith, a writer of international renown, now deceased, and Mr. John Ross Robertson, now one of Toronto's most distinguished public citizens,"

Page   355—13 lines from the top "Alta" should be in full *Alberta*.

Page   369—There is a grave error in identity in the group picture facing this page. This picture is said to represent David Trout and wife of Manfred, Alberta, but now of Bashaw, Alberta, Canada. This should be William Trout and wife, of Cowper, Saskatchewan, Canada.

ADDED PERSONAL RECORDS

The Harriet Ann Trout, or Stirling Family Tree, on page 298, is not complete in the Hunstman Branch; in addition to Mary Eleanor, who is recorded, there should be Eloise, born March 18, and died March 23, 1913. Also Edith, born November 19, 1915, and Harriett Elizabeth, born November 8, 1917.

Also the youngest son in this sister's family, Mr. John Herman Stirling, an undergraduate of the Ontario College of Agriculture, was united in marriage to Miss Marie Macdonald, daughter of the late James Macdonald of Guelph, Ontario, Canada, on June 20, 1917, the nuptials being most interestingly celebrated at St. James' Church, Guelph. They now reside on a nice twelve-acre fruit farm on Lake Ontario shore, near the old port of Oakville. This forms their present home, and will be the subject of their care.

Also, Alexander Linn Whitelaw, the youngest son of my youngest sister, Mrs. Margaret T. Whitelaw, has interrupted his responsible business long enough to form the marriage union, July 14, 1917, with Miss Mabel Wells, daughter of the late John Wells and Dr. Josephine Wells, now of Toronto, Canada. And in connection with this they both spent the first half of their happy honeymoon at Algonquin park, that large fine forest reservation in Northern Ontario, but are now at home at 100 Pacific Avenue, Toronto, Canada.

Word has been received, February 27, 1917, of the safe arrival in France of Captain Alexander Linn Trout of the 310th Engineers. He is the son of Mrs. Caroline H. Trout of Detroit, Mich.

PREFACE.

Evidently this large book is no mere genealogy. Nor is it a record of ancestry; as the little reliable information given, regarding my great-grandfather George Trout, is all that may be called ancestral. It is just a Family History, as well as a Genealogy; with constant allusion to the conditions of the times, and other incidental matters.

When this was first projected twenty-four years ago, it was intended to mainly follow down the male line—those having the Trout name. Our aunts' families, and those coming in by the marriage relation, were to receive only necessary reference; a record that would need only a good-sized respectable pamphlet to contain it. I wanted to preserve the old time stories and traditionary information, handed down by father and others, before memory might fail, or other disabilities prevent me. After making a good start it had to be indefinitely postponed, and when, after twenty-two years, by the urging of relatives it was resumed, it was with a greatly enlarged purpose, but no definite, complete plan. Such plan as may be found, gradually grew into shape as the history proceeded.

After the recital of the few facts relating to my great-grandfather, George Trout, of London, England, the record really begins with the individual and family life of his only son, Henry George; and continues until his children marry and set up their own households; then we take the line of the eldest son, and follow through the succeeding heirs to the latest great-great-grandheir; then come the other members of this oldest son's family, in the order of their ages.

This results in giving father and his family line greater prominence; and as I am the second heir and the one who tells the story, I am brought to the front more than may seem modest; and while father's story thus proceeds, the relationship to the whole is a matter of constant reference. Besides all the events are in the setting of the social, economic and religious conditions of the times; so that the narrative has breadth as well as definiteness. Thus father's line has much of the general history in it. After it is completed the next of grandfather's children's families is taken up, and the line specially, but briefly considered, till all his eight families receive their attention.

A summing-up chapter, with a tabulated Family Report, concludes the whole family story.

Ten leaves of writing paper are added, with blank ruled spaces, for a convenient and continuous Family Record.

It is not our aim to write a glorification of the Trout family, or even a good pleasing story, but essentially a *true* and *helpful* one. At least true as far as it goes. We do not record all the truth, because it is not all known; and we cannot even tell all that we know, there is not room; also the privacies must be respected. But the great salient facts in the family life, with the special characteristics must have their place in the history, though sometimes they may seem like shadows in the picture, adding lustre to the bright lights beside them.

We may well expect that mistakes may be found, and that some may feel they are not deservedly represented; possibly a few may judge that they are even misrepresented; if they could only know the careful, kind consideration that has been given to those matters, they would have charity for the writer, who thus ventures to discuss personal and family traits, often in a comparative manner; though comparisons are said to be odious.

The extended references to the mechanical careers, of both father and myself, may to some be uninteresting. The page headings, with the book title on the head of the left-hand page, and the subject treated on the right, will enable one to quickly pass over what he may not choose to read; or with this and the table of contents he may readily find any desired subject or passage.

No claim is made to literary ability. It will hardly be expected from one so devoted to mechanics; but we dare to hope that the book may be found to be fairly attractive reading.

Interest will center largely in the twenty-six Family Trees, where the relation of each one to the others is graphically shown, along with the main life dates—birth, marriage and death; also when known and practicable, general residences are noted; so that we not only may know who are our relatives, and how related; but also, where we may expect to find them.

It is to be regretted that there are so few photos of the old fathers and mothers, those obtainable are presented, with many of the later generations, in the best half-tone engravings we can procure.

While we have endeavored to interestingly bring out the relationship and characteristics of this great family connection, of about 1,070 people, the higher and greater relation to our Heavenly Father has not been forgotten. We come to this relation not by our creation alone, but by the Elder Brother, the Redeemer, the Forerunner, who passed the death portal, and ascended to the Heavenly Mansions, to prepare a place for those, of whom "He is not ashamed to call them brethren." And our final wish and prayer is—that in this Father's House there may be an abundant entrance and a glorious reunion.

W. H. T.

322 24th Avenue, Milwaukee, Wis.
November, 1916.

INTRODUCTORY

TO everyone endowed with even an ordinary measure of human ambition and family affection, a knowledge of his progenitors and relatives should be interesting. He should collect all the information that is obtainable, and place it on record for the interest and benefit of his successors. Whether highly or lowly born matters not, for in the changing vicissitudes and conditions of our American life the working man and woman of today may be the parents to the millionaire of the next generation; and the reverse is equally true.

But especially do we need the record of good men and women that we may feel a laudable pride in their connection and be incited to duty by their example, thus maintaining the family credit while being ourselves advanced in the upward way.

Hitherto, in this matter, myself and our connections generally have been grossly careless: We have lived and acted for the present solely, as if the past was of no account, since it could not be changed or redeemed; and the future benefits of those depending on us were too indefinite and uncertain to try to provide for them. The strenuous and all-engrossing conditions of pioneer life is our only apology.

This work was undertaken twenty-three years ago, and prosecuted in the spare time of the noon hours, in the drafting-room of the E. P. Allis Company, Milwaukee, Wisconsin, but the pressure of other matters shelved it to await a more leisurely time, which was certainly long in coming, but which we hope has now arrived, and this self-appointed task may go on to its completion. I now rewrite and reconsider what has been previously done.

Regarding my qualifications for this self-imposed duty, I would say that I am in the direct traditional line, being my mother's first-born, and the eldest living son of my father, who stood in the same relation in his father's family, and I have had the companionship of my older half sister, Mary, who spent the first thirteen years of her life in grandmother's family, and learned from conversation much of the earlier times, as well as some of the current events of that time. Also from my Aunt Harriet, who in her widowhood lived with grandfather, and was, more than others, familiar with their history, she being for a time my teacher.

It is unfortunate for me that I did not take up this matter earlier, when I could get names and dates and facts and figures from the persons who had more complete knowledge regarding them.

The name Trout is uncommon. My letters are never received by others in mistake. I never saw but one man of our name that was not directly related to us, that was C. H. Trout, of Indiana, a very creditable preacher. His parents were Germans, among whom the name is not uncommon; it is by them spelled Traut, but designates the same fish. There is a large family connection of Trouts, centering in Randolph County, Virginia, one of whom corresponded with me (Mrs. Mary S. Terry, née Trout, of Elmwood, Roanoke, Virginia). Their earliest American ancestor came from Kent County, England, before the American Revolutionary war, and as I have learned that grandfather said he had cousins in Virginia, there is no doubt but these are distant connections. I have met several people who knew them, and described them as highly reputable people. We present two halftones from photos of these distant worthy connections, the first being the Hon. John Trout of Virginia. The picture was probably taken about 1863. He was the father of Mrs. Terry and also of the Hon. Henry S. Trout, the subject of the second picture, and at present, 1916, is the president of the National Bank of Roanoke, Virginia. No doubt our English ancestors, as well as those of the Virginia Trouts, came from Germany, but at what time, we have not the slightest knowledge. If a lengthy pedigree were required of us, we certainly would have to hunt up or make one. Maybe with a little doubtful history, and liberal use of the imagination, we might make it appear

HON. JOHN TROUT
ROANOKE, VIRGINIA

RESIDENCE OF WILLIAM TROUT FAMILY 1843
TOWNSHIP OF ESQUESING, ONTARIO, CANADA. PHOTO 1912. (SEE PAGE 67.)

HON. HENRY S. TROUT

Son of John Trout, and President of the National Bank, Roanoke, Virginia

that a certain distinguished ancestor came over the straits of Dover with William the Conqueror, and won renown on his battlefields. But our ambition does not incline that way; it would avail us but little if it did. Better belong to God's nobility, be the modest successors of honest God-fearing parents, than lay claim to titles that are simply the shadows of power that at one time has triumphed over the weak.

ANCESTRY.

Our direct knowledge of ancestry begins with my great-grandfather, George Trout; his home was in London, England. He was doorkeeper for the House of Commons. This was quite an honorable office. He was no mere guardsman, but had charge of all such. He was an officer in livery, had the freedom of the city, and was exempt from military duty. The pay was no doubt liberal, and was the source of his moderate wealth. He had two children, a daughter named Nancy, and my grandfather, Henry George Trout, who was born June 8, 1770. He died January 27, 1852.

He was well educated, with a view to a nautical career, and in his seventeenth year, under the charge of a friendly sea captain, he made a voyage to the West Indies and return, and was seasick the whole time of both journeys. On this account his father's ambition, that he should be a sea captain, was given up. The son's preference, however, was very decided for the army, accordingly without his father's permission, he twice enlisted, and was twice bought off. Finally, seeing such a determination on the part of his son, the father bought a commission, and the son entered the army as an officer. What his rank was at that time is not known. In the war of 1812, he served as adjutant. With his regiment, or a portion of it, he came to Canada about the middle of the last decade of the eighteenth century. He may have remained for some time in the lower provinces, may have been with a body of troops in different places. He was in Toronto, when, as he described, it was a black ash swamp with a few shanties. And probably while at some of those stations, or in some way unknown to me, he made the acquaintance of Rachel Emerson and married her. She was a native and resident of Connecticut, of English parents, and it is not improbable that she may have been connected with the Ralph Waldo Emerson family, though we have no direct clue. He then settled at or near Fort Erie, where he bought two pieces of property; the first I think was a farm, a mile or two from the Niagara River; and a hotel property on the river opposite Black Rock, which had a ferry connection to the hotel; he owning both. He also ran a line of stages into the then New Canadian country, using the farm for raising and keeping horses. This was his occupation up to the American War of 1812.

EARLY HISTORY.

These were the *ante bellum* days, previous to the greatest war of Canadian history. It was the period of my father's childhood, also of most of my uncles and aunts. As far as I can learn, it was a happy period; they lived by the beautiful, far-famed Niagara, near the great expanse of Lake Erie. The Black Rock ferry was the highway of communication between the Canadian settlements and the then infant American nation.

In those days the two peoples were scarcely distinguishable; they were neighbors in a much closer sense than has been common since, being of the same blood and language, with common interests, and such interdependence as is common to people in new countries; they were practically one. My information gives no account or even hint of any tariff wall or customs' officials.

My principal informant, respecting those times and conditions, was my father. Though only eleven years of age when the war began, he had a large personal acquaintance on both sides of the river; in those days, schools were scant, and newspapers almost nonexistent. News travelled and was rehearsed by the individual. Under such conditions we can hardly conceive how much a boy's mind can grasp and retain. In the activities of the hotel and ferry, he had excellent opportunities to gather the news of the times, and some of the unrecorded events of the times preceding. Much of this he told me in my boyhood days, when I was his only companion at work. The audience was small, but the interest was great. Stories about horses, about fishing, hunting, and boating on the Niagara, and stories of the war, which I could compare with the histories, and seldom found them seriously at variance. The interest I manifested in these latter stories seemed to cause him to fear he was telling me too much, that he was arousing in me the soldier spirit, which is latent in most boys.

These conversations occurred principally during the winter of 1846 and 1847. I was then completing my thirteenth year, one year younger than he had been when the war of 1812 closed. He and I worked alone, finishing off the inside of a frame house for James McGlashan in the village of Hurontario, which is now a part of the present town of Collingwood, Ontario, Canada. It was the only time I worked alone with him for any length of time, and the memory of it is pleasant. I was a listener and questioner, and because I lent an appreciative ear, and asked thoughtful questions, I drew out his whole fund of observed facts and incidents, as well as his opinions and judgment regarding them. A previous reading of an abbreviated history enabled me to do this, and fix the relation of many of the events he gave me.

In a reply in regard to what caused the war, he said, the Americans claimed that it was in brief "Free Trade and Sailors' Rights"; the British claimed extraordinary rights and privileges on the high seas; among those was the right to search foreign, or at least American vessels, for British seamen, and if they found any, they would take them away. He gave the stories of the thirteen colonies resisting England; the Boston tea party; the battles of Bunker Hill and Lexington; the character and career of George Washington. He spoke of him as a most skilful general; also as being a good man, and especially kind and considerate of his men, as he would not place them where risks were great.

Though a thorough Britisher, father had nothing but respect for Americans in their efforts for independence and national autonomy. This was at a time when the war feeling had not by any means subsided. Politicians in the United

States, with their spread-eagle oratory, kept it vigorously alive, and of course provoked a counter spirit in Canada. This will show that he entertained no prejudice against Americans, which if he had, it would not prevent his telling squarely the truth; but his information was too general, and his ideas and mental make-up too Christian and cosmopolitan to entertain a bias or prejudice against any people. The same may be said of grandfather; as a soldier he was intensely loyal to his flag and country, but, beyond this, loved truth and justice and fair play generally. Besides this he had an American wife, who retained much of her old love for the American people. On all these accounts, father's remembrances in regard to the war and the events of the early days were much better than the ordinary unofficial information of the time.

Some of his stories were about events that transpired before his time. One, I well remember, except the names; father's memory in this respect was good, but mine is not. A party of about six U. E. Loyalists, who at the beginning of the war of the Revolution left their homes in the Eastern States, and travelled on foot through New York, which was then a wilderness, crossed the Niagara River, and came into Canada, arriving in the fall of the year. Father afterwards personally knew some of these men, and no doubt got his stories quite direct. I knew many of the descendants of those U. E. Loyalists, and one of the originals, my sister Mary's grandmother, Mrs. Frank; when I saw her in the year 1850, she was well started in the nineties, and lived for some years afterward.

When this U. E. party was crossing the Niagara, on one of the large islands in the river they observed an abundance of small wild fruits, and nuts of all the kinds common to the country; so after some prospecting for the location of their new homes, they returned to this island, and built a shanty, with a small addition for a storeroom, which they filled with nuts. They also shot some wild hogs, the progeny of some pigs that had been left by some of the early French voyagers. With this food, and in this home, they passed the winter, and came out in the spring, fat and hearty looking, but really weak and unable for toil, until they had lived for some weeks on ordinary food. Those wild hogs were for a number of years a great help in food supply of the early settlers. They were killed only in the fall. They were nearly as wild and gamey as the wild boars of history. Dogs were frequently killed by them. They were apt to charge on the hunter in a body. His only safety then was to climb a tree, or in some manner get out of their way. I recollect about him telling of a hunting party in which one of the boys was killed; whether by the hogs or an accidental discharge of the gun I am not certain; with the same party two dogs were killed by the hogs.

Father related another instance of two young men, who had gone over to the island to hunt in the fore part of the winter, and before they were ready to return, a blinding snow storm set in with severe cold. Shortly after leaving the island their boat upset, and one of the men was immediately drowned. The other, a good swimmer, and otherwise a strong, hearty man, though sometimes swept off by the rough waves, clung to the boat for five or six hours. Two men on shore heard his call, and went to him in a canoe, but the waves were so rough, and the canoe so small, they could not take him on board, so went back for a larger boat. His last words were "For God's sake, hurry!" On their return they found the boat, but the man was gone. He had been washed off, and was not able to return. The men said that when they saw him the bottom of the boat was icy all over, so were his clothes, and his hair was frozen to his coat collar. The bravery and strong fortitude of that young man, along with his sad fate, enlisted my tender boyish sympathies greatly. An event like that in a sparse population is long and regretfully remembered.

He also told stories of catching fish, not alone with hook and line, but with a seine, similar no doubt to what was done in the ancient days in the Lake of Galilee; also spearing at night with a jack light. Sturgeon were plentiful, some he speared were much longer than himself. I can only particularize one fish story of which father was not an eye witness, so it may be held liable to the usual discount, but I understand that he got the story very direct and did not regard it entirely unworthy of credence. Two boys with their parents, in the daytime, walked up the Niagara River from Queenston. In a narrow channel near the shore they ovserved a monstrous sturgeon; they stole carefully up alongside of him, and both planted their spears into his head; he would have gotten away, but the confinement of the place hindered, so they held on to him till life was extinct. Then with their spears they towed him down to Queenston, where, with help, they got him out of his native element, and into a farm wagon. When his nose touched the front end of the box, the tail reached over the hind-end board of the wagon box and dragged on the ground.

I have already referred to grandfather owning and running a stage line, and necessarily having a large number of horses, so that father was familiar with horses from early childhood. He told of grandfather importing a fine English stallion, for which he employed a highly recommended groom to attend and care for him. The groom thought he could teach the horse some fancy tricks, as if he were only a colt. In trying to accomplish his object he punished and abused the good-tempered creature till his high English horse blood could stand it no longer, so he fought the groom with such ferocity, that it was at the peril of the man's life for the horse to see him unless he was securely tied. When grandfather learned of this condition, he discharged the groom, and for a time took care of the horse himself till he returned to his usual good nature. Nearly three years after this, some officers and gentlemen called, and grandfather with a long halter led out his fine horse to show them. The barnyard was enclosed with a palisade of cedar posts set close together in a ditch, the wide gate of which opened on the street. While the horse was showing his paces at the end of a long halter, his old groom was going by, mounted, and seeing his old charge, turned in at the gate to get a nearer view of him. When about half way up the yard the stallion got notice of him; raising his head he gave one steady brief look, and made a plunge, dragging grandfather on the ground. The old groom, thinking that it was his horse he was making for, jumped off and ran for a small opening in the palisade, where a post had been pulled out, barely escaping the jaws of the horse, which snapped together at his back after he passed through, the horse running head and neck through after him.

GRANDFATHER AND GRANDMOTHER

The grandfather and grandmother that I knew must have been quite different from the active, forceful couple that conducted the hotel along with stage line and ferry opposite old Black Rock, a village that is older than Buffalo, though long since absorbed by it. My memory of grandfather was that of a medium-sized gentleman, with a good amount of snow-white hair, black eyes, and a somewhat weatherworn but kindly and decisive face. His soldier-like bearing never left him, his fine head stood erect on straight shoulders, all of which gave him an expression of quiet natural dignity, with much of the repose that becomes age.

My memory picture of grandmother was that of a large, white-haired old lady, not nearly so neatly built as grandfather, but very matronly and kindly in her manner. Aunt Harriet made her home with them, but grandmother ruled her house in her own beautiful, quiet way. It is easy to understand that a girl born and raised in Connecticut, in the latter part of the 18th century, with the bright intelligence that would suitably match a well-educated young British officer, and subsequent good business man, a woman of that kind with the intensely practical training of the times would be a match for most conditions she might meet. And it was regarded that there was no kind of woman's work or management peculiar to the times, but she could lead in it. Of course, then, she was a good cook, and there is a good story in regard to her prowess in that line.

Four American gentlemen came in a carriage over the ferry, and stopping at the hotel, they wanted dinner. It was then half past one; they said they could remain an hour and a half, and would like some kind of fresh meat. Now, fresh meat in the summer time in those days was not to be obtained on call outside of the cities. Grandmother studied awhile, thinking of what she could best do, when she observed the sow coming into the back yard with her litter of fine one-month-old pigs;

her mind then was soon made up; she would have a roasted pig; she saw a good lively job ahead and began at once. I was not told that she had any help, but think she must have had some help on the details, while she quickly handled all the main operations. Fire and hot water had to be attended to, then piggy had to be caught. She did not send out for the hired man, or gather up some boys to have a noisy squealing time and a fight with the old sow, her guests hearing and enjoying the fun and joking about the job. She got a pail of feed, hoisted the back window, quietly got the sow's attention, and when the sow got her head in the pail and the little fellows were trying to get in there too, she grabbed her choice by the hind legs and landed him inside in her strong, home-made linen apron before he thought of squealing, and after that he had no chance. His blood was soon let out, and he was into a hot bath, his incipient bristles removed, then cleaned inside and out and stuffed. While all this was in progress, the big stone oven was being heated; now the burning brands were drawn out, and piggy inserted. Other parts of the dinner were now attended to, table fully set, the dinner bell rung one hour and a quarter from the beginning, piggy on the big side dish ready for carving. The guests came in, one of them smilingly takes his place at the head of the table, saying, "Boys, this looks pretty nice." "Yes," said the others, "a nice roast, but I am afraid to put a knife into it." "Why?" "Oh! I am afraid he will squeal. I saw the landlady jerk him in through the window alive and kicking, shortly after we came, and here it is now; it looks fine and we will soon know how it goes." The carving showing it was all right and the eating proved it; so they ate and drank and praised the cook.

WAR CONDITIONS

The declaration of the war in 1812 made a great change in the conditions and spirit of the times, those on both sides of the river who were neighbors, now became enemies. Communication was cut off, and war preparation began, militia were enrolled and drill sergeants were in active duty. Home work was left to the old folks and women and children. All males from sixteen to sixty were enrolled. John Graybiel, then a farmer near Fort Erie in upper Canada (now Ontario) was enrolled and called upon to serve as militia man, but being of the Dunker faith, his religious principles would not allow him to fight. Along with him were one or two others of the same persuasion. They would not obey the order. For a long time past, in Canada, such men are exemptd from military duty, but it was not so then. The men were arrested and taken to grandfather's hotel, and tried by court-martial and fined, or sentenced to be kept under guard for a certain time. As they would not pay their fines, they were held. Shortly after this, Governor Brock came into the neighborhood, and hearing of this affair, made careful inquiries regarding their character, occupation and good standing, and ordered their release. And further ordered that any whose religious convictions were clearly apposed to war, and who remained at home, attending to their work or business, should not be molested. As he said we would need good men for times of peace as well as war. This I got from the lips of the saintly John Graybiel himself, in 1857, at his residence in Williamsville, New York. Father also told me the story.

Father told me about families that he knew, being personally familiar with the boys. The youngest in the enrollment would be only five years older than he at the beginning of the war. Those boys, though well brought up, when they began soldiering, soon left home training out of their consideration. They first took on rough, careless, swaggering ways, then learned to lie and get drunk and steal. Of course, their stealing was often only a matter of mischief or to get a change from the regular army diet, but it was clear stealing and they rather gloried in it.

One old Quaker, Ben Tuttle, I think was his name, saw a squad of boys coming around one evening and he knew what they were after; he acosted them, "Well, boys, how do thee do?" "Oh, first rate." "I say, boys, it seems to me it must be awful dry living on hard biscuit or dry bread and salt beef." "Yes, it goes pretty dry, sometimes." "Well, let me give thee some fowls, or a fat sheep for a change?" "No, thank you."

But he insisted and they finally accepted. "Some folks tell me thee steals; now, surely, thee *never* would steal." "Of course, we would not." Certainly old Ben Tuttle never had anything stolen. Another old neighbor was different; he would stay out nights and watch his property with a gun; still, he always lost more than others; some of the boys would decoy him away at the risk of being shot, while others would go in and carry off the booty. One night a small party were out and had poor success. Everybody seemed to be ready for them. The time was drawing near when they had to be in camp. They said, "This is too bad; we can't go back without something." One of them said, "Well, since we can't do any better, we'll go to Dad's, and we will get some ducks there, I am sure." Accordingly they went, and that boy's mother had an easier job counting her ducks next morning.

The people thought it pretty hard for their own militia boys to steal from them, but they could apologize for that. The boys did it for a purpose; but afterwards, when the regulars came on the scenes, they would steal at every possible opportunity, whether they made or lost by it. They were punished if discovered or proven against them, which they always managed to make a hard job. Father told of an instance, when, on a cold winter day, he was out chopping wood, a half dozen regulars came along with their long winter overcoats on and began talking to him, at the same time strategetically executing a flank movement around an axe that his brother George had been chopping with. Father missed the axe at once and charged them with taking it. He was not the least afraid of any of the soldiers, though a boy of twelve years. He was conscious of the prestige coming from being an officer's son. The soldiers knew this, too, and their respect might be judged from the fact, that grandfather's office or duty was full charge of the camp. To the charge of stealing, they replied, "Think of the saucy imp of a boy saying we honest men stole his axe; search us if you want to." And father started to search them. They stood in a circle and would pass the axe from one to the other. He showed the mark of one passage in the snow. He threatened to follow them to the barracks and complain if they did not give it up. Finally, one of them flung it to one side in the snow, and they went away.

Grandfather's hotel, or rather club house, for so it became after war was declared, the officers making it a resort or kind of headquarters. It was a place to bring American officers that had been made prisoners, some of them wounded. At times it was a small hospital. Father related that one prisoner got discouraged and tired of life, and finding a loaded musket, took it into his room and placed it at the foot of his bed, so that the muzzle was directed at his head, then pushed the trigger with his big toe; but he instinctively rolled his head, and the charge passed by the side of his face, burning whiskers and hair. The report brought many into the room. A fellow prisoner started beating him with his crutch for being so cowardly as to try to take his life and then dodge the accomplishment. Aunt Susan informed me that grandmother said that the Americans robbed them of everything in the hotel, that she had eleven feather beds, that the only thing saved out of the house was the family Bible which was buried in the ground until after the war. The house was a convenient place for either army as their turn came to occupy. One of their favorite winter pastimes was cock fighting, and for this grandfather kept a good number of game cocks. Some of those villainous soldiers were prowling around one day, and grandfather missed one of his favorite birds; he started to the barracks in pursuit; they got in about a minute ahead of him; but time enough for them to roll forward the back log of the fire and make a grave in the hot ashes for the fine little fighter, then roll back the log and straighten up the fire, when grandfather came in. He searched carefully the whole place and every man in it, and went away still feeling sure the cock was there. Before getting into their bunks for the night, the soldier boys pulled off the brands and coals from his game roostership, and brought him out, the feathers being burned to a crisp, which along with the skin was nicely removed, showing the flesh beautifully roasted; so they passed around the pieces of adjutant Trout's game cock, enjoying the delicacy, while chuckling at their smartness; and having won the victory, they did the crowing.

I must give one more thieving story. Late one fall after a number of beeves had been killed, grandmother concluded to make her winter's supply of candles, as usual then, by the old dipping process; being an ill-smelling, greasy, dirty operation, it was done away out from the house with a special fire and a large kettle. She got the help of a widow who lived about a half mile away. The two were engaged at the work till late in the evening, having made up a large stock. They would have taken them in that night, but they were not sufficiently cooled and hardened, which they would be in the morning. The women went into the house, had their tea, and the widow started for her home; shortly after that, two of those brave regulars were snooping around and spied the white candles in their racks; so they went to work and stripped off from the sticks enough candles to fill their empty haversacks, and went off; being late and most of the people in bed, there seemed to be a poor chance of their getting rid of their loads that night, but as they were going along they saw the light in the widow's house, and turned in. After knocking they were admitted; they got off a good plausible story to explain how they came to have the candles, and offered them for sale cheap. "Well," said the woman, "come here and put all your candles on this table," which was at the back side of the room, "So I can see what you have, and I'll buy them," and as the last of the candles were being lifted out, she went and closed the door, got a broom, and with the handle pounded on the board floor above, for the boys to come down and make prisoners of those thieves that had stolen Trout's candles. In less than two seconds the scamps were away with knapsacks and candles left behind, and no one in the house, but the widow. Illustrating the text, that the wicked flee when no man pursues.

WAR STORIES

Father's tales of the war of 1812 begin with General Brock's career, or Governor Brock as he was both Governor and General. Father had seen him, I think, several times. On account of grandfather's house being a central meeting place, he had opportunities of seeing officers, and other distinguished men, that few other boys had, and at his age, eleven to fourteen, when powers of observation and attention are most alert, and the impressions most lasting, this, with his truth-telling habit, make his statements deserving of respectful attention.

Governor Brock was described as a large man, genial and pleasant in manner, his speech indicating lowland Scotch origin. He was always buoyant and confident, and brave to a fault. Under his management, the war was prosperous from the British standpoint; Detroit was taken, and Michigan was held by British troops, and I think it was during his regime, but not directed by him, that General Rial with a body of volunteer Canadian militia, captured and burned Buffalo. Father said the militia men volunteered readily, as they had repulsed an attack on Fort Erie, I think, or some place in the neighborhood, and the boys blood was up after their recent victory. The burning of Buffalo, however, was in retaliation for the burning of Niagara on-the-Lake, by the Americans, a short time previous. Both were war's barbarities; but the Niagara was the worst, being done without provocation and in the winter time.

Father's account of the battle of Queenston Heights, was very definite, particularly as to the locality and nature of the ground. In June, 1856, when I was returning from the Williamsville Academy, Williamsville, New York, in company with Mary and John, Wm. Frame and his younger brother James, we had to wait in Lewiston several hours for the Toronto boat. We left Mary and James at the hotel and the other three of us went to see the long suspension bridge connecting to Queenston. We went across it. I wanted to go up on the heights, and see Brock's monument, and look over the old battle ground. They objected and I went alone, and made the most of an hour and a half before the coming of the steamer. My imagination based on father's description had pictured a more rocky precipitous hill. On the Queenston side, I saw no difficulty in ascending it, almost anywhere. The side toward the river was much more inaccessible. The leveling process of more than forty years had been going on. The forest had all been cut down, not even stumps remained. Portions of the hill showed the outcropping of rock, which in the earlier days had no doubt been much bolder. The road up the hill from Queenston to the monument, on which according to father's account, Brock was shot, was still there going up in a slanting direction as father described. He said the Americans occupied the crest of the hill and the column of British was marching up this road, with Brock on or near the head of it, when he and McDonald, his aid, were shot. He said the Americans, when firing, marched in a circle, loading their guns when turning around, away from the brow of the hill, and delivering their fire when coming opposite the road; so that a constant hail of musket balls was poured down the road on the ascending column. After the shooting of Brock, the column retreated and General Sheaff took command. According to father's information, General Brock was advised by General Sheaff, not to make a direct attack, but as father understood, Brock did not want to waste any time. He contrasted General Brock's impetuosity with General Sheaff's caution and coolness, representing Sheaff as an old veteran, that knew the value of good preparation. He quietly sent part of his force to ascend the hill much farther to the north, out of sight of the enemy, while with a part he remained to keep their attention on Queenston, and at the concerted time, the advance was made from front and rear, so that the battle soon became a rout. The only side open to retreat being the way they came, and it was impossible for a large body of men to get quickly down the hill on the side of the river and live. So out of fifteen hundred men, eight hundred were made prisoners, about three hundred were killed and wounded, and four hundred escaped wtih the help of boats from Lewiston.

The connection of the occurrences which I am now about to relate with regular history of the times, is what I am at present unable to determine; an examination of a good history would no doubt place them. Their accuracy as to fact, I have no reason to question.

An invasion of Canada was planned by a small force of Americans to take place on a certain night and a certain Captain King volunteered or was detailed with a hundred men to go ahead and clear the way. He was perfectly familiar with that part of the country, knew the location of the sentries, etc. He engaged to clear the river bank of British troops for three miles, and hold it for three hours, during which the main body was to cross the river and disembark in the early morning. He performed his part of the contracted program; but his superiors with the main body failed badly in theirs, as we shall see. About one o'clock in the morning, the night being very dark and rainy, he landed with his company below Fort Erie. The British troops were quartered in the houses, as most all of the owners had deserted them. King landed his company with perfect secrecy, and their movement on shore was so quietly managed, that the sentry was taken by surprise, and captured or killed at his post. He then placed his men in the best positions and alarmed the village, and as the British militia filed out of the houses they were shot down. At one large two-story house that was filled with troops, the dead were piled upon one another around the door.

Father told an incident of this warfare butchery to show how some men can be mutilated, and still live, and others die with scarcely a perceptible cause. He gave me the name of the first, but it is forgotten. He was a Canadian militiaman. He was running from this large house and got nearly ten rods away, when an American musket ball passed through both hips. While lying on the ground groaning, a squad of King's men came along, completing their assigned work, and a soldier, either from brutality or questionable humanity, stabbed him through the abdomen. This made him complain worse and another said, "Oh! put him out of pain," and the butt of his musket came down on his face and broke his jaw, while the first with his bayonet stabbed him again in the eye; but instead of going through the base of the brain, it came out at his ear. Some time before morning, no one knows when, he turned over, and dragged himself to the house, by his hands and arms only, and entering, went up two flights of stairs to the garret and lay on a pallet of straw. While there, a cannon ball from the American block house at Black Rock, came on its errand of destruction, and passing through the plate of the house, tore off a large splinter, which, after partly scalping him, remained sticking in between scalp and skull.

In the morning, after, the wounded were cared for, and the dead collected, and while they were still looking for more soldiers in out of the way places; one of the surgeons noticed the trail of blood on the stairs, and said some poor fellow had gone up there, and following it up, he found his man in the garret, where a close examination proved him to be still alive, but perfectly insensible. He was brought carefully down. The surgeon examined him, pronounced him a very bad case, but with a possibility of life, as none of his five serious wounds were surely mortal. They fixed him up and in less than three months, he was around again, with a deformed face, from the broken jaw and the blind eye; otherwise he was all right. He could drink just as much whisky as he ever did, and was just as wicked as before. A few months after, he was shot by an Indian in a drunken row, when one rifleball through the head, that scarcely showed a trace of its passage, instantly killed him.

Captain King, the dashing leader of this lively American advance party, after clearing the river shore for about a mile each way, was quietly waiting for the main body of his comrades to come over and support him, as they had engaged to do. In the meantime the British troops rallied, and were determined to find out what scared and hurt them so badly. They soon discovered King and his party, and before daylight they were all prisoners. About 9:00 a. m., the main body embarked in a large number of boats of various sizes, and as they were in full view of the British from the start, every necessary preparation was made to receive them. The British officers concluded that sufficient troops had been concentrated to take the whole invading force prisoners. So they drew up a long thin line of militia, a few rods from the shore, and had some good reserves under cover close by. Strict orders were given to the militia, not to fire until the word of command was given. So they waited, and watched the approaching line of boats as they gradually drew nearer. When they came within musket shot, and no command was given, the boys began to get very nervous. They were eager to pay back what King's men had done the night before. But all were not of that mind. The major of the regiment was known to be a little weak-kneed, when opposed to danger, but strong in the legs going from it. He was nervously pacing back and forward in front, when he suddenly remembered he had important business with the general, and off he started. Grandfather called to him to stay at his post; but that was not according to his ideas. He "skedaddled"—though that word was unknown at that time. Some time after this the same major was expressing some courageous wishes, that the Yankees would only come over, so they could have the fun of clearing them all out. A woman, overhearing, said, "Oh! Yes! I do wish they would come, we would have the fun of seeing those long boots running away with you over that green, making for the woods in brave style." The women of those days, had no use for a man that would not fight. The line of American boats were drawing near to the shore. The commanding officer stood upon the bow of a large bateau in the center of the line and slightly in advance, waving his long gleaming sword high in the air. He called out to be heard by his own men, and the British quite as well, "Come on, the day is ours', come on, come on." A half-breed Indian, accompanying the Canadian militia, was at one end of the line, behind a stump, close to the river. He, hearing and seeing the officer wave his sword, said, "I'll stop your bragging," so drawing his rifle on him. The officer sprang into the air and fell into the water dead. His comrades caught his body and drew it into the boat. The moment this shot was fired, every man in the line began firing. The officers tried to stop them, grandfather and others were going in front of the ranks and knocking up their muskets, and while they ceased in one place, they began firing in another, making it so hot for the Americans, that though coming up to the shore, and some almost ready to land, they turned and went back. Father was not a witness to this little fight, but it was a matter of common conversation and took place a short distance below Fort Erie. Some weeks after this, father and a number of boys went out in a boat, he was in the bow with a spear, looking out for fish, and saw something shining brightly on the bottom. An examination with the help of the spear, showed it to be a sword. So hooking the spear into the guards about the handle he drew it up, and to his unbounded joy, it was a magnificent, long sword, bright and shining, with engraved and gold handle, but no scabbard. He took it home. Grandfather told him it must be the American officer's sword. Being so long in the water and having no sheath, it soon began to rust. A British officer who had lost his sword, spied it one day, and with grandfather's permission he borrowed it, and that was the last that was known of it. Father was sorry he had not kept it hidden. It would have been such a fine memento of the great war. When the war had actively gotten under way, grandfather moved his family with the necessary effects to his farm, back from the river a mile or two. The hotel then became entirely officers' headquarters, till it became riddled by shot from the American block house at Black Rock. This block house and Fort Erie played the artillery game between them, seemingly not that either was doing the other any damage, but they wanted to keep a little busy and let no one sleep. Uncle George, grandfather's eldest son, would be frequently down about his old home; so also, would father, who was the second son. Sometimes Uncle George would play a dodge game with the American cannon balls. Their principal range was a short distance in front of the old hotel. He would run out from it into the open street, where he could get a good view of the American block house, and when he saw the jet of smoke issue from it, he would then run back up the step of the hotel, and watch where the ball would strike. When engaged in this way one day, the ball came, and plowed up a furrow in the street where he had been standing, then turning out of the ground it came up and struck the hotel, some distance above his head; knocking off some boards, it glanced outwards and down again to the street, where, after a few more capers, it came to its rest, and Uncle George went out and picked it up. An officer who had witnessed the performance went in and told grandfather, who was in one of the back rooms, and that was the end of Uncle George's cannon play.

Father gave me a number of interesting stories about the battle of Chippewa, all of which I do not fully recollect, stories of personal bravery, as usual with me, the names are forgotten. According to the description, the Americans crossed the river in the morning. General Rial, who commanded the British troops, had not sufficient force to attach them, but sent for reinforcements. General Brown of the Americans for some good reason did not attack him, but marched down to Chippewa creek, went into camp, and fortified his position. The next morning when General Rial was ready to begin the attack, he found the Americans behind deep ditches, or a thick abatis, made of the tops of trees, the ends of the branches being cut off sharp, so that no horse or man could go over or through them. At one place they had three rail fences, built very close to each other, ten feet high. The Canadian militia men said, "It is always the way, leave the Yankees alone over night, and they will dig themselves in, as secure as a ground hog in his hole." But the Yankees did not choose to confine fighting very long behind their defences, still with their cautious policy, they kept largely to the woods, in which the greater part of the battle was fought. This placed the British regulars at a disadvantage, as they were unfamiliar with the methods of bush fighting, in which the Canadian militia were about as much at home as the Americans. It was a decidedly lost battle to the British.

Father gave one story of this battle, that illustrates the style of fighting. At this occurrence, the Canadian militia were slowly advancing, crowding back the Americans, both fighting in the woods, under cover. A British major rode up toward the front line, when partly in front and a little to one side, an Indian jumped up from behind a big log and presenting his gun to the major, said, "Me Nider," meaning Oneida, which tribe was an ally to the Americans. He, of course, intending to take the major prisoner. A young militiaman, McDougall, seeing the Major's peril, jumped from cover and though his gun was unloaded pointed it and said to the Indian, "I'll shoot you," and advanced toward the Indian; who, as McDougall came close, let go his gun, and instead of surrendering, grappled McDougall and instantly threw him; but the fear of the Indian's knife nerved him to a great struggle, and he threw the Indian off, who at once ran away. But the major's turn now came in, and the Indian was shot. McDougall saw him throw up both hands and drop, and he felt a pang of regret for the brave fellow, who dared in front of their line to undertake what he did and handle himself so well. He examined the Indian's gun and found it empty as well as his own. Both had been trying the scare business, or as we say now, they put up the bluff, and neither could make good.

In a few weeks after the battle of Chippewa, the battle of Lundy's Lane or what the Americans call the battle of Niagara, was fought. This was one of the most memorable of the war, being a hard contested battle, great bravery and skill were manifested on both sides. Father sketched for me the position of the armies, and the situation of the country. He said that General Scott advanced with two columns of the Americans, not on the public roads, but in two well separated strips of woods, which reached nearly up to the British position, evidently intending to surprise and outflank them, which he almost accomplished. Major Jessup under orders from General Scott extended such a flanking movement a little before dark. (See American account.)

The British certainly had no idea of his close proximity. According to the history he had no idea that he had so large a body of British in front of him. While Scott's columns were convening where the two strips of woods united, two women who had been making an afternoon visit to some neighbors, were returning after tea, on a path through the woods. When pleasantly chatting along on their journey, they were suddenly met by two American officers, and looking around they saw, as they afterward said, that the woods were full of Yankees. They started to turn back, but the officers told them to stop, and coming close, courteously informed them, that they were prisoners. They replied, "Oh! you surely won't make women prisoners!" "Yes, we must, if we let you go, you will tell where we are, you must march with us for a while, and we'll let you go." They looked imploringly at their captors and began to cry. "Then it will soon be dark and we can't get home, we must get home to our children; we'll never tell a word about it." After a little hesitation by the officers, the women were sworn by the uplifted hand, not to tell any-one, until the next day, then they were conducted through the advancing columns and allowed to proceed on their homeward journey; which was at a lively rate. On their way, they came to a house where several horses were tied. Looking in, they saw three or four officers, grandfather being one of them. The women called out, "Why aren't you with your men?" "Why, what's the matter?" "Oh! Matter enough, get to your men." "What's up?" "We're sworn not to tell." So they jumped on their horses, and started the way from which the women came, when the women called out, "Don't go that way, for you will never get there." So they took a more round-about course, but never got to their commands till the battle was nearly over. It seemed at every turn they would come out on the wrong side of the American army. Grandfather had no special duty in the battle. He was there as a volunteer. His regular duty being the charge of the camp.

Grandfather, or perhaps grandmother, seemed to have feared that their house was in a dangerous position; because she and the family went away from it, and spent the night in a widow's small house in a glen, near the battle ground, but out of the way of the army movements. They were within hearing of the musketry firing. It was the month of July, the night was calm and the weather hot. At the beginning of the battle, they heard the artillery men knocking down the fences, and driving their field pieces over the rails. Firing began at about dark, but only at irregular intervals, until about ten o'clock; from that time till midnight it was one unceasing roar of musketry and artillery. Then it became intermittent and slackening, till 2 a. m., when it ceased entirely. Of course, there was no sleep for any one in that part of the country on that night. Next morning at sunrise father wanted to go to the battle ground, but grandmother would not allow him, until at least she heard the news. He argued with her that it made no difference, that if the Americans won and held the grounds they would not interfere with the boys; it would be all right anyway. But grandmother would not yield to his urgency, until she learned that the Americans had retreated and were away from that part of the country. Father went with boyish hopes that he could find a sword, to replace the fine one he had lost; also to get a nice American rifle. But he found guards posted on every road leading to the battle grounds, and those guards warned him to keep away, so all he could do, was to get on to the highest, nearest place he could and overlook the scene. He saw men moving about, gathering up the dead and wounded. He also saw what I have not seen referred to in any account of the battles—the fires for cremating many of the mutilated bodies of the slain, mostly Americans. He described the method by which this was done. A square pen, of chestnut rails, two rails high, was first made; this was floored over with two or three tiers of chestnut rails. On this was laid a tier of bodies which were enclosed by another pen. Then another floor of dry rails, and its tier of bodies, etc. If the third tier was laid it would be the final one. The pile was then set on fire. This is substantiated by Martin McLellan of Alton, Canada, who gave me a traditionary story from his granduncle, who was in the battle and saw and helped with the burning.

I asked my father, why this was done? It seemed to me barbarous. He said it was not on account of any inhumanity toward the Americans, for some of the British soldiers were disposed of in the same way. He said it was on account of the extremely hot weather. This 25th day of July, 1892, is an anniversary of this battle, and the thermometer stands today at noon, which is the time of this writing, in the drawing office of the E. P. Allis Company, Milwaukee, Wisconsin, at 94 degrees Fahrenheit. On such a day as this, the conditions of the bodies can be imagined, but would not be nice even to describe. But I think there was another reason besides the hot weather and the work of digging graves and burying. I think the depth of the soil above the limestone rock in that part of the country is not sufficient for a grave. It is so in other places of the same formation and no doubt was so here, as the place was not over a mile from the falls of Niagara.

This battle is claimed by the Americans as a victory; and the same claim is uniformly made by the British and Canadians. General Brown in his despatches says, that he attacked and drove the enemy from his position, captured his cannon, and a large number of prisoners, among them being General Rial and some of his staff officers. This is true but not the whole truth. General Rial was captured by his own mistake. In the dark he rode right into a body of American troops, thinking they were his own men. The British did fall back from positions in order to be in better form. A battery was captured in a brave and clever manner, but the guns were left on the field. Father told how this capture was made; a small body of troops crept up under cover of a fence along which bushes grew, till they were near the battery and practically surprised the gunners. More prisoners were taken by the British than by the Americans; also the killed and wounded by the American's account was greater on their own side, than on the side of the British. The Americans retreated, leaving the British in possession of the field, which from time immemorial is regarded as proof of victory. It is said the Americans fell back to camp in order to reform and renew the fight; that may have been General Brown's intention, but he was wounded, as was also General Scott; and General Riply, who was left to the command, evidently thought it prudent to get away as far as he could, so the retreat was continued into Buffalo. Father says, that next morning after the battle, there was not an American within ten miles of the battle ground, and the American dead were three to one of the British. This, of course, was learned from the conversation of the time, or from grandfather.

A regiment of royals, or most likely only a portion of the regiment, was afterward in the famous field of Waterloo. John Loyd, of St. Vincent, Ontario, Canada, was one of those. He told me, the fighting, in that hot night of July, was as close and hard as any he ever experienced. He said they were giving ground a good part of the night. He said the Royal's white breeches made them a plain mark for the Americans. While the blue or gray uniforms of the Americans were indistinguishable. Loyd regarded it as an undoubted British victory obtained by plain hard fighting.

The greater part of the American army fell back to Buffalo, under command of General Riply; Yet General Brown, having learned of its movements, ordered it to recross the river, and occupy Fort Erie. Which was done without opposition. They then enlarged and strengthened the work, mounted more cannon and prepared to hold the place. The British army came on, threw up breastworks and mounted artillery in order to retake the fort. So there was fighting of some sort every day for several months. A storming party of the British captured a portion of the works, and held it against repeated assaults, when an explosion occurred, which is claimed to have been accidental, destroying this portion, and inflicting severe loss on the British. Typhoid fever broke out in the British camp, which became like a general hospital. The Americans made a brilliant and effective sortie, causing great loss in killed and wounded and spiking the cannon. After this General Drummond, who I think commanded the British, retired and let the old fort alone.

Grandfather was through this whole series of fights and bombardment, and father was never farther away than to be out of reach of immediate harm. He was not always an eyewitness, but an earwitness, as he could hear the artillery firing, and the conversation about it from some who were engaged in it. He described the blowing up of the part of Fort Erie that was retaken by the British, and the death and the devastation occasioned by it, and gave the names of officers, which I have forgotten. One, who I think commanded the storming party, grandfather said was carried past him, by four men, on a litter, that there was scarcely a rag of clothing on his body, which was black from head to foot. He had been blown two hundred feet over the rampart and was picked up outside of the fort. Grandfather spoke to him, and asked if he suffered any pain? He replied, "None." He died in a few hours. These were trying times for all concerned.

The Americans, shortly afterwards, dismantled and evacuated this fort, and I think it has not been used as a fort since. This is the close of the last but one, of the Niagara campaigns. More blood was shed on this Niagara peninsula, than on any other similar portion of territory, in either of the two countries.

Before leaving this war subject, I must tell one more story. A Colonel in the Canadian militia, Fitzgibbon might have been his name, I am not sure, was well known for bravery and ability in both opposing armies. The colonel owned a farm near the seat of war. His wife and children were taking care of it, to the best of their ability, while he served his country. They commenced making hay. He obtained leave of absence and went to help them. An American officer, whose small command was not many miles away, heard by some means of the colonel's farming movement, and thought it would be a neat, smart thing to go out and catch him. The colonel had a fine farm, with a large barnyard about twenty rods from the road. A lane led straight away from the road to the barnyard, in the center of which stood the barn, broad side to the road. It had the usual large doors, and driving floor to go through it. Back of the barn was a large wheatfield, bounded by woods, the field sloping down toward the woods. One day he was on top of a load of hay, pitching it off into the mow, with his wife and two daughters storing it away. One of the girls, looking out, saw the lane nearly full of Yankees. She called out to her father, who dropped his fork and slipped down at the front end of the load, ran out between the horses and straight for the woods. One column of the men ran straight through the barn after him, two other columns went around each end of the barn, and all three columns fired at and about the time he jumped the fence, into the wheatfield. The mother and girls got down off the mow before the Americans got in, and by every means tried to prevent the firing; and as they saw him fall down from the fence they were sure he was killed, but soon after they saw the wheat stalks in motion, and a few who had not previously fired, delivered their shots. Presently they saw his head above the wheat, running in a furrow for the woods in fine style. By the time the guns were reloaded and fired the second time, he was well advanced, and was soon clear away. Like the Indians who once attacked Winfield Scott, they were sure they must have hit him some place, but they did not. Imagine for a moment the scene, when an hour or so afterwards, the father returns to that family.

An examination of the fence showed it to be literally torn up with bullets. When lying on the ground, the colonel knew how close he was to them. Father said, the reason they missed him, when the second round was fired, was that he was running down hill, and in such a situation most marksmen are liable to overshoot.

AFTER THE WAR.

After the close of the war, in 1815, there was a period of six or seven years of which I have but little information. Grandfather's business, with his buildings, stock and chattels, were almost, if not wholly, destroyed, the land only remaining. The farm near Fort Erie, would likely be his only recourse for a livelihood. There are usually hard times after a war. It was in this time, no doubt, that father was apprenticed to a carpenter and millwright. One of those generally useful men, that could build most anything that happens to be required by the times or the need of the situation. This trade was father's choice, and grandmother backed him. Grandfather thought he might not succeed in it and, it seems, preferred some other; but the two prevailed against the one. As usual, I do not recollect the millwright's name, except that his first name was Charles; and I remember this, because it was in a story that father sometimes told to show the risk that is sometimes run in scare games. This millwright boss of father's was one of those cool philosophic men, that dared to question anything that was not supported by clear and irre-frangible proof. His reasoning discarded the devil, along with ghosts and witches and other uncanny things. On this account some called him an infidel; but father never did. He respected him highly; though not religious, he was in general terms, a good man. Now for the story. On a certain New Year's Eve, in the olden time, a party of young men, who were spoiling for rough, lively fun, concluded that it would be a fine, and rather meritorious joke, to get up a good scare on the old millwright. Accordingly, they fixed up one of the biggest and cleverest of their number, to represent Satan. He had on a most satanic false face, above which was a pair of bull's horns, with their skull connection covered by the hairy skin between and around them. This was mounted on a pad on top of his head. He also had a buffalo skin coat with chains and other satanic paraphernalia, and so made his way to the millwright's home, with his companions close in the rear. It was the usual log house of the time, though a good one. The end was toward the road, with the door close to the left hand corner; at the same end and in the center was a large stone chimney. The millwright sat in a chair, leaning against the chimney, and with his right shoulder toward the fire. He was reading aloud, by the light of the fire, to his wife, who sat in front of the fire, also facing him. Satan came unannounced, opened the door very quietly, and as quietly closed it, and advanced from the dark passageway, till near the millwright, when his wife observed him. In great fright she threw up both hands calling, "Charles! Charles!" and fell to one side on the floor. Charles did not wait for more than a glimpse of the figure, arose, and bidding Mr. Devil good evening, got his hand on an old musket barrel that was used for a fire poker, and with a powerful swing, he landed the heavy breach end between the two horns and Satan dropped in a heap on the floor. Next he went to rouse up the old lady, and while engaged in this, Satan gets up and begs, "Don't hurt me, let me go," and off he went. It was found afterward, that the bull's skull was broken by the force of the blow, so that it, with its padding, was what saved the young chap from being killed.

Father had another good short story of the times, to show how a bad parental example returns upon the parent. A certain wealthy, but very unprincipled man, whom we shall call Smith, had a son, Smith Jr., twenty-one years of age. One of those early, but rare, parliamentary elections was in process. The brother-in-law of Smith Sr. was one of the candidates. The opposing candidate's name was Swazie. Freehold suffrage was the only kind at that time. Smith Sr. calls his son, saying, "Here is the deed of the Mill Creek farm, made out to you, take this with you, saddle the bay mare, and go to the polling place, and vote on it; then bring the deed back to me (intending of course to burn it) and be sure to vote for Swazie. *Not* for uncle." "All right, father," and the son went off, carrying a high head. And instead of going to the polls, he went direct to the registry office, and had the deed duly recorded. Then went to the polling place, and contrary to orders, voted for his uncle. When he returned, he handed the deed to his father, who saw the certificate of registration, and angrily exclaimed, "How dare you do that?" "Why," he replied, "it is my property." "Did you vote for Swazie?" "No, I voted for uncle," and moving away from his father's presence he coolly remarked to the amused crowd: "Well, father learnt me."

REMOVAL TO NEW HOME.

After the conclusion of the war, grandfather filed a claim with the Canadian government for his losses on its account. These claims were not adjusted for five or more years. The Niagara properties were sold, and grandfather lived for a year or two, at either Wellington Square, or Burlington, I am uncertain which. He was finally awarded eight hundred acres of wild land in the township of Erin, which at that time must have been newly surveyed, and was at least twenty-five miles north and beyond the settlements, which were mainly at or near the Lake Ontario coast. He was about forty miles north-west of Toronto. Upon this he settled in the year 1821.

Grandfather and family no doubt experienced most all the trials and hardships peculiar to the early settlers of the woods. But these conditions were so common that they were scarce worth talking about. The triumphs over them were a constant gratification, and there was the close kinship with nature, making new adaptations, and finding new discoveries, giving perpetual hope and constant buoyancy of disposition and character.

I have scarcely any information regarding the journey from Burlington to Erin, a distance of over fifty miles, if they could go direct, which was very far from being the case. When this history was commenced, Aunt Susan, who was grandfather's youngest daughter, and the only one of his family then living, gave me in a letter some reminiscences of the last day of this journey, she was then (the fall of 1821,) coming five years of age. She said the road was exceedingly bad. It would be the most primitive kind of a bush road. Everyone that could walk had to do so. She said she got very tired, and it was wet and cold, and they stopped and made a big fire by the side of the road, and they got warmed and dried. No doubt they had their lunch at the same time. She said, "When we started again, mother wrapped me up, and tied me between two beds on the wagon." Uncle John, who was the next and the baby of the family, was no doubt served the same way. "That night we came to Mr. Howe's house, which was two miles from our shanty, which your father and Brother George, built for us." She described Howe's house, or rather log shanty, as being built against a bank (no doubt clay), the fireplace being dug out of the bank. The clay thus removed would most likely be worked into a mortar to plaster on to the inside of the cobbled up sticks, that would be built up for a chimney. She said the ground was the only floor, and, each side of the chimney, seats were dug in shape for sitting near the side of the fire. The roofs of each shanty were usually made of broad sheets of elm or basswood bark. Though Mr. Howe, and possibly a few others, preceded grandfather, yet he and his boys were the really active pioneers in that part of the country. To show the difficulty of getting in supplies,

father related a journey which he made. In the fall of the
first summer in the woods, salt was wanted in the settlement
very badly. Grandfather sent father to Burlington to bring
in a barrel. He took a pair of young steers with nothing but
the yoke on them; also, an axe on his shoulder, and nearly a
week's provisions. The steers were to find their own feed
on the way. He took the most direct route possible, going
through the native woods most of the way. Just before coming into Burlington, he selected a sapling with a divided trunk
forming a crotch, like the letter "Y" with a greatly extended
stem, in the end of which he cut such a notch as would secure
it in the ring of the yoke; leaving the forked end to drag on
the ground. He also twisted some small tough saplings into
withes, and cut them off close to the ground. Having purchased the salt, he next, by means of the withes, securely tied
the barrel on the crotch of the sapling. The two ends of the
crotch, projecting behind the barrel, served as the runners of
a sleigh. It was all tied and well secured to the steers, that
wherever they could go, the barrel was sure to follow, over
logs or stones, or among thick trees, as the case might be, so
in due time he arrived safely home with his precious barrel
of salt.

GRANDFATHER'S FAMILY.

As grandfather's family was now complete, and this removal to Erin being a new beginning, it would be well to give
the names of his children in their birth order: The oldest
being George, born April 27, 1799; William, June 20, 1801;
Ann, May 6, 1803; Henry, April 4, 1805; Harriet, May 6,
1807; Rachel, October 1, 1809; Charlotte, March 19, 1812;
Susan, December 25, 1816; and John, August 21, 1819.
John was no doubt born at Burlington. Susan's place of birth
is uncertain. The other children were all born at or near Fort
Erie. This is graphically shown by the family tree on the
following page, showing his own sons and daughters in the
order of their birth and the grandchildren of his son's families.
Reference can be made to this as the history proceeds.

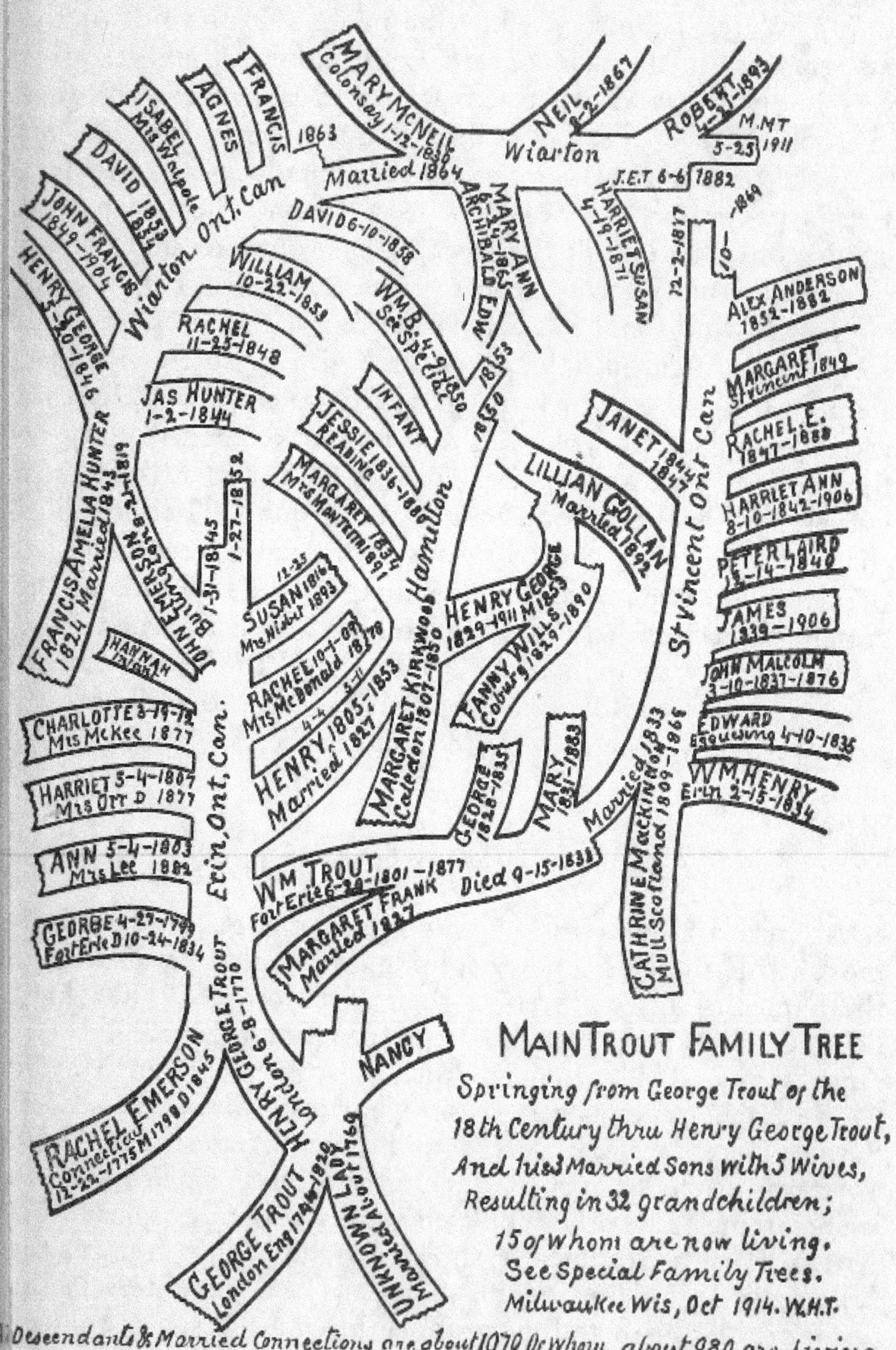
ISABEL Mrs Walpole
AGNES
FRANCIS 1863
DAVID 1853
JOHN FRANCIS 1849-1904
HENRY GEORGE 20-1846
MARY McNEIL Colonsay 1-12-1838
Married 1864
NEIL 9-2-1867
ROBERT 5-31-1893
M.N.T 5-25 1911
J.E.T 6-6 1882
HARRIET SUSAN 4-19-1871
MARY ANN 3-24-1865 ARCHIBALD Edw
12-2-1817
1869
1010
Wiarton
Wiarton, Ont. Can
DAVID 6-10-1858
WILLIAM 10-22-1858
RACHEL 11-25-1848
JAS HUNTER 1-2-1844
WM.B. 4-9-1850 See Special
1853
1860
ALEX ANDERSON 1832-1882
MARGARET St Vincent 1849
RACHEL E. 1847-1858
HARRIET ANN 8-10-1842-1906
PETER LAIRD 12-14-1840
JAMES 1839-1906
JOHN MALCOLM 3-10-1837-1876
EDWARD Esquwing 4-10-1835
WM. HENRY Erin 2-15-1834
St Vincent Ont Can
JANET 1844-1847
LILLIAN COLLAN Married 1892
FRANCIS AMELIA HUNTER 1824 Married 1843
JOHN EMERSON 8-22-1819 Butt 1792-9-20-8
JESSIE 1836-1868 Reading
MARGARET 1834 Mrs Montein 1891
INFANT
HANNAH Infant
SUSAN 1816 Mrs Nisbit 1893
MARGARET KIRKWOOD Hamilton
HENRY GEORGE 1829-1911 M 1853
FANNY WILLS Coburg 1829-1890
1-27-1852
1-31-1845
11-25
RACHEL 10-7-011 Mrs McDonald 1870
HENRY 1805-1853 Married 1827
MARGARET Caledon 1807-1890
GEORGE 1828-1831
MARY 1831-1883
CHARLOTTE 8-19-74 Mrs McKee 1877
HARRIET 5-4-1807 Mrs Orr D 1877
ANN 5-4-1803 Mrs Lee 1882
GEORGE 4-27-1799 Fort Erie D 10-24-1834
Erin, Ont. Can.
WM TROUT Fort Erie 6-30-1801-1877
MARGARET FRANK Married 1827
Died 9-15-1831
CATHRINE MacKINNON 1833 Mull Scotland 1809-1866
Married
GEORGE TROUT 6-8-1770
RACHEL EMERSON Connecticut 12-22-1775 M 1798 D 1845
HENRY GEORGE TROUT London 6-6-1828
NANCY
UNKNOWN LADY 1769 Married Alcott
GEORGE TROUT London Eng 1744-1828
MAIN TROUT FAMILY TREE
Springing from George Trout of the
18th Century thru Henry George Trout,
And his 3 Married Sons with 5 Wives,
Resulting in 32 grandchildren;
15 of whom are now living.
See Special Family Trees.
Milwaukee Wis, Oct 1914. W.H.T.
Descendants & Married Connections are about 1070 Of Whom about 980 are Living

It can readily be seen that in this pioneering year grandfather had quite a helpful force; Uncle George was at least twenty-two, father was over twenty, Uncle Henry, who was the tallest in the family, being about six feet, would be then a good stripling of sixteen. Grandmother had her sturdy eldest daughter over eighteen, and Harriet very helpful at thirteen, Rachel near twelve, and Charlotte eight or nine, each beginning to be useful, with Susan and John practically babies.

The settlers' first crop is nearly always potatoes, then wheat, oats, etc., for food; along with this they planted flax for wearing apparel, which required good hand-worked machinery to be available. Father led in this work and no doubt trained the others, as the three oldest brothers seemed to be all mechanics. They made the machines to dress, spin and reel the flax, and the loom on which to weave it, as well as the woolens that were made up into garments. Grandfather took up shoemaking. Every need of the family was supplied at home. At our first visit to grandfather's he made shoes for us little children, largely from the unworn portions of old boots, and they were good shoes. I saw them made and wore them. The boys, George, William, and Henry, built the first sawmill at what is now Erin Village, which enabled them to build the substantial parental home, which remains to this day. The boys also built the first dry goods store; I think for some other party. They also built and for a time conducted the first potash and pearl ash factory, which was a great boon to the settlers, converting the ashes made by clearing up their land into cash. This being about the only article then payable in money. This once important industry is now almost unknown in Canada. Seaweed now supplies the alkaline products.

The eight hundred acres of land were divided among the oldest boys, two hundred to each and grandfather two hundred, and for a short time they all farmed more or less, though evidently not their inclination. When over thirty-four years of age, Uncle George died of tuberculosis, being the first death excepting a child in grandfather's family and Uncle John succeeded to Uncle George's portion.

The school education of grandfather's family was very limited. Father got no further than spelling, reading, and writing, and only a moderate amount of these. There is not much to show that any of the rest did better. By personal study and no doubt, with grandfather's help, further progress was made. Aunt Ann and Aunt Harriet seemed to be well informed. Father seemed to have no difficulty with any needed calculation in business or mechanics. His evenings were used for study and reading. Grandfather had a small library of good books to which I had access, to my great pleasure. The revolutions of Europe most interested me.

Grandfather sold his commission in the regular army, I judge, shortly after the war. He was appointed magistrate soon after settling in Erin; also clerk of the division court, and the duties of these offices were so wisely and judicially administered as to obtain the sincere respect of the whole people. The magistrates of those days had a very much larger field of duty than at present. An incident is related that took place at the beginning of the McKenzie rebellion in 1837. A large party of orangemen, with their too ready loyalty in behalf of the British crown, went around the settlements and collected, by force, if necessary, all the guns and other arms, that belonged to others that were not orangemen, so as to cripple possible rebels, and keep the arms in their own possession till the trouble would be over. Complaints were made to grandfather, and all these would-be guardians of the government, were summoned to appear before him. Then after administering scathing rebuke for their presumptuous act, they were ordered to inform the owners that their guns were at Squire Trout's, and they could go there on a certain day and get them. They would have been compelled to restore them, except for the uncertainty of each man getting his own gun. My sister Mary remembered seeing the guns brought there and dispensed. She was then about six and one-half years old. Grandfather was also captain of a militia company, which he had been drilling and had called out ready for service orders, when the rebellion subsided. Father also had charge of a company in Caledon, but he was not so hearty on the job as grandfather, who at that time was a Tory. Father belonged to the reform party, the extremists or radicals of which were the Rebels.

Grandfather's religious position was that of an Episcopalian; or in the Canadian parlance of the times, he belonged to the English Church, as did his father before him. I am not certain as to grandmother's position, most likely she agreed with him. But I have heard no account of any active church connection, until after they came into Erin. The Wesleyan and the Episcopal Methodists were the religious pioneers of the times, and grandfather and grandmother at least associated with them, and continued whatever connection they had until death. Grandmother died in the winter of 1844-5; I think of pneumonia, I remember her from three separate visits. The first was in January, 1841, I remember the time, because one of my aunts explained to me, the purpose and uses of an almanac. I was looking over the one for the previous year, having 1840 in large figures on the front. I asked what the book was for and she explained it all to me, saying, "That is last year's 1840 almanac, we will soon get another for this year, which is 1841." I began counting the years from that time. On this first visit father took Edward and John and myself, the three oldest, in a cutter, from the village of Norval, where we lived, to Erin, a little over twenty miles. I rode on the seat with father, the other two were snugly at our feet. Edward got sleigh-sick, turned very sick and vomited. Father set him on the seat between us and he soon got over it. At grandfather's, the only one I was well acquainted with was Aunt Harriet, who had been my teacher in a private school at Norval. Here also I met for the first time, my bright-eyed, cheerful half sister, Mary, who was both a surpirse and pleasure to me, as we no doubt were to her. Aunt Susan must then have been at grandfather's, though I remember little about her, nor do I remember much about Uncle John, who was at home also. I have already referred to grandmother's kindly, quiet, governing ways. There was a household of at least six besides the visitors, father and we three boys. The house seemed large, there was

GRANDFATHER'S OLD HOME IN ERIN, ONTARIO, CANADA.
See description on opposite page.

From an old proof-photo, so badly faded as to be scarcely discernible, taken in 1894, and preserved by Mrs. William Davidson, of Feversham, Ontario, Canada, our artist and engraver have produced the above highly creditable picture. The modern addition on the left occupies the place of the old domestic workshop. The old active use of the stone basement has been plenty of room. The basement of the house was of stone, fronting on a side road, and was built partly into a bank about ten feet high; this formed the kitchen and dining room, which also contained one bed. In the center of the end toward the road, was a large, well-built, stone fireplace that would take in four-foot wood, with a stone chimney to the top of the house. Close to the right of this fireplace was a large stone oven built in the same masonry and with its flue leading into the chimney. The entrance door was on the end alongside of the oven and had a glass sash in its upper part; two other small windows served rather poorly to light the room. The upper or main story was built over the basement and extended back over the top of the bank about fifteen feet, forming two or three bedrooms. The large best room was directly above the kitchen. It had a fireplace connected with the main chimney. Grandfather and grandmother's bed was in a recess to the right, between chimney and side wall and the corresponding recess on opposite side of chimney, contained grandfather's bookcase and books, and business table. This was the main living and reception room, and had its front door on the side to be entered from the top of the bank. The kitchen was entered from the end on the lower level. About three rods in front of the kitchen was a beautiful perennial spring, walled up with stone, so as to be two feet deep, with a nice little creek going away from it, cool in summer and never freezing in winter. They generally kept a pet trout in it, who had his cavern at the bottom of the stones, generally out of sight, but would come at call for feeding. With hard work we could empty the spring low enough to catch him with our hands and for a short time admire his wiggling beauty. But to us boys and Mary, the bank and a hand sleigh were the most interesting of all. We could slide down hill to our heart's content; and on thawy days could roll down big snowballs and make snow men. The first visit was also extended to take in our Scotch relatives on the west side of Erin, but how we got there and how we got back to Norval, I do not recall. I think father returned very soon and left it to some of our uncles to bring us back.

MATERNAL RELATIVES

While my object now is to finish the record of grandfather's career, then to proceed to father's and others, yet there is such an interweaving of lives, in the events common to each, that as they occurred in relation to both sides of our family, so we must narrate them.

Our second visit to Erin was made in the winter of 1843, Uncle Laughlin and wife came down from Erin to visit his father-in-law (McKinmon on the seventh line of Esquesing) and then came to Norval and took mother, and us five boys, with Harriet, the baby, back with them to Erin, and I think at about the same time, father was called upon by a Mr. Connell, of Toronto, to go across the country, to the Georgian Bay, to examine and report on a mill site. We thus spent the last half of the winter visiting first with our Scotch relatives. There were four families: Uncle Donald, with one child; Uncle Munn and Aunt Sally's family of one girl, Mary, and five boys, the oldest being about a year and a half older than myself; Uncle Lachlin's family of three boys, the oldest being about a year or more younger than I; and also Uncle John's with one baby boy. They were all so close to each other, that we could walk from one place to the other, if roads were good, which was seldom the case, as it was a winter of very deep snow. It is plain that we five boys matched up with the Munn boys pretty well. I, nine years old, could help feed the cattle and do chores and then we would have all the more time for play, which was mainly sliding down hill, digging in the snow, or chasing red squirrels about the barn and fences, or catching the young cattle by the tail to give us a good run. There were no schools, or else it was too far or the roads too bad to go. At my other uncle's, I learned to thresh with a flail, and clear up and winnow out the grain with a fanning mill; we boys turned the crank and could hold the bags for the grain to be shoveled into them, and pitch sheaves down from the mow; the last was fun, but crank turning did not measure up much as fun. This was the first winter of the Millerites, the end of the world preachers. I think at that time the end was to come that year, or the next, I am not sure; of course, now it does not matter which, but at that time, with many people it was a subject of great concern.

It was a winter of great snowfall, the depth being from three to four feet. Teams meeting each other had great difficulty in passing. There were but few large clearings, and, in such, the roads were impassable. Uncle Laughlin took us to grandfather's, and we had a hard time to get there through the rough bush roads and the drifted roads in the clearings. It was only nine miles, but it took the greater part of the day to make the journey. This second visit was much like the first of two years previous. Grandfather and grandmother and Aunt Harriet were much the same, Mary and we boys had grown older. Aunt Susan and Uncle John were married. Aunt living in Otanabee, one hundred and fifty miles away, and Uncle John across the road from grandfather. Aunt Harriet's younger children, Julia and Henry, were with us. All these with mother and her six children, made a big family, and we had a lively time for two or three weeks. It was on this visit that I made my best acquaintance with grandfather's books. I also learned some more about grandfather's horse team, Myra, a gray mare, and a bay horse, Bill. Myra was well-behaved and kindly. Bill was prankish and uncertain. He would get up a runaway sometimes for a change. My first recollection of the horse was when grandfather and grandmother made us a visit to Norval, the first and only one as I recollect. They came in a wagon and rode in a double-armed, bark bottom chair, specially and strongly made for the wagon. When not required for riding out, the big wagon chair formed a good settee in the kitchen. The visit was much enjoyed by father and mother, and was a matter of much interest to us children. In regard to chairs, grandfather had a few that were very finely made, with what are called rush bottoms. I never knew such to be made in Canada. He also had an excellent Connecticut clock, the first one I had seen, with wooden wheels, but the usual coiled wire strike, which seemed to me so sweet and musical, and the nice ogee moulded and veneered case, with a mirror in the door.

One beautiful bright morning in the latter part of March, our Erin visit came to an end. We were packed into grandfather's sleigh and taken homeward, I think father was with us. The unusual, the incidents of the journey, are what is best remembered. Though the snow had melted and settled down very much, it was still deep, we had to make some roundabout journeys to get by impassable places. About noon we came to Uncle Dan McDonald's, in Caledon, Aunt Rachel's husband. Since we had been there two years before, he had built a nice addition to his house. The clear, bright sunshine, reflected from the snow, gives an uncommon brightness that is almost blinding except to good strong eyes, and the warmth is also increased by the reflection; some house flies were buzzing in the windows, and a few on the sunny side of the house outside. This brightness gave a glow and a charm to everything about Uncle Dan's place, that was in great contrast to the gloomy snowy days with our Erin Scotch relatives. Uncle Dan's boys, too, were fine fellows. There were five or six of them, I am not sure, and one baby girl, like what mother had, and her name was Harriet as well. The two oldest boys were much older than John, James and I. William, the third, was only a little older, but much bigger and stronger than I. After dinner, Uncle Dan told the three oldest to go out to the sugar bush and tap some trees so as to get sap for molasses. Being a village boy this was new to me. Edward and John, also had to go with us. The snow was deep and soft and wet with the heat of the sun, but our strong cousins dashed through it seemingly without effort, we had enough to do to keep up with them, though having the advantage of their track. John McDonald did the tapping, James and William carried the gouge and spiles. A sloping nick, or rather a pocket was chopped with an axe into the side of a maple tree; the sap would run out at the lower corner, the steel gouge was driven in below, after the gouge was removed, a wood spile that would fit the gouge cut was then tapped in, and by it the sap would be conducted away from the tree, into a trough set below for that purpose. The troughs in the previous summer had been considerately leaned on end against the tree with bottom outwards, so they were easy to reach and pull out of the snow and clean off, the inside ready for the clear beautiful maple sap, which flowed at first in a fine continuous stream, afterwards in big rapidly succeeding drops. By the time the allotted twenty trees were tapped, we had enough sap in the trough first set, to give us all big, sweet drinks, and at night had delicious maple syrup. The next day landed us at home, where school and other routine duties were resumed.

TRIP TO GEORGIAN BAY

While we were at grandfather's, or immediately after we returned, father went up to the Georgian Bay to examine and report on the Connell millsite, at what was afterwards Hurontario village, and now is the port and town of Collingwood. He took grandfather's horse, Bill, and made a special sleigh, or what is called a jumper, in which the shafts and runners are all in one piece; a simple but sure construction to get through the narrow bush roads, or where might be no road at all. By this he got within eight miles of his destination. This remaining eight miles was through the woods on snow shoes. Some parties had been there the previous summer and had erected the frame of a building. He made his examination, and purchased from some Indians or half-breeds, or French fifteen or twenty salmon trout, had them in a box frozen, and brought them to Norval. No greater luxury could have been bought for us children and mother, and the friends with whom we shared the fish. On this fish eating memory hang all the incidents connected with it; the flavor lent zest to the whole travel story. Early the following summer he went up again to commence the building of a sawmill and a flourmill. He made the first stage of the journey to grandfather's, on a borrowed horse and took me along to bring the horse back. I rode behind him. Being only nine years old mother was afraid to have me go and return so far, twenty-two miles. Father said I would get on all right and the events proved it, though there were good reasons for mother's fears. In due time we got to grandfather's all right, except that I was galled from my first long ride. It seemed very different at grandfather's, from previous visits. It was summer time, every one busy. There was no play going on. Having to return alone and be a little man on my own account, I was serious like the rest. This was the last time I saw grandmother, she died the following winter. One morning after the stay of a day or two, my horse was brought up, saddled, and a bag of various good things for the dear ones at home was tied securely to the front of the saddle, and with all the kindly wishes and affectionate kisses, the boy was set astride of the big fat horse, for the return journey. Father had told me to take my time, not to urge the horse at all, as I had all day to get home; so I started off on an easy trot, but a neighbor boy on a good smart horse overtook me, and we got into conversation, my horse, too, seemed to like company and improved his gait to match the other. I saw how easily and carelessly the boy rode and wished I could do the same. At a brisk gait we soon made the two and one-half miles to Erin village, and from the excitement of the little lively town, or his own mischief, my horse got frisky, went off on a gallop, and I believe tried to throw me; but I stuck like a monkey, and finally, though scared, I got him reined up and going quietly. I stopped at the tavern at Balinafad, got some grub for self and horse, and when mounting again, the old fellow would not come to the stump or log that I would be standing on; I finally got him between a stump and a fence, where he could not turn his head to me and keep the saddle away, so got started. Father had told me to walk down some of the hills, as a rest from riding; before coming into Norval, I did; at the bottom, however, the horse tried to spring away from me and nearly jerked me off the ground, but I kept him, and, mounting, rode into our village in fairly good style, to the envy of some of my boyish chums and to mother's joy. I have given a good deal of space to this boy journey; it was significant, being the first time I was put on my own resources. Remember, the country was only half cleared up then and I had not been over the road in the summer time. It was crooked. Father called my attention to the places of liable mistakes. I really had no trouble on that account. My green horsemanship was the main trouble.

Father's employment with Connell began in 1843, and continued until 1844, when George Jackson purchased the mill property. Father continued with him, building and improving the property until 1846, when McGlashan and Cox purchased it, Jackson going to St. Vincent and father, after building a little grist mill at a place afterwards known as Cresemore in 1846, purchased in the winter of 1846 or 47, fifty acres from Wm. Hallock in St. Vincent and we all moved there in May, 1847.

FINAL REFERENCE TO GRANDFATHER

In the winter of 1848 or 49, father made a business journey back to Hurontario and from there to Erin, to see grandfather, I accompanied him mainly to bring home some cattle from Melanethon, which were coming to him in payment of two notes.

That was the last time I saw grandfather, I think he had been sick, but was then about as usual. He was concerned about Mary's sheep. When sister Mary was an infant, some of her relatives gave her one or two lambs; when these were grown, they were put out on shares, that is, a neighbor farmer took them and agreed to double the number of sheep to the owner every three years. So it was not very long until Mary had a nice little flock of sheep. But the farmer in the same time had acquired a much bigger and better flock, as he would no doubt keep the better animals for himself. He turned over Mary's share and Uncle John took them, of course, assuming the same obligation, but uncle, like the rest of the Trouts, was not much of a farmer; the sheep did not prosper with him. The wolves killed some and he killed some for his family's needs and was not in a position to make good. This worried grandfather and also Aunt Harriet. I think a new arrangement was made about the sheep, but Mary received but little, if anything, for them. There was another matter of importance connected with Mary. Her mother, Margaret Frank, was the daughter of John Frank, a U. E. Loyalist, and as such child she had never drawn her quota of government land, two hundred acres. She being dead and Mary her only heir, the right to the land descended to her. I am quite certain this was up for consideration at that time, and no doubt father intended to look after it, but, of course, postponed it, till the government seemed to have grown tired of these deferred claims and closed up the U. E. business.

I think in the year of 1849 or 50, mother made a visit to Erin, most probably with father; of this I am not certain, but I know she brought back quite a number of mementos from grandfather's. Those most highly prized by herself and Mary and I, were some water color pictures, drawn and painted by himself. They were made from engravings in his books. The coloring was his contribution to the pictures. One was a portrait of Flavius Josephus; another the battle of Navarino; Richard Coeur De Lion in battle; the death of Prince Poniatowski, and others. He made those pictures when he was seventy-eight. When confined in the house in winter time and in bad weather. The quiet, gloomy days, when as the preacher in Ecclesiastes, states, "Those that look out at the windows shall be darkened," (grandfather had a cataract in one eye), "the days when the almond tree had flourished, and the grasshopper becomes a burden, and desire fails." No doubt in this little art work, grandfather drew on his early childhood training, making use of what he had learned probably sixty-five years before. I hardly think he picked it up like he did the shoemaking many years before this. The pictures were too good for that conclusion. No matter— here before us was grandfather's neat handiwork, and the expressions of an active, progressive mind. At an age when others had succumbed to infirmity, he would leave some mementos of his patient skill to loved ones left behind. I feel sure when giving them to mother he remembered the boys, he knew how I read the books and admired the pictures.

I framed those pictures, and kept them under eight by ten glass, and hung them up in our main living room, hoping that while we could see them they would also be well preserved. But the framing, at best, was only a boy's job, and in a large

Sept 1842
Battle of Navarino between the Russian and Turkish fleet

family of busy boys and girls, accidents would happen, the frames and glass would get broken, and for a time at least the pictures would be laid away with other old papers and get torn, or otherwise injured and spoiled. Some were kept for a long time. Now I judge none remain among us. We could hardly imagine then how precious they would be now.

October 23, 1916. Quite lately I learned that two of those precious pictures are still in existence; preserved by one of grandfather's granddaughters-in-law; then Mrs. William McKee. Now she is not connected with us, being Mrs. Davidson of Feversham, Ontario, Canada. For a moderate consideration she has passed them on to me and I shall take care that they be preserved in the Trout family indefinitely. They were made on poor paper, are yellow with sixty-nine years of time, and have been injured by partial wetting, and will be exceedingly hard to reproduce; but, if possible, one at least shall appear in the book. His signature, with date and explanatory statement of a dozen words, accompanying each.

About three or four years before grandfather died, he sold or transferred the old place to Uncle Sam McKee, who married Aunt Charlotte, and they with their large family lived in grandfather's house, and cared for him till his death, in January 27, 1852. Aunt Harriet's house, where she lived with her youngest son, Henry, was close to grandfather's, and she also gave him her very best attention and thoughtful care.

BRIEF FINAL TRIBUTE

We must now take leave of grandfather, remembering him with the most deserved affection, as the dignified Christian gentleman that he was. The dignity was not put *on* it was *in* him. His whole life was one of leadership. A commanding manner belonged to him, still he was always modest and approachable. He not only served the public as a magistrate and court clerk, and it must be remembered that a magistrate's sphere of duty was greatly extended beyond that of the present. The duties since performed by the township and county councillors lay then upon the magistrate; but those duties then were much simpler in the simple pioneer life of the times than at present. He served as notary public, made out deeds and other papers, and on rare occasions married people. He was ready for any needed service that an educated man could perform. It has been a great matter of regret that the McKee's sold the old place. It is possible that some small plot of a burial ground may have been reserved; if not, there is not one square foot of the original eight hundred acres granted to grandfather, now belonging to any of his descendants; but that is Canadian, as well as American style.

GRANDFATHER'S CHILDREN

We will now proceed with brief records of the lives of grandfather's children. Uncle George was the oldest, and all I have learned regarding him, is already previously embodied in the life of the family. Father William Trout comes next. After Uncle George's death he becomes the oldest son and heir in the family line. His boy life has been brought out already quite fully; also much of his young man's work in the early experience of the family in Erin. His personal history now begins. Grandfather conveyed to him one full lot of two hundred acres, which was one fourth of his allotment. Father cleared up a small portion, and put up a small log house, on it. I saw the ruins of this in 1843. The next step was to get the occupant for the house, the life partner who with him would begin a new family life. Everybody married those days. My uncles and aunts were not unduly hasty nor did they prolong the single life. Generally marrying in the early or middle twenties. Father went into the next township, Caledon, about ten miles away, for his bride. He found Margaret Frank, daughter of John Frank, a U. E. Loyalist, and brought her to share his shanty home with him. This must have been about the year of 1827, when he was twenty-six years old. Of this union George Trout and Mary were born, Mary's birthday being February 5, 1831. On November 15th, this same year, Margaret Frank died, and father was about one and one-half years a widower, the two children being cared for by grandfather and grandmother. George died in July, 1834. The cause of his death was peculiar and most regretable. It was haying time, and people in those days thought that whisky was necessary for such hard work in hot weather: A boy was sent to the village with the jug to get whiskey and George was sent with him; the jug was corked with a piece of corncob. The boys found that by turning up the jug, big drops would leak out, they held it up and sucked the cork several times. They arrived at the field, delivered the jug, and Uncle John sent George to another part of the field to find and bring a hay fork. He went and called out that he could not see it and also that he could not see anything. They found him in a bad state, took him to the house where his young life of six years was quickly snuffed out. The older boy was not seriously affected. Father and mother were ten miles away. Somebody was careless. No wonder we now have laws against children carrying liquor of any kind.

Mary remained with grandfather till the summer after grandmother's death, when father brought her home to live with us in 1845, when she was in her fourteenth year; and we boys, particularly myself, felt proud to have an older sister, who afterwards became like a second mother to us.

RELIGIOUS LIFE AND CONDITIONS

Father had a very distinctively religious life, which began about this time. In the new settlements of Canada, the Wesleyan Methodists were the religious pioneers. Grandfather and all his family attended their services. In those days there were no churches, and but few school houses; meetings were held most commonly in private houses. Large meetings were held in the open air, by the edge of some woods, or on a barn threshing floor. Father attended those Methodist meetings and offered to become a member. These were the days of penitent bench procedure. People were expected to pray in those days or be prayed into the pardoned condition, when with a paroxysm of joy, the assurance would come; and this was attributed directly to the Holy Ghost. Father undertook the praying process and followed it conscientiously and diligently for months, but there was no forthcoming assurance of pardon. He began to feel despairingly about the whole matter; when he incidentally heard of a few families that met in a private house some distance away, that were not Methodists. One Donald MacLaren was the leading man in the group, and Peter McArthur was another. They were Scotch Baptists. Their method of teaching, rather than preaching, impressed him favorably, and he continued attending; and began to see that the Message of the Gospel of Christ was primarily to the understanding, the heart, the conscience and the will, as well as the emotions; and the place to look for pardon, after rendering obedience, was in the promises of God, and not in our individual feelings, which were only a result or consequence of the pardon, but not the cause, or not even the evidence of the cause. It was not very long after this that father was baptized—immersed, in one of those beautiful spring creeks of Erin. A Christian baptism like this had not yet taken place in all that part of the country. He was well known, he said people came from twenty miles around to see William Trout baptized. It awakened a great deal of interest as well as prejudice and hostility.

It would be well to note further the religious conditions of the times, and to note how a few good men, though independent of each other, left their impression on the religious situation. The Wesleyan Methodists have already been mentioned, there were two or three other Methodists bodies, these seemed to be the most active religious forces in the community. Besides the different Presbyterian bodies were numerous; also The Church of Scotland or Old Kirke; and the Church of England, known in the United States as Episcopalians. Though Canada, strictly had no state church, yet in the allotments of the public lands of upper Canada, a certain percentage was set aside to assist in the maintenance of schools, and another much large percentage, I think one-tenth was set aside for the support of a Protestant clergy. The English Church, being the national church in England, regarded itself as having the same rights under the flag anywhere. The Old Kirke, though more modest, was disposed to regard itself in the same boat; but the other religious bodies, not only refused a share of these

funds, but insisted that *no* religious denomination *should* receive them; that churches and denominational colleges should
depend alone on the voluntary support of their adherents.
For twenty years or more this was the great political question
of the time. It was part of the discontent that caused the
MacKenzie rebellion, of course, the reform side won. You
will observe I have not mentioned Baptists, they were very
few. And as for those now known as Disciples of Christ or
Christians, there were none. But almost simultaneously, starting at several different centres, in this new liberty-loving
country, with its great lakes, broad rivers, immense forests,
and unbounded horizons, most naturally it would seem that
those who had tasted of the liberty wherewith Christ makes
free, should go forward, and shake off the trammels of religious creeds and religious usages, and the semi-sacred influence
of great names behind such things.

It is not to be wondered at, that alone with God and
nature, and a sparse humanity, that they should fall back to
THE BOOK, to the supreme authority, there to study out
their course, and in a helpful, brotherly way with others like
minded, to follow it. Donald McLaren, was not just one
of this type, he only partly led the way, but others would not
stop where he stopped. Father could see the plain beauty of
apostolic preaching and apostolic ordinances. But he failed
to see Calvinism interwoven with them. In that he tried to
teach his teacher, but failed. But beginning in that little
Highland Scotch congregation, many went out into the larger
liberty of the children of God.

JAMES BLACK'S BEGINNING

Canada had a still more effective acquisition for religious
teaching and progress in the person of James Black, who left
Scotland early in the second decade of the century, a young
man and a Baptist; he settled near the present town of Guelph,
and taught school, and true to his Christian responsibilities,
he opened a Sunday school and taught the Gospel and its
duties from the New Testament. In a year or two he saw
there were a number ready for Christian baptism. He wrote

back to Scotland, to a mission board, to send out an ordained minister to preach and baptize. One was promised, but was several years in coming. He did not wait but kept on with his good work, and added preaching to his teaching, till quite a number were ready to take upon themselves the name of Christ, and enter his service. His study of the New Testament showed him most plainly, that no consistent follower of Christ was debarred from preaching the Gospel or administering its ordinances. Accordingly, after receiving their confession of faith, he baptized the penitents, and formed a Christian Church in apostolic fashion; and had it going in good working order, when finally the Baptist missionary came, and proclaimed Brother Black's course to be wholly unauthorized, his converts illegally baptized; and that they must now be baptized by himself, as a lawfully ordained Baptist minister, in order to be a correct Baptist Church. And from his point of view the minister was right. Did Brother Black acquiesce? Hardly. He briefly, but courteous told him to keep his holy hands off, or words to that effect. These people were already Christians and there was not the least need of their becoming Baptists. So Brother Black left him to go elsewhere and make his Baptists out of the raw material. This was in the early times of A. Campbell's work in Pennsylvania; Brother Black knew nothing of it then, but began to learn about it shortly afterwards. Brother Black raised a large family of fine sons, and though a farmer, continued preaching most successfully, throughout his whole life, which ran up into the nineties; a constant pattern of purity and goodness. The marks of his influence are laid deep in the records of Canadian Churches of Christ. There were other Christian noblemen of this same type; about whom I can do little more than mention them. Elder John Menzies of Norval, who was an old man when I was almost a baby, but a vigorous preacher, and was said to be a walking concordance. Another notable highland minister, was Dougald Sinclair, the man who baptized my mother in Scotland. His home and sphere of influence was much farther west, in the township of Lobo. So far all these were Highlanders, and while they talked English finely, yet could preach in the Gaelic when called upon. Wholly different from these was one that was associated with the congregation near Norval, a north-of-Ireland man, Stephens, by name, a man of fine education and culture, who resided for some time in New York, where he was a member of a congregation of disciples or Christians, that was started directly, or indirectly I am not sure, by one of the Haldanes of Scotland, from whom A. Campbell received much of his initiative. The father of Isaac Errett was also a member of this congregation. Brother Stephens had a family of seven sons and four daughters nearly all being grown and more or less influential and effective in the spread of the Kingdom of Christ. One more of those old pioneers should be mentioned, that is, George Barclay, of Pickering. His ancestral home being in Fifeshire, Scotland. Like Brother Black his work began near the beginning of the century, the effects remain to this time, not alone in the churches east of Toronto, but in the lives of his children and grandchildren and great-grandchildren. In all those large families of this olden time that would average about ten children each, there were no imbeciles or malformations, nearly every one counted up to his full measure, and filled his honored place in society.

This large digression from the family story has been necessary for a correct setting of the events and the social and religious conditions of the time. While father was never demonstrative or bold or showy, yet he was never misunderstood regarding his Christian duty. After his baptism and association with the congregation, his place was with it every Lord's day. Old friends and acquaintances who had been used to doing their visiting on Sunday would call on him. He pleasantly informed them that he and wife were going to meeting and would be glad to have their company. Though it might be against their inclination they would most likely go, and a few occurrences of that kind settled Sunday visiting between him and his friends.

WILLIAM TROUT SECOND MARRIAGE

Father was studious and attentive, not only in the acquisition or ordinary knowledge, but especially in what related to his millwright or machinery and builder's work. And when he became a Christian, the Bible and religious literature was added to his course of study, and as a matter of course he advanced beyond his fellows and was able to enlighten and encourage others, so he became a speaker and continued progress made him a preacher; that is, he preached on Lord's days and worked on the working days, which was his usual course throughout his whole life.

I have no doubt that it was through this congregation that father became acquainted with mother, who, though often referred to previously, now should have an introduction and further reference, along with her people as we proceed. She was Cathrine Mackinnon of Mull, Scotland, born on Easter Sunday, 1809, the date not being otherwise determined, she came to Canada with two brothers and a sister and other relatives about 1827. She lived a year or two in Toronto, as servant in the home of James Leslie, publisher of the Toronto Examiner. Afterwards for several years with her own relatives in Erin. I have already referred to Dougald Sinclair who had baptized her in Scotland and also her brother Laughlin, it is easy to see that they would gravitate to this Highland Scotch Baptist congregation. I know she was intimately acquainted with all of them. And most certainly father and mother for a few years at least belonged to them. However, before either saw the other, she had been notified by some wise friends that he was to be her coming man. So we may judge the interest she felt when first he drove up to the place where she was, with a dashing gray team through the deep snow. But at first sight she did not like him, so I heard her remark to a lady friend. Evidently the dislike was very short, as the liking was certainly lifelong. Incidentally too, I discovered that my aunts regarded the match of their clever oldest brother, with a young Scotch girl that could not speak good fluent English and was unfamiliar with the ways of the coun-

WILLIAM TROUT   CATHRINE MacKINNON TROUT

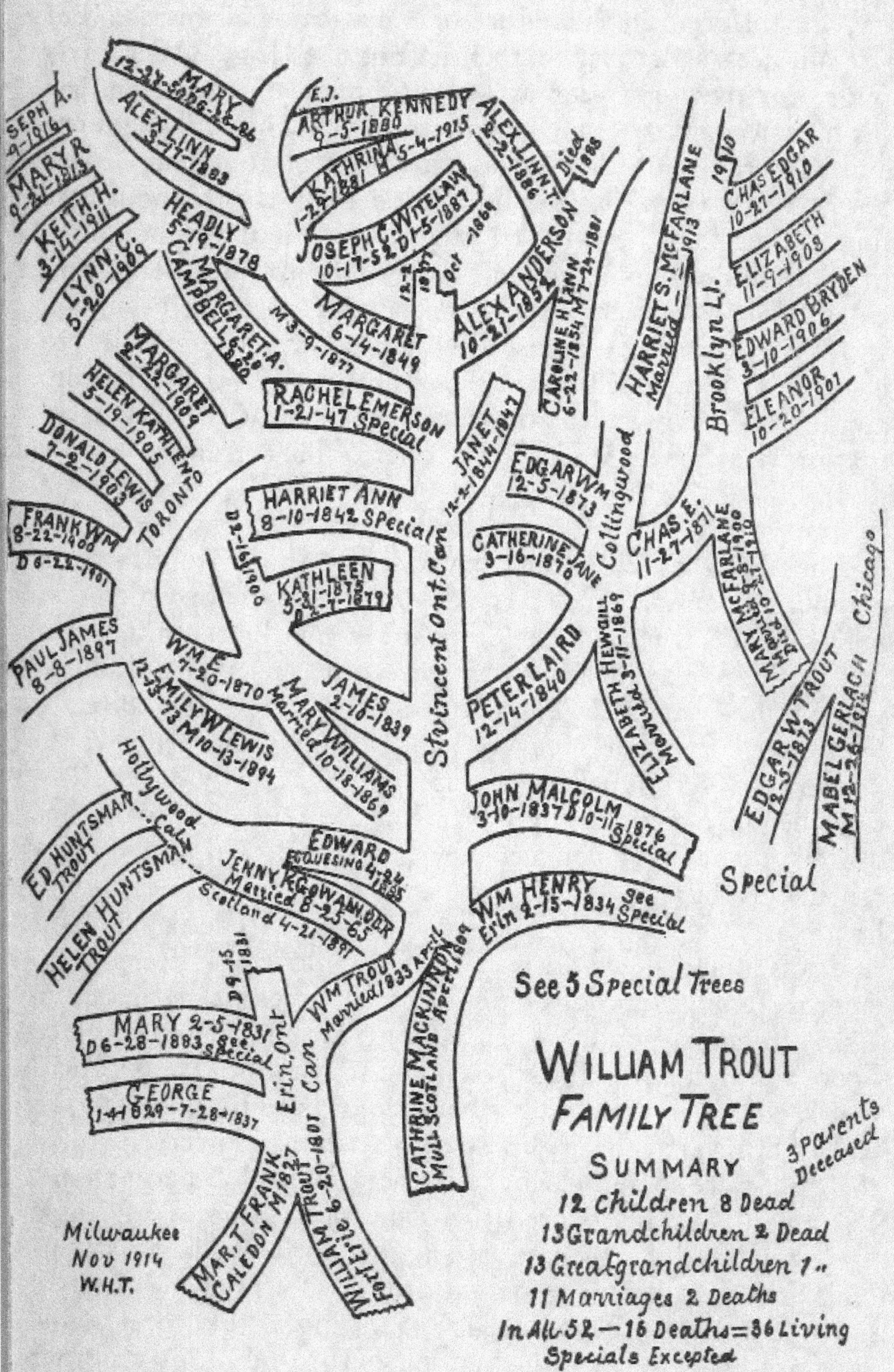
SEPH A.
9-1916
MARY R.
9-21-1913
KEITH H.
3-14-1911
LYNN C.
5-20-1909
MARY
12-27-5006-16-84
ALEX LINN
3-77-1883
HEADLY
5-19-1878
CAMPBELL 6-29
MARGARET A.
M 3-9-1877
MARGARET
6-14-1849
MARGARET
2-22-1909
HELEN KATHLEEN
5-19-1905
DONALD LEWIS
7-2-1903
FRANK WM
8-22-1900
D 6-22-1901
Toronto
PAUL JAMES
8-8-1897
E.J.
ARTHUR KENNEDY
9-5-1880
KATHRINA
1-25-1881 M 5-4-1915
JOSEPH C. WITELAW
10-17-52 D 1-5-1887
RACHEL EMERSON
1-21-47 Special
HARRIET ANN
8-10-1842 Special
D 2-16-1900
KATHLEEN
5-31-1875
D 5-7-1879
WM E.
7-20-1870
EMILY W LEWIS
12-23-73 M 10-13-1894
JAMES
2-10-1839
MARY WILLIAMS
Married 10-18-1869
ALEX LINN T.
8-2-1886
Died 1888
ALEX ANDERSON
10-21-1852
1877 Oct -1869
JANET
12-2-1846-1847
St Vincent Ont. Can.
CAROLINE H LINN
6-22-1854 M 7-24-1881
EDGAR WM
12-5-1873
CATHERINE JANE
3-16-1870
CHAS. E.
11-27-1871
PETER LAIRD
12-14-1840
ELIZABETH HEWGILL
Married 3-11-1869
JOHN MALCOLM
3-10-1837 D 10-11-1876
Special
Collingwood
HARRIET S. McFARLANE
Married 1913
Brooklyn L.I.
CHAS EDGAR
10-27-1910
ELIZABETH
11-9-1908
EDWARD BRYDEN
3-10-1906
ELEANOR
10-20-1901
1910
MARY McFARLANE
M 2-8-1910
EDGAR W TROUT
12-5-1873
MABEL GERLACH
M 12-26-1915 Chicago
Special
ED HUNTSMAN
TROUT
Hollywood
Cala.
HELEN HUNTSMAN
TROUT
JENNY R GOWAN ORR
Married 8-23-65
Scotland 4-21-1897
EDWARD
M COUSINS 4-7-1885
WM TROUT
Married 1833 April
CATHERINE MACKINNON
Mull Scotland April 1808
WM HENRY
Erin 2-15-1834
see
Special
See 5 Special Trees
D 4-5-1881
D 6-60
MARY 2-5-1831
D 6-28-1883 see.
Special
GEORGE
1-4-1829 - 7-28-1837
MAR. T FRANK
Caledon M 1827
WILLIAM TROUT 6-20-1801
Erin, Ont. Can
Fort Erie.
Milwaukee
Nov 1914
W.H.T.
WILLIAM TROUT
FAMILY TREE
SUMMARY
3 Parents
Deceased
12 Children 8 Dead
13 Grandchildren 2 Dead
13 Great grandchildren 1 ..
11 Marriages 2 Deaths
In All 52 — 16 Deaths = 36 Living
Specials Excepted

try, as something in the nature of a matrimonial mistake, but like mother's short dislike, this did not last long. After marriage, for over one year at least, he made his home on the farm. I do not say that he farmed much, the millwright or builder's trade and farming do not work well together. I was born on that farm, but did not long remain there, about that time father sold the farm to Hugh McMillan and bought a small mill site about ten miles south of grandfather's, and entered into a partnership with a reputably good business man, and then father gave his attention more unreservedly to mechanics. So, much against her judgment and inclination, mother bade farewell to the farm, and afterwards regarded that move as the beginning of a series of misfortunes.

FIRST BUSINESS VENTURE

They bought a site about ten miles south of grandfather's and built a dam on a nice large creek, at one side of which was built a small sawmill, at the other side a small grist mill, while up on the bank, on the right were other needed buildings. Our house was also built up on the bank and directly overlooked the mill pond and mills, and nearly the whole property. Here is where my first observations and recollections begin to come into our life story. There are many important occurrences connected with that place that I do not remember, but the whole property scene is distinct in my imagination. Were I a landscape painter, I could put it on the canvas and it would be an artistic picture. The stream emerged from the woods on our left, at which place there was a small natural pond. Then curving around, it cut into the opposite bank, rendering it steep and precipitous, probably 30 feet high. This was the farther side of the mill pond; at the end of which, to the right, stood the mills; down stream to the right were some clearings of other people. A magnificently timbered forest covered the country. Game of all kinds was abundant. I remember seeing a fine stately buck, with his long branching horns, come out of the woods beyond the mill pond, and stand close to the edge of the high bank, for a while, as if studying the whole situation before him. At another time I met a doe, at a short turn of the wooded road, not more than twenty feet ahead of me; she did not seem to fear me any more than I did her. I went back to tell mother, while no doubt she went back to look after her youngster. We were only afraid of bears and wolves, and these were rarely seen. If father went to hunt up the cattle he took his rifle and would often bring home a deer. That was the way summer fresh meat was supplied.

Our house was built on the sloping bank in two parts; the kitchen evidently being built first, its bank end was dug into the bank, so that it was an easy job from the rear to climb onto the roof. There was a stone chimney with fireplace for cooking. Evidently after this a larger and better room was built, as the main living and sleeping room. This was heated by a large box stove, made in Glasgow, Scotland, the same being connected with several important incidents in the family history. The first of which was when living in this house, I being about four years old. Edward and John, my younger brothers, were with me in the cradle, not far from the stove, rocking; a neighbor's boy older than I, came in, and wanted to share the cradle with us; but I would not let him. He was ugly, and pressing his foot on the cradle rocker as it came forward, upset it against the hot stove. I came against it with both hands and I think pushed the cradle back. Edward came against it with one side of his face, so that the skin was left on the stove. John's head touched it, making a spot about one inch and a quarter in diameter, where hair never grew. Edward had a glazed looking scar for many years, and it is yet quite noticeable. While I know that the palms of my hands were burned, yet I have no scars. Five years afterwards this stove caused the loss of father's workshop and tools and in twenty-five more years the loss of a sawmill and turning factory, to myself and partner, C. H. Jay.

ACCIDENT—CUT KNEE.

A few months after this burning incident, father was repairing or making some change in one of the water wheels; and in using an adz in an awkward place, cut his knee very badly. This was in the forenoon, he was helped to the house and had the wound dressed as well as the common conditions would allow. His own skill in that line was good. When his men came in to dinner, they wanted instructions about setting the water wheel in place, and properly securing it. He soon saw that they did not understand the job and would most likely do it wrong. He said he would go down and show them. Mother stood in the doorway and tried to prevent his going, but failed. Much of it had to be done under water, where the conditions were not easy to determine, and required good judgment to meet; so he got into the water and remained there for over two hours, directing and assisting until it was all properly done. A sharp pain began in the wound before leaving the water, that was the beginning of three months constantly in bed with great suffering and another three months in the house. It was one year's time before he could lay away his crutches, and then had a stiffened knee and occasional fever sores on the lower part of his leg for the remainder of his life. And according to the old saying, "Misfortunes never come singly." The firm was somewhat in debt, and the burden of the business now rested upon his partner, who seems to have thought that the job was too heavy for him, and his best course was to gather at least what cash he needed and leave the country, which he accordingly did, leaving behind him all obligations.

There was no bankruptcy act those days. No receiver could be appointed, who would step in between an unfortunate debtor and his creditors, and say, "Hands off and take your share when I give it to you." The partner's leaving was the signal for every creditor, with a matured claim, to place it in the courts, for immediate collection. The first few judgments and notes might get their claims, others must wait. So, before father was out of bed, bailiffs were driving off the cattle. I remember seeing this, seeing how determined the cattle were not to leave the place. I remember mother's tearful explanations, which I could not then fully understand. There was nothing left that the law would allow to be taken (and it was pretty drastic), that was not taken. That was trouble, real and deep; but we children knew almost nothing of it. I am surprised now that I remember so little. Other creditors and larger ones had to wait for the sales of the real estate, some creditors were considerate and gave time, in fact they had to be. It was not until eleven years afterwards that every debt was paid; the final of some accounts with costs and interest was four times the original debt. Mother was my informant on these matters more than anyone else. While as children our real needs seemed to be always supplied, yet we knew no luxury, in food, or dress, or amusement.

NORVAL UNDERTAKING

As soon as father felt able to resume work, he went to the village of Norval, about ten miles farther south and took a three-year's lease on a large flouring mill. The mill was not in good condition. He repaired it, hired a miller and a helper, and with himself serving as head miller, ran it night and day, during the busy season—the winter time. Here he made money wherewith to pay debts and made good progress. At, or before, the end of his term, he built for Col. Adamson, the proprietor, an addition to the large mill, with a complete set of machinery for making oatmeal.

Father had made a beginning in Norval before the family got there. I think it was Uncle Laughlin who moved us. It was in the winter time. We were not there many months when brother James was born; some few months after his birth, we moved to McNab's large old house close to the mill. I was then in my sixth year. The big mill was an immense interest to me. The only thing I remember about the little mill in the back woods, was the way when a certain slide was pulled up the beautiful white flour came down and filled up a large tray. But this was a merchant mill, all was on a grander scale. And from the big wheel house at the bottom, to the peak of the roof, it was filled with machinery. I asked no questions, I bothered no one, only wanted to be left alone and investigate, and lest I should be hindered, I kept out of father's sight, and out of the miller's way. After I began to get used to the mill, as a whole, I undertook methodically its several parts and their relation to one another. I soon settled on the true beginning place, that was the wheel house. So, down between dark stones, walls and heavy timbering, I found my way to the big water wheel (old breast wheel style), where, through the gate, the water went into the buckets, Chug! Chug! as each came for its share of the water load, that bore down that side of the great wheel, and turned it and thereby drove every moving part in the mill. So, for a long time, part of my daily occupation was to fully study out that mill. When it was pretty well mastered, I began to explain it to mother and it alarmed her to think of the way I had been going around, she thought I would be in the office room of the mill only. Of course she told father, but it was no news to him; he had seen me often when I did not know it and divined my purpose and saw that I was taking care. Some time after this, when I was satisfied that I knew every part of the mill and its use, I looked through a hole in the side, where a piece of board was broken off and saw in the dim light a large finished room, so I crawled through the hole to examine, and found this room had a conveying or hopper bottom; then I got into it and found a hole at the bottom, with some wheat in small corners. Here was another mystery for me; and I found also a hole above, evidently to let wheat in. As the hopper sides were pretty steep, it was not so easy to climb out, as to slide down. It occurred to me that no one knew where I was, but I was not the least alarmed, a barefooted boy can climb out of most anything. My after examination showed me the weigh hopper above this temporary store room, where the farmers' wheat was weighed in, when purchased, and at the conveying bottom was the foot of an elevator, whose head was in the highest peak of the mill. Wheat went from the bottom to the top, and was then turned into a conveyor, which ran along under the ridge of the roof, and spouts from this conveyor let the wheat into bins in the upper story, from which it could be spouted and conveyed to the millstones for grinding. Here was a whole fine system of machinery, that I had entirely overlooked.

To many people these boyish experiences may appear like a great exaggeration, but such is not my style. This will not seem so strange, when it is remembered that I was the oldest of mother's family, and she had others to care for quite as well as I. Edward was only fourteen months younger than I, and John only three years; so when I began to care for myself I had the most welcome leave to continue; and that early acquired ability and initiative never left me. This with an evidently inherited mechanical tendency, explains my forwardness in child mechanical study.

As a sample of the slow hard ways that money was earned in those days, I would cite an unexpected visit that Uncle John McKinnon made us. He arrived one winter night about eight o'clock, having left home, nearly thirty miles away, at three o'clock in the morning, with his ox team and sleigh loaded with twenty bushels of wheat. Of course he carried the necessary feed for his oxen for both journeys, and had to give them good time to rest, and feed by the way, and he provided in the same way for himself. It was a cold long journey of fifteen hours. And as a matter of course he brought some good sweet things for the children. Father got his oxen in the stable or shed. The next morning the load was sold. I kept along with Uncle John, being interested in the sale, and heard all the bargaining, and being a new experience it was remembered. The standard price was three shillings and six pence per bushel (seventy cents). Of course uncle wanted the full price. The buyer, with a standard sample in one hand, and uncle's wheat in the other, showed that uncle's, for want of plumpness in the grain, was below the standard, and cut his price one penny, three shillings and five pence. Uncle haggled hard for three shillings and five and one-half pence but could not get it; so the twenty bushels were sold for three pounds, eight shillings and four pence or thirteen dollars and sixty-seven cents. Uncle John was only a small farmer; a few small sales like that would make up his year's total of cash.

This and the reference to myself is rather a digression from the main story of father's life.

At the end of the three years' term of lease, the mill was given up, and millwright and other work taken up. The oatmeal mill was completed, the sawmill was thoroughly repaired, a new flume and water wheel built for the mill; and a distillery was built for Col. Adamson. This was a matter about which father had some conscientious scruples, and mother considerably more. Though neither were so well decided then as afterwards. Liquor was then generally regarded as useful, its harm coming from the abuse. Moderate drinkers could belong to the churches. Father recognized this state of public opinion, though he was teetotal, and watchful for the welfare of others. One day a drinking man started home with his grist from the mill. Father watched to see if he would pass the tavern, as he knew the family needed the flour, but the toper had to stop; father saw him begin to take off one of the flour bags; then father started up street, and though lame, ran as fast as he could (I saw him running). The flour was taken into the tavern and the door locked before he got there. He claimed admission but could not get it. He turned the team back, and took the remaining bags into the mill, put the horses in a shed, and sent word to the family. Then a friend came, and thanking father, brought the flour to its proper destination. I think it was in my seventh year when the distillery was built. It did not interest me like the mills, as there was no machinery in it. It had a large cylindrical boiler set in a brick arch; and some immerse tubes, and pipes, etc., and a peculiar mean smell. The distiller was a young man, a friend of ours, and boarded with us. As had been usual, mother sent me to the distillery for yeast one morning. New whiskey was being made and the distiller was having it tasted by way of test by some men then present, when a tablespoonful or more remaining in the bottom of the cup was thoughtlessly handed to the boy. I drank one swallow, not liking it, and started home with my yeast, having nearly a quarter of a mile to go. When about half way, my head began to swim. I found I was becoming drunk. I fell down and spilled my yeast. I remember this part well, but not much more on the rest of the way home. When I got there I lay down on the floor and fell asleep. Mother came in and found me, with empty tin pail, smeared with yeast and dirt, looking pale, and could not awaken me. She felt somewhat alarmed, but undressed me, and put me in bed, and let me sleep. I awoke before dinner, and told her what happened. She then saw the danger I had gone through, and when the distiller came to dinner he got an awful scolding.

Father, mother and friends discussed the distillery building business, and the conclusion reached was that as liquor was so much more of a curse than a possible good, he, for one, would never do anything to aid or abet this essentially bad business. Temperance societies were then practically unknown.

RENEWED CHURCH RELATIONS.

At the little mills in the woods there seemed to have been no religious meetings, but very shortly after our coming to Norval with father and mother and smaller brothers, I was taken to my first meeting. It was held in the large farm house of Elder John Menzies, who has been previously mentioned. The Elder preached, as was generally the case. This was about a mile and a half from Norval. We went quite regularly, generally depending on the kindness of some of our friends to bring us in a sleigh or wagon. Probably after about a year's meeting in the farm house a nice log meeting house was built, by the roadside on Menzies' lot, which was the home of a good congregation for a long time. Father now gave increased attention to studies and reading on religious subjects. He subscribed for and gave financial help to the "Christian," a monthly published by W. W. Eaton of St. John, New Brunswick. Also was a subscriber to the earliest issues of the Millennial Harbinger, and purchased the publications of Alexander Campbell. So that he soon became second to the Elder in the leadership of the congregation. I have heard him relate how the old man, though known as a disciple or reformer, held to some of his old Baptist usages in the examination of candidates for baptism. He retained the old hard catechetical questions that a well taught candidate might answer but many others could not. At a certain examination conducted by the old man, father modestly challenged the right and propriety to ask such questions and pleaded for the plain acknowledgment of Jesus Christ as the son of God. The old man sat like an old judge, listening thoughtfully, at the same time was almost unconsciously cutting tobacco, and filling his pipe; when this was completed, and a coal placed upon it, he went out, saying, go on and have it your own way. That was the last of any critical examination of baptismal candidates.

PROMINENCE OF NORVAL CHURCH.

In those beginning days this church was one of the most prosperous in all our Canadian brotherhood. I think it was here that the first June mass meeting was held, at least I know of none other that was earlier. They began about 1842. Brethren came from Erin, Eramosa, Toronto, Pickering, Coburg, and West Lake, and Dorchester and Lobo on the west, and with scattering members between. At our first June meeting we had at least four from Ohio. William and A. S. Hayden, Dr. Belding and Dr. Robinson, these were then all comparatively young men. A. S. Hayden led the singing, and I think did nothing else. Several of our new, now old, tunes were learned at the meeting. One young preacher from Ohio, who came I think in the winter time, I remember most distinctly. His name was Williams, of medium size, dark hair and eyes, but not a dark skin. He gave the first discourse that my boyish heart fully took in. It was the story of Jesus. I had read the gospels not once or twice, alone, and had committed portions to memory, but had no connected idea of the whole; this he gave me. Though then not nine years old, I did not seem to miss a sentence.

In those times father also made a notable journey to Ohio. He was absent for about a month, during which he attended a monster June meeting at Bedford, where they had a great tent, that was then used I think for the first time. It would seat two thousand people, and there were other means besides for accommodating the immense crowd. About ten years ago, Brother Charles Louis Loos gave a description of this meeting, which tallied well with father's. He never seemed to grow tired of telling of that most extraordinary assemblage.

This would be about 1842 or 1843. Those were immense evangelistic rather than business meetings. In fact evangelism was about the only business of the churches and active members of the time. Our publications and incipient colleges came in for some attention.

SPECIAL EVANGELISM

It was about this same year, that a letter, or some communication, came from some small weak churches in Prince Edward county, asking for evangelistic help for a month or more. This Norval, or more properly Esquesing church took the matter up as a business consideration at the conclusion of the morning meeting. On that day, as visitors, there were present, Alexander Anderson of Eramosa, a rising young forcible preacher and James Leslie of Toronto, the publisher of the Examiner. After some discussion and consideration the meeting decided to send Brother William Trout and A. Anderson to the help of the Prince Edward county churches. Thus far there had not been a word said about money. So much was done those days without cash, particularly in the way of preaching that no one seemed to have thought of it. But with the city brother—Leslie, it was different. So he rose up and said, "Brethren, you have not provided for the expenses of those brethren, nor for their time, this should be done at once, and I will give one dollar toward the fund," and accordingly stepped forward and laid a Spanish dollar on the end of the long table. A few others who had cash, also laid down their quota. Others promised till there was about sufficient for likely needs.

As soon as father and Brother Anderson could arrange matters, they started on their journey of about one hundred miles. It was stage and steamboat, till they were welcomed at their field of work. It was in the summer time, and in a beautiful part of Canada, well settled with an intelligent, fair-minded people, more, or less ready for the reception of new teaching, such as our brethren were known to give. The message was strange to many, as were also the messengers. Manifestly they were not clergymen; they assumed no airs of that sort. Their preaching was an example and a plea for the simplicity of apostolic times, as well as calling sinners to repentance. In fact, their greatest work was to clear away the rubbish of false ideas, piously entrenched, and plant the plain gospel in the heart. I cannot say now just how well they succeeded; but they had good meetings and a good many baptisms. Almost every evening there was preaching at some place, both were singers as well as preachers, so each had the alternate change of work. Many years after this, when father died, Brother Anderson wrote his obituary which will be added in its proper place. He referred to this journey and said that father was the most agreeable preaching companion he ever had. Brother Anderson always felt handicapped by his high pitched, monotonous voice, which came in great contrast to father's clear, easy, well-modulated style. This was a matter of remark by the people. Though Brother Anderson seemingly could not improve his voice, yet he became one of Canada's great preachers. When the time came for them to leave, Brother Anderson asked father how much money he had; the reply was three York shillings (thirty-seven and one-half cents). Then father quizzed him in return and he replied one British shilling or twenty-five cents. This was the remains from the Norval collection. One brother arranged to take them next day to the port, where they would get the steamer, and a certain doctor gave them two dollars each, which brought them to Port Credit. There was still enough left to pay for their dinners, and then they could walk fifteen miles home. This was an easy job for Brother Anderson, but hard on father with his partially stiff knee. Brother Anderson came on ahead, possibly hoping to get some help for father. He told mother of father's coming, so she and Edward and I went to meet him, and found him on foot and though tired he arrived all right; and thought nothing of it, but told much of their good meetings. This latter part of it was told more fully by Brother Anderson after father's death.

This four weeks' preaching tour was the only one of the kind father engaged in during his active life. Nearly thirty years after this, when about seventy years old, and he had given up active labor and business, the brethren in Prince Edward county, many of them remembering his former visit, wrote him to come and spend a winter with them. This he did, not a full winter, but several months of easy preaching, in which he was cared for as a father, which in a sense he was to some of them. They then had learned that preachers had needs. He came home from his journey, improved in preaching, and in health, and in appearance, proving what I have settled, that well graduated mental activity and health go together.

BUSINESS CONTINUED

Father's working and business career has been carried along to the completion of the distillery. After that he did various contracts. One was building a fine two-story house for William Clay, the leading Norval merchant. Father rented an unused small store, and turned it into a work shop, and when not otherwise busy between contracts, he made horse sleighs, and cutters of different styles, in this way keeping his few men employed. When Clay's house was about one-third done, this shop by a little thoughtlessness of one of the men, took fire and burned completely with the loss of tools, and considerable lumber, the frames, sash and doors of Clay's house, and other stock, putting father back to the poverty stage once more. He was so crippled financially that I think he had to give up the Clay contract, as I have no recollection of his finishing the house.

That fire was a second bankruptcy, while in the course of a good effort to recover from the first. The calls for payment of immediate debts could not be met by the remaining slender assets.

As old Jim Chambers used to say, "there was no nothing, to do nothing wee (with)." There were no tools, no lumber, no immediate prospects of work, no credit, except such as might depend on father's skill and pluck, and the latter then was at a low ebb. Friends connected with the church saw his plight, and raised a purse of fifty dollars to buy the most needful tools. So with a borrowed horse and cutter he went to Toronto and laid out the money.   In those days, while general prices were low, tools were high. The fifty dollars did not go very far. Among the tools was a short, thin, well-made cross-cut saw for use in framing. Our friends that winter made a great wood bee, and supplied us with several years' wood, but it was all in large logs, which had to be cut up and split, and with father's and mother's direction we boys used the saw to cut the logs in stove lengths; then at noon or night father would split them for us; or mother would have to get someone to do it. At first it was play to use the new saw, but it soon became real work. We could play out in the stormy days, but we could not work in them. We kept that saw for twenty-five years.

It was on this Toronto trip, that the acquaintance of Mr. Connell was made, and the prospect of employment on the Georgian bay loomed up. The dark cloud then began to show a silver lining, and the arrangement with Connell that nearly two years afterwards brought us all to the north was good, so the loss of the shop was a great gain, at least to the family, which was father's and mother's great concern. Father's first northern journey has already been referred to. About sixty miles of nearly unbroken forest lay between the frontier settlements more or less connected with Lake Ontario and the Georgian bay. There were little settlements at a few points with long stretches of woods between. Through these a road would be blazed out by some good leading bushman, who would know enough of the country to keep as clear as possible of swamps and big hills, and have favorable places for fording the creeks and streams. Fortunately on that route there were but few large streams. To undertake a journey like that with no kind of certain route, and end up where there was no settlement would have appalled a great many, but not father. It was simply a matter of course to him.

So I reckon it was in the winter of 1843 and 1844 that this journey was made. A report of the conditions regarding the mill site at Hurontario was no doubt forwarded to Connell at Toronto, and work commenced in the spring, father going up in the early summer as already noted. During this summer of 1844, a well-constructed sawmill was built, capable of sawing 2000 feet in ten hours, which was reckoned about the best performance a gate mill could do, and there were no others in those early days. Following this a large flouring mill of two run of stones was next built, and after mother and we children came in the fall of 1845, a large grain storehouse was built. While father was conducting this work on the Georgian bay at Hurontario the first active settlement and building up of the town of Owen Sound was proceeding. I think this began perhaps two years previous to the Hurontario settlement. Alexander M. Stephens, son of Brother Stephens, already mentioned of Norval church, and John Miller on the town line south of Norval, being among the earliest settlers. In this early period father worked for John Ingles at Sydenham Falls, two and one-half miles up the river from Owen Sound, at the first mills built there. I cannot locate the time when this was done, but he worked several months. While father was in the north, and for a year or more previous, we lived in the lower part of the house of James Mitchell, a tailor on the south hill above Norval. While living there, one evening John Miller called on mother. Having just come from Owen Sound, he knew that mother would be glad to hear any news from the north. So he happened to come in when we boys were having our big romp before retiring. Mother had no difficulty in quieting us in the presence of a big man, a stranger to all but mother and I. She began by apologizing for her noisy, rough boys. "Oh!" he said, "that was all right, boys that did not make a big noise were no good." There were five of us, counting baby Peter tumbling around. He said he liked to see a crowd like that. I thought he was a rare, nice man, and knew boys all right. Mother enjoyed his compliment as well as the news he brought. (See old residence of 1843, opposite page 3.)

STEPHENS'S FARM.

Early in the spring of 1844 we removed to a house on the Stephens farm, a fine, well-built and well-finished log house, which was built for J. D. Stephens, the eldest of the Stephens sons. He built it for himself and bride, Anna McHenry, and in it, his first son, Tom, and daughter, Annie, were born. This house was pulled down in 1912, and a brick residence built on the site. Previous to the dismantling, one of Elder Menzies' granddaughters, remembering that it was once the home of the Trout family, took a photo of it, and sent the picture to my sister, Margaret, in Toronto. It appears on next page. It was well finished inside, three rooms below and two above. Note the old-time mortar still holds between the logs, though seventy-four years old. J. D. Stephens moved to about nine miles from Hurontario where he purchased a large farm, and married Mrs. Frame, to whom their son George was born, now a successful merchant in Winnipeg, Manitoba.

This Stephens's residence was interesting to us, because it was on a magnificent large farm. Wm. A. Stephens was the farmer, a gentlemanly, kindly, fine man; boys were never afraid of him. He took pleasure in being instructive. The season we were there, he said he would have over 2000 bushels of grain, mostly all wheat, besides hay and other stuff. The wild pigeons were so numerous that they would come down and literally cover the shocks of wheat. A man would be kept shooting to keep them scared away. All this harvesting was done by the old-fashioned hand methods, grain was cradled, and grass cut by scythes. The horse rake for haying began to be used. Men were hired in the North by J. D. Stephens, and sent down to work on this farm, in that way we were making acquaintances with future friends and neighbors. After coming to this house in the spring, mother made spring bitters from burdock roots principally, which were adjudged to be good for the purification of the blood; and to keep the bitters from fermenting, as well as to render them more palatable, a certain proportion of whisky was added. This was placed in a covered tin pail, and we were to drink a small tin cup full each morning. I felt satisfied that a few tin cups full would make me drunk, and had a curiosity to know what being drunk was like. The incident with the yeast did not teach me, because it was unpremeditated, and I was very young, in my sixth year, and at this time in my tenth year. So one forenoon, when mother was absent, I drank at intervals several tin cups, watching the effect. The first noticeable change was the uncertainty of maintaining balance, and along with this, though not observed at the time, but in my after consideration, was a dead carelessness as to what I might do. The melting of the winter snow had made a large pond in a low portion of the meadow not far from the house, and on it we boys had made a raft to shove and paddle around the pond. So there I went, and started paddling around, though nearly falling in a few times. I did not quit, till at last I had to jump in to save a fall, and was waist deep in cold water. I then waded out and went to the house, and into a bed room, shut the door behind me, and threw myself on the bed. I don't precisely remember all this, but it was done. When mother returned some little time after, she found all the rest all right, but did not see me, she wanted to know where I went. The boys said they saw me on the pond, so it was examined, and every other likely place without result. Of course, she did not telephone to neighbors; but thought I might soon turn up, but happening to go into this bed room, she saw me stretched across the bed, very pale and cold and wet, she was alarmed at my appearance and condition, and with difficulty awakened me, and demanded me to account for myself . I explained, not fully, however, that I had drank too much of the bitters, got a little tipsy and fell in the water. Though she let me understand her great anxiety and warned me strongly, yet she blamed the bitters more than me, and threw them out, and no more whiskey ever went into the bitters. I needed no further lesson as to getting drunk.

As special events and landmarks, my recollections were the births of my younger brothers and sisters, and the houses in which they were born. James was born in the first house in which we lived in Norval, Peter in the second—the big McNab house, Harriet in the third—the Mitchell residence, and Janet in this house on the Stephens farm. This was in the second year of father's working in the North, so far from home that he managed to see us scarcely twice in the year. He was thus absent when Janet was born. Mother notified me a short time previous, that she would call me up some of those nights to go to the neighbors for her, and that I was to do it promptly. There were no explanations, none were needed. I had more intelligence on that job than mother imagined. In due time I was called out past midnight one dark night, to go first to Mrs. Nixon's about a quarter of a mile away, then to another, a little farther off in another direction. I made the round and was back shortly after Mrs. Nixon got in, was then sent to bed upstairs. In the morning when we all got up we heard considerable commotion in the large bedroom below; but we were warned to come down to the cook house and kitchen and stay there. Of course, we heeded the warning, but there was curiosity, and a key hole, and I had a peep, and saw a nice little baby being dressed by Aunt Harriet. She also saw the light stopped from the key hole by a peering eye, and ordered an apron hung over it. She was always sharp in guessing, and heading off on our boyish tricks, but she was too late that time, and I had advance knowledge of an interesting secret; which after breakfast was common to all, when our new little sister was introduced to us. As far as I have been able to understand, there has been a similar course, that is, no doctor with all of mother's ten babies.

There was no regular mail route between Georgian Bay and Lake Ontario settlements. The only way we could get letters to father was by incidental travellers going up to that part of the country. Anybody would carry letters, and deliver as far as he conveniently could, or put it in the hands of others that would deliver. Mother's only school education was in Scotland, where she learned to read Gaelic fluently, and learned to read and write English before she could talk it, which manifestly was scarce half learning it. Being always in contact with English speaking people, she improved in the talking and reading; but scarcely any in the writing. So in writing to father, I had to be her amanuensis. She dictated, I wrote. One afternoon she got word that W. A. Stephens was going to the Georgian bay, and would start at sunrise next morning, and would carry a letter to father; so as soon as I came from school, I had to begin writing, and excepting for supper and necessary work, this was continued till bed time. It was then finished, but too late, she considered for me, to go a seven-eighths of a mile journey, part of which was through a strip of green woods. So she sent me to bed, and would awaken me at break of day to take the letter. So I was awakened, she said light was beginning to break in the east; we had no clock. I started, it was awful dark then, in the woods, but when I could not see, my bare feet could feel the path; so I got to my destination, and rapped and rapped, and waited and rapped; finally Mr. Stephens got up, took my letter, and told me it was between one and two o'clock, and I better go to the cook shed where there was a fire, and wait till morning. I did, and waited till I got tired, and started back home in the dark. Mother heard me coming in and apologized most sincerely. I went to bed and had a good sleep by morning.

We had no newspapers, but mother learned of Morse's experiments in telegraphy through Stephens, I judge, and told me the wonder of sending news on a wire in an instant from one city to another. I wanted to know how, but she could not explain.

We were a mile and a quarter from school, but I think winter or summer we never missed a day, that is, Edward, John and myself. I remember going when teams would not venture. It was just a pleasant heroic job for us to climb over snow drifts.

THE McNAB FARM

We remained in the Stephens house just about one year. The whole place except the old family home was sold; and nearly everyone went to Georgian bay. We moved in the spring to a small house on a farm of Alexander McNab, to remain until such time as father could get ready to have us move North.

This change was all right to us, but not pleasant to mother, but there was no complaint. Father came to see us in the summer, and brought Mary from grandfather's to live permanently with us. This was hard on Mary. Conditions at grandmother's were nicer, and better than ours, she knew no other; so to be the only girl in a family of five boys, the eldest three years younger than herself, and a stepmother and two little girl babies was certainly different and not pleasing. She did some quiet crying, and expressed her feelings to me and no one else. I was proud of my big sister, and did what I could to please her, and we all soon got along pleasantly.

Alongside of us was an old-style Scotch farmer, Geordie Hamilton. He had two girls about the age of Ed and I, and smaller boys. He and mother arranged that Ed and I should go and help in harvesting. He would have no new-fashioned, wasteful methods on his farm. He reaped like Abraham and the old Greeks did, his fields were a beauty, the grain stalks thick on the ground with heavy heads all even on top, yielding in the neighborhood of forty bushels per acre. His girls could reap nicely, but he would not let them teach us. He did it before us, and explained every detail, then made us go through the stunt. Well we learned to reap, but reaping was hard work, to young, growing boys. I could hold up to it fairly, but Ed was not so good. There were one or two men reapers that could beat the boss, who was seldom with us. The girls could outwork us, but when we would get with our row to the far end of the field it was not hard to persuade them to rest, and I set to work with my knife to make whistles out of big oat straws, or we made reeds out of split straws, held between thumbs in such a way that by blowing strongly through the slit we could make quite a scream, so we soon had a full organized quartet band, and to our surprise it was heard but not appreciated far and wide. The mother at the house heard it, and it took her some time to determine where the weird music came from; then the humor of the thing caught her; but the old man was not struck that way, at least he did not show it. He was cross about it. However, we spent a week or more having a good living and a good time, even if the work was hard. The trouble was the ripening of the grain would not wait on us, so other and stronger hands had to use the sickles. We went home and the girls helped their mother.

Alex McNab had two farms, one constituting his beautiful home, which lay across the Credit river from the village of Norval. Along the stream on the front was a beautiful meadow, which gave a fine perspective to the large white house and farm buildings, with orchard and grain fields behind, and back of all the wooded hills, with the mixture of hardwoods and dark evergreen pines and hemlocks. This house was ruled by one of the most kind and motherly spirits I ever knew, she knew that active boys were never short on appetite. Many a good piece of bread and butter she spread for me. She had a son Harvey, about a year and a half older than I. He had the advantage of me in strength and experience, but I was ahead of him in school, and could help him in study, so we evened up and mated fairly well. He was kindly and would not see me imposed upon; but as for moral stamina he seemed to have none, and that I knew better than anyone else. The farm on which we lived was a half mile from the McNab farm. Harvey had to bring refreshments to the men in the fields. I helped him, and had a share of what was going, and occasionally helped in such work as a boy could do. Mr. McNab thought it necessary in the harvest time to give his men a moderate amount of whiskey in the afternoon. He most frequently brought the bottles. At the first drinking time, I was offered a taste, but refused. He said, all right, he did not want to encourage boys to drink, though really doing it by example in giving it to his men. Toward evening we had to gather up the refreshment baskets and bottles; there was sometimes some left in them. Harvey would take a drink, and insist it on me, too, and I generally yielded though under conscience protest. After harvest, when the school term had begun, mother concluded not to continue us with the Norval school, as the teacher was not regarded near so good as a new teacher in the school nearly two miles away, wholly in a farming community. I knew some of the boys and liked them, and was glad to get rid largely of Harvey, and others that I knew were bad, though for peace I kept in with them. The new teacher was a Scotchman, but speaking perfect English. He had a long rod, but it was used for pointing and other purposes, not for punishment. He was a big man, and could put on a fierce look, or be kindly, as suited. Could scold most witheringly, or be humorous and sarcastic, but always positive; we never misunderstood him. We studied aloud, and a fair-sized schoolhouse was packed full of children. He used monitors to help. There was a constant din of voices, and it was a perfect beehive of mental industry; and when out for play, that had to be as thorough as the school effort. He saw to it that every one dropped into their play niche as well as their study niche. As a consequence we advanced twice as fast as in any other school I ever attended. Each evening the school closed with two large spelling classes. The schoolroom was hardly big enough to stand them in; and nothing besides was done. The one who spelled a missed word correctly, went up to the other's place in the class. We, Edward, John and I being new scholars, had to begin at the foot of this spelling class. I was the lowest; but every night in the week we climbed, and Saturday evening (our holidays were only alternate Saturdays) were at the top, I first, Edward next, John third. Then the teacher began a most scathing lecture to that class. "To think of three boys not so big as many of you, coming from another school and in one week standing at the top." Of course, we felt good, but I felt sorry to see the other fellows get such a lecture. Over six weeks after, when moving away from that part of the country, we passed by the school, the teacher came out to bid us goodbye, said he was glad he had had us as his pupils, and complimented mother on her family in a way that swells a mother's heart.

NORVAL REMINISCENCES

I have thus anticipated our departure from Norval and its associations, almost all of which are matters of pleasant memory. There were boyish escapades and breaches of parental command, and its resulting discipline, that can only be regarded as pleasant, by the better results that followed, or that ought to have followed, for I felt sometimes that punishment had missed its mark. There was no question of our parents' conscientious duty toward us, and they invoked help from on high to fulfil it. Father had family worship every day when his home life was anything like regular, and in his absence mother often supplemented it. The Scriptures that I have committed to memory at mother's instigation were mostly done in Norval, and are still unforgotten. The river Credit, a rarely beautiful stream, was a great interest to me. I early learned to swim, and to fish, and supplied our table with many a meal with the prince of fishes, my speckled namesakes. I felt no danger in wading while fishing, as I knew the river so well and could swim, but friends would see me in what they regarded as dangerous places and report to mother, giving her great cause to worry, and me trouble when I got home. My best explanations could hardly convince her that I was reasonably safe all the time. The baptisms in connection with our Christian congregation were all in the river. There were no baptistries in the whole country. I think I witnessed most all the baptisms that were administered when I was there, several of them in mid-winter. Our house was generally the dressing room, and father the administrator. The most notable and best remembered was that after a big meeting held at the Stephens home, in which the people filled the house and surrounded the door. The preaching was by some outside man, possibly Green. It was summer time. I was then in my eighth year. After the preaching, most all the congregation went through part of Ostrander's pine woods, and down a steep hill to the Credit, a full third of a mile from the house to the place of baptism; and such a place I have never seen before and never will again. The big hills and immense tall pine trees that in the valley tried to equal their companions on the hillside, and that completely shut out the sunlight, the clear flowing wide river showing dark in the restricted light, and the people on the bank who seemed like bright pigmies in the greatness of the place. It impressed my childish mind with awe, and enabled me to since understand the feelings of our great American poet who wrote, "The groves were God's first temples." In this sublimely beautiful place seven or eight were baptized. I distinctly remember the tall girlish form of Ellen Stephens, afterwards Mrs. D. L. Layton, as one of them. I remember well too how I regarded the action of some thoughtless boys who threw sticks into the stream for the dogs to swim after. It was to me like rank desecration; however, a word of admonition stopped it.

GEORGETOWN WORK.

In referring to father's various sorts of jobs, when being in Norval, I omitted to mention his work in Georgetown, which was five miles northwest from Norval. He built a large over-shot water-wheel for George Kennedy, also made patterns for his foundry, also a smaller water-wheel and other work for Travis, a chair and furniture maker, from whom father bought a nice rocking chair, my preference, on account of the scroll-shaped arms. John McIntosh was going to Georgetown with his sleigh, and took Edward and I with him, to see father and the place where he worked. When the chair was bought, Edward and I shoved it along the snow-covered street to T. C. Stephen's store, there to wait till McIntosh came to take us and chair home, which is now in William Sterling's home. At the store we made our first and very pleasant acquaintance with D. L. Layton, a young man from Nova Scotia, afterwards to be a life-long friend. Father also worked for William Barber and Brothers, about the first manufacturers of woolens in upper Canada. We boys used sometimes to walk up there to see father, and deliver some message. The factory was certainly the most wonderful thing I had ever seen; the spinning jennies were the greatest wonders. Father had rebuilt two of them. The larger self-acting *mules* were then unknown. The friendship formed with this great Barber family was continued. I shared in it at Streetsville thirty years afterwards, and Edward continues it to the present time.

NORTHERN JOURNEY.

A friend of father, Findly McNaughton, came from Hurontario to Toronto, and father engaged him, to come and superintend our journey to the North. So friend McNaughton engaged James Menzies and John McIntosh, with their horses and wagons, to take us by Toronto to the Holland Landing, from whence we would go by boats and a *portage* journey the remaining distance of sixty miles to Hurontario. This was in October, 1845. To pack and manage our household goods for a journey of one hundred and thirty or one hundred and forty miles was no small task, but mother managed it some way so that we got there all right. It was a great journey for us in those times, really the first we ever had. We boys and Mary enjoyed it doubly, both in prospect and process. The interest of the journey really began when we got on to the Dundas Road. This old government highway was built almost in advance of settlement; between Toronto and Dundas, it was part of the main artery of travel, beginning at Brockville, taking in Kingston, Toronto, Dundas, and on to the west. This was a fine graded and macadamized road. Our teams with their loads could make some speed. There was nearly continuous travel here, and it greatly increased, and the macadam surface of the road widened as we reached Toronto. Loaded teams had their place on the right hand side of road center, in whichever direction. Fast going teams kept the outside right hand. When night drew on, the steel *caulks* of the horseshoes would strike fire on the broken granite and flint; the wagon tires would do the same, but to a less extent. There was a perpetual tramp of horses and a rattle of wagons that was exciting to us in a great degree. Coming in on Queen street, Osgoode Hall attracted our attention. It had then a large tin covered dome, that shone in the moonlight. We were told that was Lawyer's Hall, which was the old name; and it probably then was the only building in Toronto deserving particular attention. On the northwest corner of Yonge and Queen streets. we put up for the night; and slept as boys can; but in the morning we were up and dressed early, and away down to the harbor, to see the steamboats and ships as we called them. We were back before breakfast and went again, taking Mary with us to see the sights; and as we did not leave till after ten o'clock, we had some good idea of Toronto's appearance in 1845; at least I had. Going out north on Yonge street, the beautiful residences and well-kept grounds, along with the historic places, connected with the rebellion of only eight years before, were the matters of interest. The night following we stopped at Bond's lake; where in the morning, on my own account, I took my first boat ride, and soon had others with me. Near Holland village we had four miles of awful mud; we had to hire an extra team for each wagon, and they knew how to charge for their work. It was *awful* mud, Edward undertook to cross the road and got stuck, could pull up neither foot. John went to help him, and also got fast. I, standing on better ground, got hold of John's hand, and pulled them out. We arrived at the steamboat landing on the Holland river too late to get the boat, and had to remain there two days. Peter McFee kept the storehouse and wharf. He had a small rough boat, and paddles, that we boys got permission to use, and Mr. McNaughton took some pains to show us how to handle it. I did not like the looks of that sluggish, dark-looking, marshy-banked stream, so unlike the Credit. Even if one could swim, and I was the only one that could, it would still be almost impossible to get through mud and marsh to any standing place, so we were careful in and about that boat; but it gave us a good time for the two days' stay. The night before leaving there was a fall of eight inches of soft snow.

At length we were on the steamer Beaver, a short, flat-bottomed tub with side wheels, and we were going down the Holland river. Down would be hardly proper in this case, as there was no appreciable current, but we were going toward Lake Simeon. At every short bend the steamer would run her pug nose up onto the marsh and stop, and the men stationed at the bow would shove out their long cedar poles with their roots on them, cut off a foot or more from the trunk, this root end would press on a large surface of the soft marsh, making a half stable base to resist the pressure of the men pushing the boat around into the channel. As there were many of these bends, the steamer seemed to be standing half the time. At some places the whole marsh seemed to be afloat, as the waves from the steamer heaved it up and down.

When we came to the open lake we had steady going, and in about six hours from starting, we landed at Barrie. Here on the wharf were two boats' crews, that had come from

Hurontario to meet us, to carry us and our staff as well as some goods for Mr. Jackson, Hurontario's main proprietor. Their boats were left at Willow creek, nine miles from Barrie. We put up at Bingham's hotel, and Bingham's teams took us to Root's, an accommodation farmer's house, where travelers could stay. The remaining three miles, Root was to take us with his ox teams. This whole portage road of nine miles, was opened out by the government in 1812, and used to transport military supplies to the Upper lakes. Our men saw two very heavy anchors left by the side of the road in that war time. The last mile or two of this road was a causeway in a swamp, and was so rotten and uncertain that no one would venture horses on it, for fear of getting their legs broken, and being rendered useless. Oxen, being slower, could feel their way better, and, if injured, could recover. We had to remain about two days at Root's, waiting, I judge, for the goods. We saw oats brought in from the field, late in October, after there had been a snow fall of about ten inches on them, when in our country the latest crops were in six weeks before. We thought we surely were getting far to the North.

Our embarkation on Willow creek was another new experience. Our smaller boat was over five feet beam by about eighteen feet long. The larger was over seven feet beam by twenty feet long. It appeared much too large for the cedar swamp. The surface of the creek was nearly level with the swamp. The willow bushes grew on each side and touched each other in midstream, but our boats by paddling or pushing as might be required moved lively down the stream. In a few hours we came into the large Nottawasaga river, here the long oars could be used, and we made better speed; but night soon came on and it became very dark, and though a lookout man was kept in the bow we began to hit dangerous snags; so it was deemed prudent to go ashore, and camp till the moon rose about midnight, and then proceed; so with a great fire, that illuminated the great high trees, making them seem bigger and higher than they were, we spread out blankets and were soon asleep. It seemed but a short time till we were

turned out, the moon was shining on the river; our things
were gathered into the boats, and cold and sleepy we proceeded on our voyage. At daybreak we passed an Indian
home, John Jack's, a neat lodge in a little clearing, by the
bank of the river, which was broad at that place. Shortly
after that we went down three miles of rapids, where good
boating skill and caution were required. Our big boat grazed
bottom twice. At the end of the rapids we passed Carthy's
sawmill. Only a mill and a house but no settlers to be seen.
Soon after this we were at a portage, where the roar of the
stormy lake could be heard, so there was small probability of
our making the lake journey, and we might be detained two
or three days at the mouth of the river, now only six miles
away. On this account, a man was sent across this portage to
Hurontario seven miles away to get and bring provisions to us
at the mouth of the river. In the remaining journey down the
river, we had a narrow bank of sand hills on our left, separat-
ing us from the lake, on the opposite side a sloping woodland.
At the mouth of the river, our men and we boys got out, and
climbed the sand bank to view the condition of the lake. The
men decided that their boats could not live through the heavy
breakers meeting the current of the river, and accordingly
must wait till the storm subsided. While moving around over
this sand hill, one of our men picked up a musket ball, and,
looking around, others were picked up. I found one or two,
so did most of us, and the question was where did the balls
come from. Some of more knowing ones had heard there
had been a battle there, between Americans and British in the
war of 1812. Besides this, on the opposite side of the river
we could see the sunken wreck of a large schooner, the masts
of which were burned off, the bow and stern only being above
water. Some of our men with their boats went out and got
onto the bow, and could shake the whole vessel. I would have
been with them if I had had half a chance. I saw it then from
a little distance, and again the following year. Our balls were
American musket balls, fired from two vessels out in the lake,
at the British schooner that we saw inside of the mouth of the
river, as the records will show.

We had left our home at Norval Monday morning. This was near noon on the next Sunday, we had nothing to eat since the eve before. Mother had provided plenty for us, but the men fell on to our store and cleaned it out. We were surely hungry then, when we found there was nothing to eat.

It was finally decided that we three boys and Mary, and two of the men should go on foot around by the beach, to Hurontario, twelve miles away, and the remainder stay till the storm subsided, and come by the boat. So we started along the smooth sand beach; near the water it was hard and made easy walking; but we boys kept up playing a game with the waves on the shallow sloping beach, the waves would run four or five rods up the beach and retire the same distance; we would follow out the receding wave, which was easy, till we met the advancing wave, which required our best speed to keep ahead of it; but frequently we would be caught, and get wet, perhaps to the knees. Four or five miles of that began to tire us. Mary's sense was too good to indulge in that risky play.

When about half way on our journey we met father and Duncan Menzies, son of the elder, going to meet mother, also the man on horseback with the provisions for those left behind. The last five miles was a stony rough beach, sometimes we had to leave it and walk in the thick brushwood and over streams on a log or pole. Mary could not do this, so she waded. Near the evening we got to our destination; but Oh! so tired. I guess I never will be more so, till I tire out altogether. Edward was helped by the hand, and John had to be carried for a while. The McNaughton family cared for us most kindly, and we were soon all right; the second day after this the boats arrived, and in a good log house we set up our family life, in a small new village, on the lonely shores of Georgian bay.

NEW HOME BY THE LAKE

It need hardly be said that our new northern life was interesting to all of us. We had father with us now all the time, and there were excellent friends, George Jackson, the proprietor, a rarely gifted clever man, the proprietor of the whole place, who was afterwards member of the Dominican Parliament, with his wife, a fine English lady, but no children. These were as democratic as any of the rest of us. I had the reading of any book in his library, which, though small and choice, was very large to me. He would question me on what I had read, and was pleased to get good answers. He and wife, with the McNaughtons, Comptons, and father and mother, made a small Christian congregation of eight, that attended worship every Lord's day, father generally presiding. All the men could share in the exercises. Of course, the women had no sort of a part, but singing, and were but little good at that. The youngsters made up for them pretty well, but were not encouraged, as they should have been. There were just five other families, who, though attending sometimes, seemed to think our meetings too good for them. Father's work was in finishing a large storehouse which was begun after we arrived, and keeping the mills in the best possible condition. Not being needed much the following summer, he got a job of putting in a run of mill stones and bolting machinery, in an addition to the back end of a saw mill for Nulty & Webster, eighteen miles south and east, on the Mad river. Duncan Menzies and I went with father. A horse and cart worked its way through the woods with the tool chest and our belongings.

This was just a hole in a heavy thick woods of the Mad River Valley. In enlarging the clearing they had to be careful to prevent trees falling on the mill. I was the only boy, except a three-year-old, the son of the only woman, Mrs. Bennet, a widow who got the meals, and made the beds for the dozen men about the place. She afterwards got help when the work increased.

This excelled every other place I ever was in for pestilent flies, from the nearly microscopic gnat, through all the grades of black flies, musquitoes, deer flies, cattle flies, grey horse flies, up to the great, red-bellied blood suckers, as big as a bumblebee. We generally kept *smudge* about where we were working, having it in some old kettle or pan. The dried fungus that grows on rotten logs makes a smoke the flies can't stand, and it is not so bad for men. Mad river had an abundance of fine trout, and, of course, I liked fishing; but then was the time, when absorbed in catching fish, for the flies to catch me. When pulling in the beauties, I would suffer the flies till nature could stand it no longer, with gnats and black flies crawling through one's hair and going down inside your shirt, biting all the time, and musquitoes sticking their bills through your summer clothes all over. I would wade ashore, throw down the rod and myself on the ground, and roll over, fairly howling with pain. Three days before we left we had an inundation of flees, which for the time outdid the flies; but our mill was done and we gladly retreated. The pleased people were the settlers coming in with a bushel or so of their new wheat on their backs to get flour and have good bread, which perhaps they had not tasted for a month, living on potatoes and milk and butter and greens. That mill was the simplest, most original thing for grinding and bolting flour that we ever made, perhaps father's little mill beat it. However, it served its day finely.

It is easy to imagine that after a three months' absence father and I had a cordial welcome home, and we enjoyed it equally. I found the boys, Edward and John, had become regular water dogs; they had learned to swim. They had gotten roof troughs from a torn-down shanty, and each boy in town had a boat of his own. The little harbor swarmed with craft. Mr. Jackson had sold his interest to McGlashan Bros. & Cox Co., the latter, a swearing rough man, being superintendent. This was a great change. The village adopted the style of the boss. Under Jackson's regime, oaths were not heard. Under Cox's, they were common. Sister Rachel was born this summer of 1846.

Father built a nice dwelling house for McGlashan, as referred to previously, that he never occupied.

In the fall of 1846 Owen Sound became a good market for lumber, and Hurontario had abundance to sell, so a big scow was fitted up to carry it. It could sail before the wind and but little else, without being pushed by poles or oars, which was rather impracticable. One trip was made in the summer time all right. The second time the scow was blown out past the Christian island and to the north shore, seventy or eighty miles from her destination. It was feared the scow and its two men were lost. A good sail boat and two good sailor men were sent to find them; they went to the Christian island, and returned, not learning anything. They were too superstitious and fearful, so father was sent with them. He made thorough work, and found the lost men more than half way home, and soon returned with them, leaving the scow in the nearest harbor.

SECOND HOME BY THE LAKE

After Mr. Jackson left, father had no interest in Hurontario. It was the same with all the better citizens. Compton, after a year or two, went back to Toronto. The Hallock and McNaughton families went to Wisconsin in the summer of 1847. In the spring of that year father moved to St. Vincent, having purchased William Hallock's place of fifty acres, three miles north of Meaford, on the lake shore. This suited mother immensely. It was the beginning of a farm, and it fronted on the lake close to it, so that it reminded her of old Scotland, and the sea; and, as a matter of course, a very natural place for Trouts, who could also catch their splendid namesakes in the clear lake before us.

But as a farm it was not very inviting, four or five acres were irregularly cleared; there were no fences, and no cultivated portion, a small log house and a small log barn, and four or five more acres chopped and slashed down. Father spent a month or two with us with our first hired farmer man, to start putting things in order, and then went off to work at building. He made a small dwelling house for Mr. Jackson at the end of his store. D. L. Layton was clerk for Mr. Jackson; father built a small nice house for him, into which he brought his bride, Ellen Stephens, I think in the winter of 1848 and 49. In 1848 Chantler's big mill was built, and a sawmill for John Wilson of Sydenham. I worked on Layton's house and Chantler's mill, and a short time at Wilson's, and in midwinter father and I made a visit to grandfathers, being the last time that we saw him; this has been referred to in grandfather's career. In the summer of 1850 father built a flour mill for Wilson. I as well as Edward worked on this job. I had access to two bound volumes of Mechanics and Engineer's Magazines owned by Duncan Sinclair, and, when leaving, father purchased them for me. They were published in Glascow in 1841 and 1842. One of them had a picture of a flying machine, a monoplane, with a propeller and an engine and boiler, but it is needless to say that it never flew; but they were on the right trail.

Since I am practically giving the story of my own life along with father's and the family, it would be well to refer to some of the journeys made in those days, when boys and everyone else had to be good for all their capabilities.

In moving to St. Vincent, in the spring of 1847, father and Ed and I, with a good boat, made the first voyage with some of our belongings, in the early spring, before the ice banks and the ice fields were entirely gone. With sailing and some rowing, we made the twenty-eight miles in the day. The second journey the whole family, except myself, went in the boat. I, with Norman Hallock, a boy of my age, thirteen, were to drive up the cattle, that is one yoke of oxen and three cows. The first eight miles they had to be driven on the beach, a good part of which was a wide sand beach, a part narrow and rocky, and some places we had to drive through the woods. This first end of the journey, the cows were determined to turn back on us at every possible chance, and it took most of the day to get the advance of eight miles to Brazer's bay, where lame Tom Stephens with his large family lived, and where we remained all night. They said I was driving cattle all night. There I first saw Maria Frame, a beautiful, slender, red-cheeked girl, a year or more older than I. On the next day the cattle were much more easily driven, but we often had a very blind road, that was scarcely distinguishable from the open woods through which it went. There were only three settlers on this remaining twenty miles; we made it in the day.

In the summer time, milk cows and working oxen were the only animals we kept close watch of. Young cattle might be seen occasionally, when the snow came, in the fall, they would come in. Our oxen, not being used for some time, strayed away. We found one ox four miles off. The other had left him; he had been raised in a different part of the county, thirty miles off, in a straight line. It was my job to find him. I traced him from one settlement to another for fifteen miles, in the direction of his old home. Sometimes I would be away from home nearly a week. The old women were my best informants and advisors. They would tell me which way to go, and where to inquire, but told me I should never attempt to hunt the woods. I hardly needed that advice. They said, "A strange woods would be risky enough for a good man, let alone a boy." One woman came with me, and started me to the next settlement two miles away, on a blaze that she had made by scraping the bark off the small trees with a carving knife, so that you could follow those blazed trees ahead of you and come out all right. Now she said, "If you should lose this blaze, you know the river is on your right hand, and you can keep along within sight of it, and you'll come out all right." I was told, "Oh yes, we saw that ox with our young cattle, but you can't tell where the cattle or he is now, he may be halfway to Osprey, where he was raised, you won't see him till snow falls." I went home and reported; then was sent to Osprey with Hiram Mallony for company, a boy about two years younger than I; we went to Osprey and notified the former owner of the loss, and to look out for him, and let us know. This was done, and when winter came on I went and got him. In the course of the fall, father had sold both the oxen to Wilson Mallory as beeves; so Hiram Mallory and I took old Buck, his mate, a fine old fellow, to Owen Sound, eighteen miles in a straight line, but those old roads were never straight. The central part was great stretches of solid woods. Owen Sound had Hill street and Poulett street fairly well opened; houses and stores were among the trees. Our ox was delivered to Hiram Kilborn, who had a tannery near the site of the present swing bridge. I was unexpectedly pleased to meet my old Norval teacher, William Miller, also some of the Stephens's. Next morning, being Sunday, Valentine Brown, an apprentice of Kilborn's, who was two years or more my senior, and a chum of his, got a boat to show us around. We went down the Sydenham, and up the Indian river, as far as our boat could go, both being in their native original beauty; also to the Indian village, and Boyd's wharf, and back to Kilborn's. Tine, as he was usually called, regarding himself as a town boy and us as backwoods kids, tried to fool us once, and nearly succeeded. After dinner we two boys legged it smartly back home. In a new country, as that part of Canada was at that time, there were constant demands on one's initiative courage and endurance, boys and men, and women as well. We were ten or twelve years behind the earliest settlers; we had an easy time, compared to them. Some of them encountered nearly every sort of hardship that humanity could suffer.

THE PIONEER HOSTELRY

I must diverge from my main story to tell about one old couple of the olden time, whom everybody in all that region up into the fifties knew. I never heard his first name, he was known as Brock, sometimes old Brock, and often by way of compliment, General Brock, after Canada's old war governor. His wife's name was Electra; and an adopted orphan girl's name was Clarissa. He was a true woodsman, and did not care to be anything else. He advanced into the woods nearly twenty miles beyond settlements. A nice, low log house was built and covered with troughs. An acre or two of land was cleared, so that he could raise a patch of potatoes, and corn and some wheat, of which he could use but little for want of a mill to grind it. A sparkling mountain stream a few rods away, that did not freeze in winter time, supplied him with the best water. He kept a few pigs that could root their own living most all the time, winter or summer. A few head of cattle, with the help of some beaver meadow hay, could do the same. He was not much of a hunter, but little skill was needed to occasionally bring down a deer. The wolves and bears were sometimes hard on his pigs, often chasing them up to his door, but this did not worry him.

Seemingly nothing disturbed him. From some of his biggest log heaps he burned a little lime, with the mortar of which he plastered the chinks of his house, and built his broad, low chimney, and whitewashed the house inside and out. Large flag stones from the creek formed the hearth, and a few in front of his door kept away the mud. Split planks formed the house floor, so with all its crudeness there was a good measure of neatness and comfort. He had three or four little log shacks for his stock. I think only one had a roof on it. On the other there were poles thrown across, and a stack of beaver meadow hay built on top served for a roof and a hay mow. Also the hay was supposed to be out of reach of the cattle, but they learned to climb up aainst the side of the house, and pull off the hay all around; and if the snow got deep they would be able to reach higher and get most all of it, but that did not matter, it only saved the trouble of feeding them. It was evident that at the first he must have had some ambition to keep a house of accommodation. The place was admirably suited for it, being on the surveyed line of a great government road; but he never seemed to prepare for it. When settlers began coming in, and had to stop at his place, he gave them the best help he could, and generally let them pay their own price. When crowded too hard, he managed to build a small addition to his house, and an increase to his stable room. Had he squarely met the needs of the times, he might have been well-to-do. Finally when the whole country was well settled up, the settlers petitioned the government to grant him the lot on which he lived, which was done. They also clubbed together, enlarged his clearing, and built a good log house, where the two could live with comfort, but the backwoods style belonged to them, and stayed by them; and Clarissa, the girl, now becoming older, and though always short on sense, still had enough left to help ease down the mortal exit of the old folks, and take her chance for care on the kindness of neighbors. I first met these folks in the fall of 1847 when hunting the ox. They had killed a pig a few days before, and had cured the body meat, and were living on the extras. That night for supper we had the feet. There was just one foot apiece, we picked the bones and counted them, and in answer to their questions I told the progress of the settlements, and from the occasional newspapers could give them the news of the times. They contributing their share, thus old and young, we were all nibbling, chatting children, comfortably enjoying ourselves together.

ST. VINCENT CHURCH OF CHRIST

Father was never long in any place without seeking religious affiliation or making some. So considering the prospect in St. Vincent, he thought the likeliest way was to renew his old acquaintance with old Elder McLaren, who had baptized him in Erin. The old man, with several sons and daughters, had come north in advance of us, and along with a few neighbors of like mind, met as a Baptist congregation, at McLaren's point or later cape Rich, which was six and one-half miles north of us. We had a boat which we used for a little fishing, and as our principal means of travel. So after we became settled in our new home, and there came a Sunday of nice weather, father and the whole family took the boat, and we rowed up to the point. We got there before their meeting time, and were most heartily received, as old friends should have been. At the meeting father was called upon for the principal speaking. There was no communion service that day. They said they had no wine. By a pressing invitation we remained to dinner, and throughout the afternoon, getting home for supper. This Sunday journey was made several times during the summer. They were always kind, but religiously not approachable. Father finally asked one of the members if they refrained from having communion on his and mother's account, and was told that was the case. So he abandoned that effort, and endeavored to start a meeting in our own house. I don't remember the first meeting. I think probably Brother Layton was the only member besides father and mother. But father advertised himself and some neighbors came. Then the acquaintance of John Williams was made, who was another member, then Richard and Joseph Cox, members of the McLaren Church, called in on us two or three times, and afterwards joined. Before this we built an addition to our house, and had a living room eighteen by eighteen feet that was regarded as fine for meetings. Also meetings were held at Brother Williams, and Mrs. Williams and Mrs. Wm. McDonald were baptized in the Big Head river at Williams. Not long afterwards at the same place James Dunn was baptized. The next spring, the last Lord's day in April, 1849, sister Mary and John took up the matter of the response to the Christ call, John taking the lead. Mary talked the subject over with a neighbor girl, Mary Mallory, who was already on the same move, but her uncle said she must leave his home if she did. I learned of all this, and judged it was my time to fall in. Father asked each of us separately why we were taking this course. John and Mary answered because they wanted to obey the Savior and have remission of sins. My reply was that I knew it was the right course, and I might as well being it now (cool philosophy as usual). Father was not pleased with my reply as well as with the others. Neither was I pleased, and after long, hard thinking concluded that I was not ready for such a great stop, but when the time came to act, my will dropped itself on the right side. There were a number of others besides us to be baptized. The baptisms were to be in the lake in front of our place. I went with father in the morning and showed him the best place. The settlers learned of all this and spread the information widely, and our house was crowded not inside alone, but outside as well. Next Sunday morning after this, Mrs. Layton, when passing the house where Mary Mallory lived, saw her in the garden and beckoning her to the fence, asked if she still wished to be baptized. She said, "Yes." "Then come with me and you will not want a home." She climbed over the fence and came to the meeting. Her uncle saw her baptized, and true to his word, told her Monday morning to get her clothes and get out. She had a better home than the one she left and the conviction of duty done.

Quite frequently men that father hired, or apprentices, became Christians, or if denominationally so, they became Disciples of Christ; it was almost uniformly the case with girls employed by mother, and it was the same with others. I have referred to Mrs. Layton who cared so kindly and helpfully for Mary Mallory who after a few years left her, agreeably to both; and Sister Layton engaged for her help a young tall slim girl of fifteen years, Jane Clark, daughter of one-eyed Clark, of Euphrasia. He was the oldest of six brothers, that had lately come from northern Ireland. Each taking up two hundred acres of land in one settlement in Euphrasia. They were big, strong men, and orangemen, who are always a self-assertive and superloyal crowd, ready for fight if fighting was to be done. These Clarks were for a time the terror of the settlement; particularly at logging bees or barn-raisings. This Clark daughter when she began with Mrs. Layton had little besides good native energy and natural good sense; but she learned not only good housekeeping but books and writing, as Mrs. Layton had her devote an hour each day helping her in her rudimentary reading and writing. All this time the story of Jesus was not left out, and Jane Clark was soon a candidate for baptism. She lived with Mrs. Layton three years and went home again. But once in a month or two she would walk the seven miles to Meaford on a Saturday evening and remain with Mrs. Layton over night, and as had been her custom would come with them the remaining three miles to meeting. Not long after this, we heard she was married, and for nearly three years we never saw her. We thought most likely she had been reabsorbed into the old Clark style. But one Sunday morning at meeting time, being out in our yard we heard loud strange bells in the distance. We knew most every one's bells by their tone, and watching we saw emerge from the woods a fine span of big grey horses, and as they trotted on in fine form, we saw a bran-new handsomely painted farmer's sleigh. The driver we saw was a stranger, and the woman was veiled, and to our further wonder, they turned up to our house, and when landing in our yard, we saw we had Jane Clark, her two babies and her husband before us.

They had bought their new sleigh the week previous, and this was their first ten-mile journey in it. It is needless to tell how welcome she was in that congregation. The young man, modest and quiet, simply looked on, but took it all in. Some years afterwards, Jane wanted some preaching in Euphrasia and in a short time a congregation of second generation Clarks and their connections and others was formed, Jane Clark's husband, (I have forgotten his name) being one of the leaders, and I know it continues to this time. This is a sample of the close home missionary work of the early days. Now-a-days this work is done away beyond arm's lengths. Not individualistic, but in the aggregate, by our chosen representatives. Social distinction now cuts off our employees, particularly if they are house workers; a great many ladies don't want their servants to be in the same church with them. Mrs. Layton justly regarded herself as at the top of whatever might be called society in Meaford, but this did not hinder her from recognizing the wide and high level of Christian democracy, where all mistresses and servants, male and female, all are one in Christ Jesus.

RELIGIOUS WORK AND BUSINESS.

The Trout family history is closely interwoven with the history of the St. Vincent, afterwards the Meaford, congregation of Disciples of Christ. Also other small efforts in that direction, at places where father had jobs of work. When at Wilson's mill, meetings were held at Archibald McLaren's, a son of the old man, that refused father communion with him. This son had a Disciple wife, so he was openminded to new settings of the truth. A small congregation was formed there that continued about ten years. We built a barn for W. Whitelaw and he attended meetings and was baptized as well as nearly all his family. At Durham, where we had a large contract of mill work for an estate of which T. J. Leggett was the Manager, similar work was done. On father's first business visit, after the business talk was completed, Leggett inquired as to father's religious affiliations. Father replied that he was a Disciple. "Well," Leggett replied, "I judge we are all disciples, or at least we ought to be." "Yes," father returned, "we certainly ought to be." But Leggett wanted further definition and father went on setting out the Disciples' position. Coming to baptism, he interrupted father: "Do you mean to say that you immerse people, that is burying them entirely under the water?" "Certainly I do," said father. They were on the bank of the Saugeen river. "Now do you mean to tell me, that you would take a fine lady out there and bury her under that water?" "I do." "Well! Well! that is an unheard of thing to me." Yet, I think it was less than three months till he and wife were so buried in the same river. A small body met at Durham, Mr. and Mrs. George Jackson being among them, they continuing for the six months or more that we remained there, and for a year or two afterwards.

It was the fall and winter of 1851 and 1852 that we were at Durham. Previous to this time we had a barn building time. One for John Ward, Peter Emory, William Laycock, Bryan Laycock and James Laycock and two for Whitelaw. Also a big fine house for Whitelaw in the later half of 1852. And in the early summer of 1852 we built Walter's grist mill. This was thirteen miles from the lake, and three miles beyond the nearest settler. A mill built for two runs of stones, but only one put in by us. A mill with only one iron wheel and shaft—the stone pinion and spindle, and only one belt, which drove the smut machine. It was wooden shafts and wooden geared wheels throughout the mill. This old style was excusable when it is understood that there was not a passable wagon road into the mill. The stones and gudgeons being brought in in the winter time. Our Sundays were spent exploring the woods and waterfalls if the weather was fine; if not, they were spent in reading the few books we brought in with us. In the winter and early spring of 1853 we built a flour mill for C. R. Sing in Singhamton; from this job I was sent alone to do some repairs to a sawmill on the Batteau Creek for Marshall Stephens—my first job without a boss. The only work I can think of for the summer of 1853 was Neeland's barn. There was other work of importance, but I do not remember it. But in the early part of the winter, father, John McInnis and I, went to Creemore to get out the timber for a big three-run merchant mill, and also to get out timber and build a sawmill on eight hundred acres of land that father bought, I then coming twenty years of age, hewed all the timber, for both those mills. Though moderately tall, I was the lightest of any of my brothers, seldom weighing over one hundred and fifty, often less, but this winter's work will not be forgotten. During the first two weeks every principal part of my body had its turn in being most painfully tired. The axe usually weighs eight pounds, the work is done in an inclined position, the weight of body resting mainly on one leg. Sometimes all the strength of arms and body were needed, again only light strokes were required, but always the axe was worked and sustained in a position more or less strained.

After the first two weeks, however, I got seasoned to my job, and, as my work was constantly improving both in quality and quantity, it became more interesting. The memory of those grand and seemingly illimitable forests of great pines and magnificent hardwoods is even now inspiring and stimulating.

Up to this time, 1854, father's experience and judgment in matters of business and mechanics had met successfully every demand made upon them. His work showing good skill and judgment and always bringing satisfactory results. But it was largely pioneer work or its immediate outgrowth, which his progressive mind was equal to. But now we are coming to a time when the progress of the country is leaving the pioneers behind. A time when the educated and city-trained engineer and millwright was needed. This new merchant flour mill was the second of its style in that country. It was to have iron shafting nearly throughout. The sawmill we were building was also an advance on former mills. It was to be driven by a large slow-running pitch-back wheel, necessitating intermediate machinery to obtain the necessary speed for a good smart mill. As it was built for ourselves we considered every possible economy in construction. To its great detriment, we cut down all we could on the foundry and machine shop bills, making wooden pulleys where we should have had iron. After starting, some changes were found necessary, and the mill was set to work. Uncle John, who had considerable former experience in old style simple single-geared mills, was appointed to run it at a certain rate per thousand feet of sawed lumber. Father being good for important repairs. There were frequent breakdowns, which discouraged both father and Uncle John. In the meantime, J. D. Stephens and Marshall had an eye for the property and made father a good offer to purchase, which he accepted and which, so far, was good. Then in the latter part of the summer of 1854 we began the construction of the big flouring mill. Aunt Harriet was mistress of the big boarding house. Her oldest son, Sam, worked for father. Her youngest daughter, Julia, and Cousin Rachel McKee were the helpers, and a pair of sturdy girls they were, particularly Julia, who would not object to an occasional wrestle with her boy cousins and would sometimes give us a fall. Edward Orr, another son who was married and in business, conducting a tannery and shoe shop in the village, and Henry, the youngest, was with him. These, with Uncle John and family only five miles away at the sawmill, made altogether quite a respectable Trout connection. Besides these we had a visit from my sister Mary, and one from Cousin Henry Trout of Buffalo, and Aunt Ann with her daughter, Anna Lee, and granddaughter, Isabella Cotton; also a short visit from Mr. Zelotes Cotton, who was twice the son-in-law of Aunt Ann, and an almost unwelcome visitor at this time, because he came to conduct our esteemed relatives away. I felt rather abashed in the presence of my finely-dressed and cultured, city-raised cousin, Anna, who was about a year and a half older than I, but I was pleasantly reassured, as by her preference I enjoyed her lively company. This visit has been well remembered by all concerned in it. The towering pine trees of those magnificent and extensive old forests were a constant source of attentive wonder to our visiting city relatives.

THE MECHANICAL SITUATION.

There is no intention of giving a history of our mechanical work, and mill building, and it would hardly be fair to look on it from the eminence of sixty years of progress. The principles of mechanics were well understood by father, and seemed so obvious to me that I seldom saw the need of studying them. On this account what we could plainly understand we had little hesitancy in undertaking, so, in regard to the iron shafting for the mill, father purchased an old Bull lathe with a slide rest that had been burned and was said to be well refitted, also bought the round rough bars of iron for the shafting to be turned on this lathe and fitted to the wheels, etc., that were bored at the machine shop in Oakville more than a hundred miles away. Father had seen iron work done, and could handle a cold chisel and file fairly well, but nothing more and there was not a man in his employment that knew anything about it. I had a book knowledge of the various processes, and understood that turning iron with the old hand tools called for expert long practice and a skilled hand, but to set a-going and to operate a self-feeding lathe seemed as simple as rolling off of a log. So I was to be the iron worker and having father's consultation as was needed, I made a long wooden frame and mounted on it the head and tail stocks of the lathe, and the slide rest, and had it all nicely painted and was proud of it.

Our blacksmith was a Scotchman from Glasgow, and he was no discredit to that leading mechanical city. He came in one day when I was getting ready for work, and looked at it. I thought I saw a look of disgust on his face, so, to make sure, I asked him what he thought of the lathe. He looked at me with an expression of half pity, walked up and took hold of the tool post and shook every joint in it, called it a d——d old rattle trap, and other mean unmechanical names and went away. I was annoyed and said to myself, "It is just his old prejudice against everything Canadian." But it did not take long to see that the blacksmith was right, and though I did not know what good work was, yet it was plain that there could be no satisfaction till that slide rest was somewhat perfected; and at every opportunity I kept working at it till it became measurably dependable. But what shall I say about the fits? Ah! the less said the better, a real good fit was only a chance exception, and as I also did the key fitting unless a wheel or pulley had to be taken off, no one else knew what kind of a job it was, and when seen there was no one knew enough to criticise me. I certainly did as well as I could, and thought it was at least passably good; and as we ran part of the mill before I left, the work held while I was there. Though afterward much of it had to be replaced or refitted. Some years afterward I perfected the old lathe and made it do its best, which was good standard work; then the memory of the old work was no pleasure; and then, also, father began to see that in mechanics at least he had better take a back seat.

While working at that Creemore mill in the fall and early winter of 1854, before we got our mill enclosed and could work in it, in the long evenings I got restless for good reading. I had been using chance cash in the purchase of books, phrenological books receiving the most attention, and I received the phrenological journal, published by Fowlers & Wells of New York. That fall they began the publication of Life Illustrated and offered large bonuses in the way of books for new subscribers. I felt an interest in the firm and its publications. So I could see the chance for a lot of books and a free weekly paper for myself; accordingly I took my samples and started out in the long dark evenings, through mud sometimes, or deep snow, as it happened. Settlers were scarce, so good distances had to be covered. I usually did my canvassing going outward; and when bedtime came, and no lights were in the houses or shanties, I turned for home, getting in often between eleven and twelve. Father would sometimes hear me (as I slept with him), and inquire where I had been and what I was doing. I would tell him, and he would reply, "If you think you must have the books, pay for them straight, and quit this long night work." But I got up my club and got the books without calling for money. I had gained some reputation as a phrenologist. In an idle time, if the boys were short on diversion, they would get me to feel their bumps, and point out their characteristics. In those days, lectures on phrenology with its kindred studies of mesmerism, physiology, hygiene and sociology were one of our main sources of information and amusement; the lecturers would fill a hall sometimes for two or three weeks, five nights in the week. They called attention to the old Greek motto:—"Know thyself," or as Pope has expanded it:—"Know then thyself, presume not God to scan; the proper study of mankind is man."

SCHOOLS AND BOOKS.

We moved up into the northern woods of the Georgian Bay country when I was eleven and one-half years old. Previous to that time my opportunities for school education were good. The first two schools might be called private schools. Parents combined, and employed a teacher, and paid their share of expense for each child that was taught. The school house was any convenient building or room that could be easily gotten for the purpose. Mother used to tell us to study hard and learn our lessons well, for the school cost so much money. However, soon after this, through the help and direction of the government, good school houses were built and teaching given on fairly good modern lines, so that Edward, John and myself were good proficient scholars for our age. In the North, what few schools were started were too rudimentary to be of any value to us. Our education would have stopped, were it not for taking a weekly Toronto paper, and having access to the few books we could afford to buy, and those few we could possibly borrow.

We had also the habit of discussing the public events of the time at our table.

But father had always determined that our school education should not be so limited. Accordingly, he corresponded with A. S. Hayden, who has been previously mentioned, and who was then (1854) principal of the Hiram Eclectic Institute, of Hiram, Ohio, in regard to a course of study for us. I remember the cordial, nicely written, friendly answer he received. Accordingly, about a month after I attained my majority, which was on February 15, 1855, it was determined that my older sister, Mary, Edward and Julia Ann Orr and myself should spend the long spring term as students in Hiram.

The extent of sacrifice on the part of father and mother was not much considered then. Like other young people we were always in the foreground of our picture. Father and mother and Aunt Harriet Orr were all in the background. They had not only to dispense with our help, but also to meet the great expense connected with the undertaking. Mother had to do without her main help in the care and work of a large family. Father was then in the busiest time with the Creemore mill job, it was within a month or two of completion. I was a leading worker; Edward, though working with us, was not mechanically disposed but decidedly inclined toward business, so he kept the time of the men and business accounts; thus in sparing us father was losing his most dependable men. Also Aunt Harriet was dispensing with her most trusted help in conducting her large boarding house. But we heard no complaint, all were glad to see us go. The Northern Railway of Canada, then in course of building, had trains running within twenty miles of Creemore, at which point our green Canadian quartet started on its more than four hundred-mile journey. Edward and I had been to Toronto, but the girls had never seen a railway.

The institute provided rooms for light housekeeping, so we brought with us bedding, and a few necessary cooking utensils and dishes. We had all our allowable baggage in the shape of three big boxes or clothes chests. There was some kind of checking system, just what it was like I don't remember, but we had no faith in it, and there was no through checking. We were determined to see those boxes go on the cars, and come off and on at every change. This anxiety brought us trouble at Buffalo. The Penfield Bus Line agent came aboard the cars to sell bus and baggage tickets to any part of the city. After a good deal of explanation, he convinced us we ought to buy from him and we did so, surrendering our checks. He told us that when the train finally stopped we were to get out and get into one of the yellow busses we would see, and it would take us to the Cleveland Depot about a mile away. We saw the busses all right and knew the orders, but particularly the girls wanted to be sure of the boxes, so we watched and saw them come off the cars and being placed on the transfer trucks. Then the agent who sold the tickets spied us and called out, "What are you doing here?" Then looked out at the street and saw the last bus leaving. He scolded us and we deserved it. "Now," he said, "you will have to walk, or ride on the trucks." Of course, we would not do that. The walking was no trouble if we only knew where to go, but at the most we could follow the trucks. Some private hackmen offered to take us over very reasonably; but Edward said, "Will you take those tickets in payment?" No, no, he could not do that. But another scamp told Edward he would take us over and take the tickets; so we bundled in giving our hand baggage to him and partner in the *boot*. We arrived at a hotel just back of the depot, where he told us we could go in and occupy the sitting room, till the Cleveland train went out, then we were to identify our baggage and check for Cleveland. The girls went in. Edward presented the tickets, but they would not receive them. I went to the other fellow in the *boot* for our hand baggage, but he would not give it to me. They wanted more than twice what others had offered to take us for. We refused to pay and threatened police, but we had not seen a policeman and were not sure of the outcome if we did.

So, most grudgingly, we paid, I think, three dollars or three dollars and fifty cents to get possession of our hand baggage. That is the fee we paid for getting our eye teeth cut; an operation that never had to be repeated. We were so mad at Buffalo that we never spent another cent in it. Cousin Henry who then was but a short time married was living there, but we could not find him. We might have found his shop had we tried, but we sulkily stayed around that hotel and depot till our train went out in the evening. It was over a twelve-hour ride to Cleveland and an easy one to remember, because it was so rough and uncomfortable.

We slept a little, I would rouse up at times, and was amused to see everybody's head bobbing up and down or swaying to either side. The old style light rails and poor fish plates made the old-fashioned fish plate music, that our younger folks now know but little about. It was an incessant, "clackity clack, clackity clack," varying in speed as we went up grade or down. But it brought us to Cleveland in the morning. We left our Canadian forest country with three feet of snow in the woods. At Cleveland there was none. On the way to Hiram, the remains of large drifts lay along the fences; and when, at Ravenna, we left the cars for the highway to Hiram, we met another extra tax on our funds. The usual stage rate was twenty-five cents, but on account of the terrible roads we had to hire a special conveyance, paying one dollar for each of us. We were landed at the Hiram hotel, kept by Orrin Brown, but it was no hotel reception they gave us. No relatives or friends could have received us more kindly than they. No others had come so far for that term as we, and there were four of us. And after a three-days' journey, with such a reception, our feelings can be imagined without any attempt at description. We were simply at home, and had a fresh lesson in Christian relationship. The following morning, Sunday, we went to the Disciples or Christian meeting house, we did not call them churches in those days. A good old frame building, probably the first Hiram had. There was a large, pretentious, tall-steepled, Methodist church there then, but there is none at all there now. The third Christian church building, a splendid brick structure is near the site of the original building. That Sunday morning Professor Munnell preached, and I clearly remember the whole tenor of his discourse. It was a rousing warning message to parents, based on Samuel's denunciatory message to Eli: "Because his sons made themselves vile and he restrained them not." There were no smooth words in that discourse, the weight of parental duty was not lightened. The object of the sermon was to wake up parents to their duty regarding the summer Sunday school. We did not have Sunday schools in winter time then.

ACADEMY COURSES.

In entering the institute we started with advanced courses in the common branches. There were boys and girls in our classes, not near full-grown and it was easy to see their pleasure when sometimes they scored a point over the big fellows. My extended reading gave me a standing, not alone in the class, but in our society clubs or fraternities.

That spring term in Hiram is the brightest and best remembered picture in memory's long panorama. Nearly two years afterwards Mary, John and myself followed up our Hiram beginning at Williamsville, New York, where Brother Munnell was principal and Joseph King assistant. Here also was a most interesting and valuable season of progress.

Returning from Hiram we stopped in Buffalo about three days, and had our first acquaintance with cousin Henry Trout and wife, which was as pleasant as our former passage through the city had been disagreeable. Also Edward made the acquaintance of the Bryant and Stratton firm of business colleges. Nothing eventful occurred on our homeward journey. The great change was that in our absence the Northern Railroad had been completed to Collingwood, which seemed rapidly growing to be a city. A line of steamers were chartered to maintain daily connection to Chicago. There was a sudden boom in land values in and about Collingwood that set people nearly crazy. The next season the passenger steamers were taken off the route and the boom measurably collapsed. Two small steamers were on the route to Owen Sound. One good one could easily have done the business. Father had told us to take Captain W. H. Smith's boat, which certainly was the most primitive steamer I ever saw on our Great Lakes. There was rough weather on the lake when we arrived in Collingwood and the captain would not start out, but, according with his prediction, the wind settled in the evening and we made our twenty-four mile voyage to Meaford in about three and one-half hours. Of course, we had a warm welcome home and by our friends. While we never learned the art of putting on airs, we certainly felt and made ourselves of more importance. I know that I put more system and thoroughness into everything I did.

MILL SITE PURCHASE.

Father had purchased two hundred acres of heavy timbered land about a mile and a half up the river from Meaford and about five miles from our home on the lake shore north of Meaford, upon which there was very extensive water power. He was depending upon the proceeds of the sale of the sawmill and his right to the eight hundred acres of land in Tossoronto to meet the payments on the new purchase. It was as stated before, a boom time. Yet the two hundred acres at twelve dollars per acre was regarded as a moderate price. It was very much what is called broken land, the river, which was from seventy to one hundred feet wide, meandered across our lot from side to side. The contour of the hills on each side, which were one hundred and fifty feet or more in height, generally coincided with the course of the river, so that we had a deep, narrow, crooked valley affording no extended view from any point, and in which the storms that swept the hills were scarcely felt. While father was elsewhere engaged he directed me to go into this valley, examine the mill site he described, and I would afterwards have the help of two young men in clearing a small spot and erecting a log house to live in, till the site was made available and a sawmill built. One beautiful forenoon in the last days of June, 1855, I entered this interesting woodland retreat. The leafy vegetation was at its height and every available space seemed filled, and the bird life with its music, in those times so abundant, was at this part of the season only beginning to subside. What with hill, and dale, river and fountain, birds and abounding vegetation, it would seem that my irrepressible love of nature would surely be satisfied, and measurably so it was; for here, though only seven-eighths of a mile both east and west, were lines of settlers on fair public roads; and north or down the river a mile and a half the new town of Meaford, having then over one thousand inhabitants; yet in this leafy seclusion I wandered around for over two hours without seeing the first sign that any sort of humanity had ever been there before me. It was like an exploration into some unknown wilds, and that was its great charm. After awhile I came across a place where some of the settlers had come to the river and had got some of the large smooth flag stones from its bottom to make hearthstones for their open fireplaces. A hearth of only one large fine stone was a pleasure to the housewife, and a matter for boast on the part of the good man who procured it. You may wonder how they got those large stones out of the thickly wooded valley and up those steep hills. A good smart yoke of oxen and a triangular or crotch stone boat tells the story. Such an outfit, with the stone lashed on to it will go anywhere where the oxen can pass.

I spent the day there planning the future course of our work. Afterwards, with the help I built the body of a fair log house with cobbled gables and an elm bark roof; I am uncertain as to the construction of the floor, I think we had the ground only for some time. The young men and I made it our sleeping and dining room. Also a pair of flying squirrels proposed to live with us; and we did not seriously object till they began to take a share of our bread and butter without our leave. Then we had the fun of chasing them one or two evenings, till they left us for quieter quarters. Had I been the true naturalist, like Burroughs or Muir, I would have insisted on our making companions of them, and would have taken up the study of flying squirrels, maybe to the detriment of mill building.

I only began this work in the hollow. The shanty was not finished by me. I don't know if a shanty ever is or can be finished; whether good or bad, it is always only a temporary structure. However, it got some sort of finish. The roof kept out the rain while I was there. Afterwards, when a cooking stove was brought in and Mary installed as the pioneer shanty keeper, the sheets of bark in the roof began to shrink up and curl in every possible way, on account of the heat; so that when the first shower came, it put out the fire in the stove, and the shanty was dry only in spots. Mary thought her patience had been drawn upon far too heavily; she wisely threw up her job and went home till better conditions prevailed. Afterwards the bark roof and the whole structure was fixed up so that five or six of us spent the winter in it without serious discomfort; and after the sawmill got running it was transformed into a fair standard log house.

After our returning from Hiram, while I had been assigned to start work on our new mill place, Edward was sent about forty miles from home, to look after the accounting and labor-work of a sawmill then in course of contruction for John Strathy. John McInnis, our senior apprentice, but now a journeyman under father's general direction, had the main charge of the job. When I came he would leave, and I should remain to start the mill and run it, in order to prove its working up to the terms of the contract. Then I should get an acceptance from Strathy and leave; and begin work at Boyd's mill in Owen Sound. This was all carried out according to program and contract; but Strathy would not give the acceptance without seeing father; and father was on a journey to New York. I persisted, but he would not yield. Perhaps he was short on the cash that should accompany it. However, I was determined we would hold the mill and he should not use it. So I locked up and left the mill, and went to Boyd's. In due time, after father's return, Strathy settled.

A peculiar incident connected with this Strathy job is worth noting. Near the close of the work, father had several hundred dollars in money to be sent there to pay off the men. James, then about fifteen years old, was to be the messenger. The roll of bills was put in a good vestpocket and secured there by two pins. When within ten miles of the end of his journey, he felt for his roll and found the pocket empty, the discovery fairly weakened him. He did not know what to do, but at last concluded to come and let us know; so, near dark, he came in, looking the most dejected mortal one could ever see, and while he felt so bad because he lost the money, we shared some of his feelings with him. In two or three days the men must all be paid, and cash had a value, in those days about two and a half times greater than at present. He was sure he had it when about eight or nine miles from home, and thought most likely he lost it when he got off the horse and was walking over a causeway about thirty miles back. Next morning by daylight he was on the return journey. We felt sure he would not find it on the much traveled thorough-fare, so, here, while he kept a wide open eye, he made some speed; but on the less frequented part of the road, he took time. Coming to the causeway was his last hope, so he got off and kept the horse behind, slowly walking and examining every space between the logs. Finally he saw a portion of his roll, where no one else would have seen it; and he returned to us as happy as he was before dejected. It was a strange loss and a remarkable find.

NEW YORK JOURNEY

This New York journey, that has just been referred to, was one of the notable events of father's life. It would be a notable event in those days in most any man's life, except that of a wholesale merchant. Father had been buying his Burr millstones and bolting cloths from John Gartshore Company of Dundas, Canada, but in 1854 for the Creemore mill, he went to Buffalo, and purchased from G. T. Noyes and Company with advantage. In 1855 requiring four pairs of Burr's and corresponding sets of bolting cloths, he concluded to buy in New York, and timed his journey so as to be there during a convention of the American Bible Union, of which he was a member and which was then engaged in translating the New Testament and the book of Job into current English. He spent over a week in New York, mainly at the convention. Met and heard Dr. Conant and other Bible Union celebrities, whose names I do not remember. Among the younger men and somewhat lesser lights were Isaac Errett, and others rank-ing with him. This Bible Union in its incipiency was largely Baptist, and one of the speakers rather pompously referred to it as being always only Baptist. One of our brethren, whose name I forget, rose up after him and courteously called his attention to figures in the membership list, and to the presence of Disciple brethren on the board; and further said, "To whom do we go for financial help when funds are low, if not to our Disciple brethren, who liberally respond?" This so manifestly represented the sense of the convention, that the former speaker rose up and respectfully apologized.

Here was a sample of Christian Union sentiment, giving itself expression in a great common effort for the clearer understanding of the Word of God.

The American Bible Union did a great and good work in its time. For a long time I carried one of its pocket Testaments, but its work has since been overshadowed and is now almost forgotten.

The millstones were bought without their plaster backing, thereby saving in their first cost and their freight, the backing being put on at the mills. The saving in the price of the stones and cloths more than made up for the time and cost of the journey, besides having the enlargement of mind resulting from the great convention.

WORK IN OWEN SOUND

I worked on the sawmill for William Boyd for six weeks or more till the mill was started. It was nearly half built before I came. It was an unsatisfactory job, a piece of patchwork all the way through. There were no good steam sawmills those days. The engine and boilers gave greatest trouble. It was a pleasant change for me to be the boss on the job in the town of Owen Sound, when there was so much good company and town privileges.

We also had an interesting job two or three miles south of the town, the McInnis mill. A run of stones for flouring and a run of stones for making oatmeal, with corresponding bolting machinery for each. Father had the entire contract of building and machinery. Work began on it in August, 1855, while I was at Boyd's. About the first of October I joined them. We had a preacher from New York state working with us. In all we had about seven or eight men on the job. Our sleeping room was a loft in an oat kiln building. We had it passably well fitted up with table and chairs, and candles for reading and writing; and to make it more Christianlike the young preacher started us in having a Scripture reading and prayer before retiring, which was never to be later than ten o'clock. There were only three or four that would conduct this service, but the rest even if not professors fell in readily with it. Some of the evenings we would have some lively amusements, but when bedtime drew near the reading and prayer was decorously observed. Father had a bedroom in the dwelling house. Our minister left us after about two months, but the prayers were kept up till after the mill was enclosed and the work had to be hastened by working long evenings.

This was an exceptional style of mill. A large beautiful spring of sparkling water sprang out from the side of the rocky hill, and was conducted a short distance by race and flume to the high pitch-back water wheel inside of mill, on which the water, acting by gravity, turned the wheel and drove the mill. A small quantity of water falling as this did, nearly thirty feet, would furnish considerable power. The wheel was thirty feet in diameter by four feet in breadth, the largest in diameter of any then or since built in Canada, as that style of wheels was soon afterwards superseded by the turbine.

This mill was completed about January 1, 1856, and the men employed were discharged. The one apprentice of that time, Thomas Crispin, returned home with us and we began the building of our sawmill on the Big Head river, where I had built our log house the previous summer. Roads had been cut out through the woods, and the steep hills ascended on the slant with one side of the road dug out and the other supported by logs. The headrace had been cleared out and the head protecting dam and flume built, and some timber prepared for the mill. A small log stable was built and first used as a workshop. Snow lay fully two feet deep over everything; and snow was falling on an average at least every other day. There were Edward, T. Crispin, and myself who worked regularly as mechanics, father not being regularly with us. My brother John and Uncle John, who had moved his family from Tossoronto, worked with us in different capacities. Besides, there were one or two laborers employed all the time at digging and wheeling in making the dam and work of that kind. In fine days we worked outdoors, and in very snowy days we crowded the little shop.

The frame and piers of a good bridge were built over the river, but it was all carried away by the spring freshet and ice jam that accompanied it.

Though working under difficulties and hindrances, the mill was started in the month of April. Father having intimated that in time it would belong to us boys, I paid special attention to its construction, and the millwright work was excellent. Had the machinists' or general iron work been as good, all would have been good. I introduced some automatic features in place of hand operations formerly used that saved exertion and time. It was a good mill; and during the first summer lumber was in good demand at a good price.

After the mill had sawn the lumber for its own roof and floors, and a new roof for our log house, Edward and I left to begin the Gardiner flour mill job, in Arran township, Bruce County, about fourteen miles west of Owen Sound. The frame of a good-sized mill was up, which we were to enclose and finish, and put in two runs of stones, with the necessary machinery. John McInnis was again with us, and we hired also a few transient men. I had entire charge, and made a good mill. The trouble was that it was too good, or rather, too good-looking; while the quality was kept up, too much show and style was added, which, of course, added to the cost and cut the profits. On a visit to us, father saw this, and regretfully pointed it out; and what annoyed me most was that the proprietor did not care much for fine work. It took a long time for me to put the artistic entirely in the background, and the mechanical in the front. When I had skilfully accomplished that, good economy and good appearance coincided

After the flourmill was finished the sawmill was entirely overhauled, and lath-making machinery added. I had expected it to work better than it formerly did; but it disappointed me. However, thinking I had done my best, Ed and I left for home. The proprietor, Mr. Gardiner wrote father complainingly about it. Father questioned me carefully about the whole construction and was satisfied I had not made the best application of the water to the wheel. So with a horse and cutter we arrived there in one day, and next day we made the change to father's old-style way, and the mill started very fine, and Gardiner finally, though unsatisfactorily, settled up. Six hundred dollars was due us. Father then rather than go to court accepted less than one hundred dollars. He had no use for law.

WILLIAMSVILLE ACADEMY COURSE

After our sawmill was completed, father built an addition to it, and purchased and installed a carding machine and fulling mill, costing altogether over one thousand dollars; and this business in wool and cloth was carried on as well as the mill. So there was considerable to look after in the Trout mill hollow, and his boys were his main dependence in this supervision. But they had got a good taste of education and were anxious to continue. John had followed up the little school advantages he had with private study, and taken out a teacher's certificate, and had been teaching one or two seasons; so he with the rest of us older ones wanted to go forward, after our Hiram start nearly two years previous. While we were on the Gardiner job father learned that a large new academy was being built at Williamsville, New York, ten miles east of Buffalo, of which Professor Thomas Munnell of Hiram was to be the principal, and Joseph King and Mrs. King, assistants. This being one-half nearer than Hiram it was determined that we should attend there. Accordingly, at the beginning of the winter term, Mary and John left for Williamsville, and Edward shortly after left to commence a course in Bryant & Stratton's Business College in Buffalo.

When I got through with the Gardiner job, according to the reckoning, I also was ready for the Williamsville journey. Father then saw and felt his plight, with mill and farm on his hands, as well as other business, and only two not yet fully grown boys, James and Peter, to help. He gave me some extra consideration to stay and take care of the mill; but I gave it no thought and, though it seemed hard, it was surely the best; so I left for Williamsville about the middle of January, 1857. About twenty weeks were spent there, and precious, well-remembered time it was. Everybody in the neighborhood of the academy seemed to be friends of the students. There were nearly two hundred and fifty. Most of them were graduates from the common schools, who had begun with the fall term. A few were from the high schools. It was like one great democracy of freshmen.

Our professors were highly interesting people. Prof. Munnell, being the principal, who, though pleasant and agreeable, carried himself with a certain dignified reserve that never invited familiarity. He was an excellent teacher and an always interesting and forceful preacher, and was the main dependence of the Williamsville Christian Church. Brother and Sister King had some exceptional regard for my sister, who, with John and I, were invited frequently to their rooms for good confidential talks. Before leaving in June he and Brother Munnell urged me to become a preacher, and for some time I so determined; but our home situation compelled me to stand by it so long, that I gave up the purpose. During a two weeks' vacation between terms I went to Buffalo to look for work, so as to help out our expense account. I got carpenter work in the morning at one dollar and thirty-seven and one-half cents per day. I thanked the man and told him I wanted millwright work, which would afford me much better wages. The man kindly informed me where I would most likely find it. I found it hard to make the bosses believe I was a millwright. I looked young and slender, though twenty-three and had a study-paled face and white hands. Toward evening I went into a large mill that was getting a thorough course of repair, and they wanted a man. I talked to the boss millwright; he soon became satisfied I would suit him. I told him I was a student, and had no tools. He said they would fix that all right. I was to go into the office, and get liberty to work, and he would see that I got the tools and a fair wage. I went in, saw the bluff old proprietor and stated my errand. He scanned me up and down. "Got any tools?" "No, but there's no trouble in getting all I want." "Don't want anybody without tools," and turned away. That was the first day in my life that I ever looked for work and it was a lonely time. I went back and took the job offered in the morning, at one dollar and thirty-seven and one-half cents per day. I boarded and lodged with the boss himself at a saloon costing about forty cents per day. This was a well-conducted Dutch saloon, the only one with which I ever had anything to do. It is hardly necessary to say that none of my money went over the bar. This two weeks' vacation work was a good rest from study. While I regarded it as almost a discredit to work for one dollar and thirty-seven and one-half cents per day when if that old mill owner had decent sense I might have had two dollars, I still had that advantage over the other young men, that none of them could earn near as much as the little I earned.

We entered Williamsville society through the introduction of friends with whom father and mother had made previous acquaintance. This was obtained at one of those general meetings of our brethren, always and still held in June, and, therefore, called June meetings. This particular meeting was held at Jordan near the Niagara Falls on the Canadian side. When nearing its destination, the Canadian train connected with a train from New York state, and a good number of passengers got aboard from it. Mother watched them filing in and told father she felt certain there was a good number of our brethren among them, and pointed out the suspected ones, and insisted that father should go and find out; which he did, and thereby verified mother's judgment. Here he met John Gotwalt and wife, and John Graybiel and wife, and a good number of others. After his introduction father introduced the whole Canadian contingent, among which was Aunt Harriet, so that the short remaining part of the journey became a lively acquaintanceship meeting.

Father and John Graybiel's meeting was like a renewal of an old acquaintance; he being the one previously mentioned as being held under guard in grandfather's hotel on account of his peace proclivities. Though Graybiel was very much older than father, yet the interest of old associations made them equals. Also as their peace principles and lively interest in the affairs of the Kingdom of Christ entirely coincided, there grew up a decidedly mutual high regard; and we young folks at Williamsville were the fortunate successors to all this.

I should also relate here, that, at the close of the meeting, father and Aunt Harriet obtained a horse and buggy, and drove over the country seeing the landscapes of their childhood, enthusiastically relocating the places of important events of their early memories, and noting the changes of forty or more years.

Williamsville is an old village, older than Buffalo, so father maintains, which is quite likely, as farmers would need a village before they would need a port. A steady, clear-running, respectable creek flows through it, and falling over a limestone ledge of twenty feet or more, makes a beautiful cataract, and a very easily controlled water power. John Graybiel left Canada shortly after the war of 1812, and secured good property in Williamsville around this little cataract; and started large works for the manufacture of wrought iron bars, and special forgings, using the system and methods common at that time. For a time the business succeeded, but better situated shops with the later improved processes put iron in the market cheaper than he could, and he shut down. These fine old works were intact when we were there in 1857, and were a matter of great interest to me, as was also an old-fashioned iron foundry making stove plate.

There was also a paper mill, a large tannery, and several flour mills in and around it, so that when weary of study there were for me some interesting places to visit, but I generally went alone, the preferences of others not coinciding with mine.

Besides Father Graybiel's peace principles, which were then very common among disciples and continued so until our great Civil war, he had other radical views on this and similar matters. He said the Christian was in the world, but not of the world. His duty was to obey, but not be a part of the government. Consequently he would not accept any office, neither would he vote, and to be consistent with his theory he would not be a citizen, and I very much question if he was.

I told him I thought it was the Christian's duty to persistently try to make the world, as well as the church better, if he could. He said, we had nothing to do with the world, but to preach the gospel and live it. I said I thought we would get on slow if we allowed the wicked to rule all the time, but to him it was only a reason for greater effort in his line. I said when we all become Christians we will still need a government to regulate us. "No, no," said he, "In that blessed time we all will do the right and need no law. His general goodness and weight of years, as he was then an octogenarian, caused me to yield, rather than the weight of his arguments. Sister Graybiel was a great mother, not alone to her five or six daughters, but she held a high motherly place in God's Israel, as well as in the whole community. That the "women keep silence in the churches" was generally observed in this olden time; but sister Graybiel's voice was not infrequently heard in both exhortation and prayer in our prayer meetings. Mary Graybiel, our pioneer and greatly respected woman missionary, was then a half-grown girl in her common school studies. Tobias Witmer, the farmer surveyor, and the willing and efficient song leader, and teacher for the church and the Academy, also cannot be forgotten; his friendship was maintained, and was reciprocally strong with us all till his death over ten years ago. Ah, these were bright happy days in the growing springtime of life, unfortunately too soon to be ended. Our commencement day came on with an extended program of examinations and exercises for the benefit of parents and friends, and in the evening a sympathetic public filled the large hall. A good program was well carried out, and having the valedictory, my turn came, and looking over that large expectant crowd I felt for the first time, the speaker's elation when he receives attention, and is master of his subject. Why I was chosen for this, I never knew. My brother John was a better speaker than I, perhaps the best in the Academy. I think it was my general good judgment that commended me. Whatever it was I am pleased to say there was no one disappointed. Whatever we had gained, little or much, that was the end of our school days. We turned our way homeward. Part of the journey, my jaunt up to Brock's monument, has already been referred to. Nothing of note occurred on the way except my anxiety to investigate the superbly new and odd style of engines on the Lake Ontario steamer. On going below, the fireman wanted a gift, so they could get liquor as compensation for my privilege of looking around. Besides not liking to spare the money, I had a pretty strong conscience against giving money for drink. They threatened me, and looking around, I saw a man wiping a broom in some dirty oil, and then started to wipe up some soot with it. I sprung up the ladder, but got one good swipe of the broom on my back. The condition of my coat can be imagined. Mary and I cleaned the coat as well as we could, and a clean duster covered the remaining dirt. She said I was served just right for fooling around.

RESUMPTION OF WORK

Edward had with difficulty, on account of ill health, finished his business course, and got home two months ahead of us, but with health so much impaired that it took six months to recover.

His trouble was a goiter, and the drastic iodine method of curing it was used. He was so saturated with iodine that it could be distinctly scented on him three or four months after he quit using it. He was not sick, but weak through the summer. He was for a while running the sawmill; I came along by the mill, and he wanted me to roll on a moderate-sized log. I readily did it, then he said, "I have to work easy, and then rest every hour or two. I keep this sheepskin to lie down upon for a rest every little while. You used to study medical books, and water cure, and such things. Now, if you will prescribe a course for me, I will follow it, and see if I can recover strength." I reminded him that he used to make fun of me for reading such dry stuff, which he admitted; so as requested, I laid down a course, a daily cold bath in the middle of the forenoon, showing how it should be brief if he felt weak; afterwards to rest comfortably for a while, and drink water only. He carried it out, and in a month or so the smell of iodine left him; and in less than three months he began gaining flesh, taking on for a while four pounds a week, and has kept good health ever since. He now gives more attention to health matters than I do, all to his advantage.

Arriving home we found business conditions uncommonly bad. There had been poor crops the previous year, farmers could not pay debts, all the money that could be gathered went to Toronto, toward paying merchants' bills, on some of which time had to be extended. Father's principal job was the building of a storehouse with a horse power elevator. We turned in on this, and it was soon completed. We also did some work on an extension of the wharf, which with the storehouse was the expenditure of township money. A large barn built mostly by Edward and myself was our only private contract. While laying out this frame, I had the measles, but laid by only one day. Most of our family suffered badly by them.

In this year of 1857, after the Crimean war, business was not only locally but generally bad, and hit father very severely. His mill contracts were unpaid, and as many of them had been full contracts, in which he was liable for the machinery and much of the material, the loss was heavy. Two of the firms he built for became insolvent.

He had to mortgage his property heavily or take the same course. His strength and activity began to diminish. In partial explanation of all this, it should be remarked that father's aptitude was for mechanics, not particularly for business. He trained himself for the former, but not for the latter. Most of the people in those days thought such training was hardly necessary, so it can easily be seen that he was likely misled as to the condition of his own business. However, here was a situation to be met, and we boys had to step into the breach.

John had a settled ambition to become a lawyer, so after leaving Williamsville, he diligently kept up private study, and in the autumn engaged to teach a good school; and having marriage also in contemplation, as a debt raising help he had to be left out. The job then mainly devolved on Edward and me. He shortly afterwards engaged with James Beaty as general agent for the Toronto Leader, receiving his pay by commissions; and he was soon earning nearly as much as all the rest of us, all of which beyond his personal needs was directed to clear off the debts, amounting to nearly five thousand dollars; and in the course of a few years he cleared off our home property, which was principally turned over to him. After a few years from this time in 1857, James took up different agencies, working them in the winter time when farm work could not be done, and succeeded so well that he was able to purchase back from Ed the major part of the home farm.

A NEW VENTURE

One day, in this trying year of 1857, we had been making hay, and at the noon hour were resting in the shade. Father says to us, "Boys, what are we going to do this winter? There seems to be no building job of any kind, and there is scarcely anything that we might make that will bring money." And holding up a rake, said, "Can't we make hay rakes?" I grabbed the idea and said, "Yes," though not one of us had ever seen a rake manufactured, or been told how it was done, neither had we a dollar to spend on any new undertaking. But we had an abundance of good timber, and the water power to work it, and the skill and most of the tools to make the machinery. After our haying and our little harvest work was done, I quietly began feeling my way toward rake construction. Father, some years before, had split out some choice samples of fine hard beech with which to make planes. I brought some of these to our mill, and first made a pair of simple hollow mandrels for turning round and pointed fence pickets, and we sold a small quantity. The mandrels were made of wood, and rotated in wooden but babbitted boxes, and were driven by a good home-made belt. The cutting tools were made from a piece of broken cross-cut saw, cut out and heated in a fire of hemlock bark made in the stove, and forged into shape on anything that would suit for an anvil. Wooden screws served us often finely for bolts, but our cutters must be held by a neat small iron bolt, also other forgings we knew we must have. So we found that the leading smith in the town wanted good turned neckyokes and whiffletrees, which we were well-prepared to furnish, and were ready and anxious to take our pay in blacksmith work. So, step by step, with required special machines, made of hardwood, and a frame for tapering the handles, which was mounted in our ordinary wood turning lathe, these and many other machine contrivances, that persistent ingenuity would suggest, enabled us to get out for the summer of 1858, three hundred dozen rakes, which were sold and delivered to merchants in our county, at from one dollar to one dollar and seventy-five cents per dozen. Pitchfork handles and hoe handles were sold along with them. In those times the winter season was the active business time of the year. Farming operations were suspended, except chopping down the forest, bringing saw logs to the mills, anl splitting fence rails. It was the time for journeying, marketing, and general going about. Roads that were practically impassable in summer time, were well travelled in winter. What little cash was in the country was all in circulation, and the bartering peculiar to the times was active. The winter of 1857 and 1858, though exceptionally dull on account of the two crop failures and the general business depression, yet was as active as the limited possibilities of business would allow, so that the real hardships likely to follow were not felt till the spring; then it was that many families could see no source for their living till the new crops would come in. Our township council, advised by the assessors and tax collector, prepared for the situation, by using the credit of the township to repurchase the wheat stored in the general storehouse, and distributing it to those who might want it for seed, or for food, and adding the account to their taxes for the ensuing year. When this was all done, there was still likelihood of future need, to supply which there came from Chicago some good shipments of corn meal and grown flour, which were sold and distributed along the Georgian Bay shores.

That was the last time I remember eating what we called grown bread.

Our present generation knows nothing of it. When woods abounded all over the country, rains were more frequent, and sometimes we had wet harvests. Then grain, in sheaf, or shock, left to further ripen and harden would swell with the warm moisture and sprout, and start growing. If dry weather followed, that growth would be arrested; and if the growing process had only started, bread could be made of it, but it would be sweet, and soft and pasty. If the sprout had well started, it was only fit for hog feed, or the distilleries. In the 1857 harvest much of the western wheat was thus grown.

This spring of 1858 was the quietest possible kind of a time. Everybody looked to the ground for a living. Gardens were planted to their limit. Every acre of farm land was made productive. But the problem with a great many was to squeeze through till the new growth matured. There were father and mother, James and the three younger girls on the farm. Mary, Peter and myself with occasional other help were at the mill. John spent his Saturdays with us at the mill or at home, except frequent visits to the residence of Edward McMillan. Edward was seldom with us. Alexander, then quite young was our messenger boy. John Raymond, a man with a large family, was engaged to run our carding machine and fulling mill. The spring and summer time was the carding season; but enough cash or produce did not come in to support Raymond's family. When the tight times would come, as frequently they did, there were in all three houses of from sixteen to twenty people with only one to look to and that was my humble self. The humility of the situation can be understood by any one who has ever undertaken to collect money, or something to live upon, from good solvent people who had but little or nothing to pay. I certainly felt like a poor forcing beggar, and would have preferred a horsewhipping to that sort of duty. As the spring advanced, we succeeded in getting out an early batch of rakes, which were placed in some of the largest stores in Owen Sound, and for which we received payment in groceries and some cash. Then our living problem became quite easy.

In due time, when the wheat crop was harvested and known to be by far the finest and most abundant of all the previous years and the price also good, you may be sure there was a thankful and happy people, who never afterwards had a renewal of any thing approaching that trying year's experience.

From the foregoing the reason will be manifest why I was diverted from my preaching purpose formed at Williamsville. Paul was under necessity to preach. My necessity lay another way. I was the oldest son and my father's namesake, so I must stand for his honor and the family interest. My known efficient line of work was mechanics, which evidently I must continue. Edward was my second in the same purpose but ahead of me in money efficiency, toward its accomplishment. No one blamed John for striking out for himself, it was the best course in his judgment and was so respected. He soon after married and went to Toronto.

To start a nice little business like the manufacture of rakes, without a knowledge of it, or money to meet the cost, simply studying it out, and inventing and making the cheap machinery to accomplish the work, which successfully met the needs of the trade, and helped to carry the family and others through a severe crisis, all in about eight or nine months, was deservedly regarded as no small creditable accomplishment.

Based on the experience already gained, and some knowledge of the methods of other manufacturers, we proceeded to replace, as fast as we could, our temporary machinery for something more efficient and stable. Cast and wrought iron took the place of wood, old processes with their machines were discarded for those more effective and economical. This course was kept up for two or three years. The carding and cloth-dressing machines were disposed of, which gave more space for our new work. Also an addition was built which doubled the capacity of the shop, and the business was placed on something like a permanent footing.

When our friends would want an afternoon's holiday, they would come to see and admire our (to them) wonderful shop.

In the year 1861, the heirs of Wm. Laycock, from whom father purchased the mill property, began to press for the

JOHN MUIR IN 1866

JOHN MUIR IN 1913

final payments, and we had no means to meet them; they foreclosed the mortgage, and took possession of the property and ran the saw mill, leaving us the free use of our shop, and second claim on the use of the water power, and the liberty of cutting hardwood lumber on the land. This arrangement continued two years, and Charles Hugh Jay and myself formed a new company, Trout & Jay, to carry on the business of harvest tools and other articles of similar manufacture. About the same time, the Laycock family found they were running the mill at a constant financial loss; so they quit working it, and offered the property for sale. Receiving no offer, they again offered it to us on such favorable terms that it was repurchased by Trout & Jay, who at once began arranging for a more thorough and systematic conduct of the business, with prospects of a fair degree of success.

THE COMING OF THE MUIRS

About this time (1863), on one midsummer day, a grown-up beardless boy called at our mill applying for work. I asked him how he came to look for work with us in our secluded valley. He replied that he had tried all over town to get work and failed, and was advised by several that our place was the likeliest to find it. I told him our spring rush was over, and we had then nothing for him to do. His fine, boyish face and frank open manners interested me. I said to him, "You are evidently a stranger in this part of the country?" "Yes," he replied, "I am; my brother and I are students from Wisconsin University at Madison, and we are spending the summer vacation here in Canada botanizing." A couple of my farmer customers were standing by, and that big new word "Botanizing" aroused their curiosity. "What's that?" "Why," I said, "the boys are examining and studying the different kinds of plants." "What for? For medicine?" "No! but for knowledge." They looked bewildered, but said no more. He explained that his brother and he found it best to separate for a while, and meet again at a certain town, but somehow they failed making connections, and each was no doubt hunting the other; also his money was about all gone, and he must

find work till he could get word from home or from his
brother. I again regretfully told him I had no work, nor
could I tell him where he would get it. He left, and in the
evening I was surprised to find him working for the man who
was running the sawmill. I said to him, "I am glad you got a
job." "Oh, just working for my board." "Is that all? Why,
you come with us, you'll get better board and at least a dollar
a week." "Thank you, I shall be glad to do so." So I soon
introduced Mr. Daniel Muir, of Portage, Wisconsin, to my
sister-housekeeper, and he soon became to us, not a needy
young tramp, but a most welcome companionable guest. He
remained with us about six weeks; then through a few home
communications his brother was finally located, and he left us
to join him, and they continued their journeyings for a couple
of months longer until winter was likely to set in, and snow
would cover up nearly all of the plant life. They had not
returned to the Wisconsin University because of a positive
order from their parents that Dan should remain in Canada
while the military draft was enforced in the northern United
States, and John, his elder brother, being of manhood age, was
urgently requested to remain with him. While John's feelings
did not coincide with their wish, yet especially for his mother
and Dan's sake, he complied. So now on the approach of winter, like the squirrels and marmots and bears, the great question was, "where shall we den up?" not in the inactivity of the
two last mentioned animals, but with the common characteristic activity of the squirrels, the Trouts and Muirs as well. So
the question was not alone, "where shall we go?" but also,
"what shall we do?" (The Muirs' never knew idleness.) After
John had proposed several places that fell under his observation, and were considered, Dan suggested our mill place. It
would be as much like a winter den as they could find, and
though the place was not our family home, yet a good part of
it would be there; and that we were a studious, well-informed
lively lot of boys and girls, some of them school teachers, and
they were all in touch with others of the same style; and we
had a large shop in which they could likely have employment,
or they could work in the woods getting out logs for the mill.

Dan's proposal carried the day. One evening, after returning from town, I met our former good boy friend, Dan Muir, who at once introduced me to his brother John, who after a few minutes of general friendly chat laid before me their situation very much as I have outlined it above; and hoped we might make some mutual good arrangement in regard to work for the winter, at least such that would be profitable to us and helpful to them. After due consideration an agreement was made, and their first work was to assist in building an addition to our shop, or rake factory as it was afterwards known. They remained with us altogether a year and one-half, or until near the close of the war, when Dan went home and John remained to complete a contract which he had entered into with us to make one thousand dozen rakes and turn thirty thousand broom handles. The broom handles were turned and stored in every available space about the factory for final seasoning, and a good start made on the rake contract, when one stormy night, near the first of March, 1866, the factory took fire; and sawmill and factory with broom handles and partly manufactured rakes all were completely destroyed, and no insurance. We had recently paid the second payment on the property, which was now forfeited. We had accounts to collect, and debts to pay, one of which would about balance the other. A good span of horses and wagon was the only firm property left to us. We settled with John Muir under the peculiar circumstances as equitably as only Christian brothers could. I don't remember the exact figures of the account, somewhere about three hundred dollars, and after paying him what cash we could scratch up, enough to carry him a good journey into the United States, he cut down the account to two hundred dollars, taking our individual promises to pay, each one hundred dollars, without time limit and without interest. A few years afterwards in San Francisco, when relating some of his experiences, he showed these notes to his friends, who derisively asked him when he expected payment. "Never mind," he replied, "those notes will be paid." Laughingly, they responded, "Won't you kindly let us know when you get the cash?" They regarded it as a good, soft joke on John. Not long afterwards he wrote me that he was contemplating marriage, and that he never began to feel poor till he faced the calculations regarding it, and also intimated the acceptability of the promised fund. Though poor enough myself, I got together a hundred dollars and sent it to him. Muir at once showed his jibing friends the cash, and had the laugh on them, who said, "Well that is pretty good, there is one Christian conscience in the world, but that is only one, wait till we see the other paid." "That will be all right, too, one of these days," replied John, and so it subsequently proved.

APPRECIATIVE REFERENCES TO JOHN MUIR

The first winter of John Muir's stay with us he regarded it as likely to be the only one, so he took up no special course of study, but gave us pretty freely the benefit of his fine conversational powers. He was making acquaintances with us, and we were endeavoring to fully understand him; and when it comes to measuring up and determining the extent of the capabilities, disabilities, liabilities and various other abilities of a gifted young man, who had the advantage of about three years' university study and training, and a continuous study of nature's great book as well, it will be easy to see that we had much the hardest sizing-up job. It was easy to admire, but to understand and appreciate him required some knowledge of the subject matter of his studies and his modes of thought. Though ardently devoted to science, as well as the study of nature, yet the agnostic tendencies that had their beginning about that time found no sympathy with him. With him there was no dark chilly reasoning that chance and the survival of the fittest accounted for all things. On the contrary, that God "cared for the sparrows of the air and the lilies of the field," was something that his kindly nature could most readily understand and heartily appreciate. He examined nature with a lover's eye, and he saw not only an All-Creator, but an All-Father and Protector. In temperament and parental training between myself and he there was much in common. In my thirteenth year I read and studied Goldsmith's Natural History, to which was added Brown's Anecdotes of Animals. Though Goldsmith could hardly be called a naturalist, yet he could write interestingly on any subject which he treated, and when I read Goldsmith I was certainly in close contact with nature and with very little else, such as the native woods and waters of Canada can exemplify. So that Goldsmith at the least helped to make me an interested observer. Not a studious, methodical systematic persistent observer like Muir, but one that had always an interested eye with regard to what was going on about me. Beside this I had from childhood a strong bent for astronomy, mastering as well as I could all accessible information regarding it. In this Muir and I more nearly mated. He was a real live inventor, while I was also so regarded, yet I felt I could not by any means take rank with him, but I was easily awarded the lead in practical mechanics, as my experience, if nothing more, would have justified. But John and I were not the only frogs in that little pond, there were others there to croak as well as we. There was Mary, our steady housekeeper, who had also been a teacher, and three other sisters, one or more of whom would come from the home farm, or the schools where they were teaching, and visit us on Saturdays along with other teachers; also my business partner, C. H. Jay, who lived with us, and Dan Muir and my brother Peter, who was a great reader and never forgot anything; all young lively intelligent people, with common aims and purposes, and yet each with his distinct individuality, which, in discussion, was often decidedly pronounced, but which rarely became ungentlemanly. If, as Garfield said, that Mark Hopkins and a good student sitting on a log would make a university, so I should think that John Muir, though himself then a student, and others learning and contributing, our log house in the mill hollow might modestly claim the same dignity.

I have referred to similarity of temperament, and parental conditions and environment between Muir and myself. These would account for my tendency to invention and mechanics, as my father was at the least a good mechanic, and my ability was largely acquired; but with John it was altogether different, his father was in no sense a mechanic, yet with the seeming absence of the hereditary impulse, and the usual necessary training, both of which I had, he showed himself to be a real born inventive designing mechanic. While still a small boy, he began fixing things about the house and farm, and later while still in his minority, took methodical and regular times out of each morning's sleep to construct special clocks and other intricate machines of his own original design. In this I am not dependent on his or anyone's story because I examined the constructions.

When John Muir made his rake and broom handle contract with us, he also made a proposition to be given the liberty of improving the machinery as he might determine, and that he should receive therefor half the economical results of such improvement during a given period. An arrangement of this kind was entered into, and he began with our self-feeding lathe for turning rake, fork and broom handles and similar articles, which I considered nearly perfect; by rendering this more completely automatic, he nearly doubled the output of broom handles. He placed one handle in position while the other was being turned. It required great activity for him to put away the turned handle, and placed the new one in position during the turning process. When he could do this there would be eight broom handles turned in a minute. Corresponding to this I had on the floor immediately above him a machine that would automatically saw from the round log, after it was fully slabbed or rounded, eight handles per minute, but setting in the log and the slabbing process occupied about three-eighths of the time. This, with keeping saws and place in order, cut the daily output to about two thousand five hundred. John had his drawbacks in similar ways, and at best could not get ahead of the sawing. It was a delight to see those machines at work. He devised and started the construction of several new automatic machines, to make the different parts of the hand rakes, having previously submitted and discussed them with me, from which our intimacy may be judged.

Like all others who have made much of themselves, and much for the world of humanity, Muir was a most diligent student and systematic worker. He would make inroads on his time for sleep and recreation. In fact, for the latter, there was no time allowed. What fun we had was generally caught on the fly. For him, seven hours was the allotment for sleep, that was from ten in the evening to five in the morning. The encroachments were made on the first part of the period, when the study became more especially interesting; an hour or two was not considered, and the clockwould strike eleven or twelve before retiring, but that made no difference about the rising. That was previously determined, and unalterably fixed. His bed was mounted on a cross axle, sustained by two high pedestals, one on each side, and nearer the head than the foot; so that if the foot was not held up it would fall and lie on the floor, and the bed would be reclining at an angle of about forty-five degrees. A rod screwed to the ceiling, and hooked to the foot, sustained it in the level position.

At night, however, a special trigger was affixed to the rod, and sustained the bed. A string connected the trigger to his specially constructed clock, which at the determined hour, five in the morning, would pull the trigger, and release the bed, which would instantly fall, leaving the occupant in a half-upright position, with his feet on the floor. If he lay crooked in the bed, or crossways, he was apt to be rolled out sharply to the floor. Our house had only board partitions, ordinary sounds could be heard in every room; so that when John's bed fell it was a wake up signal for all in the house; but if we heard a double shock, which would be caused by a roll out, then we had the signal for a good laugh on John, and he had further jolly reminders of this at the breakfast table. Charlie (Mr. Jay) generally led off in these jibes.

When the bed fell, an arm swung around, into the fingers of which had been placed a match, which in swinging, rubbed over a piece of sandpaper, and being ignited, came to rest over the wick of an oil lamp, perched in its regular place on a shelf. The lamp was thus lighted with the fall of the bed. A sponge bath in the tub was the next move, then dressing, which was followed by study, till breakfast time. Then the day was for work except the noon hours, when there was always the handy book, and place to turn to, and if there was one minute or five minutes before eating, it was used in reading; and it was the same after dinner for the remainder of the noon hour, unless some very interesting topic was started at the table that must be extended beyond the meal.

MUIR IN INDIANAPOLIS

Soon after the burning of our mill, as has been previously mentioned, John Muir left us, and went to Indianapolis, Indiana, and engaged with a wagon manufacturing firm; they soon discovered John's ability in fixing things, and gave him the care of all the machinery. After he had been there about four months, one day, while unlacing a belt, using the tang end of a file to pull out the laces (such as I have done hundreds of times), in which he had a hard pull with a sudden release, which allowed the strain on his arm to plant the tang of the file into the center of his right eye, causing the vitreous humor to run out, it was thought the eye was totally lost; but with highly skillful treatment, and eminent "vis naturae" or good healing force, his sight was fully recovered. An angular corner in the pupil of the eye was testimony during his lifetime of the entrance of the file. He had about one month's confinement in a dark room, and was gradually brought to the light. While in this confinement, as he remarked to me in a letter, he had the grandest opportunity for prolonged meditation. He decided that life was too short and uncertain, and time too valuable, to spend it mending belts, and sharpening saws. While he was looking after wagon-making machinery, God was making a world; and if his eyesight was spared, he would devote his time to watching the process. Accordingly, about six weeks after the accident, he settled up with his employers, paid his bills, and started a cross country journey on foot, from Indianapolis to South Carolina. He rather avoided the ordinary roads, preferring the woods, river banks and mountains, plant and general nature study being his object. At Charleston he had a weary time waiting for money from home. South Carolina had scarcely begun to recover from the devastations of the war, food was scarce, and very limited was the money to buy. He took his abode in a half-ruined church outside the city, from which for six successive days he made his anxious journey to the post office, for the needed money that was to come from home. When it finally arrived, he continued his way southward through Florida, then over into Cuba, making the double journey through its extent; then taking in some of the West India islands, he crossed the isthmus of Panama, and took steamer for San Francisco, from thence he started for the mountains. In order to fill up his depleted exchequer, he engaged as a shepherd for a large flock of sheep, the migrations of his flock enabling him to see the country and pursue his studies, which were never lost sight of. Shortly previous to this, Yosemite valley had been discovered, and its possibilities as a great wonderland for tourists estimated. A company was formed, a stage road projected, and a hotel was to be built in the valley. The inaccessibility of the valley called for a sawmill to be built on the ground, in order to make the lumber to build the hotel. Muir was in touch with all this, and convinced the money magnates that he could build the mill, a simple structure, which, when satisfactorily completed, he ran, until the hotel was finished. Then, except for Muir's residence in it, the mill was of no further use. He had built his bachelor's den in the back end, up under the roof. It was a bed room, kitchen and dining room, as well as a naturalist's studio, and museum of botanical collections and interesting curios, natural and mechanical. It was reached by a ladder and a plank stretching across the wide space from one beam to the other. I am describing it from his letter and my sawmill knowledge. It seemed as primitive as a cliff dweller's home, yet he had city privileges. He had an acqueduct system, by which constantly clear sparkling water flowed through his room, or rather headquarters as he traveled the mountains. He now began to be known as a magazine writer and lecturer, and scientific and literary celebrities from Eastern America and Europe, visiting the Yosemite, called on him, pleased to enjoy his humble hospitality and his enthusiastic, enlightening conversation. Early in the seventies, when in the reading room of the Mechanic's Institute, Peterboro, Canada, in looking over one of the leading magazines, my eye fell on a well-illustrated article, captioned "the Glaciers of the Sierras." Glancing over it, I inwardly remarked, "That style of writing and those sketches make me think of Muir." I then began at the beginning, enjoying the reading, thinking how much it was like Muir's talk; and at the end was most agreeably though not wholly surprised to find my friend's brief name appended to it. He was and always is just plain John Muir.

A life like this, so interestingly interwoven with ours, hardly calls for an apology for the extended references which I have made to it. What I have given is only a brief introduction to a great career. He became the great mountain explorer of America, giving particular attention to finding the location and action of the great glaciers, from the arctic circle to the gulf of California. Often for months at a time he never saw the face of humanity. The masterly mountain sheep, that spurns all but the loftiest crags, and bears and deer and the birds were his principal acquaintances; but he was never lonely, to him all nature was alive, and told a never-ending charming story. Woods and winds and waters had their ceaseless music. Even quiet, restful, sleepy winter occasionally broke out into the howling storm or booming avalanche or the shaking earthquake, which were regarded as only demonstrations of nature's great power and fulfillment of God's purpose. But I must leave off. Those who would like a further acquaintance with this fine old friend must read some of his charming books, "The Mountains of California," "The Forest Reservations of America." Young folks will be delighted with his dog story, "Life in the Sierras" and "Boyhood Life." There are several other works, all charmingly written, and can be had at most of the publishing houses.

About two years ago I received one of his specially good friendly letters, and I turned it over to my son to read, after which I said to him, "Now you are a business man and understand the money worth of things, can you put a value on that letter?" He reflected a moment and said, "Oh, I give it up." My reply was, "So do I." And so it is always, genuine friendship never gets down to the dollar measurement.

THE PASSING OF JOHN MUIR

The above lengthy reference to my much-esteemed old friend was written nearly a year ago, and was thought to be all that might be said regarding him; and this is interjected on account of the fact that on December 24, 1914, after a summer of irregular health conditions he contracted pneumonia, and in a few days died. The next morning I read the account in our Milwaukee paper; it had been telegraphed to all the leading papers in the United States. It was an overwhelming surprise and disappointment to me. In a prolonged journey to the Pacific coast in 1911, I expected to make him a long visit; but before I arrived there he had started on his great South American journey. Failing to see him in 1911, I wrote him in the early part of 1912, stating that I had planned a visit for the summer of 1915, if health and strength permitted, not mainly because this was the summer of the great exposition in San Francisco, for that was to me a second or third consideration; seeing relatives and friends was the main purpose, and as the time drew on, and it was arranged that our general missionary convention would be in Los Angeles in the same summer, the interest of the trip became much greater. Of course, the exposition, then going on, was a most extraordinary show—a great beautiful mass of matter, that in some sense might represent spirit; but grand as it undoubtedly was, it was still only a fleeting show, while Christian friendship is eternal and abiding, and as we draw near the sunset of our brief day, we appraise the values of things, by their relation to the things unseen, yet enduring and eternal.

John's reply to this letter of mine is the one referred to at the close of the previous paragraph, regarding which I asked my son to adjudge its value. Now that John is parted from us, everything connected with him becomes doubly dear and valuable. On this account I introduce a copy of this letter, so that relatives and friends may share the pleasure of its reading with myself.

Martinez, May 10, 1912.

Dear William Trout:

In trying to clear away the huge talus of letters a year high, accumulated while I was in South America and Africa, I find your long interesting letter of March 15th full of good news.

I'm always glad to hear from you. Friends get closer and dearer the farther they travel on life's journey. It's fine to see how youthful your heart remains; and wide and far reaching your sympathy, with everybody and everything. Such people never grow old. I only regret your being held so long in mechanical bread winning harness, instead of making enough by middle age and spending the better half of life in studying God's works as I wanted you to do long ago. The marvel is that in the din and rattle of mills you have done so wondrous well. By all means keep on your travels, since you know so well how to reap their benefits. I shall hope to see you when next you come West. And don't wait until the canal year. Delays are more and more dangerous as sundown draws nigh. I've just returned from a long fruitful trip: first up the Amazon a thousand miles, and return to Para; thence to Rio de Janeiro; thence to Santos, and inland four or five hundred miles, in the State of Parana; thence back to the coast at Paranagua. Thence to Buenos Aires, stopping at many interesting ports by the way; thence across the Andes to Santiago; thence south five hundred miles up through grand forests to the snow, where I found Arucaria imbricata, a wonderful tree forming the strangest woods imaginable. Thence back across the Andes and Argentina, to Montevideo; thence to Teneriffe. Thence to Cape Town, Africa; thence one thousand three hundred miles northward to Victoria Falls, where I found Adansonia digitata, another wonderful tree; thence to the East Coast and Beira. Thence to Mozambique, Zanzibar, etc., to Mombasa; thence to Victoria Nyanza, Entebbe Jinji, to the head of the Nile. Thence back to Mombasa, around the north end of the continent to Aden, and home by the Red Sea, and Naples and New York; thus crossing the equator six times on a journey about forty thousand miles long. Hope to tell you about it some day. In the meantime, I am, ever faithfully, your friend,

JOHN MUIR.

Yes, John hoped to tell me his great travel story, and I, as earnestly hoped to listen and talk it over with him, much the same as I did in the year of the great earthquake, when he had a year or two previous made his globe circuit through Europe and Asia and the islands of the Pacific and back home again, a much longer and in every way a greater journey than the one described above. I have this letter. But I did not heed his suggestion, that it was *"dangerous to wait, we being too near sundown."* I thought the danger lay all on my side.

I was four years and two months older than he, and was not near so hearty and strong, though on account of his weather-beaten face from the outdoor life, he looked quite as old as I, who for forty years past have spent nearly all my time indoors. I felt sure that if we failed to see each other it would all depend on me. But we never can tell, and while many of our troubles show advance signs of their coming, pneumonia, old people's greatest foe, gives no previous notice. It comes without warning, and even with the vigorous, often makes short work.

While the public press of the whole country and the magazines made more or less extended references to his death, the Pacific coast papers showed an interest and sympathy much beyond all others. Some of my friends sent me copies or clippings. But I could not rest without more direct information. I had an acquaintance with the younger daughter at her home; my youngest daughter Lucretia who accompanied me on that journey and Helen Muir, being both near the same age, were generally cordial chums. They had their daily horseback rides and other enjoyments, while their fathers had their times together at home. Mrs. Muir had died some years before this. Wanda, the elder, had just been married, and was away on her bridal tour. I did not see her. Shortly afterwards, Helen also married, and now, not having the address of either of the daughters, with their new and unknown names, I wrote my letter of requests and condolence to the Muir estate, expecting it to reach at least one of the daughters, and most kindly and cordially Wanda (Mrs. Hanna) answered it, besides sending special printed matter and clippings. This good letter follows:

Dear Mr. Trout:

    I must thank you for your very kind letter. Although I have never met you, I feel that I know you as a friend, for my father so often spoke of you with regard and affection, and talked of the times when he was with you as a young man. His death was a great shock to us all, for although he had been very frail for a year following an attack of the grippe, and been very sick last July he seemed somewhat better when he started south to visit my sister on the 17th of December, and we had no idea that the end was so near. He had often spoken of having only a short time left to finish his work and had put all his affairs in shape, but seemed cheerful and hopeful to the very last, and was talking of his work when his health suddenly stopped without any warning or suffering.

My father's Alaska book was nearly completed at the time of his death and will soon be published. There are a good many other notes and manuscripts that probably will at some time be edited and published in some form, but as yet no decision has been made as to how they are to be used.

The botanical and geological specimens are still in our possession. Some of them, no doubt, will be given to some scientific association; and some of them we will keep. He made no disposition of them himself.

My father had three surviving sisters and two brothers. My sister, Mrs. Buel A. Funk, lives at Dagget, San Bernardino County, California, and has three little boys. I have four boys. If you come to California in 1915, or at any other time, I hope that you will visit us. I am deeply sorry that you did not do so while my dear father was still with us.

Thanking you for your sympathy, and your long friendship for my father.

Sincerely,

Wanda Muir Hanna,
(Mrs. Thomas R. Hanna)

Martinez, California.
January 31, 1913.

I have already referred to eulogistic articles in the magazines in regard to John Muir. I will now refer to only one, that of Theodore Roosevelt in the Outlook. During his last presidential term he made a visit to California, and, as a matter of course, visited the Yosemite Valley; and, as a further matter of course, took along with him John Muir as the best guide and exponent of the beauties and wonders of that wonderful glen with its surroundings, the big trees, etc. In his mention of Muir in the Outlook, the president so nicely refers to his beautiful simplicity of character as well as his accurate knowledge of any subject of his attention and study. The president told of the encampment under the big trees, and incidents of the journey as they related to Muir; and Muir, in conversation, told me the incidents as they related to the president. A great crowd of editors, reporters, politicians and others, accompanied, or rather, followed, the president on this mountain journey. They not merely wanted to see, but to have the prestige of being a part of the president's great Yosemite party. Muir regarded them as an unmitigated nuisance, and no doubt the president partially shared his opinion. At the great Sequoia Grove, Muir suggested that they quietly give the party the slip, and let it go forward while they would remain behind and encamp alone under the canopy of the towering Sequoia Gigantiae. To this the president promptly agreed. The manager of the party was let into the secret, and he left them what was needed. I remarked to him that an event like that, alone in confidential chat with the president of the United States, in such sublime surroundings, was something long to be remembered. "Oh, yes," said I, "Did you sleep much?" "No, not very much." "Then you did a lot of talking?" "Well, I did the most of it." "What was it about?" "Oh! I stuffed him pretty well regarding the timber thieves, and the destructive work of the lumbermen, and other spoilers of our forests." "How did he take it?" "Well, he did not say much, but I know and so do you, how he went for them afterwards."

While it was a good time for quiet conversation, it was also a grand opportunity for great meditations. The towering majesty of the great trees, as enhanced by the fire light, and their immense age, as proven by Muir's count of the rings of one that is fallen, show them to be as he says "respectable saplings when Adam was young." They are undoubtedly the oldest and the largest living things in the world.

John Muir held a doubtful attitude to what is called spiritualistic phenomena, telepathy and such occult beliefs as are enlisting the attention of psychologists so largely at the present time; yet there occurred with him a remarkable presentiment, vision or dream, whatever one may call it, relating to the death of his father.

It was near the last of June, 1896, when he gave me the narration direct. The occurrence and his father's death were in the same month. He told it quite circumstantially, but the details are not well remembered. However, one night in the earlier half of the month he had a very vivid striking dream regarding his father, seeing him in bed, and likely to die. He was strongly impressed with the idea that he must go to his old Wisconsin home at once, and began getting ready. The following night he had much the same vision. His older brother, David, was then living in California, John went to him, and told him he had the most certain impression that their father would die about as soon as they could get to see him. David made light of his premonitions, but finally concluded, since John was surely going, and at the best his father might not live much longer, that he would go with him, and they started at once. At Omaha, Nebraska, where their younger brother, Dan, resided they stopped off and soon persuaded him to accompany them. They arrived in Portage City, Wisconsin, and in time to have a recognition and some conversation with their father and a day or two afterwards he passed away. John did not regard this as a chance dream, but a real presentiment.

The only thing approaching that in my experience, was in the town of Owen Sound, Ontario, Canada, forty-five years ago. One summer morning about eight o'clock, a farmer, while plowing in his field two miles from the town, was fatally shot by a man in ambush. That very time I was at work in a shop, and was suddenly impressed with the mental sight of a crouching man firing a gun at another man. I was just as much startled as if I had heard the report. I turned around and said, "Somebody is shot." I would have regarded it as a freak of the imagination, had not my sister come in a half hour afterwards and related the occurrence, having gotten the news direct from the messenger who came in on horseback for a doctor.

On his return journey, John Muir notified me that he would be at our Union Station at a given time, and requested me to meet him, which I did most cheerfully. After the greeting he apologized for taking me from my work to meet him, saying he never could trust himself in the cities, they were man's arbitrary building without any intelligible common plan. "But," said he, "you might put me down in any dark valley in God's mountains and I could soon find my way out. If you come across a man's face in the dark and feel his nose, you know where to find his mouth." On the street cars going to our home he told me the story of the presentiment regarding his father, which I have given, regarding it as extraordinary. He remained with us about twenty-four hours. The children greatly enjoyed his talk. None of us retired till midnight. Mother and I were complimented on our family. "See those fine big boys of yours, and I have no boys. They are scarce with the Muirs, there may not be enough to carry the name."

He left us to join a commission in Chicago, appointed by President Cleveland, on forest reservations to be made in different parts of the United States. This occupied his attention for a year or more, and was the subject of his largest and best book.

Well, his day is past, but his story is not told. A life so full of great service cannot be fully told. No one knows it all, except it be himself and his Creator. It is all finished and in the great record, and he passes on with the closing. One of his Eastern literary friends sublimely pictures this in three magnificent stanzas. Though we might criticise the phrasing, the imaginative sweep overpowers us, except the last three lines which approach the common place. Chas. L. Edson of the New York Evening Mail is the poetic author. He makes a characteristic answer for John when he says: "John o' the mountains says, 'I knew'." That is, I have been watching, I have seen it.

> John o' the mountains, wonderful John,
> Is past the summit and traveling on;
> The turn of the trail on the mountain side,
> A smile and "Hail" where the glaciers slide,
> A streak of red where the condors ride,
> And John is over the Great Divide.
>
> John o' the mountains camps today
> On a level spot by the milky way;
> And God is telling him how he rolled
> The smoking earth from the iron mold,
> And hammered the mountains till they were cold,
> And planted the redwood trees of old.
>
> And John o' the mountains says: "I knew,
> And I wanted to grapple the hand o' you;
> And now we're sure to be friends and chums
> And camp together till chaos comes."

From *Collier's Weekly, January 16, 1915.*

Collier's editor continues, "Of course, John Muir and God are friends. Muir fraternized with the birds of the field and forest, and chummed with the squirrel and the bear. He rhapsodized over the beauty and sweetness of the flowers, and communed with God through the redwoods and pines. His life was a glorification of God's original handiwork."

John was familiar with his Bible, God's revealed will, as well as nature's book. It was his child study and was ingrained in his mental make-up as his writings abundantly testify.

We must now reluctantly part from our friend and his story and again resume the family narration.

TROUT & JAY BUSINESS CLOSED UP

Besides the family references, in Muir's and our own story, but little of note had occurred. Father had spent one winter in very serious sickness. Just previous to this time, Charles Jay and my brother Peter had put in a winter term at the High School in Owen Sound. Now, after our mill was burned, it was deemed best to separate. Each one to make the best possible shift for himself. As C. H. Jay had been in charge of the business end of our firm, he was left at home to settle up accounts, and also made another settlement with the Laycocks, by which we retained the millsite. Oil had been discovered at Oil Springs and Petrolia, a year or more previous, and thither people were flocking as if there were gold mines. To the original property holders it was as good as a gold mine; and possibly the same to a few sharp speculators. Many of the operators at first made good money, only to encounter great loss afterwards, unless they were able to hold out till steady prices obtained.

I headed for Oil Springs by way of Toronto, and since I was only about twenty miles away from the residence of my sweetheart, Miss Jennie B. Knowles, at Dunbarton, Pickering, I determined to make the short journey east and and see her. As we were not then engaged I had some anxiety to know the state of her mind toward me, after the adverse change in my financial condition. This proved to be all right, and, though at the bottom of my poverty, I proposed. While I got only a postponement, it was an encouraging one, which in due time came out all right.

OIL SPRINGS VENTURE

At Toronto resided my two next younger brothers, Edward and John. Both were married and held responsible positions in the Leader newspaper office, and had made good acquaintanceships with some of the leading business men of the city. I was introduced to two of them, and my Oil Springs prospect presented. They seemed to read me pretty thoroughly, and cautioned me to lay off my modesty; that I would no doubt be good at once for any demands made upon me; and I would soon come to it. This was needed and I profited by it, for when arriving at Oil Springs I soon found good employment in a machine shop though not a well-trained machinist.

This Oil Springs experience was like a new beginning for me. I was among strangers. Nearly two-thirds of the operators and half the working men were Americans. Mostly from the new oil districts of Pennsylvania. New people and interesting new conditions prevented loneliness. Still there was abundant time for meditation. Full thirty-two years of my life had passed and I was seemingly only a beginner. I saw that it would be better to leave business alone. The ability to earn good living wages, while working for other people, and the freedom from anxiety, connected with such a course, along with my distaste for business, and my relish in the study and practice of mechanics, determined me to be an employee, rather than an employer. But at that time I was not properly prepared to judge. Excepting while working for father I always had the self-direction of my work as well as that of other people. I did not then know what it was to be under the inconsiderate direction of a meanly disposed boss who had no decent regard for common human rights. Just a little taste of this sort inclined me for a time to reverse this decision, as will be seen by our further experience.

After being in Oil Springs about six weeks, my partner, C. H. Jay, also came, like myself to work independently, as best he could. I had some solicitude regarding him, being younger than I, and having no mechanical experience except such as he had gained in the few years working with me, which was so different from what he would be called upon to do. After his arrival he spent a week before getting a job and in the meantime was carefully observing and studying what he saw, and this habit he quietly kept up after he obtained employment, which was with a gang doing general repair work. The boss of the gang, like many others at the Springs, was only a respectable bluff. When he came across a difficult job, he would give his men a chance to suggest his method of procedure; and he began to look to Charley as the likeliest of the lot, and he was not mistaken; but it was not Charley he called him, it was Mr. Jay, and Mr. Jay was soon in good regard by both boss and men and to my surprise he got as good pay as I did; which all goes to show the advantage of playing the owl, tactfully—thinking hard and looking wise. But Charley had an uncommonly good practical mechanical sense, as was afterwards very fully proved. He was always ready to handle in a masterly way any difficult job that came before him.

When I came to Oil Springs in March, 1866, crude oil was about five dollars per barrel. The previous fall and winter it had been nine dollars. It was regarded that its use as an illuminant was only fairly begun, that good prices would surely be maintained. Five dollars would be the summer price and in the fall higher prices would return, but the price kept steadily falling, and the business prospect gradually growing worse. Wells that were costly to run were shut down. But this was regarded as only temporary. It was expected that the fall and winter would surely bring enhanced prices and a resumption of business. Late in the month of June, Mr. James Campbell of Thornbury, Ontario, a friend of ours, had a fire loss similar to ours. His dwelling and store were burned. Having learned the machinist trade, he concluded to fall back upon it, and came to Oil Springs to look up his chances. He met with Mr. Jay and myself and we jointly considered the prospects of business. We decided that

Oil Springs was a declining town, and Petrolia, seven miles away, was a rising one; so an arrangement was made to combine our small means and efforts, build a machine and blacksmith shop, for general repair work for oil wells. Mr. Campbell was our main dependence for cash, we were to furnish our horses and wagon, and our work in getting a building erected and ready for business. Accordingly, about the first of July, I left my Oil Springs employer, bought a good chopping axe and borrowed a broad axe, and with the privilege of cutting in a certain woods, began chopping trees and hewing the timber for our new shop. This was lonesome, hard work, usually done by a group of at least three or four persons. Mosquitoes were more or less constant in their annoyance. In about three or four weeks my timber was hewed and drawn to the site for building. A few men were employed, the building was framed, erected and enclosed, ready for service early in September. Also the timbered foundation for a good house for Mr. Campbell was laid and the kitchen portion of the house roughly completed. About the last of August, Charles and I had a brief vacation. We went home, where I witnessed the marriage of my sister Mary and Charles Jay, father as elder of our Meaford church, being the officiating minister; and he served in that capacity for most of his children. It was my pleasure, not the bridegroom's, to accompany the bride to her home. He took the horses and wagons across the country, while I went with my sister around by the railway. Charley always had the team under his charge. The kitchen of the intended Campbell residence was to be our home, at least, temporarily. It was certainly unpretentious, but that did not mar the happiness of its occupants. No one could accommodate herself to a new and trying situation any better than Mary; and she could do it with a light heart. Charles was the one that worried. He began to see and keenly felt that he had brought his new wife, to begin business with the prospect of certain failure. We were ready; had a good blacksmith and helper employed; they fitted up the shop with the necessary tools in good shape, and I got the machine shop ready for work. But the work would not come. I went around and called at the wells and talked up business and got a few orders which were soon disposed of. We found that the operators were quietly shutting down their plants. Oil had lowered to one dollar per barrel, and no buyers. We struggled and kept going for a month or two; till late in November, two flowing wells were struck. One of them being a gusher, flowing two hundred barrels of fine quality oil per day; and the price went down to twelve and one-half cents per barrel. I attended meetings of the operators and learned the hopelessness of the situation. Mr. Campbell came, a council of war was called and we decided to surrender. It was a gloomy conclusion to my married partners; but except for their sakes I was not disturbed a moment. We dissolved our partnership. As Campbell had put up most all the cash, he was awarded the shop and property. Charley got the horses and wagon back and I contented myself with a beautiful little English foot lathe, which had cost in England fifty pounds, but we had purchased it for eighty dollars. Mr. Campbell went back home. Mr. and Mrs. Jay back to Meaford to make a second beginning. I remained to finish up a little work; pay off our two men, put away tools, board up the windows, pack up my little lathe and personal belongings, lock up and leave. Which I did one early wintery morning about the first of December, at the end of twenty-four hours of continuous hard, anxious work. Thus ended my last business experiment. Manifestly it would be a most restful change to go to Pickering and see my sweetheart, which I accordingly did, and spent a few days most pleasantly; and after a day or two in Toronto with my brothers, I went to Meaford, and remained with the home folks for nearly a week. Then I answered an advertisement for a woodturner in Owen Sound, I knew the proprietor of the shop and he knew that woodturning was not my regular work. I told him when applying I could do good work but would not be speedy till I had some steady practice. He engaged me at decent wages, and I worked for him about three months. Then I engaged with Christie of Owen Sound as a millwright. This brought me once more to the backwoods at my old calling, which I had quit about nine years before.

My father's apprentice and my former chum, John McInnis, had charge of the job of building a nice small grist mill at Colpoys Bay, about fourteen miles north of Owen Sound. I was to work under him, as he had in former times worked under me. But in either case we accounted ourselves equals. The land had been open for settlemnt only about three years and was then pretty well occupied. Each settler had his little clearing with its small log house, and general shanty conditions. Of course, there were discomforts, but no complaining. In their neighborly democacry they were a most happy lot of people. Skating on the ice of the bay or sliding down the hills in moonlight nights, or small evening parties in the larger houses, were the leading diversions for the young people. I shared very little in these amusements. Religious meetings were generally in private houses, or in a school house, of which at that time there were very few. I attended, as did most of the people. There was only a bi-weekly mail, and in stormy times once a week. A postman carried everything on his back; the mail was mostly letters, of which I contributed probably the biggest individual share. My friends and relatives and most particularly my sweetheart got them. She took nearly a year to decide for me. I did not worry, feeling sure it was coming.

In the early part of June, 1867, we got through with our mill work, and I returned to Owen Sound, working first as a machinist and afterwards as a patternmaker for David Christie. While there, I designed and built a special lathe for my former employers, Chatwin & Comely, to automatically turn the old style round bed rails. This was a good step in advance of the practice of that time.

MARRIAGE—TROUT AND KNOWLES
(See on following page Wm. Henry Trout Tree.)

In the early part of November, 1867, came the pre-arranged time for my marriage to the handsome, buoyant, good girl I had courted for nearly three years—Miss Jane Barclay

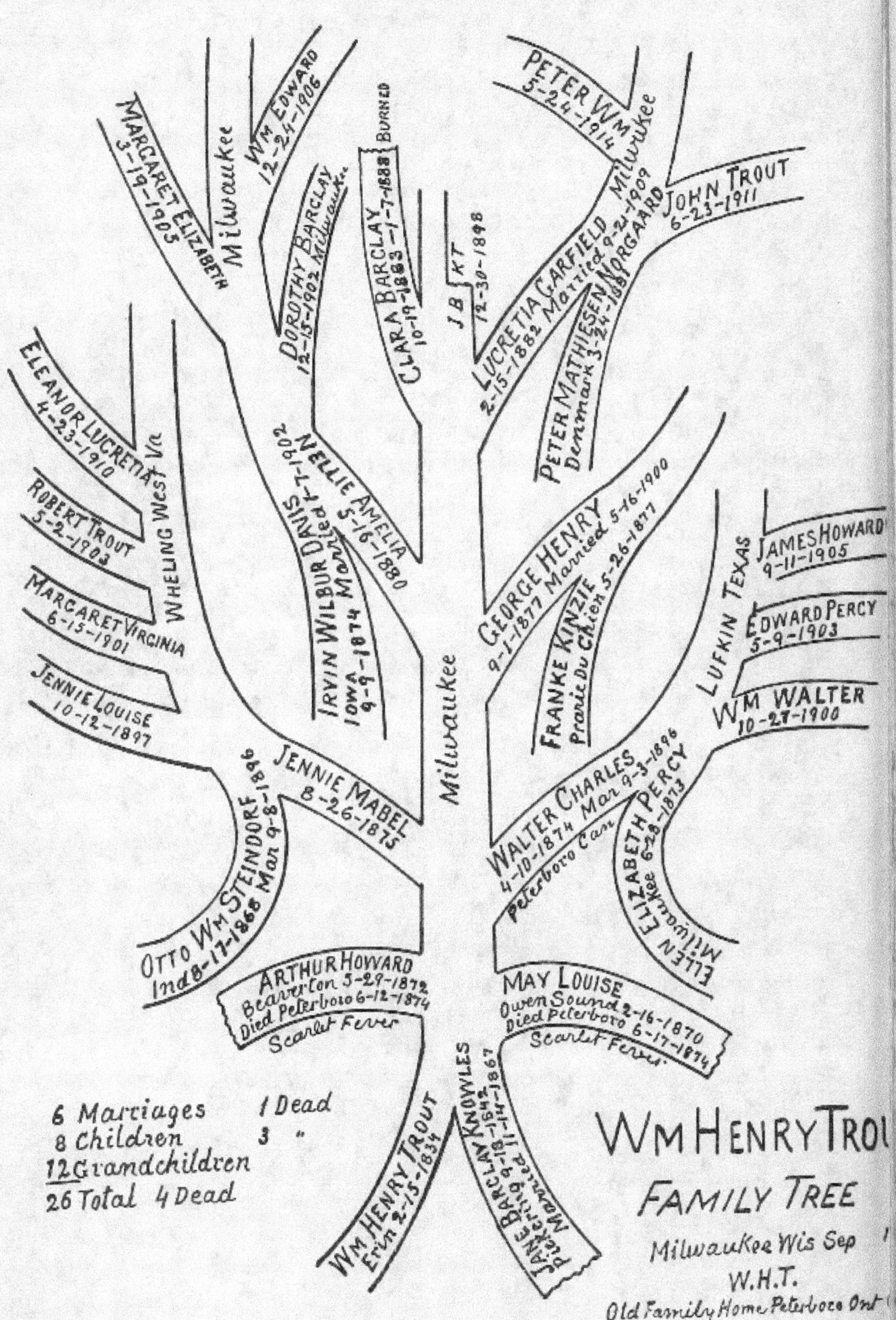
MARGARET ELIZABETH 3-19-1905
Milwaukee
WM EDWARD 12-24-1906
DOROTHY BARCLAY 12-15-1902 Milwaukee
CLARA BARCLAY 10-19-1863 — 1-7-1888 BURNED
JB KT 12-30-1898
PETER WM 5-24-1914
JOHN TROUT 6-23-1911
LUCRETIA GARFIELD 2-15-1882 Married 9-2-1909 Milwaukee
PETER MATHIESSEN NØRGAARD Denmark 3-24-1889
ELEANOR LUCRETIA 4-23-1910
ROBERT TROUT 5-2-1903
MARGARET VIRGINIA 6-15-1901
JENNIE LOUISE 10-12-1897
WHEELING WEST VA
NELLIE AMELIA 5-16-1880
IRVIN WILBUR DAVIS Married 7-7-1902 IOWA 9-9-1870
GEORGE HENRY 5-16-1900
9-1-1877 Married 5-26-1877
FRANKE KINZIE Pravic Du Chien
JAMES HOWARD 9-11-1905
EDWARD PERCY 5-9-1903
WM WALTER 10-27-1900
LUFKIN TEXAS
Milwaukee
JENNIE MABEL 8-26-1875
OTTO WM STEINDORF 1896 Mar 9-8- Ind 8-17-1868
WALTER CHARLES 4-10-1874 Mar 9-3-1896 Peterboro Can
ELLEN ELIZABETH PERCY 6-28-1873 Milwaukee
ARTHUR HOWARD Beaverton 5-29-1872 Died Peterboro 6-12-1874 Scarlet Fever
MAY LOUISE Owen Sound 2-16-1870 Died Peterboro 6-17-1874 Scarlet Fever
WM HENRY TROUT Ervin 2-15-1834
BARCLAY KNOWLES 9-12-1842 — 1867 Married 8-18-1 Catharine
6 Marriages   1 Dead
8 Children   3 "
12 Grandchildren
26 Total   4 Dead
WM HENRY TROU
FAMILY TREE
Milwaukee Wis Sep
W.H.T.
Old Family Home Peterboro Ont

JANE BARCLAY KNOWLES TROUT
AND TWO ELDEST DECEASED BY SCARLET FEVER

Knowles, daughter of Abraham Knowles, a well-to-do farmer and much-respected citizen of Pickering, Ontario, Canada. Miss Knowles's mother was the daughter of Elder George Barclay, the pioneer farmer preacher formerly mentioned. Ten dollars were my wages per week then. I knew I was worth more, and tried hard to get a promise of a raise after marriage, or at least not later than the first of the incoming year. I got everything else that was pleasant and hopeful save the direct promise and had to content myself with it.

I drew from my accumulated wages held by the boss, one hundred dollars, with which, and a small sum left from former payments, I started for Pickering. I took my father and sister Harriet with me. My journey was about one hundred and forty miles, and theirs one hundred and twenty. I bought a fine broadcloth coat and pants with satin vest, which I have still, all finely made in one of the leading clothing houses of Toronto, for twenty-two dollars; also a fine Tweed suit, silk mixed, for seventeen dollars; felt hat and shoes cost me four dollars and fifty cents; other clothing incidentals, two dollars and fifty cents; the whole totaling, forty-six dollars.

Father, sister Harriet, and myself arrived the day previous to the wedding. My brother John and wife Eliza came on the wedding day. As the numerous relatives and friends of the bride lived mostly in that locality, the spacious parlor and adjoining room were well filled with guests. Father was the officiating elder (he never would allow "Reverend" prefixed to his name, nor would he give it to anyone else); he had a form of marriage somewhat to his liking, but not well written out. With his leave I took it, improved the order and style a little, and gave it back to him on good paper with good bold writing. The obligations on each side were in mutual terms, there was no "obey" in it. The ceremony was at noon, and with such style as befitted a good farmer's home. My brother John took the second bridal kiss. The usual kisses, good wishes, and congratulations followed; after which the guests moved to their places at the feast in the long dining room, where on the long and broad table there was such a profusion of the good and luxurious things of life as liberal hearts and good cooks could furnish. Nearly two hours were spent in enjoyable eating and lively conversation. In the course of the afternoon, when guests began to separate, goodbyes were in order, and the new joining relation was the cause of some affectionate and tearful partings.

The Trout portion of the party took a train back to Toronto; the bride and groom to continue their wedding journey to Niagara Falls and Buffalo, and to the old academy and friends in Williamsville, New York; visits to relatives were made en route. There was a short return visit to the new parental Knowles's home. Then came the final leave taking, and the start on the Northern journey, taking in my father's home, giving old friends and relatives and mother, a short joyous acquaintance with her new daughter. Another half day brought us to our new home in the town of Owen Sound, there to assume married life's duties and responsibilities.

Our first residence, previously rented by myself, was a three-room, small brick house, with full-size, stone-built cellar and wooden lean-to for a kitchen. There was also quite a large lot, which made a big potato patch, for this we paid four dollars per month, or about one-tenth of my wages, which is a very much lower ratio than is usual nowadays; twice that or more is common. Our first Sunday was at the little brick church, where all were not only brethren, but personal friends were easily remembered. After the meeting, when the usual handshaking is in order, it will be easy to imagine that the bride, Mrs. Trout, would be a center of attraction; and my ability, which was never good for making neat graceful introductions, was greatly tried. When Mrs. Miller, who was formerly a Stephens and an old-time friend of our family, was being introduced and informed that Mrs. Trout was a granddaughter of old father Barclay, said no further commendation was needed. Brother George Miller, always the wag of his company, expressed his great pleasure in making her acquaintance, but was very sorry to be obliged to inform her that he must have her arrested. She looked a little astonished, and gave me an inquiring glance, but he, continuing, said, "You see I am the fishery inspector for this Georgian Bay district, and you have been catching trout out of season." Canadian people are generally decorous, in church, but this broke the bounds of church manners; at that time the laugh was explosive and loud.

Our first two years of married life were spent in Owen Sound, and upon the whole happy years they were. Our first little daughter was born there, May Louise, a bright, cheerful, joyous, lively sprite, that enlivened our home for nearly five years; and departed a few days behind her younger brother, after a visitation of scarlet fever. At Owen Sound we began to meet the various problems and necessities of family life. Being the eldest of my mother's family, I had the best opportunity to learn them, and how father and mother met them. My business experience was also a help. But our problems, financial and otherwise, were not like theirs. Like every other pair beginning the family household life, we had to meet our own conditions. Some are fairly prepared by previous observation, good study, and hard consecutive thinking. Others who may have been brought up and trained in standard ways consider that they will, as a matter of course, be ready for every problem when the necessity arises. Such was the case with Mrs. Trout. Her father was not only provider, but was also mainly the spender, or the one who made the purchases; and, being a farmer, these were usually on credit. If income from crops failed to meet the bills his credit was good. A six-month note settled it. The mother regulated the house, and made good use of what was furnished. Everything moved like clockwork. Boys and girls worked by uniform routine, without responsibility or care; and though seemingly ready, yet they were not educated and well prepared for the eventualities of life. I felt that my success in life largely depended in following out and making the most of my mechanical proclivities. Besides working ten hours per day, and occasional work in the evenings, a good part of other evenings was devoted to study in order to be ready for the many underlying problems, that were likely to be met in the progress of my work. This made me a dull companion for my young and lively wife. On this account I often relaxed; but my steady purpose was to make myself as valuable as possible to those who might employ me, so as to get the best wages I could possibly command; and turn over the whole or such part as might be needed to my family business partner, to expend as she might deem most advisable. As man and wife are partners, this is obviously the true and proper course, which does not prevent each from advising and helping the other, as may be needed; but it leaves each free in his or her sphere of duty, to make the most of it, and thus gain the mutual respect that springs from their well-directed though divided effort.

LOCK INVENTING.

In the summer of 1869, Robert E. Stephens came to Christie's foundry to have some new style gate hangings made, presenting some free-hand pencil sketches and verbal explanations as to how they should be made. With Mr. Christie's permission I took his sketch, simply as ideas, and embodied them in the best form I could to accomplish his intended purpose; made good drawings with which he was well pleased; made the patterns and had the work completed to his great satisfaction; and he had it patented, and in the summer of 1913, I saw in Owen Sound a gate mounted with them.

This being regarded as a good serviceable piece of work, he came to me with some ideas regarding a lock, or rather a lock latch, asking me to work it out, and he said, "We will halve the results between us." I did so, on my own time, producing a good simple gravity lock latch, which he claimed as his own, and proceeded to apply for a patent. I maintained that it should be a joint patent; but he insisted that it was his idea, and the idea was the whole thing, and that my consideration would come in with a share of the profits. In other words I was to content myself with an indefinite promise. Instead of doing that I set to work and got up a more improved form, and made application for my own invention on it, hoping to keep clear of his; but our claims collided and a trial before an arbitrator's court was declared, which I had not the funds to stand, so the matter was abandoned. In the meantime, however, the inventive bee had got into my bonnet, and kept buzz-

ing about locks. Also shortly after this, a cousin of Mrs.
Trout, Randal Bently, visited us, and locks with various other
inventions were the subjects discussed. He told me what the
Yale Lock Company, then in its beginning, were undertaking.
This was a spur to further effort, so I gave my whole time to
locks, most enjoyably spending a good part of one winter on
them; and drew on a small fund held by my father-in-law,
Abraham Knowles, for the benefit of Mrs. Trout when she
might need it for our living. I made some good practicable
locks, and applied for patents, and sought means to manufacture without any kind of good prospect, so I abandoned the
whole undertaking in disgust. Some months afterwards, however, when putting the iron work into the Owen Sound registry office, I made a fairly good burglar-proof lock for it, which
it still giving perfect service. The fifteen dollars received for
this, and the lock and business experience gained, was all I
received for my expenditure of time and money. It might not
have been wise, but it was not regretted. The unfortunate
thing about this lock business was the estrangement that resulted from it between me and the Stephens families who had
been lifelong friends; but this was of short duration.

SPECIAL REFERENCE TO MOTHER.

Father's health about the years 1865 and 1866 seemed to
be completely broken, obliging him to keep to the house in
winter, with occasional long terms in bed, suffering mostly
from chronic diarrhea. We regarded his tenure of life as
short and uncertain, so also did he. On the contrary, mother's
health seemed exceptionally good. The younger of her children, being well grown and helpful, and the elder ones beyond
her care, she had more leisure, which she employed in helpful-
ness to her neighbors, particularly the young women starting
in their household and family life. On account of this, and
her previous well-known kindly ways and general character,
she was held in such high esteem as occasionally surprised herself. An instance of this occurred in relation to old Nathan
Duxbury, or "Daddy Duxbury," as he was usually called.
The old man was well up in the nineties. He was a local

Methodist preacher, a good old soul, whom everybody highly regarded. He became sick, and mother wanted to visit him. Not being very familiar with him and his household, mother invited her neighbor, Mrs. Neeland, a prominent lady in the small Methodist congregation, to accompany her. Mrs. Neeland, being an ex-school teacher, with a fine, wordy style of speech, could make a fine prayer and tell a glowing experience. Mother regarded herself as occupying the second place. Mrs. Neeland, so well known and associated with him, must of course take precedence. But the old man would not have it that way. The greeting to Mrs. Neeland was formal, mother's was cordial. As conversation was waning, he asked mother to read a chapter and then to pray. She felt disconcerted by the preference, as Mrs. Neeland could do both in a more dignified and ready manner; but she accorded to the old saint's wish, read the chapter, talked about it in connection with the promises, offered the prayer, bade the old man goodbye for the last time, and they both left. This may seem to be an incident of small account, but it shows the confidence in character, as against clever wordy declamations and church relations.

About the year 1866, the crofters or small farmers were evicted from their holdings in the north of Scotland, in order to turn large portions of that rough mountain country into great game preserves, so that wild deer might graze on the little fields where the crofters raised their slender living. These poor struggling people were sent out by the shipload to seek new homes in Canada. Some two or three hundred were landed at the port of Meaford. A large empty storehouse was allowed them for a temporary residence. The active men, those who could talk a little English, were scouring the country to find employment, and a place to begin family life. The rest, mostly women and children, remained at the storehouse. Father and mother were at Meaford one day, and being ready to go home, mother proposed that he would drive around by the Stevenson storehouse, so she might see those new arrivals of Highland people from old Scotland, which he did. She got out of the wagon, and went up into the wide doorway; they observed some one darken the door, but paid no more attention. They knew no one, and felt that no one could be interested in them. Mother saw them variously engaged, sitting on their boxes, or on the floor with their children; then she called out in Gaelic: "Kem a ra hin dugch?" ("How are you today?") The effect was electric; all were on their feet in an instant. A stranger was speaking their own language. They all started to meet her, crowding around, so that in a few minutes, as father said, mother could not be seen. They unmistakably showed their joy at meeting some one of their blood, that in their own language could tell them about the new country. It was with difficulty that she broke away from them. She showed them her house upon the curved shore of the bay three miles distant, and for some weeks, nearly every day, small companies would make her visits to get instructive help. "A touch of nature surely makes all hearts akin," and "blood is thicker than water." Scotch clannishness and Christian kindness make a strong helpful combination.

Christian worship was to mother what it should be to all, spiritual meat and drink, and communion with the Heavenly Father. We could not regard her as a singer, neither did she; but she sang, and it was with the spirit and the understanding, even if imperfect as music. In the devotional part of the worship she seemed to lose herself. It was much the same with the preaching, she never complained of long sermons; and in those old days they generally were long. I used to think the end was never coming; but to mother the end came like an interruption of her rich meditation. I have heard her say to the preacher, "Why did you stop so soon?" It was the same with her reading of the Scriptures, they engrossed her whole attention, they were truly sacred to her. She was not by any means fluent in speech, yet her strong conceptions of divine love, and her human sympathies, seemed to give her the soul of the orator. Father was a good talker, clear, logical, and loyal to conscience and duty. Mother's thoughts and feelings took higher flight into the realm of the spiritual and sympathetic.

She was our first teacher, teaching us our letters and first spelling; but as previously mentioned, Aunt Harriet began very early with us, teaching a private school in one room of our house at Norval. I heard mother at different times state, that my brother John could read easy portions of the New Testament when he became four years old. The Testament was one of my first books; and the first chapter of the Gospel of John my beginning reading lesson, the first half being committed to memory, as were also many other portions of the New Testament, with some of the Psalms, Proverbs and Ecclesiastes. The whole Bible was read through before I was nine years of age. The stories of the mighty men, previously told by my mother, with their journeys, conquests, battles and sieges, were more specially interesting. If she felt pride and quiet satisfaction in her ten children, they certainly have cause for great gratitude for such a dear, good mother. In the summer of 1867, mother made her last visit to relatives in the township of Erin. While there a decided dropsical tendency developed, and she was advised to apply to a certain doctor in Guelph for counteracting medicine. On her way home at Toronto the prescription was filled. On delivering the medicine the druggist gave the cautionary remark, that the medicine should be given with watchful care, as it was twice as strong as usual, and the doses twice as frequent. Some time after returning home, she began taking the medicine and the dropsical tendency was overcome. But in a month or two paralysis of the left side set in, which for a time prevented speech or general movement. Though doctors may differ, they often stand by one another, but our family physician regarded the strong medicine as the main cause of the paralysis. The paralyzed condition greatly improved, but she never recovered good speech or easy movement. In the course of two years and a few months her final sickness came on—a combination of the paralysis and dropsy. Her scattered family received notice to gather in. Though she could not talk she showed her pleasure as each newcomer appeared. Edward was the last to arrive; mother was then unconscious. My sisters felt anxious that she should know that we were all there.

Father and the ten children were on the three sides of her bed. Harriet said at last, "We must try to arouse her." So going close to her head she distinctly called out, "Mother." At the call she started up as from a vivid dream, looked around at us with some appearance of recognition. Then Harriet used the remaining few moments most considerately, bringing each one up for the final handshake and kiss. Fearing that she might not recognize us by sight she introduced each in his order. Here's father. Here's Mary. Here's William, etc., until all were presented. Soon after this the unconscious condition returned, also the usual stertorous breathing, and in an hour or more mother passed into her final sleep, a sleep that knows no earthly waking. But:

> "Asleep in Jesus (is a) blessed sleep,
> From which none ever wakes to weep;
> A calm and undisturbed repose,
> Unbroken by the last of foes!!
>
>   Yes,
> "We shall sleep, but not forever;
> There will be a glorious dawn;
> We shall meet to part, no never,
> On the resurrection morn."

Thus it was that mother passed away in her sixty-first year, much sooner than we had looked for. The home center of affection was gone, but there was no complaining. The children were now all grown people; Alex, the youngest, being seventeen. Each was providing for himself. School teaching was usually the first occupation, particularly of the younger members; and it deserves remark that school trustees had little or no hesitations regarding a Trout teacher. Father was the only natural occupant of the old home, but since he was not able to work, or care for it, he left it, and made his home with Mary (Mrs. Jay) until his death, eight years afterward. The home center was thus transferred from the old farm to the home of our oldest sister, until every one of us had homes of our own. Not long afterwards Edward sold the old residence portion by the lake. James already owned the rear, the best and much larger part.

In the fall of 1913, I made my last visit to this old hallowed locality. The great primeval forest of former times was non-existent, except a few straggling patches in the valleys or hill-sides. But the great distinctive features of mountain and lake, hills, creeks and rivers still remained, and compelled constant observation. Most of the old buildings were replaced by new, but many of the good old barns and houses that father had built, we boys being his main help, were still serving their use-ful purpose. A host of memories would rise at every turn. The big boulders and shade trees by the roadside had their story, till the mind is overwhelmed by the multitude of the moving pictures of the past. It is fortunate that we best re-member the best things, so these good memories have a refin-ing and happy influence. But you say this is only sentiment. True, but sentiment is the spice of life. True again, but spice is only trifling luxury. Yes, but the great comprehensive sentiments, respecting God, humanity, home and heaven, are no trifles, but involve the great questions of our common and also our immortal life. Compared to these, what we shall eat, drink and wear, though necessary, are really the commonplace considerations. They are the material needs, the "things seen, which are temporal." The others are the "things unseen, which are eternal."

As we six boys were all there together after mother's fun-eral, we rightly judged that such might never happen again, so we concluded to have a group picture; and the small photo-graph that follows this was taken. It was the best the limited studio could give us. Not long afterwards our four sisters had a similar group picture taken, which is also appended; also the pictures of father and mother taken about one year before she died.

NORTH SHORE MOVE.

Late in the fall of 1870, with prospects of work in the foundry looking exceedingly slim, I received an offer from Allen Gunn, a lumberman operating on the north shore of

SIX SONS OF WILLIAM TROUT

John M.   Alexander A.   Edward
James   William Henry   Peter L.

Georgian bay at what is now known as Algoma, which then besides the mill had only three dwelling houses. My duty was to repair and improve the mill during the winter, so as to be prepared for good service the following summer. I was to be paid two dollars per day, with free steamer passage, free rent and firewood. It was a good offer, and, with the superintendent, I was taken up to see the mill and determine its needs, so as to prepare for our work. On returning I reported the situation to Mrs. Trout, who regarded it with great disfavor. The idea of leaving a nice town and friends, and put in a winter on a lonely shore with lumberjacks and Indians, had no terror for me; but this was a real terror to her. I showed the advantages, my agreement, and our necessities, and pleaded that we must face every undertaking in our lives squarely and bravely. She assented in a rather half-hearted way, and we packed up the groceries and food we would need for the winter, and the most needed pieces of furniture, and some books, and stored the rest of our things; and I got our boxes to the dock ready to go on the steamboat when it should call at our port, which on this trip would be late in the night. As our house was empty, a kind neighbor took in Mrs. Trout and baby; and as she had been very busy and wearied, it was advised that she and the baby go to bed early, and have a good sleep before the boat came, which she accordingly did. I had still much to look after, and when after ten in the evening the boat came, and I saw the freight and wood that had to go on board, I knew that at least an hour would pass before she would start out. I went up and told Mrs. Trout to be ready to come to the boat in three-quarters of an hour; so, with the help of our good neighbor friend, she and the child were soon dressed and aboard the boat. Most of our things had to be left behind for the next trip. It was a rough night in the sheltered town, and no one, better than our captain, knew the stormy nature of the weather out in the main lake, and with the immense load of freight, and large list of passengers, he no doubt felt his responsibility. Accordingly, he delayed starting till such time as would allow him to pass the stormiest portion of his trip in daylight. At the gap, we had to lay by till near evening, under the lee of an island till the storm measurably subsided. Mrs. Trout and baby were seasick, and helping them disturbed me a little. But few wanted breakfast. Dinner also, when under the lee of the island, was not fully attended; but at supper time, sailing under the shelter of the great Manitoulin island, everyone seemed to come to a most hearty appetite; and the dining room was a most pleasant meeting place for all our passengers. There were women and children aboard, but my good fortune was in having the best looking young woman, and the only fine young baby, of the crowd, both being a matter of considerable interest. After this fine steamboat meal, the lively conversation and companionship of ladies and gentlemen in the rather crowded cabin was very enjoyable. We had another day's sailing on one of the most picturesque routes of America, and on our third afternoon arrived at our destination. It was a dark, gloomy day, with misty rain. I pointed out the place to Mrs. Trout, and her countenance fell. The few unpainted, barn-like houses, irregularly built, old mill, and partly broken old wharf, all with a gloomy sky and a background of rocky hills and burned woods, made certainly a forlorn and most discouraging looking prospect. We had to descend from the boat onto a big scow in order to land on the old wharf. Everyone in the place was there to meet us, and receive the things landed from the steamer. There were only four women, the mistress of the big boarding house and the helper, and a half-breed French woman and her young sister. I knew them from the previous short acquaintance a few weeks before, and introduced them to Mrs. Trout. The French woman, Mrs. Madore, had no children, so her heart warmed impulsively to the baby; she wanted the privilege of carrying her, which, of course, was granted; and proudly and kindly she did it. The others made themselves as helpful as they could. We had our first meal at the big boarding house, where the baby and its young mother made no small sensation. The married men of the crowd thought I had one over all the rest of them. But I felt this was no good place for us to stay, so we walked the short distance to Madore's house, and asked the privilege of living with them till our household stuff would arrive. This was most gladly given. He seemed to think that we were conferring on himself and family a benefit by our company. He was pure French, which was not very common, could read and write and had traveled, she never saw a school, and could speak only French and poor English. We remained with them over two weeks, and they would not accept one dollar for their kindness. He said that was their style, and that I might travel the whole north shore among their people without money.

The second or third day after we began housekeeping, a nice, clever Indian came and offered mother a fine, big fish, for which he wanted some bread for a sick girl he had; she gave him two loaves, nearly four pounds of bread, and was surprised that he did not want more, as is usual with Indians. Each was mutually pleased with his bargain. When I came in at dinner time, she showed me the fish, and asked what kind it was. I said I was not sure. It looked exactly like a whitefish, but I never saw one even half as large. It weighed just eight pounds. However, I said it is surely a good fish, there is no danger of that. On returning to work, I told the men about the fish. They said, "That is a whitefish all right." But I replied, "It is so astonishingly large." "Oh, that's not very big." Then each began telling of some that were larger. The biggest that was heard of was eighteen pounds, but several claimed to know a fisherman that packed a half-barrel, one hundred pounds, with seven fish. That was regarded as a settled fact. Certainly the fish on that north shore of the lake were greatly superior in quality and size to the south shore fish.

This Indian was a rare one for that time. He was a Christian Indian, while many on the north shore were pagans, and others nominally Catholic. He spoke excellent English, and, as I learned, had put in a term or more in the Wesleyan College at Coburg. His dress was largely the white man's style. His squaw was in her usual Indian fashion. His wigwam, or tepee or lodge, as we might call it, was half a mile away on dry elevated ground, far from stagnant water; so he would be little troubled with mosquitoes, though he was in the midst of a thick grove of evergreens, which effectually warded off

the winter storms. The wife and I made him and his family
a call one wintry Sunday afternoon. He had an outer room,
through which we passed to the large living room of his well-
made wigwam. There being no door, there was no doorbell
to ring, nor latchstring to pull, as in a white man's shanty. But
there was no need of any of this, for his dogs gave warning;
and he was out to meet us, and conducted us in, pulling aside
the skin curtain, that admitted us to his family living room.
The fire was on some stones on the ground in the center of the
room. Broad rush mats were laid on the ground on three
sides of the tent space, on these the squaw and family were
squatted. I think a box was brought in for Mrs. Trout, who
sat with her baby on her lap. The Indian and I stood. There
were two girls, and two bright, little boys. The oldest girl,
about seventeen, was the sick one. She sat with the rest,
though in the last stages of tuberculosis. The squaw and
family could only talk the native language, so Mrs. Trout
could only observe and listen to our conversation. The inquiring eyes of the squaw and the family were directed to the baby,
whose white skin was such a contrast to their swarthy faces.

After presenting some delicacies Mrs. Trout had brought
for the sick girl, which were most gratefully accepted, we
made our exit homeward, she having witnessed the best representation of Indian wigwam life that I ever saw. In two
months after this the girl died, and the Indian came to the mill,
and asked for some one to make him a coffin. I was told by
the superintendent to make up a rough box coffin. I worked
as hard as I could for three or four hours, and finished a neat,
properly-made coffin, with lid to screw on, and filled full of
fine pine shavings to form a bed for the corpse. I set it off to
one side, and the proprietor came along and saw it, and
scolded me for wasting good lumber and time for a no account
dead Indian; but I did not care much, I knew that live Indians
had kindly sympathetic hearts, and respect for their dead, as
well as white folks, and I made the coffin accordingly.

Our winter in that region had a lower average temperature,
but was, I think, less stormy than the usual south shore winters.

The lake softened the keenness of the north wind for those on the south side, but to us it had the dry snappy character that belongs to the real arctic winds. Zero weather was common. On two occasions the temperature went lower than our thermometer would register. Our houses were built to retain the warmth, but we could not keep the frost out. Our little May slept between us, and would feel too hot, and kick herself out from under the clothes; and the next morning, after one of the severest nights, we found one foot swelled, without any possible cause, unless that it had been frostbitten in the night. A characteristic letter from my esteemed sister Harriet refers to this, and other conditions of our northern secluded life, which will on this, as well as her own account, be now introduced.

St. Vincent, February 7, 1871.

Dear Brother and Sister:—

I have only a few minutes to write, as I did not know till just now that Duncan was going to Meaford, and it scarcely seems worth while to talk to you for so short a time, and you so far away.

I am glad to hear by Mary that you are both well, and the new little fish doing so well too; but it must be a strange place you have gone to, when she would get her foot frozen. I hope you will be rewarded in dollars and dimes for your winter's privations, for I am sure they are numerous. There must be quite a bit of the pioneer about you, Jane, in fact you are right brickish. I certainly trust you will not have cause to regret it. I suppose the next move all around will be to Beaverton; that makes me feel kind of chicken-hearted, or else like going too. The worst is the thought of father going, but it really seems that we must take things just as they come, and calculate that our backs will be fitted to the burden. Our family have seen so many changes, in so short a time, that it really seems as if the time has come for us to have changes and trials such as we never had before; but there is nothing like facing all with a stout heart, cheerfully doing, as near as we can determine, whatever is best and right, and blessing will follow. There is an unseen hand governing all our events, and an eye always upon us, and an ear always open to hear whatever our wants may be, or wherever our lot may be cast. These, the greatest of all privileges, you have, though so far away in the North above Spanish river; and how cheering it is that there is no place on earth to which we may go, however remote, nor no circumstances, however dreary, but we have His presence. Not a hair of our heads can fall without His knowledge. Doubtless the rest have told you of the little angel in disguise that winged its way to our domicile a few weeks ago in the form of a little son (William T. Stirling), Duncan's heir. He is a small beginning for a man, but if he lives, and keeps on growing as he has done so far, he will make it out in stature anyway before a great many years pass away. He is a pretty strong little fellow, but was most awful poor, almost as poor as Birde (Bertha Jay) was. He was somewhat troublesome at first, but is proving better every day. Dun-

can is going now. He sends his warmest love to you both; mine, too. Write soon. The rest will have told you all the news. Affectionately, your sister,
HATTIE.

That hastily written letter is characteristic of Harriet, sprightly thinking and sisterly affection.

MAIL SERVICE.

From the last voyage of the steamer in the last week of November until Christmas was a period without any mail. The deep snow by land, and the slushy, half-frozen condition of the water in the bays and among the islands, prevented all long distance travel. After the lake became fairly well frozen, then the dog trains were started; and we had fairly good mail service every week or ten days.

The government had three trains, with two men (half breeds) to conduct each train, while one pair made their journey, the other two rested. Their double journey was about three hundred and forty miles. They were well paid, and a good prize was given for the gang that made the quickest journey. I do not remember the exact time of the best double trip, but the daily average was sixty-seven and a fraction miles per day. They certainly were the greatest boys to go that I ever knew. The short dreary days of the midwinter, with its heavy snowfall, made certainly a dull period. Mrs. Trout and myself were then thrown upon each other more exclusively than we had ever been before or since. The oneness of man and wife had a chance to mature, and there was time for reading, letter writing and study. The purest kind of water, perfect fresh air, and good food with hard work, kept us in the best of health and good spirits.

NORTHERN SPRINGTIME.

When the bright, sunshiny days of March came, and the south winds blew, melting away the snow, we began to make short Sunday journeys over the rough country, extending them as the springtime made the walking better. They were all

FOUR DAUGHTERS OF WILLIAM TROUT

MARY

HARRIET ANN

MARGARET

RACHEL EMERSON

necessarily limited, as we generally carried our little one. Some of my tramps with the other men were all-day journeys, but all were interesting, the immense hills of solid granite rock, some gray, others red, and others nearly black, all crowned and covered more or less with a great variety of different colored mosses and scrub evergreens, which lodged on every possible shelf. Among these rock hills was a system of beautiful lakes, the outlet of which was the stream that furnished the power for our mill.

There being no limestone, and very rare deposits of clay, this water was the pure type of nature's distillation, beautifully soft and transparent. The whole country was so different from the stratified limestone formations of the south shore, or Manitoulin island, the flat sky line of which could be seen in the usual clear days; while the sky line of this shore was a continued series of hummocks.

In the early spring, long before the ice went out of the bay, our mill started sawing, which called for much watchfulness and hard work for a time, to keep the machinery in best going condition. With the noise of the mill and lumber piling on our renewed dock, our hamlet took on a more lively and inspiring activity. The second day after the ice went out, a large, three-masted schooner appeared on the lake horizon, and soon beat its way into our port; and tying up to the wharf, began to take on a load of one hundred thousand feet of lumber, which occupied three or four days. We made the acquaintance of the officers of the vessel, and the captain invited us, along with the mill superintendent, to spend an evening with them on board his vessel. Interest in Mrs. Trout and our baby largely accounted for this invitation, which after five months' nonintercourse with the outside world was greatly enjoyed, and the more so, as captain, mate and purser were all good Christian gentlemen. It was a novel visit for Mrs. Trout, as we had to climb and descend a rope ladder on entering and leaving the vessel.

After the mill got running in good shape, and I was not so much needed, Mr. Peter Murray, a mill proprietor of Blind river, seven miles north, wanted my help in changing and repairing his mill. With the consent of Mr. Gunn, I undertook his work. He came for me with a sail boat. We had a brisk wind off land, which was changeable and uncertain, as such usually are, requiring watchfulness and skill in handling our craft. He was captain and steersman, I was the man before the mast, attending to sails. We had a fine exciting run. The only fault was its brevity. In some of the squalls our boat laid over so much that the lee gunwale was several inches below the water surface, but she tore through at such a rate that the water could not enter.

We had formed the acquaintance of Mr. Murray in the different calls that he had made to the mill and house during the winter. We seemed to understand and appreciate each other from the very first call, and this soon ripened into a warm friendship; and if anyone wishes to really know the fine value of intelligent, responsive, Christian friendship, let him be cut off as we were on the north shore, and when he meets a congenial spirit, he will know how to appreciate him.

In my absence the first steamer of the spring arrived, and with it two government timber inspectors. One of them knew me, and they made our house their headquarters, giving good respectable company for Mrs. Trout, and paying well for what they received. They roamed the woods every day for a couple of weeks, and found that Mr. Gunn had been cutting outside his proper limits, so they seized the whole output of the mill, till proper settlement was made.

On my return from Blind river our dear little May, who had previously learned to walk, now could run over the soft sandy ground wherever she pleased and of course became increasingly interesting.

After a few more weeks of service with Mr. Gunn, I had my final settlement, drawing the largest lump of wage money I had ever drawn at one time before or since. In the early days of June we started on our steamer trip back to Owen Sound. The bright afternoon we boarded our vessel was a contrast to the gloomy day we left it six months previous.

We were happy in the thought of getting back to friends and more civilized conditions, but we met those already when we got into the steamer's cabin and on her upper deck. A long list of passengers, men and women, like ourselves, were returning from their northern shut-in winter. A few were acquaintances, but it mattered not, all were friends.

In the course of the afternoon a thick fog enveloped us, and as we were coming among the islands, speed was at once reduced to a few miles per hour and the whistle tooted frequently. A lookout was placed far out on the bow. A sailor with sounding line was on the forward part of the vessel and each sounding was recorded as given. After an hour of this experience, the engines stopped and the steamer came to a standstill, and we were to wait till the fog lifted. To some who seemed annoyed by this, the captain replied, better to wait while we are afloat than to wait on a rock. But our delay was quite short. The fog grew thin and in a few minutes all was clear with bright sunshine and blue sky, and the captain's good judgment was manifest, for on every side of us were the beautiful rock islets, like the tops of the land mountains, projecting their peaks above the calm water, and how lovely they appeared in their beautiful spring dress. Flowers and mosses and fresh tipped evergreen shrubs, on the rounded crowns of those protruding islets, suggested flower beds both of rare and varying beauty; their reflections in the placid water giving depths to the picture. Emerging as this panorama did from the fog, gave it an enchantment not to be forgotten.

That evening after a luxurious supper, all the passengers repaired to the cabin, where our captain called on some leading singers to sing and a Roman Catholic priest to play the small organ that was kept on board. He was in ordinary dress and besides laid off his priestly manners. He played the music for our Protestant hymns with as much evident zest as those who sang them, wife and myself being among the active ones. We had a splendid time till late in the night. A quick, uneventful trip brought us to Owen Sound, where, after settling up accounts for previous fall purchases and making a few visits, we took our furniture and goods out of the store, and had all shipped to Beaverton. We remaining over for a few days at St. Vincent, where only James and Harriet with their families, and Margaret, were still remaining. We also settled the last of some half uncertain old debts, which were paid more for the sake of our good name than for their real obligation.

BEAVERTON PROJECT.

Some of the enterprising citizens of the town of Beaverton on Lake Simcoe determined to have an agricultural foundry and machine shop, and knowing Mr. Jay's business and mechanical ability, invited him to build and manage the whole undertaking. Accordingly, he moved his family from Meaford to Beaverton. As father was living with them, he accompanied the family. An arrangement had been made with me, while on the north shore, to assist in the plans and construction of the plant, and in the course of regular work, to be the patternmaker. A large machine shop was erected forty by sixty feet and two stories high. Parallel with this, twenty feet away, was the moulding shop or foundry, and a building twenty feet wide connected the two. In the course of three or four months business was commenced, and in about four months after this the foundry took fire and burned to the ground. As the buildings were all connected, and the town had no fire company or fire appliances, it was regarded that all would surely go. The fire broke out about nine o'clock in the evening. The whole townspeople, men, women and children, gathered and stood awestruck with uplifted faces, watching the great high cone of flame and sparks as it shot toward the sky. But one of the town officials saw that the machine shop could be emptied of its stock and machinery and that much saved. He was a big man with a voice like a roaring bull of Bashan. He called on the men to come on and clean out the shop, and the women and boys were to carry water to prevent the shop taking fire, as long as possible. So everyone began to make himself as useful as he could. The shop pump and other pumps were kept a-going. The fire was fought in the connecting building; and when the big shop began to smoke, from the great heat, water was thrown upon it from the windows, from which most of the sashes had been taken. In a short time the building was emptied of its contents. Then efforts were redoubled to save the building. But, at the same time, more than half the upper side of the building burst into a sheet of flame, which running upwards passed over the eave projection like a reversed waterfall. We thought we were surely beaten, the heat being so great, we could hardly stand to poke our heads out of the windows. But well-directed water thrown by many hands, extinguished the flames, and we saw that the charred surface absorbed the water, so that it would not readily ignite again; so we saved the main shop, while the foundry was completely destroyed and the connecting building almost wholly so. It was the most heroic accomplishment of that kind that I ever saw. Next morning the citizens gathered again and carried in the heavy machinery they had so ruthlessly pulled out the night before. It had, however, suffered much by the change.

This fire was a severe blow to the company, and accompanied by the fact that we had spread out into lines of work, in which we could not compete with the large shops, this compelled us to narrow its sphere and curtail expenditure. This made it advisable for me to leave and find employment elsewhere, as I did in Peterboro in the early summer of 1872.

I feel that I should not dismiss this year in Beaverton without further reference to father. Mr. Jay and I felt that in coming there we were entering into a large and hopeful undertaking. Father, though in his seventy-first year, felt likewise, he was as buoyant and hopeful as his boys, but in quite a different line. While Mr. Jay and I hoped to carve out a business and mechanical career with at least good moderate success, he was building himself up with the hope of starting a Church of Christ. So in the large house we all occupied, a large room was set apart to be the place of meeting, and his family, that is, myself and Jane, and Charles and Mary, were to be, with his lead, the nucleus of a church. There was no use in raising objections, or asking to wait for a better start. The first Sunday we were all together was the first meeting day, and besides Jay's two children and our little one there was no further audience. We went through the usual routine of worship. Though father was physically unable to work, his mind was alert, and like Paul at Athens, he talked in the market place or anywhere with those who met him. His hearers would admire his knowledge of the Scriptures and his ability in argument, because they could not match it, and they would let it go at that. To go to the good auld Kirke on the Sabbath day and have some good Scotch whiskey on more or less frequent occasions satisfied their minds and palates so well, that a change could not be considered.

An advertisement for a machine shop foreman brought a Mr. William Smith to our house. After the business talk with Mr. Jay, and a mutual satisfactory arrangement had been completed, father began sounding him on the religious situation. He was found to be a good solid well-versed Scotch Presbyterian. So father lined up against him some of the Scriptural positions that he could so nicely pose and the discussion was long and earnest, but kindly and considerate. Smith realized that for the time at least he was beaten; but felt sure that when he could review, and place his arguments in more orderly form, he would come out all right. A few weeks afterwards, when he began work with us, the whole subject of their differences was gone over again, and Smith surrendered, and a week or so after, he and his wife were baptized in Lake Simcoe, and our church numbered seven, and I think that was the extent of the Beaverton Church of Christ. Mr. Jay remained in Beaverton a year or two after I left, and after turning the whole management over to Smith, he and family with father returned to Meaford, where he entered into business with my brother James.

REMOVAL TO PETERBORO.

As before mentioned, I had struck out for a new job. I went to Peterboro and engaged with an agricultural and foundry firm of which J. R. Davis was the manager. I was the leading and for most of the time the only patternmaker. Here was my first experience with architectural castings and with George A. Cox, afterwards the great railroad king, Member of Parliament and president of the Canada Life Assurance Company; who, though rich, and I only a good skilled workman, yet through work I was doing for him there arose a mutual respect, which was undiminished by the fact that though he with others strenuously urged me, he could not enlist me as a politician in his behalf. Afterwards, when he had removed to Toronto and was president of the Street Railway Company, he must have acquired a similar greater respect for my brother Edward, for neither by argument or the prospect of material advantage, could he prevail on him to change the course of the Monetary Times in regard to Sunday street car service to suit his interest.

This Peterboro beginning was momentous in more ways than one; I was away from old associations; both of family, friends, church and politics. I was free to readjust myself and family religiously, politically or socially. I had been a Liberal Conservative. My employers and new friends were in the Reform party.

As there was no congregation of Disciples to unite with, the question came up, "Should I unite with some other body or stay out altogether?" The latter possible choice was admitted to consideration because of my knowledge of the scientific discoveries of Darwin, Huxley and Tyndall, and the possible deductions therefrom, seemingly so hostile to current religious belief. The most extreme of which was the confidently expressed opinion, that "Given matter and force all things could be accounted for." This manifestly assumed the question in dispute, that is, mind or spirit. Which was regarded if not in some way material, at least a product of matter; and they seemed likely then to make their contention good. So that for a time thoughtful believers were uncertain as to their standing.

However, the second or third Sunday after coming to the town, I attended the Baptist Church. At the close of the preaching service the pastor announced that a meeting to attend to the Communion or Lord's Supper would immediately follow this, to which other Christians were invited. Though greatly surprised, I said, "That means me," and remained. But seeing the members reseating themselves compactly in the center row of seats, said I, "This looks like close communion, I better wait," and seated myself to one side. A venerable old deacon came and inquired if I were a Baptist? I replied, "No, but I am a Disciple." "Do you wish to commune?" "If there are no objections, I would be pleased to do so." He went and submitted the matter to the pastor, who gave me an approving nod, and I took a place among them. Later when I was ready to move Mrs. Trout and family to the town, without any further formality, we continued to work and worship with them quite heartily for eleven years. We were often earnestly entreated to become formal members, but as our position was that of Christians only, we could not curtail our freedom by becoming Baptists.

This at first was a Scotch Baptist Church and attended to the Lord's Supper every Lord's day, according to the regulations of close communion. A good Englishman, Brother Gilmore, while their pastor, indoctrinated them with open communion principles, which cut off their fellowship with the regular Baptist churches, and left them independent. Since we left, however, they have been regulated back into the full fellowship.

With regard to politics, I gave the claims of the Reform party a new, and as unprejudiced consideration as I could, only to settle back more decidedly in my Conservative position, opposed as it was to boss and friends and fellow workmen.

After a year's residence in Peterboro, the combined position of draftsman and foreman patternmaker, in the William Hamilton Company's shop, became vacant, and I applied for the place, and secured it. I had been preparing for advanced work and here I had it in plenty.

There was no agricultural work, such as had received my attention for more than two years previous; but heavy sawmill machinery, large engines, water wheels, power force pumps, and steam pumps, transmitting machinery and architectural work. Scarce any of this was beyond my ready comprehension, but nearly all of it was beyond my experience. I had unlimited faith in mechanical principles and the action of forces, and boldly struck out machine designs on a calculated basis, without much reference to previous methods of work, or standard forms of construction. My first object being to fully understand the nature of the required duty; then to make the readiest construction for its good performance, eliminating the superfluous, and retaining the essentials in their simplest form. While this generally resulted in improved and more efficient construction, yet it was always more or less in the nature of new experiments, which are accordingly costly. To this feature my boss, Mr. Hamilton, gave his attention, as well as to see the certainty of results, his attitude being uniformly skeptical. So with his careful conservatism as a drag on my eagerness, we most always "made the spoon" and did not "spoil the horn." But the spoon had to be improved, or changed to suit its varied uses, and this was a source of weariness to the boss, who wanted something to manufacture steadily, for a special good price, without drawbacks, instead of that the good had to be made better, and the better to attain the always impossible best. This is the law of progress. It requires a long time with constant skilful effort to standardize an intricate machine. Sawmill machinery had not then even approximated it.

The eleven years of employment with the William Hamilton Company, were notable years of progress. They were in the middle period, the last of the thirties and the forties of my life, the period of greatest power and activity, when one can do the most work in the least time. In the winter of 1874 which ended my fortieth year, I took lessons under an itinerant teacher, who claimed to teach bookkeeping and business forms, and arithmetic. Also free hand and mechanical drawing. In the first three studies he was proficient; but in the last two, a sham. The bookkeeping, etc., and arithmetical drill were helpful, and I enjoyed what I thought were my last schooling days; but twenty-one years afterwards, I took with much greater pleasure and decided profit a university extension course in astronomy.

FAMILY SICKNESS AND DEATHS.

This 1874 winter also saw the birth of my second son, Walter Charles, and the nearly fatal sickness of Mrs. Trout, which followed it. And in the early summer, before she fully recovered, our two older children, May Louise, and Arthur Howard, died of malignant scarlet fever, with only three days intervening. The little boy was the first to catch the fever and the first to go, and the afternoon of the funeral was made a half holiday by the shop, when the men and boss attended in a body; and the same sympathetic consideration was repeated four days afterwards at the little girl's funeral. This was not specially on my account. It was their usual kindly custom.

The death of two beautiful healthy active children was a matter of interest beyond my circle of friends and acquaintances. Believers in special providences endeavored to discover God's purpose in this affliction. Evidently regarding the doctrine of providential discipline as something to be guarded and sustained. I do not so regard it. I do not regard God as slaying our children, or permitting them to be slain by scarlet fever, for the sake of setting our affections more on the future life, and the matters pertaining to it. However, such considerations ought to result from trials of that disciplinary character.

"All afflictions for the present seem not joyous, but grievous; nevertheless, afterward they yield the peaceable fruit of righteousness, to them that are exercised thereby." In this way our religion affects our daily life and makes us resigned to losses that we cannot prevent. Had my children made a raft by the river side, and floating over deep water, had been wrecked and drowned, the loss would have been the same, and also the duty of resignation; but we would not charge God, or his providence. We would charge ourselves as parents with carelessness in allowing such a risk, or if we had forbidden such a course then we would charge the unfortunate outcome upon the disobedience of our children, and the papers would report "Accidental death by drowning." Instead of this supposed case, where every cause and consequence is easily understood, there were in the actual case elements of mystery—our children associated with only our immediate neighbors, none of whom had the scarlet fever. There were one or two cases in a remote part of the town, and evidently one at least of our children in some way caught the contagion, or, as we would say nowadays, absorbed the fever germs, and though surviving the fever burning process, they finally succumbed to the load of poisons left behind. Thus it was with our dear little ones, they were worn out in the abortive effort to get rid of the poisonous load. Now all this came upon us without warning, and without our knowledge or any means to resist it. The children unconsciously met the disease germs and we could not stay their destructive progress. An unseen enemy invaded their bodies and overpowered them, and we parents, though doing our best, were only witnessing the painfully struggling process. We could know all about the drowning but of this we could know nothing. We may ask, "How is this?" and "Why should it be?" We are not yet able to answer, but let us not be impatient, but wait till we find at least a partial answer, as has been done in diphtheria and typhoid, etc., and not charge it to a special visitation of the Almighty, who wisely and kindly controls his creation "not by special, but by general laws." While, "He saw that all was good," our knowledge of many things must be greatly enlarged before we can see the reason why. And while we are realizing that, "All things work together for good to them that love God," let us also reverently watch and study the working. The patient old patriarch Job, in his sublime trust, said: "Shall I receive good at the hand of Jehovah and not evil?" No doubt he regarded both as special to him; but to us it comes in the broader sense from the dispenser of all things: "Who sends the rain on the just and on the unjust" and for whom "fire and hail, snow and vapor, and stormy wind fulfil his word."

About two years after this brother John died, October 11, 1876, and was buried in Toronto; and the year following father's death took place. At neither of these was there a complete family representation. Rachel was at her distant home in Sioux City, Iowa. I think James and Peter were not present. If I am correct, all the rest of us were. But at father's funeral in Meaford all except Rachel and John, who had gone before, were present. Also Uncle John. Six sons bore mother's coffin to the grave; but in this instance there were only five, but there were two sons-in-law to help; and I, the eldest, was placed at the rear to direct the movement. Thus was he buried on a cold December day, in the presence of a large concourse of town and country people.

Father's health was moderately good up to about one month of his death. During the previous summer and fall he had frequently spoken in the congregation. The cause of death was a prolonged spell of pneumonia, or as it then was called, inflammation of the lungs.

Father has been brought so often before us in this family biography, and mother's story told solely by myself, that I will now introduce a dear old-time friend, Alexander Anderson, late of Hamilton, Ontario, Canada, to give us the final word in reference to father. Brother Anderson's tribute is rather lengthy, and some of his story has been previously told; but now it is the much-loved Anderson who is telling it, and for his sake, as well as what he says, we will listen. It is from the Bible Index of January, 1878.

OBITUARY BY ALEXANDER ANDERSON
The Late Elder William Trout

Died at Meaford on the 2d day of December, 1877, in the 77th year of his age, Elder William Trout, one of the pioneer preachers of primitive Christianity in Canada. My acquaintance with Brother Trout dates back to the autumn of 1835, and I may say of him what Jaocb Creath said of John Smith— "The first time I saw him I took him to my heart," and through an acquaintance of forty-two years he never lost the place I gave him in my affections. I felt all along and feel today that he was worthy of the confidence I first received in him. He had, a few years before our acquaintance began, been immersed upon profession of his faith in Christ, and had united with a small congregation of Scotch Baptists in Caledon under the care of Elder Donald McLaren, and soon began to take part in the public exercises of the church, and from the very first manifested a strong attachment to everything that was Scriptural, and as he had now learned that he had before been led by human wisdom and tradition, he determined now to take no step but where the word of God clearly marked out the way. His religion was not one of fits and starts, but a constant leaning upon God and the word of His Grace, and a determination to follow truth wherever it led. Some few years after these events narrated above, Brother Trout moved to the village of Norval, and became connected with the church there. Here the writings of Alexander Campbell, and other writers of the reformation, fell into his hands. These he read with pleasure and profit, and found that in the knowledge of the Bible they were far ahead of even the Scotch Baptists. At Norval, Brother Trout was ordained one of the elders of the church. Here he found his right place; his Scriptural knowledge, his wisdom, care and patience, and his aptness to teach, eminently fitted him for that position, a position he filled to the day of his death, with honor to himself and profit to the congregations under his care. The church at Norval, at the time I speak of, saw the period of its greatest prosperity under the eldership of Trout, Mitchell and Menzies. It became one of the strongest, if not the strongest, church in Canada. What love, joy, peace and harmony; but, alas, haw changed things are there now. My heart aches to think of it. About this time they had a visit by a preacher from New York state, by the name of Green, under whose preaching a great many were added to the churches; and, shortly after, Brother Trout was sent by the brethren to Ohio, to one of their yearly meetings, to try to get a proclaimer from there to labor for us in Canada. He got one, but he said to the writer on his return, he was the only one I could get, but not the one I wanted, nor the one best adapted to our people. By this time the churches in Eramosa and at Norval had now thrown aside their human name, and called themselves Disciples of Christ. Brother Trout assisted greatly in bringing about this result. He began also to hold meetings some distance from home, and to preach the Gospel to sinners with considerable ability.

About this time we had our first co-operative meeting at Norval. We had messengers from six churches, Athol, Hillier, Pickering, Toronto, Norval and Eramosa, and perhaps Erin, I am not sure (and the two Haydens and Doctor Belding from Ohio as speakers—*W. H. T.*). We had a very pleasant good meeting.

The brethren from Prince Edward county wanted help. The churches were not doing well. Brother Trout and the writer were unanimously appointed to go there and labor for some time. I was the first to speak, and frankly stated, that however willing to go, it was utterly impossible for me. I had not the means to go with, and I judged Brother Trout was in much the same situation. Upon this the brother from the city, (James Leslie—*W. H. T.*), stood up and said, "Let every man in this house put his hand in his pocket, and lay his money down here on this table, to send these brethren to the work to which they are appointed." Then he laid down a silver dollar. Thus the large sum of nine dollars was collected to send two men some two hundred miles by steamer and stages to be a month away from home. But we started, got as far as Coburg by steamer; again when we came to pay our last steamboat fare, we lacked five cents of the sum required. Brother Trout said, "That is all the money we have." The purser asked, "Is that all your money?" "Yes, sir, every penny." He said, "Oh, well, you look like two honest men, and we will let you go with it." Well, we agreed with him about the honesty, and were glad to get thus to our journey's end.

We stayed three weeks in the county, and labored hard with meetings, often twice a day, got the brethren reconciled, the difficulties all settled, and some twelve additions to the churches; and now the brethren are taking us out to Wellington, where we are to take steamer again to Toronto, and not a penny in the pockets of either, and not one brother or sister so far has mentioned money to us at the village. Brother Trout came to me smiling and asked, "Have you got any money?" "No, have you?" "Not any. How are we going to get home?" "I don't know, here are the brethren coming to bid us goodbye." And in doing so, Brother Platt put four dollars in my hand, and Brother Lambert put thirty-seven and a half cents into the hand of my venerable brother. Four dollars paid the fare to Toronto, and we had the rest to live on for twenty-four hours; but with the kind hand of God about us, we got safe to Toronto and were penniless. We went to a brother's house in the city and stated our case. He gave us one dollar and seventy-five cents, which paid our steamer fare to Port Credit, and we had each twelve and a half cents to come home with.

In parting with Brother Trout I said to him, "If I outlive you, I will tell of this preaching tour, and how much we made by it in a worldly point of view." (I have heard the story from both.—W. H. T.) And now that I have told it, the thought strikes me that in the Book of God it may amount to more than any tour he ever made; and I am happy to state that Brother Trout was not discouraged, for he went back to Prince Edward several times after that. But in order to do this, I expect sister Trout had to deny herself a good many little comforts she ought to have had; but today I believe they are both saying, "No, dear Lord, it was not too much. Oh, that we had done more for Thee who stooped so low to lift us up to such wonderful bliss!"

Shortly after these events, Brother Trout left Norval, and went North to the shore of the Georgian bay, just then being settled. A few of the brethren went also, and here Brother and Sister Trout, with four others, began to meet as a congregation; and this was the beginning of the church at Meaford. Brother Trout and D. L. Layton took the oversight; and it has been, and still is, one of our most prosperous churches. Here Brother Trout lived and labored in the Gospel for thirty years. His family and the church grew up around him. His converts to Christ are scattered all over that region, and many of them have passed to their eternal rest. The church looked upon him as their father in the Gospel, and always listened to his wise counsel and instructions, which were always according to truth; and the consequences were union and peace, and joy in the Holy Spirit, and the number of the disciples greatly increased, and here his labors closed. No doubt the church will miss him much; and though of late years he was not able to take the active part he formerly did, he was present when possible, and had words of cheer and comfort for the brethren.

Brother Trout was twice married. With his first wife I was not acquainted. By her he had two children, a son and a daughter; the son died young. The daughter is still living; and with her he had made his home since the death of his second wife, who was an excellent and pious Christian, with whom I had a good acquaintance. Her maiden name was Catherine MacKinnon, and well did she fill her place as an elder's wife; she was always ready to assist and encourage her husband in his efforts to serve the Lord, and to cheer the hearts of brethren and sisters who visited her home. By her he had six sons and three daguhters (and one daughter who died in childhood—*W. H. T.*), all surviving except the beloved John M., the late proprietor of the *Monetary Times*. Brother Trout was never rich. He at one time made considerable money, but spent it freely in training his children, to whom he gave a liberal education (accounted so at that time—*W. H. T.*). Some of them are now occupying honorable positions in the world. He had also the pleasure of seeing them all become members of the Christian church, not only that, but useful members, trying in some degree to follow the example set before them; and when he got old and feeble, his children showed the most tender regard for him, anticipating all his wants and needs for his comfort. God bless them, a great contrast to the heartless manner in which some children in Canada treat their aged parents. Brother Trout died of congestion of the lungs, and at times his mind would wander as is common in that disease; but when called back, the Scriptures were his constant theme, and he would keep repeating text after text of the most cheering and comforting portions of the word of God. Thus passed away one of our truest men, respected in the church and out of it, by those who knew him; but he rests from his labors and his works do follow him.

Brother Trout for a short time, farewell. I feel that I have done poor justice to thy memory, but I hope what has been said may be accepted by all concerned as a trifling tribute of respect, from one who loved thee much, and was thy willing fellow laborer in the Gospel.

Rockwood, December 24, 1877.   A. ANDERSON.

Thus, one by one, we leave our dear ones behind us, or rather they pass on before us, and we in our turn follow in the great procession. If there were no resurrected Christ, it would be a dismal ending; but with Him there is the prospect of a bright reunion, and a new beginning in a NEVER ending life.

So for the present we leave them to continue the family story.

EDUCATIONAL

Peterboro had a Mechanic's Institute, with a library, both organized according to act of Provincial Parliament, so that it received a government money grant from the school fund, on account of maintaining evening classes in mechanics and allied studies. It had a president, vice-president, secretary, and board of directors. I joined it, and in the winter of 1874 and 1875 taught classes in mechanical and architectural drawing; and continued this for eight years. I was vice-president for several years. We had the association of professors from the Collegiate Institute who taught arithmetic and English.

We also had a large reading room, well supplied with current mechanical, scientific and literary journals. All this, with the well-selected, loaning library, made a good, practical and pleasurable center of culture in which I shared, both in receiving and giving; and in common with good teachers have enjoyed seeing my student boys take good responsible positions and hold them creditably.

At the close of one of our exhibitions of the winter's class work, I was placed on the final part of the program for a lecture on mechanical design. Before I began the lecture, a few not interested left for home. At the close of the lecture, which was illustrated by drawings, I gave the opportunity for questions. The principal of the Institute said his interest had been so intense that he could not frame a question. Another professor said, "I remained here out of compliment to Mr. Trout, expecting to hear dry details of mechanical principles; but I am most agreeably and greatly surprised, for he has given us in excellent form, not alone the practice, but the poetry of mechanics, and given us a fine outlook upon the engineer's field of imagination."

CORLISS ENGINE WORK.

While in the service of the William Hamilton Manufacturing Company, a contract was made with the MacLaughlin & Moore Milling Company, of Toronto, to furnish a steam plant and Corliss condensing engine, twenty by forty-two inches, with a guaranty of economic consumption of two and one-half pounds of coal per horse power per hour. This was regarded as a degree of economy seldom attained. For every ounce of coal above that consumption there was a large specific forfeit of so much from the contract price; and for every ounce of reduction below two and one-half pounds there was a similar premium above contract price. Manifestly it must be of the finest design and most careful workmanship. The time for delivery was rather short; and drawings and patterns had to be made. As I was sole draftsman and boss patternmaker, it is easy to see on whom the main responsibility rested, and while it did not rest lightly, it was certainly borne cheerfully; for a good, heavy, hard job always gave me added interest. Being the first job of that style, the boss would be satisfied if we got out even. In due time the job was completed, delivered and finally tested; and the certified consumption was two and eleven hundredths pounds of coal per horse power per hour, and the added premiums gave us a good paying contract. In this engine contract and its results, there were a good many satisfactory elements—the location of the mill was on the harbor front of the large growing city of Toronto; a fine advertising point. On this account the bidding for the job was keen, and for William Hamilton to capture it from older and wealthier engineering firms was no trifling victory to begin with. Then to raise the performance record to such a high step, was the crown of the undertaking. The other fellows had to take off their hats and congratulate old Willie on his success; and when afterward I met those high-brow engineers who think they hold all useful knowledge under their hats, I could meet their banter with effective counters that hit their weak spots. That small job raised our shop to a rank before unattained.

THREE MONTHS IN MILWAUKEE

Great business depression prevailed in Canada in the year 1878 and 1879. Our shop ran on three-quarter time, and we made extensive improvements and enlarged shop space, to be ready for better times in the future, which were slow in coming. And we further had to submit to a reduction in wages. I told Mr. Hamilton I would submit to the reduction only while I had to. He replied that was all right. In the summer of 1880 I met Mr. T. J. Neacy, a traveller for the Filer & Stowell Company of Milwaukee, who manufactured lines of machinery similar to William Hamilton. I wrote the Milwaukee Company, applying for a draftsman's position, and referred to Mr. Neacy, and received a favorable reply, with a good offer. Mr. Hamilton was willing to advance, but not to equal the Milwaukee offer, which I then accepted on a three month's trial. Before leaving, Mr. Hamilton was willing to equal it, but then it was too late. However, before the three months expired, Mr. Hamilton felt warranted in offering an advance of fifty cents per day above Milwaukee price; so I returned home.

This Milwaukee three months' engagement was an interesting and improving time to me. It was the biggest city I had lived in. Its novelty was increased by being so preponderately German and Polish. The shop was larger and slightly more systematically conducted than William Hamilton's, which is faint praise. The superintendent, John E. Fitzgerald, was my first Milwaukee friend, and remained a friend until his death. Albert Cunningham was the second and was faithful till he lately passed away. I saw the stress of the presidential campaign that elected James A. Garfield. I made the first blue prints of the Filer & Stowell Company, and did the same for William Hamilton on my return; using the formula first published in the Scientific American, making my own blue print paper. And with occasional visits to the shops of the E. P. Allis Company, I observed and studied their advanced engine and sawmill machine construction, in which the Company was the leader of America. But I was away from my wife and family, and when Mr. Hamilton's letter came, that called me back, I was a happy man.

When leaving for Canada, and bidding the officemen and superintendent good-bye, the latter said, "Ah, Trout, you would never get away if I had the fixing of your salary."

I entered the old shop again with much more prestige than I left it. It was known that I came back with a good advance, which insured me a fine standing with the men. The mill proprietors all realized the advantages, of even my brief term, of American experience. Shortly after my return, one of our ambitious young news reporters sought me for an interview, to bring out what little might be of interest in my Milwaukee experience, and in my then leading position as designing draughtsman for William Hamilton.

While he referred to the proprietor and the whole shop force in very creditable terms, still I was the subject of his special write-up, as a great mechanical engineer, and the main schemer in the construction side of the business; and he was just about right, only he swelled it up too much. He made my conferees and even the boss a little jealous, who all took some comfort in grinningly quoting to me the magnificent terms used by the reporter.

American style of sawmill machinery was certainly ahead of Canadian, but in those days both were in the experimental stage, and so were a matter of much interest to me, because of the prospect of improvement; and in this we had the backing of the mill men. They had commendable patience with any change that offered fairly well. I invented new improvements in some machines, on which, according to the old idea of general proprietorship, Mr. Hamilton claimed the patents. I protested, and hotly argued the matter, backed as I was by the patent law. Had I pushed the question, I could have beaten him; but there was not enough in it. He afterwards frankly admitted that his course was wrong.

THE WINNIPEG MILL

In the winter 1881 and 1882 two friends called at my house in the evening, just before I came in from the shop. Their business in Peterboro was to obtain machinery for a sawmill, to be built in Winnipeg, Manitoba; and as they afterward told Mr. Hamilton, they did not know him, but knew me, and had come on my account; and for that reason, came first to my house, to talk the matter over with me. They were Samuel Saunders, superintendent, and Mr. Elvidge, millwright. Mrs. Trout met them at the door, and after Mr. Saunders had introduced himself as an old boyhood acquaintance, and Mr. Elvidge as a more recent friend, they were shown into the parlor. Then she went back to prepare supper for two guests, as well as the family. The children in the kitchen had their curiosity excited; so Walter, the oldest, ran through the hall to the open parlor door, made his observations, was greeted, and ran back. Then Jennie, the second child, did the same. George, too, had to satisfy himself; and lastly, Nellie, the two-year-old, toddled up to see. Then the friends bursts into a loud laugh, "An alternating boy and girl, a designing draughtsman's family sure enough." And as I shortly afterwards came in, they finished the laugh on me.

Well, they gave us a nice contract for a complete circular mill—boilers, engine and all machinery for the Sprague Lumber Company. A month or two afterwards Mr. Elvidge came to our shop, and anxiously inquired for a millwright to build the mill in his place; as the Stearns Manufacturing Company of Erie, Pennsylvania, had offered him the superintendency of their business on the Pacific Coast, and they wanted immediate acceptance. It evidently might be a good life job, and he earnestly endeavored to be relieved of his contract with Sprague; but there seemed to be no millwright open for engagement; so I told Elvidge, if no other man could be got, I would go up and build his mill. He slapped me on the back, with, "Oh, Trout! that is the move. I will be forever obliged to you, and Sprague and Saunders will be perfectly satisfied." But I said, "Mr. Hamilton won't be willing. He won't consent." "Oh!" he said, "I'll make him." He accordingly went into the office and eloquently pleaded, showing the advantages to me of a magnificent two months' vacation, and the fresh millwright experience I would get, which would be of such general advantage in my regular work; and he prevailed. The old man said I might go; and Elvidge left in happy mood. But the old man reconsidered, and finally relented; so calling me down to the office, he said, "It's no use Trout, you can't go, you are one of the men around this shop that can't be spared. Elvidge must get somebody else." My reply was, "I am sorry, Mr. Hamilton, to find you coming to this conclusion, as I am sure this job would be to my benefit, and yours, too; and all I have to say further is, that I am going." "What, Trout! has it come to that?" "Yes, just to that. You will please govern yourself accordingly." "Well, Well!"

I had a great interest in our immense expansive Northwest, and wanted to see the ambitious new city of Winnipeg, where a few are said to have made fabulous fortunes; and others had lost in booming the city nearly to death, the people being speculatively crazy.

The first of August, 1882, I left to begin work on the mill. The only route then was by way of Chicago and St. Paul. In the early morning of the fourth day from Peterboro, we crossed the boundary, going back into Canada. It was cold, a thin sheet of fog covered the landscape. Drops of water bent down the tall grass, and drops were falling from the roofs of the cars, but it had not rained. It was only the cold, heavy dew. After breakfast in Winnipeg at eight o'clock, when I began to feel comfortably warm, a young man in shirt sleeves came in, looking flushed, and said, "We are going to have another hot day." I thought to myself if this is hot what sort of cold weather do you have? But I found in walking around for a half hour or more that it was what I would call pretty warm weather. At the mill I fitted up a somewhat sheltered place to do some necessary drawing, and felt no serious heat; and was surprised to see in the evening paper that the temperature had been up to 98 degrees. Next day at drawing, I scarcely perspired, though the temperature had touched 101 degrees. A pleasant breeze blew, and the dry, clean air carried off the perspiration as fast as it came; and at evening the paper I had been working on all day was clean, and my hands and linen were unsoiled; with the best conditions in the cities, dirt is manifest in one hour of work. This clean, dry atmospheric condition of the Northwest saves the sensations in the extremes of either heat or cold.

In building the Winnipeg mill there were matters that would be interesting to mechanics that I must pass over. Mr. Saunders had been a mill superintendent for many years, and felt competent to criticise, if not to direct millwrights; so when he found me taking short cuts and layouts he had not seen before, he felt scared and protested. A certain peculiar belt drive he declared impossible. I said it could be done, and would work perfectly. "Oh, yes, I know, Trout, you theorize and calculate, but I go by practice." "Wait," I said, "till the calculations fail, then come to me."

When the mill started, he carefully examined every movement, found everything going perfectly; then he owned up.

Some of the other mill proprietors complimented Mr. Sprague, saying, "You ought to be a happy man, your mill goes every hour of the day, week in and week out, turning out its regular good quota of lumber continuously, while our mills are shut down one-third of the time for repairs."

Twenty-four years after this I went through Winnipeg, and, of course, stopped to see the mill. Mr. Sprague, the former young man proprietor, was sitting at his desk, a hoary-headed man. I knew him because I expected to find him there. When I announced myself, he promptly remembered me, and greeted me cordially. Putting on his hat he said, "I know you want to see the old mill." He showed me the front part as I had left it, log haul, logway, carriage and circular, humming away in the old steady fashion, and the engine, too, on its original foundation, running its lively old chug, chug, for twenty-four summers. Its cylinder had never been rebored, and the circular arbor boxes had never been rebabbitted. The two boilers had renewed grates and furnace lining, but nothing more. All this signified not only good initial construction but steady, careful attention as well. The same engineer that started the mill was there still on duty, a white-haired man, deservedly conscious of his fine record. The lumber finishing end of the mill had been changed, and a resawing and a planing mill added, with the necessary power plant, all under the care of the old engineer, who had such help as he needed.

To return to the narrative of 1882, the mill was finished early in October; and I was paid $5.00 per day with board for the time of construction, the best pay I had ever had up to that time. It was a satisfactory job for all concerned.

SHORT TERM OF PRAIRIE LIFE.

The Dominion land policy of the time was very liberal, granting free homesteads to every male citizen. When the Winnipeg boom in city lots subsided, the craze turned to the agricultural lands of the province. Everybody went for a homestead, till nearly all the best available land of the province was taken up, with scarcely any show of settlement. Many never intended to settle, but held their claims to transfer to some jumper for a consideration. I was importuned by many friends to go and locate a half section, that I could do the settlement duties and follow my trade; and then at the least would have a fine property in reserve for my children. The prospects and the baits held out were alluring, but this Trout would not bite. However, when near the station to take the train for home, a young man, running, overtook me, and said, "If you have the least idea of entering for land, I have a proposition that you will be sure to consider." "Well, what is it?" "I have a half section in the Turtle Mountain district, and I have a good chance on a half section in the Souris district, which I prefer, but I can't hold both." "What's the matter with the first one?" "Nothing, only it is farther from settlement. There is one family close by it. I will take you there at my expense, and you can give me any nominal consideration." I turned with him, and we took the first train west to Brandon, where I found three of my Scotch cousins, Donald MacKinnon, hotel keeper, who had a claim near the one I was to see; also John Munn, and John MacKinnon, real estate men. From there, by a lazy little Indian pony and buckboard, we started on our sixty-mile southern journey, taking the well-traveled trail to Souris, where we stayed in a good-sized farmer's village overnight. Its new country character may be judged by the fact that on the previous night a skunk, having regard to his prior right, took possession of a residence, and drove the family out. It was a case of eviction without due process of law, and in the end his skunkship got the worst of it. But everywhere the buoyancy and hopefulness of the people were persistently manifest. There was hard work, but abounding health and strength to stand it.

We left Souris at daybreak. The fall and winter days are very short up there. We crossed the Souris river, a large, sluggish stream, and through a beautiful, slightly undulating country all day. There were one or two springs of nice water along our trail. These are rare enough to be precious. Our destination lay four or five miles to the left of our main trail;

and the trail leading off was too blind to follow in the night; and as the possibility of spending the long night on the prairie did not commend itself to us, we discussed the one possible alternative. Two families had a month or two before moved in and settled, as near as my companion could judge, two and one-half or three miles southeast of our position; if we could strike their residences we would be all right for the night, and could finish our journey in the morning. We decided to venture, though still running our chance of the long cold night on the prairie. We took our direction to a certain point on the horizon, and at every elevation scrutinized the landscape; and at the dusk of evening discovered some stacks of hay where men were working, and we soon found the houses, and shelter for the night. The next morning we arrived at the residence of our neighbor Frenchman, who had spent the previous winter there, and had a good acquaintance with prairie conditions; and, like all the rest, was enthusiastic in behalf of the country.

That morning we drove around the boundaries of the lot, locating the corner stakes.

It was a mile long and a half-mile wide, a magnificent piece of good land; and the prospective ownership certainly gave one a swelled feeling. There were more small sloughs than I cared for, but it would make a good stock farm. We went back to the Frenchman's to dinner, and that afternoon I tried to think on both sides of that land question. I put the prairie farm against the town and the shop, but the prairie had the best of it; and before evening I arranged for the transfer of entry to myself. Really there was no transfer. My companion went with me to the Government land office, at Deloraine, and relinquished his claim, the land going back to the government; then I was on hand to make the next claim, which was not accorded me till after thirty days. During this period I built up the walls of a sod stable, and built for the Frenchman a simple style of boat, to be used on the lake, which was simply a big slough, about three miles long and nearly a mile wide, and had in it a nice wooded island, where he got some of his wood. The lake was over a mile from his house, and but a short distance from one corner of my lot. It was the lowest part of a broad, flat valley, and its water, like most of the sloughs, was brackish. At that time of the year there were thousands of wild geese and ducks on its bosom and about its shores. Their honks and quacking, when I first came, made one continual chorus day and night. Cranes and herons were also common, badgers and skunks and gophers were all over, with muskrats about the lake and the big sloughs. Occasionally we met a big ground squirrel and prairie hens. Though I could shoot fairly well, I was no sportsman. My interest in this abundance of wild life was more like that of the naturalist, but this did not hinder enjoyment in the eating. On the fifth day of November we went to the island, to get wood and shoot game. The second heavy frost of the fall had the night before frozen the water on the small sloughs, so that a man could walk over them. Except around the edges, the lake was open, and a few belated ducks were swimming around near the shore in search of food, which must have been mostly vegetable, as there was nothing deserving the name of fish in the lake. When we had ferried ourselves over to the island, the Frenchman and his son took their axes to cut the wood, and gave me the gun to shoot some ducks. Altogether, there were about a dozen in scattered groups on one side of the island. I soon got my first shot, the most favorable one, as I turned over three ducks out of a nice, little flock. The next thing was to get them. The dog had followed me, and was willing enough to go into the water; but did not know enough to bring in the ducks. The boat was on the other side of the island, so I took off my boots and socks, and rolled up my pants as high as I could, and waded the ice-cold water, fortunately getting the ducks without wetting my pants. I wanted a towel then awful bad for my cold, wet legs and feet. Not long after that I got a couple of shots with one duck for each shot, and had the same cold wading again. The ducks then all left for safer parts.

When I came back to the men I was complimented on my bag of game. Soon after we had our noonday lunch, choosing a place where we could be sheltered from the breezy north wind, and get the little warmth that might come from the low slanting rays of the November sun; and while we were making the best of our brief meal, a big, lonely mosquito came around singing his old song, to see if there was anything in it for him, which simply shows the extraordinary persistence of all manner of life in that far Northwest. After eating, we took over to the mainland our first load of wood, and the young Frenchman shot a couple of muskrats on the passage. By choice I remained on that side, where near an open piece of water I could observe the industrious muskrats at work. Two of their houses were about a gunshot away. I got an easy position on some hay in the wagon and kept still, and soon noticed them come out and look around; and judging no one was likely to disturb them, they proceeded with their work, which as far as I was enabled to see, consisted in stripping off the surfaces of some of the strong rushy grasses that grow in the water. Besides we found some places where they had burrowed under the soft, turfy sod on the margin of their ponds, to get certain plant roots, which certainly would be more tangible food than what I saw them gathering. They evidently kept their stuff in a cellar of cold, wet storage, where they had to dive for every meal in the long, dark winter, with two or three feet of snow covering their house, and four or five feet of ice over their ponds, often freezing them close to the bottom. It would seem to me those lively, industrious, orderly summer workers, who, having reared their family, and gathered in their winter store, ought to have more capacious quarters for their long, dark, pent-up winter life. Their one-room life must be awful dull. They ought to have an amusement hall. Perhaps they go visiting under the ice. When our men came over from the island with their final load of wood, they shot three or four more of these intelligent little workers; and when our wagon was loaded up, we started for the house, arriving in the twilight. When I first came to the Frenchman's residence, which was just a good, comfortable, sod shanty, with an outer and inner apartment, the old man, in telling about the game, said, "There is a strange thing here, the muskrats don't smell musky." I laughed and said, "That surely is strange, a muskrat and no musk." He said, "Boy, go and get the skins for the gentleman." The boy soon brought me a big armful of skins, and laid them on my knees. I owned up there was no musk there; and that evening I noted that on the newly killed animals there was no smell of musk, though in every other respect they were just like the ordinary musky muskrat. When we got home the women expressed their pleasure at the good number of rats. I said, "Are you going to cook them?" "Why *sure* we will. Muskrats make the best kind of meat." While the skinning and cleaning was being done, I was examining the anatomy of these strangely interesting animals. The head was of the greatest interest. The lower jaw was not a single bone into which the teeth were inserted but two separate strong bones, one on each side, jointed under the skull in the usual way. Then running out long in front of the head, each bone terminated in a short incisor tooth, so close to its fellow of the opposite bone that the cartilaginous joining was not readily noticeable; and what corresponded to the grinding teeth in other animals was one pearly white plate about seven-eighths of an inch long by one-fourth of an inch wide, finely serrated into little pyramids of about one-sixteenth of an inch dimensions. There was a corresponding plate on the upper jaw, and two long incisor teeth grew out from the skull, to match the large lower teeth. The little chipmunk has pouches at the back part of his mouth, to carry his load of nuts to his little subterranean home; but this fine, wagtail swimmer carried his bundle of grass held by the great teeth in the front of his mouth, till arriving at his home, he dives and stores it in one of his subaquean chambers. We call him a rat, what a misnomer. Rats are filthy, and will eat carrion like a buzzard, but this dainty fellow is a constant bather, and a strict vegetarian. Add to all this his building ability, provident habits, and general alertness, and we have something that seems almost too human and too good to eat. But our French women suffered nothing from sentiment; they knew the art of making muskrat pie, which I can certainly certify was by far the most richly delicious meat pie that I ever had a share in eating. The splendid duck pie we had a day or two later did not nearly equal it.

The ducks, too, were of great interest. They were strangers to me. Unlike our fish-eating ducks on the Great Lakes, they, like the rats, were vegetarians, and had better flavored meat; and words cannot describe the extraordinary rich, rare and beautiful iridescent colors and tints of their magnificent plumage. How I wished I was a taxidermist, so as to mount them in lifelike form and preserve their beauty.

The conditions of pioneeer prairie life have much that is highly interesting, and much that is ordinarily regarded as unpleasant; but the pioneer takes all as a matter of course, and thinks little of inconveniences or discomforts. His conquests over nature are a constant inspiration. I was out on this prairie fully one month, doing considerable walking most every day; and with the exception of plowing the sod and drawing the cut sods to the site of my stable, the work was my own. For many years I had not been used to hard muscular effort, and the wearisome effect of real hard work was at first very discouraging. For instance, one morning I got the use of a scythe, wherewith to cut some of the tall grass, and put up a little stack of hay, to be used in the spring for roofing my stable. For over twenty years I had not handled a scythe, and I was pleased with the first few strokes, to find I had the old swing and good motion that results in good work. I put my strength in to it, as I had to, because the grass was about breast high, and as thick as it could grow. I cut a wide swath pretty lively for about one rod, and then was so completely winded that I threw myself down on the heavy swath of cut grass and panted. I said, "What's the use, undertaking to farm and can't stand five minutes mowing." But before I left the prairie I could walk all day without serious fatigue, and do hard work with most anyone.

On November 10, 1882, I paid the fee, and was entered as the occupant of my lot, intending next morning to start on the sixty-mile journey to Brandon on foot and carrying an ordinary grip bag. I went to the oldest, nearby resident farmer, who was in the third year of his occupation; he was from Ontario, Canada, as were most all the settlers in that part.

I could be at home anywhere, and anyone would entertain strangers, giving the best that was handy, for which the stranger might pay according to his good will and ability. That evening I learned, that by waiting till the day after the morrow, I could ride with a neighbor all the way to Brandon, which I concluded to do. That night I had a comfortable sleep on a lounge in a good house, the best for over a month; as at the Frenchman's I slept rolled in a quilt on a bundle of hay, with my coat for a pillow. That last day of waiting, the eleventh of November, was what father used to call a pet day, that generally presaged bad weather to follow. It was calm, and not a cloud in the clear blue sky; men went about with their coats off, like in the summer time. That evening a party of land prospectors came along to stay all night; so the farmer gave them and myself some quilts, and sent us to the hay barn, to make ourselves as comfortable as we could. That was quite a commonplace job for me; but the building, being airy, and the night cool, I kept most of my clothes on, and slept finely the fore part of the night; but at midnight there came a fearful wind that shook our light shack, but not the beds, for we lay on the solid earth. The wind currents inside were so strong I could feel the hair moving on my head, and withal it was severely cold; with the best tucking I could do, it was scant sleep for the rest of the night.

At the first show of day we turned out with the hope of finding a warm place. A rain barrel was our common wash bowl, which I was greatly surprised to find not frozen. After a good substantial breakfast I climbed onto a moderately loaded wagon, finding as comfortable a seat as I could. I was poorly provided against the weather; had a light wool tweed suit, summer underwear and light overcoat. That forty-mile cold wind seemed as if it blew on my bare skin. As the day wore on the wind increased to more than a fifty-mile gale. I got one of the horse blankets to wrap around myself, but seemingly no amount of covering would keep out that penetrating wind. It blew as steady on the great prairie as it would on the wide ocean. We made a forty-mile journey with only one stop. In the evening the wind subsided, and with it our discomfort, though it began to freeze. We stayed overnight at Souris, and next morning the frozen mud would carry our horses. We got to Brandon at noon, where there was plenty of good civilized comfort; and I did not feel the least bad effect from the severity of the day before. Spent the afternoon and evening visiting my cousins, John Munn, John McKinnon, and Donald McKinnon; also Peter Mitchel, an acquaintance from childhood. The next day I took the train for Winnipeg, where, after concluding some details at the government land office, I called on friends; and making a final visit to the Sprague Mill, I started for home, via Milwaukee, and by boat to Grand Haven. At Grand Rapids I laid over most of a day, to visit our old Peterboro pastor, Brother Mulhern, and Dan Frazer; also at Detroit I stopped over a day to see my brother Alexander and wife and the Linn family. I also stopped at Toronto. I never had looked so hearty in all my life. I certainly never felt more so. One hundred and forty miles of further railway journey brought me home to Peterboro, where after nearly a four months' absence a welcome awaited me, which I was prepared to enjoy most heartily; besides furnishing my contribution of enjoyment to the dear ones who had so long awaited me.

RESULT OF TRIP.

This millwright, prairie and other experiences were both new and profitable. My Milwaukee three months' experience, two years previous to this, was a great advantage, particularly in the line of machine design and shop practice, but this three months' Winnipeg experience was wholly different; it was millwright work which, excepting the work of two different winters, I had not done for twenty-five years. My advancing education had been largely on the information furnished by other millwrights, and, of course, lacked the positive character of first hand knowledge; but when, as I sometimes hear in the South, "he has been and gone and done it," then one knows what he talks about, and in other people he can soon distinguish stiff bluff talk from good plain information. In other words, it gives self-poise, or the mastery of one's self, as well as his subject. In resuming work in the drawing office and pattern shop, I had readier judgment and a finer grip.

CHANGE PROPOSED IN HAMILTON'S BUSINESS.

Mr. William Hamilton began his fine business with a small shop and few men, he himself always doing his ten hours' work, at lathe or vise, and often more; and always did his bookkeeping for the day before he slept. With increase of business he had to cut out his personal work, and also give the oversight to foremen; but he never lost sight of the details. He was the general inspector, and scarce anything escaped him. Little use was made of written orders, memory had to be vigilant; so there was often trouble which worried the boss, and passed on to the foreman, and also disturbed the men. There was a manifest need of some business system, that had not yet been evolved. Mr. Hamiliton was then sixty years of age, he was called old Willie; and though hale and hearty and active, realized the uncertainty of life, and his need of at least a measure of relief from his heavy responsibility.

His business was in perfect condition, the property unencumbered, no loans, funds in bank, by which bills were promptly met, and discount saved; so he had nobody's leave to ask for whatever he might choose to do. He was satisfied that as far as running the shop was concerned he had three dependable men: George Munro, his son-in-law, the superintendent; Andrew MacFarlane, machine shop foreman; and myself as draughtsman and foreman patternmaker. Another man for outside work was needed, to hunt up work, make plans for large mills, and take the contracts, and if advisable to supervise their construction. A young man by the name of Hall (his first name I have forgotten) was chosen. He had taken an engineering course at McGill University, and had superintended the building of two large mills in Quebec province. He was induced to give up some excellent prospects, and come into the proposed new firm of the William Hamilton Company. Mr. Hamilton's plan was to capitalize his business, issue stock, assign one-sixteenth to each of his four working partners, who would receive yearly dividends, beside their regular wages, and would pay interest on their stock until the dividends or installments paid for it. There was also, I think, a further privilege of stock purchase, but a final reserve must be left of fifty-one per cent, which would descend to his son. But his business and other friends got around him, and persuaded him, that he was unwisely giving away his property. The plan failed to provide for losses, and it was postponed indefinitely and never carried out. Hall turned a trick against the old man, and became the manager in a sawmill firm in Western Ontario.

VERMILION BAY MILL.

Business in 1883 opened poorly. We had but one small mill contract, to be delivered by July 1st, at Vermilion Bay, on the Canadian Pacific railway, about midway between Rat Portage and Port Arthur. Cars were running on the railway line, but it was not open for regular traffic. I obtained the superintendence of the millwright work, on terms similar to what I had at Winnipeg. This suited my plans nicely, as according to the terms of my land entry I should go onto it and break up and put a few acres in crop. Accordingly, the fourth of May I landed in Winnipeg, intending after inquiry to finish the remaining journey to the farm. I met, however, an extraordinary change in conditions. Branch railway lines, that were supposed to be built in a year or two, were indefinitely postponed. The government's new regulations blocked all transfer. Land had no value. The line to Turtle Mountain, which would help me, was indefinitely postponed. It was certain not to be built under four or five years. To hold the land by periodic visits, and raising small crops that might not be marketed, all without my family, was not to be considered; neither could I put my wife and family of young children on that lone prairie, away from schools, society and Christian church influences. I did not go to see it, for fear the prairie fever might catch me again, and change my resolution to give it up. Having relinquished the farm project, I now had time on my hands until the Vermilion bay job was ready. At the Sprague mill I installed a friction nigger or log turner that occupied me several days. I then traveled over the city for nearly a week, and could find no possible suitable employment. It was the second and last time in my life that I sought work, the first having been already mentioned as at a vacation when attending the Williamsville academy. Those two experiences were enough to give me a hearty sympathy for the poor fellows to whom such humiliating and disappointing experiences were common.

Having thus failed in getting work, I determined to go to Minneapolis, which was then becoming a great lumbering and manufacturing center. I could be reasonably sure of the kind of employment I wanted there. I called on Saunders at the Sprague mill to bid him goodbye. "Here," he says, "I want something that will count the logs as they come into the mill. You can make it." "Of course I can." "Well, there's a job, go ahead." Neither he nor I had ever seen one, but he knew that I was good for it. I spent the rest of the day at the drawing board, and the next morning got a piece of scrap timber, and began the construction; and in a few days placed the counter on its post of duty, and it served its purpose most admirably. It would give the day's count, if desired, or a continuous count up to ten thousand. Now I said, "What is it worth?" Said he, "Make your price." "Well about twenty-five dollars." "All right." "Now," he said, "you can easily put one in every mill in this town." Which I did, though it was not easy. The last manager I served challenged me to make a machine to measure the output of lumber. I saw that it would be a complicated undertaking, but I addressed myself to it. Board measuring of standard thickness and length was simple. And multiplying by increased thickness, though difficult, was practical, but to account for the third dimension, the length might be said to be impractical; and besides all these was the matter of quality, which only the human judgment could determine. Though excellent thought work and drawing had been lavished upon this, it had to be given up. I had plenty of time, and enjoyed that sort of work, which was at least indirectly helpful.

The first of July drew near, when I should begin the Vermilion bay job, and I went down there, arriving before Boss Murray, who was to be general manager. The mill frame was up and roofed, and the framer's contract was about completed; but evidently Murray had been playing double with both he and I, for he, the framer, said he had been engaged to remain and put in the machinery, and there was no doubt that he told the truth. Neither of us had a scrap of writing to back our claims. For my own sake, as well as the good reputation of our shop, I was determined to do the work. So the framer and I calmly talked the whole matter over, he saw that, having designed the machinery and engine, and planned the mill, I was the logical man to do the work; and he probably rightly suspected that Murray intended to play him off against me, so he considerately left for his home in Ontario.

While waiting for Murray I set up a drawing board, and began the design of a perfectly balanced steam gang, that I had studied out, or, more briefly, invented, in the wakeful morning hours of the long nights on the prairie in the previous October. This was a valuable invention, though ahead of the demand, and would have been a success had it been pushed. A similar one, by William Wilkens of the Stearns Company, seven or eight years afterward, had a good run.

Canada is justly regarded as a very decent moral country, but this Vermilion bay situation was the toughest hole I ever set foot in. It was a great railroad camp. There was a fine ridge of gravel for road ballasting. Several steam diggers were constantly at work loading gravel trains. Mackenzie and MacDonald, the railroad contractors, were the owners of the mill, so the mill gang was part of the general crowd. A few men that had families had separate residences. All others boarded at the main camp. On my first day at dinner, a burly, big fellow sat near me, with both eyes blackened, skin broken, and cut in a dozen places, his face swelled out of shape. One of our mill gang told me there had been a hard fight three or four days before, and that fellow had got the "lickin." It did not seem to disturb him much, and it seemed to be regarded as an ordinary occurrence. Two and sometimes three girls of the demimonde occupied a small house by themselves, and flaunted their presence about as they pleased. Two gentlemanly fellows occupied a shack by themselves, in order to cure up, if possible, from the consequences of their former licentious indiscretions. One fine man, younger than I, though bearing his part with the rest, was different; and noted the difference in me, and became my friend, was very intelligent, and interested in good things. We often spent Sundays together. We had no books, and but few papers. Conversation was our main interest. Friends are valuable where they are scarce. Sunday was my correspondence day.

We mill workers had a sleeping house by ourselves. Beds were on the sleeping car style. My berth was an apper one. There was a hanging lamp and a table under it. Cards were the standard amusement of the evening. As I did not play, and there was little chance for anything else, I retired early; and from my high-perched bed could look down at the players, and see what hands they held. I had the finest opportunity to learn, but I could not be interested enough to try; so the pleasure from cards is unknown to me, and I have no sense of loss.

This was a country of beautiful lakes, and Vermillion Bay was one of the finest. The coarse, sandy soil supported a rather slender growth of timber; the logs were small, but straight and long. A small circular saw, fifty-six inches in diameter, and light carriage was what suited the situation. It was a small mill with excellent machinery, and as it had good men to handle it, it became known as the fastest mill on the line of the Canadian Pacific Railway, and another small addition to the reputation of the William Hamilton firm. In the tree-tops near the mill, I saw what was to me the last lonely specimen of the American wild pigeon. I saw him several times during two days. He had no mate. If he had a race memory, how forlorn he must have felt, for in my boyhood days birds of his feather were so abundant that their flight would sometimes darken the sky. They were often caught by springing a large net over them, after they had been decoyed to a prepared feeding ground, by the use of a captive or "stool pigeon," one of their own species, whose feet were secured to the end of a long rod, which was operated by men under cover at the edge of the ground. They bobbed the pigeon up and down, making him flutter as if feeding over the ground; then his fellows in the treetops would come down in a steady stream, till the feeding ground would be fully covered with them; then the net would be sprung down upon them, often catching several hundred. The next thing was to kill them, which was done by crushing the base of the skull between thumb and forefinger, or breaking their necks; as their heads were sticking up through the net, this was quickly done. Then the net was lifted to its former elevation, the dead pigeons gathered up and taken to one side, some more grain scattered on the ground; and when the men had got back under cover, they were ready for a repetition of the operation. The birds who had witnessed the recent catastrophe had flown, so there would be a period of waiting for fresh ones to come to the treetops, when the same stool pigeon would be made to coax down some more unfortunates. On foggy mornings they would fly low, we sometimes then could knock them down by rapidly swinging a long pole as the flock passed by. That was also a fine chance to shoot, not directly, at them as they were coming toward us; ordinary bird shot would not then penetrate their closely packed feathers, but if we fired at them after they had passed by, we could then bring down sometimes a half dozen at a shot. In the spring and summer they helped out our larder finely. Pigeon pie was not then a luxury. Some people salted them down. The mornings and evenings were the times of their greatest activity in flying and feeding. In the middle of the day they would be found in the thick shade of the trees, or by the side of some stream, or on the lake shore drinking or picking up gravel. In these positions we could sometimes get fine shots, by standing up under cover; but it was not the busy ones on the shore that we had to look out for, but the sentinel, an old cock pigeon perched up on a high, dead tree, where he had a good outlook, and could warn his associates of danger.

In the early midsummer we would see the first of the new broods, known by peculiar young feathers and imperfect tails. They were a sure and easy game for the hawks, but it was not so with the old ones. I was once a nearby witness to a close chase of this kind. A hawk, quietly sailing overhead, evidently concluded he would try his skill and wing power on a lone cock pigeon perched on a pretty high tree, that grew on the side of the hill on the top of which I was standing. The hawk made his downward dart, and got almost onto the pigeon, when he started for the ground in a spiral course, the hawk being within two or three feet of him all the way down, till the pigeon landed in some thick low bushes, and the hawk gave him up. It was the speed of that short flight that astonished me. They tore through the air with the noise and speed of a skyrocket.

It seems almost incredible that such an abundance of beautiful energetic life should have perished from the earth. The last and only known specimen has recently died in captivity near Cincinnati; and there is a standing prize of several thousand dollars offered for a pair.

Well, the Vermilion bay job was satisfactorily completed, and a settlement made, the best I could get, which was not satisfactory. I got the specified wages, but had to stand the loss of time waiting for them, and expenses. A good kick at headquarters amounted to nothing.

The would-be millionaires, who stick their chins in the air, and see only the few they want to, are quite willing to privately profit by the meanness of their underlings, and pretend not to know it, and of course will not search it out.

LAKE VOYAGE

About the middle of October, 1883, I took the eastbound Canadian Pacific railroad train to start for home. At Port Arthur we were to take one of the Canadian Pacific railroad's staunch sea-going boats, through Lake Superior and Huron. When our train arrived at Port Arthur, a great storm was on the lake, and our boat was several hours late arriving; and the storm also prevented her starting out on schedule time the evening after. I used the spare time to visit my old friends, the Woodsides, and see the running of Port Arthur sawmill, in which the men at work seemed half asleep. The storm having somewhat subsided during the night, we made a start in the morning; and while for a short time in moderately calm weather our passengers were on view, either on the decks or in the main cabin, I noted a fine group of people. But shortly after we were encountering the high rolling billows of Lake Superior; then all the ladies and half the gentlemen repaired to their staterooms, to try and settle or "cast up" as their feelings might determine.

A few acquaintances and I took pleasure in going over the boat where we pleased. However, the storm increased, till toward noon we began to ship some heavy seas. The center of a boat is the place of least motion, but at that part the crests of some of the waves would be level with the main deck, and the succeeding trough twenty feet below. At one o'clock in the afternoon our captain decided to lay by for a time, in a cove on the lee side of Silver island. This was a rocky islet, not a hundred acres in extent, projecting up from the deep waters of Lake Superior. Our vessel came into the quiet cove so close to the rocky shore that the gangplank would reach it, and the passengers all got off. It gave the seasick folks a fine interval of relief, and the place was highly interesting. There had been a very prolific silver mine, rather under, than on the island, as shafts and galleries had been sunk in the rock several hundred feet below the lake level. Work was then suspended. There were good houses but no occupants, except a care taker and his family, to whom our forced call made a cheerful break in their lonely time. Though the wind was high, there was bright sunshine, and we spent a pleasant afternoon, climbing the rocky cliffs and seeing the mining machinery. In the evening everyone enjoyed the luxurious supper, particularly those who lost their breakfast and had no dinner, after which, the storm having measurably subsided, our steamer pursued her course. That night and the next day it was still rough, but toward the second evening it became quite calm. A plain, old gentleman from the western prairies, with his arm in a sling, seemed to know a great many of the passengers; and with those he did not know he made acquaintance, and introduced unacquainted ones with one another. He discovered the singers, the piano players, and those that could recite, tell a good story, or make a speech. He got these folks together, and arranged a program for the evening.

Had two young lawyers debate for twenty minutes, each on one of the live political topics of the time. There was a spontaneity and freedom that admitted snatches of good conversational wit and humor. On the whole, it was, on a large scale, a fine informal superb parlor entertainment. It would be easy to judge how I enjoyed it, after three months' roughing, with rough people. Many of the others no doubt had similar experiences.

The third evening we entered the St. Mary river, and passed through the locks on the American side, which was a matter of interest. Twenty-four hours more of sailing, through the lower St. Mary and Lake Huron, brought us to Sarnia, the termination of my voyage; but the steamer proceeded on to Buffalo. I took the Grand Trunk train for Peterboro, joyfully arriving home after an absence of five months, hoping that it would be the last; it proved to be the last long term.

I found work in the shop scarce, with poor prospects. One or two men and myself repaired patterns.

I started a better system of numbering, locating and caring for patterns. Also corrected drawings, which, with occasional small jobs, kept us going most of the winter. One day in March, 1884, I went to Superintendent Munro with the usual disturbing question: "What next?" He looked puzzled. I watched him a moment. "See here," said I, "I'll relieve you; I want to do some drawing for myself, and will stay at home for a few weeks." "That is a good idea," said he, "and when you get back we may have some new work." Accordingly I made up my time report, gathered up my instruments and left; and went to work to put in final shape some proposed new improvements in circulars with top saws, and make a drawing for the patent application.

RETURN TO MILWAUKEE

In the course of three weeks a letter came from Milwaukee, asking me to consider a re-engagement with the Filer & Stowell Manufacturing Company. I regarded it as a providential good prospect in a decidedly dull situation. I replied, asking for their best offer, and the return letter assured me four dollars per day, which I accepted; and came direct to Milwaukee, arriving in the first week of April, 1884, leaving Mrs. Trout and family to come when I had hunted up a house for them, and settled my Peterboro obligations. Mr. Fitzgerald, the superintendent, my former friend, who had now been most instrumental in bringing me back to Milwaukee, was about to engage as a traveler for the E. P. Allis Company. He told me I had come to the shop in the right time, that he would very shortly begin with the E. P. Allis Company; and there was no likelier man than myself to take his place, and that I must be ready to jump right into it. I was entirely ready as far as purpose and will was concerned, but not being familiar with all the details of office and shop procedure, I was really not prepared. That I regarded as a slight matter, if I only had the authority and support of President Stowell, which he, as I afterwards saw, wisely withheld. He knew it was an untried responsibility for me, and held off. Mr. Hamilton had business in Chicago, and came by Milwaukee to see me, and see a good American shop in much the same line and style of his own. He told me that Mr. Stowell had talked with him regarding my being superintendent. He did not state the purport of the conversation, but advised me to be careful about undertaking it, that I was doing well as a designing draughtsman, and could succeed in it. Afterward Mr. Stowell told me that Mr. Hamilton said I was a good dependable worker regarding myself, but not good to get the most out of other workers, which I inwardly knew to be true. Besides, I never felt either pleasure or pride in being boss, so I resigned myself to the work for which I was best adapted and could most enjoy. My expectation was that Mrs. Trout and family would follow me in the course of a month or six weeks. But about the time they would have started, Mrs. Trout fell severely sick, and though she soon got better some more weeks elapsed before she could undertake the long journey. I would have gone back for her, but the cost of the double journey, and the loss of time, which would amount to about seventy dollars, would disrupt our slender finances so badly that I felt I couldd not afford it. I wrote to her brother, Richard, to go to Peterboro, and help her start on the journey, which was the main part of the trouble. This he kindly did; and Mrs. Trout and her six active little children, the youngest being a baby just trying to creep, the eldest in his eleventh year, all arrived in due time in Milwaukee, our new home. The unbounded activity of the three eldest children was the cause of much anxiety to the mother; but she had the interest and help of passengers and trainmen and boatmen on the journey. After setting up our home in Milwaukee, there was thereafter only one or two short periods of absence from my family.

Mr. T. J. Neacy, the leading traveller, and an active stockholder, assumed to determine much of the company's policy. He set up a poor mouth story in regard to business, and as a consequence that we all must submit to a reduction of pay. I protested, and said I would submit only when I had to. Soon afterwards, Mr. Stowell spoke to the same effect. I told him I had done nothing toward making a change, but if that was coming I would do so at once. I wrote the E. P. Allis Company, giving my lowest wages at four dollars per day, and referred to their traveller, Fitzgerald, who happened to be present when my letter was read by the sawmill department superintendent, George Hinkley. Fitzgerald certified to my ability, and I had a prompt response to come on at once. I finished up in a day or two the general drawing of a floating sawmill, and began work with the larger and better firm, and where the working conditions were greatly improved. With the Filer & Stowell Company I was under continual stress, having to look after too many unimportant things, that were more or less continual annoyance. With the E. P. Allis Company I had good design drawing, my first work being the designing of the first band mill the company constructed. Band mills for sawing lumber were then an experiment. Our first mill was running inside of four months after my engagement. Mr. Hinkley went out to witness the start. On his return to the office, he was asked how the new band mill was going. "Going like ———," was his profane reply, which was characteristic of his style. That was a little dubious, so he explained by reporting the first hour's sawing was better than the best records previously made; and our band mill business soon got beyond the ability of the company to promptly meet the demand.

THE EDWARD P. ALLIS COMPANY

As my engagement with the Allis Company was to me a great change—and a very much advanced step—it would seem advisable to digress and refer to it more fully. The William Hamilton and Filer & Stowell firms employed only about one hundred men each, while the E. P. Allis Company employed about fifteen hundred men; so it can be readily seen that while the rule of thumb might in a moderate extent be admissible in the former, in the latter there must of necessity be a more or less finely developed system of designing, draughting, contracting, ordering, supervising, constructing, and assembling the work; also shipping, erecting at destination, testing, settling up, and collecting the final payments.

All of these steps in this great business process had to be supervised and wrought out by different individuals, often a great number of them. The business of each was not only to do his own work absolutely correct, but as far as possible to watch out for the mistakes of the fellows who preceded him; and detection of such was a mark of merit, and to pass over a mistake to others who followed was a demerit. But sometimes mistakes would run the entire gauntlet without discovery, and would not be found out till the final erection of the machine; then it often would be a serious money loss and discredit to the company.

My backwoods bringing up helped me in the way of initiative in meeting new conditions, and in some way I seemed to have an intuitive understanding of the principles of mechanics and the relations of parts of machines to the whole. This, with a good long working experience for one of my years, made me proficient in designing new work, for which I received the highest draughtsman's wage in the sawmill department. A thoroughly difficult job was always the most interesting. It was a pleasure to scheme and plan and bring out new and simpler forms that were better adapted to the needs of the required service.

MILWAUKEE CHURCH OF CHRIST

This digression is carrying my personal experience ahead of the general story. Fully more important than my shop career was our family and church life in Milwaukee. The first began with the arrival of Mrs. Trout and children, July 6, 1884. The second began in a tentative way in the fall of the same year. Previous to this our irregular church attendance was with the South Baptist church. We were requested to join, I told the pastor of our easy relation with the Baptist Church in Peterboro, Canada, that we never formally united, yet worked with them cordially for eleven years. He replied that the course of the church was wrong, that we should have become members, which practically meant that none but regular Baptists could be in any way connected with his church. Realizing, as we did, the freedom and broader sympathy of the Christian position, we could not entertain the idea of becoming denominationally Baptists; and we found that there were eight or nine in the same situation as ourselves. The most pronounced and active among this number was Mrs. Mary J. Allen, an old Disciple from her girlhood in Scotland, a rare, cheery, kindly, motherly woman whose efforts were hopefully directed to the establishment of a congregation of Christians or Disciples of Christ in Milwaukee. Through my brother Alexander in Detroit, we were introduced to George I. and Mrs. Lindsay, who had shortly been married in Detroit, and were then residing in Milwaukee. Mrs. Allen

hailed our coming as two more substantial helpers toward her
cherished purpose. About the month of October in that year,
1884, James H. Stover and wife with a small family moved
to Milwaukee, to conduct a life assurance business. As he had
been a preacher at South Bend, Indiana, he also was anxious
to see a good working congregation. Whether Sister Allen
discovered him, or he discovered her, I am uncertain. However, she invited us to come over to her house to meet Brother
Stover, and we found him to be a lively, interesting, young
man, of evident good ability, and also anxious to have a good
successful congregation in Milwaukee. But successful it must
be, he was not disposed to lead or help in a forlorn hope;
and as he was well acquainted with William Sherman and the
Mathews brothers and sisters, who had considerable wealth,
he considered there was a reasonably good prospect for a fair
active congregation. A brother, McDonald, who managed
a business college in the Iron Block, corner Wisconsin and
East Water streets, gave us the use of one of his rooms for
our first meeting, which was really only a getting together to
determine what might be done. Brother William Sherman
seemed the most interested of any of the men. He had come
early, and was keeping count as each entered. When Mrs.
Trout and I, with our two youngst babies, one in arms,
entered, he exclaimed, "Why, here we have nineteen now; this
begins to look like real business," and showed his pleasure
accordingly. He was assured that was all that we might
expect, and after some general conversation we had prayer,
reading of the Scriptures and short hopeful talks, from several
of those present, myself included. As we were about to conclude, I proposed a hymn, "To Him that loved the sons of
men," announced it from memory, and started the tune;
and was surprised at the lack of spirit in the singing, so I
finished with two stanzas. I afterward learned that Brother
McDonald had requested that there be no singing, as there
were other office rooms occupied in the building; and though
it was Sunday forenoon, he did not wish it to be known that
he was holding religious meeting in his rooms, all of which
shows the irreligious spirit of the times. Milwaukee is very

decidedly irreligious now, but then aggressively so, as in those days Bob Ingersol and other lecturers were abroad, making open attack upon Christianity. Bob's squibs and coarse jokes were quoted in the shops and offices, obviously with the pleasure of the majority. I for one at least had scant sympathy for Brother MacDonald's complaisance to this spirit. At that meeting we decided to continue meeting for mutual exhortation and worship; and obtained the use of an assembly room in the then poor Young Men's Christian Association building for an hour and a half on Sunday forenoon, until such time as we might find more permanent quarters. This was occupied for a couple of months without cost, and we were notified to find some other place, as further meetings might appear like a preference to us as a denomination. Accordingly we engaged a vacant store on Grand avenue between Fifth and Sixth streets, and continued there throughout the winter of 1884 and 1885. In the course of the winter we opened correspondence with Brother Moffet, president of the Home Missionary Society, and he made us a visit. We announced his coming in the newspapers, and invited any or all Disciples of Christ, residents or sojourning in the city, to be present. This brought out Miss Louise Mathews, and two or three others. That Lord's day we had two good meetings with Brother Moffet, and he left on the following Monday or Tuesday; and our meetings continued more hopefully than before. Our wealthy landlord, Mr. Wells, a good, thorough-going Methodist, would occasionally drop in to our meetings, and one day said to us, "You brethren ought to advertise and come out stronger before the public. You have ability and I like your message. It is good. But your light is now under a bushel, the situation is good, you ought to fill up this room." I heartily agreed with him. In a sense the others did too, but disliked to expose our smallness and were afraid of failure.

We wanted to start with some prestige and good prospects. We wanted a Pentecost without pentecostal courage and preparation. However, we held to our purpose of mutual edification, and though our meetings were small they were highly interesting, each of the half dozen or more men contributing his quota to the main purpose and the good fellowship of the small assembly.

One dull, hazy Lord's day forenoon, Brother William Sherman toward the close of the meeting made a very important announcement that would most favorably affect our work in the future. As Brother Stover, our best speaker, was not then present, in the afternoon I hasted over town to see him, I asked regarding his absence in the forenoon meeting, "Oh, I did not just feel like going this morning." Mrs. Stover interrupted with, "Why did you not say plainly, you were discouraged?" "Well, I judge I might be with some reason." "No, No!" said I, "no reason at all!" "Oh, we will find you fighting in the last ditch as a matter of course." "Ah," said I, "you have no idea what you missed this morning, something to give us great hope." Then I gave the purport of Brother Sherman's statement, that though we were a small body, yet he regarded us as likely to be steady residents of Milwaukee, and such as would be a good hopeful mucleus, which, if favorably placed, would grow into a good permanent congregation. That there was on the south side a neat, small chapel, and a parsonage on the same lot, ready for our occupancy as soon as we would be prepared to enter; and that we might continue to hold and use the property free of all costs, as long as we could maintain a pastor and keep up regular meetings. This magnificent proposition struck him, as it did the rest of us, with joyous surprise; at the same time we felt our weakness and inability to readily use to good effect those fine advantages.

The following Lord's day we took the matter under advisement to determine what we would do about it. It was no matter for hasty judgment. There was the respectable remnant of a good congregation meeting there every Sunday. A Sunday school was also maintained. The pastor had the reputation of being, to say the least, a very clever minister, and after a four years' trial with a constantly dwindling congregation, he was giving up; only asking the use of the house every fortnight on Sunday afternoons, so as to keep his remnant together, and preserve his standing as a minister, until he could find something better, or slide into some secular employment, which he finally did, by becoming a mining stock agent, with the final inevitable collapse and loss attending such a course.

We were supposed to go in and make a success where there had been a bad failure. A square look in the face of this would ordinarily be discouraging; but not so with our small and humble but confident crowd. We understood the cause of the failure, and felt that we had a better mission, and a more commanding message. The brief story of Mr. Hoskins is, that he as a Methodist Episcopal minister had charge of the Ashley M. E. church. He evidently felt himself to be a growing man, broadening out so widely that he could not see the narrow view of saints and sinners, or Christian and non-Christian, and under his love and care all were God's children (which in a sense is true, but not exclusively so). He had no place for an atoning crucified Saviour, or a resurrected Saviour and Lord. He did not get very far in this direction without encountering the opposition of some members of his church, and fellow ministers, who endeavored to hold him down to standard Christian teaching. But his enlarged ideas gave him the swell head, and an oratorical tongue, so he proclaimed his views with great zeal, and when the Ashley M. E. congregation got too hot, and a church trial became imminent, he and his adherents pulled out, and formed what he called the "Union Gospel Church Congregation." Evidently thinking he could play the same role in Milwaukee, that Professor David Swing was accomplishing in Chicago. He issued stock at five dollars per share, and sold it to any buyer, and with the proceeds bought a lot, built the small neat church and parsonage before mentioned, and began services in it. Also got out a church covenant, doctrinal statements and regulations, such as a temperance or an ethical culture society might do, paying no particular attention to Scripture precedent or teaching. Brother William Sherman had been observing this, and, at the start, thought possibly something good might come out of it; accordingly he bought liberally of the stock, and became superintendent of the Sunday school, which he attended to faithfully and well throughout the four years of its life under Hoskins.

The plan of building a church and organizing a congregation on a stock basis, might seem to be wise, as there was in the undertaking a definite common money interest, which along with the supposed spiritual interest and zeal that a religious organization should possess, might be judged to make a strong incentive toward union of purpose and effort. But the reverse of that was the result. After two years of existence there were two great factions incriminating ach other in violent terms. One of the parties finally gave up, and each one of this party sold his stock, Brother Sherman being the only buyer. This process continued for about three years or more, until the congregation finally disbanded, and about the whole of the stock was in Brother Sherman's possession. Being practically the owner, he could turn the property over to our use and benefit. Fourteen years afterward when we determined to build a new church, and found our old situation unfavorable and wanted to sell, we found that we had to hunt up and purchase the little remaining outside stock, and turn it all over to Dr. Sherman, the legatee, who would then extinguish the Old Union Gospel Church Association, and as we were carrying out his father's intent, he would give us a deed, so that we might dispose of the property and apply the proceeds on our new lot and building on the corner of Seventh avenue and Walker street, where at the present time, 1915, there is a good influential congregation of about three hundred and fifty members. Eight years ago, a good contingent of our congregation colonized and is now the Second or East Side church of Christ of about one hundred members, finely housed in a twenty-five thousand dollar building.

Possibly some of our relatives and friends who may read this Milwaukee church story, may regard it as a needless digression from what claims to be a Trout family history. In answer to this, I would say, that the Trouts and their connections are quite generally and decidedly church people. In getting reports from families I ask for their church connection. The usual answers show a relation with some of the

Protestant Evangelical bodies. To my knowledge there is not one Roman Catholic; but oddly enough one Mormon comes in by the marriage gate. So it is quite manifest that the beginning of a Christian church in Milwaukee might readily be a matter of common interest. The names Christian, Disciple of Christ, Church of Christ, or Christian Church are all common, not denominational, and we don't wish them to be used with regard to us in a denominational sense; although frequently we can't help it. We wish to be on a primitive New Testament Christian ground, not only in name, but in the faith of Christ as the Son of God, and the Divine Saviour of men. This is common ground to which all may come; and they *are* coming. Peculiar denominational beliefs are being left in the background. Most of the old dividing doctrines are forgotten. So that this church beginning story might be welcome even to some who might differ with us.

But there is a more direct reason for emphasis on this topic. Of the eight families descending from grandfather, Henry G. Trout, four of them were associated with congregations of Disciples of Christ or Christians—my father's (William Trout's) family; my uncle, John E. Trout, and family; Aunt Harriet Orr and many of her children; and Aunt Charlotte McKee and her husband and children; all members of the Christian Church. And since we are now following William Trout's line we might again refer to him as one who preached and worked at the millwright trade for a living. The necessities of his trade called for a great deal of attention, but equal or even greater consideration was given to attaining a good knowledge of the Scriptures and subjects relating to the kingdom of Christ and faithfully and effectively presenting them to the people. My conscientious, kindly, loving mother was a most helpful backing for him. Every one of his ten children with their married partners followed the example of the parents; with the grandchildren also in the same line; and now the great-grandchildren are starting in on the same well beaten upward trail. Not one, so far, has decided to be anything else than simply Christian.

SELF REFERENCES.

On this subject I should ask to be pardoned for going more into details regarding family and myself. As stated previously, I once determined to be a preacher, but necessity turned me aside, and I lost the chance of spoiling a good mechanic to make at least a fair average preacher; but that did not stop me from doing a little preaching as opportunity called for and time allowed. In those beginning days except at our midweek meetings I seldom attempted public talk. In our Meaford church meeting there were too many good speakers and too many possible critics. It was much safer for my slender reputation to go to some of our mission churches, where preachers were seldom heard and good common talk was well received; so I frequently went out into the township of Collingwood, where the Walters and Colemans lived, eleven miles from home. This was just a brisk Saturday evening's walk, leaving after supper and arriving between eight and nine. There was still time for a good evening's visit, while Sister Walters would be finishing up her Saturday work and preparing for Lord's day. In those days it certainly seemed as if woman's work was never done. But Sister Walters never worried. She could keep her work going on and maintain good conversation at the same time, and while the few remaining jobs were being finished, a second supper was also in preparation, which was eaten about midnight. It may be asked when was my sermon prepared? Possibly the topic was determined upon before leaving home, but generally it was all thought out on the journey. I have been so constituted that I could do my best thinking on foot. Many a good mechanical scheme has been devised on a two- or three-mile journey. When in the employment of the Allis-Chalmers Company, often have I sat at the drawing broad mentally facing a seemingly impossible machinery problem; I have then risen up and walked the round of the shops, and coming back about twenty minutes or half an hour, I would have the mental entanglements cleared away, and a likely working plan evolved that would meet requirements. Similarly in the consideration of most any interesting subject, mental alertness and an active imagination seemed to coincide with an easy measure of bodily exertion. This is no new discovery, the old Greek philosopher, Aristotle, was a peripatetic or walking teacher. And our modern Nazarenes or Holiness people, have, in place of a pulpit, a platform twenty or thirty feet long, on which to perambulate back and forth, while they work up their ecstacy, and deliver their emotional harangues. But, after all, I found the best final sermon study method was to go out on a Sunday morning, to a secluded place; where, seated on a log, with a pocket Testament, one could anchor his thoughts on the inspired Word; or, better still, to grasp the inspired idea, expand it, adapt and apply it to our present needs and conditions. The attention I received with the kindly welcome always given me, and the reflex good effect upon myself, were all I ever received, or thought of receiving. When one of their children died they sent for me to conduct the funeral. This is commonly regarded as a decidedly priestly function; to a retiring, unpretentious young man it did not appeal. Could I have induced any one else to properly take my place, I would not have gone. But I did go, and without any regular form (which I did not want). I attended to the duties connected with it, to the evident satisfaction and comfort of those concerned.

A most peculiar instance of this kind occurred in Milwaukee. Captain Richardson, who sailed one of the steamers of this Milwaukee port, though not members, his wife and he frequently attended our meetings. Nearly twenty years ago he died. Before passing away, he made the request that I take charge of his funeral; and after his death Mrs. Richardson notified me of this request, and wished me to serve. It was a great surprise. I could not understand it. I never had acted in the capacity of a minister in Milwaukee. As an elder, I had frequently presided at the Lord's table and always had a part or took charge in the prayer meeting, but to be called upon to take charge of a city funeral, especially of one so well known and respected as the captain, seemed preposterous. I went to the good lady and explained my situation. She understood, and with some difficulty secured a minister to lead in the matter, while, on account of the request, I was to assist. He attended to all the details very nicely, and gave us a short, but good, characteristic funeral discourse, while I followed for ten minutes or more, speaking rapidly in my pointed practical way, regarding the lessons we all should learn from that and similar events. My direct, energetic remarks were in striking contrast to his easy, well-finished utterances. A few years ago, in Lufkin, Texas, where for five months I was the main dependence in keeping a congregation of Disciples together in regular meetings, I served in the capacity of a preacher, as well as elder, to a greater extent than at any previous time of my life. During that time, I was called upon to conduct one funeral—an old brother who had run the race and finished his course. This incident caused me to be addressed, a number of times, as Reverend, which, if I were a minister, I would repudiate, as most all of our Christian ministers do. The term Reverend is applied in the Scriptures to God in Psalm 111, 9, and to no one else. Ministers are brethren like the rest of us. Their special duties do not constitute them a separate class or clergy: "Be not ye called Rabbi (or Reverend) for one is your teacher and all ye are brethren."

I have referred to father as a preacher, and have given no small attention to the role of his eldest son in the same line, and while we are considering this religious and preacher phase of life, we must not forget my third brother, John M. Trout, he certainly was the most effective public speaker among us. He, too, preached and bore his part in the Toronto church. What he would have become had not his active life been cut short at forty, it would be hard to determine.

Alexander, the youngest, outstripped us all as a preacher. While still a young man he held several evangelistic meetings with good success; and the church at Plum street, Detroit, will not soon forget the efficient help he gave it. He, too, prematurely passed away in the neighborhood of forty. Both lives, though short, were successful in the attainment of the transcendant aims and ends of our responsible existence.

WHAT GOOD IS IT?

The people in the days of Malachi, the prophet, said, "It is vain to serve God, and what profits it?" This so-called practical age asks the same question, but in briefer form. "What's the use?" Or, "What good is it?" Or, in the still shorter old Roman form, *"Cui bono?"* I will not deign to argue this question. I have referred to my parents and to brothers and sisters who have passed into the great beyond. Whose lives are measured, not by wealth alone, but by character. Were they a success? And those that yet remain, are going forward in the same line. Is there any profit in it? Can we measure its value? There is certainly great lasting satisfaction. What is that worth? But let us continue. I have two sons and three daughters, all are married and all except one have families. Like their predecessors all are in the Christian church, along with seven of the twelve grandchildren. All are strictly temperate as a matter of course. Only one indulges in a moderate use of cigars. Of my father's descendants or connections only two or three use the weed. No smoking-room is needed where our relatives meet. Regarding my boys, one son is the Bible School superintendent in a Texas church. Another son is an elder in an Ohio church. The oldest son-in-law is an active deacon in the First Christian church of Wheeling, West Virginia; another son-in-law is chairman of the church board of the First Christian church of Milwaukee; and the third son-in-law is also a deacon in the same church. The wives of all, in respect to church activity, are mates for the men. Three of the men are good singers; one especially so. We can't brag of the women in this respect; but three of them are good players on the piano. Most of the grandchildren offer well in singing, some of them will surely lead their mothers. With George and the local talent we may have, when we meet together of an evening, we are assured of a rare pleasant time. I should also mention that my three daughters, two daughters-in-law and three of the granddaughters, are all life members of the Christian Woman's Board of Missions, and it is no idle membership either. They, however, will disclaim credit for this, and charge it onto grandpa, and since he also is the recipient of a similar life membership he feels disposed to own up. A Junior Endeavor Society, of Lufkin, Texas, planned and started to make a good class offering to the Christian Woman's Board of Missions. The youngsters had been several months gathering the funds and were greatly pleased when it was told them that the twenty-five dollars had been paid into their bank. Their teacher and leader, Mrs. Megginson, then instructed them to decide on their choice as to who should have the life membership. Different ones suggested names but none could command a majority. At last Brother Trout was mentioned and the membership was unanimously granted him. The certificate, now framed, is hanging on the wall behind me—the children's testimonial of regard for the old man. A matter of small account, you say. Yes, Yes, but how pleasant is the memory of it. Again the old question comes up, "What profit is it? What is it all worth?" And again we postpone the answer.

Some people's lives are built on the purely selfish principle of getting all they can, and letting nothing go. They see only one small, narrow, view of life. The little space in which they enact their brief by-play. The matters that affect society, the church, the state, and the nation, are only seen through the narrow slit of their selfish wants.

There is another class that are good getters, and good spenders, but it is all for their own pleasure and enjoyment. If they should ever go to church, it would be on that principle. Catch them in the right way, at a favorable time, and you may get some loose change from them.

There is another class, and they are to be found in all our churches. They have a small idea of a moral obligation, and respond to it in a small way with some regularity. Poor souls, they might do better, if they could see further. Another set of people see the obligation, and are willing to give, but not more than their share. If others chip in good, they will do likewise. This is not so bad. It evens up. The Apostle Paul would not have others eased, and certain willing ones burdened. There is another type with a vision and a conscience to see and determine the line of duty, as between God and himself, without regard to his fellow men. He determines on a certain percentage of his income which must be regularly devoted to God and the good of humanity. May his tribe increase.

The final and highest class is made up of those who realize they have been "bought with a price," and have agreed to the purchase. They are sold out to the service of the Master, who went about doing good, and accomplishing the work of the Father who sent Him, which was His great work in behalf of humanity. The one who has realized His purchased ownership has long since forgotten his obligation as a matter of percentage. He regards his property and powers as a trust, and uses for himself what he needs to keep him in effective service, and the rest is devoted primarily to the extension of the Kingdom of God, which also meets the highest and greatest needs of humanity. Would you annoy him by asking, "Does it pay?" If he deigned to answer he might tell you that the joy of service was beyond all other possible consideration. If you should press the question of profit further, he might reply in the Christ phrase, "It is more blessed to give than to receive," or in Pauline terms, "Godliness is profitable for all things, having the promise of the life that now is, and of that which is to come." Godliness does not necessarily mean God perfection, but God likeness, which is a growing progressive quality, that climbs Godward, as we learn and practice His will. And with it goes the comfortable long life, which is but the preparation for the greater and enduring life that is to come. That is the way it all works out. Godliness not only enhances the value of life, by making it more truly and richly enjoyable, but this good life is lengthened; else, why are ministers as a class the highest in longevity?

But to come down to actual matter of fact everyday personal experiences, I have found myself walking home in the evening from the draughting office, after a day of hurrying, worrying work, feeling thoroughly wearied, and have said to myself, "This Wednesday evening others may go to the prayer meeting, but I will stay at home tonight." However, after a good supper and the resultant refreshed condition, the prayer meeting was simply a matter of course, and the walk of a mile or more was of no account. And as for the meeting, the singing, prayers, Scripture reading, and the talks relating thereto, which would bring out the great ideas of the lesson, that would cover not only the varying conditions of our everyday life but were infinite in their scope and eternal in duration, such great considerations would lift us out of the rut of what otherwise would be everyday drudgery, and make our lives more like a story of triumph. We all have known working men, and professionals, too, who were beset with blue Mondays. These are not necessarily dissipators.

Indolence will bring it on, or the reverse, a continuance of work on Sunday. That color has not been clouding my view on the first working day of the week. I wholly forget work on Sunday. Attending Sunday school, church meeting and evening preaching, is such a helpful change from the taxing routine of the week previous, that I always could begin again with a feeling of increased mental activity, enabling me to dispose of more work in a given time than on other days. This is bringing religion down to help out good working conditions, with the resulting gain in dollars and cents. Verily, "Godliness *is* profitable in all things."

My father's godliness was profitable for his children. He had a wide acquaintance with good men, which I, being the oldest son, shared more fully than the rest. Besides this, he took our religious papers of his time, The Christian, published by W. W. Eaton of Nova Scotia, and the Christian Baptist and Harbinger, by A. Campbell of Bethany, Virginia, and other local publications; which, along with good books, constitute a fine mental legacy, and has made a grand beginning an incentive to further progress, and this progress in the main has been carried forward by all his children. My position in the family necessarily giving me somewhat the lead, and feeling the pressure of the spiritual and moral forces behind me, I found it a great pleasure to yield. Added to this, my travels in later years, and my frequent attendance at our great

conventions, where the highest interests of the life that now
is, are the great topics of consideration, in connection and
correlation to the greater life to come, all of them enhanced
the uplifting effect. Active working interest, along with the
great souls who are persistently and continuously on this
supreme job of promoting the growth and enlarging the
boundaries of the Redeemer's kingdom, this enlivening partnership, with those that "work together with God," lends to
us a power that triumphs over the bodily ills and adversities
of life, staying the perishing of the outward man, while the
inward is renewed day by day, enabling us to understand that
farther reach of the human, when it stretches into close touch
with the power divine, as expressed by the prophet, "They
that wait on the Lord shall renew their strength. They shall
mount up on wings as eagles. They shall run and not be
weary, and shall walk and not faint." This is the grand outcome of the profit of godliness.

A COURSE OF INVENTION

This family history seems to be proceeding in a somewhat
irregular manner, not so much as a narrated sequence of
events, but as topics or subjects relating to the family and
myself, since I am the writer. The most frank apology I can
make for telling my own story is, that I know it best, and hope
that if it is truly and well told, it may be found interesting,
instructive and helpful; and if judged otherwise it can easily
be left unread.

I have already made several references to the possession of
a fair measure of inventive and designing ability, and have
good reason to judge, that this was the main cause of my
prompt engagement with the Edward P. Allis Company,
which has been previously mentioned, as well as the general
character and style of my twenty-two years' service.

Now, however, I shall confine myself to one important feature of that service—inventing and designing.

Reference has previously been made to my first job, the
new band mill, by which I became known among the draughtsmen as the band mill man. Our department superintendent

and I had crossed the lake, and examined two or three new mills in Michigan. On our return, he sketched out for me what he regarded as the best type of mill, it being on the general lines of those we had seen. I pleaded that the Edward P. Allis Company, being the great leader in so many lines, ought to have a distinctively characteristic style, differing from all others, and carefully sketched out such a mill, embodying new constructive features and different form, yet easily and cheaply made. While he claimed his own plan was the best, he saw that mine had merits that should not be ignored. He called in Mr. Reynolds, the general superintendent, who was one of the leading mechanical engineers of America. He then laid the two sketches before him without saying who made them, seemingly desiring to have it understood that both were his, but Mr. Reynolds was not deceived; after a little consideration and some questions he pointed to mine, saying, "That is the best," and with no small pleasure I won my first quiet score over my boss.

After our first mill was made and running very satisfactorily, among our many orders we had one that was to have friction feed works to operate the carriage connected with it, and I was told to make the adaptation. Instead of that I invented a style to specially meet the needs of the situation. My superintendent did not see this, till the drawings were finished and explained to him, and he approved them. Afterwards when the patent application was made, he claimed not only all improvements in the band mill, but the feed works as well, though he had never ordered or seen the latter drawings till they were completed, yet he made the declaration that he was the inventor. As he evidently expected, I remonstrated against such a course, and he was prepared for his defence, with as much of the air of a dignified judge as he could assume. He began in a slow, deliberate manner to explain the usage of the company regarding inventions, that I as an employee was engaged in consideration of my ability in this direction, and paid accordingly, and the work I did was according to his orders and direction and final approval, and as the company could not as such be said to invent, some-

one had to claim the invention, and the heads of departments
were the only logical ones to do it. But I said, "What about
the feed works, which you neither ordered nor directed?"
"Well, I accepted them or they would not be made; and the
Company pays for the patent." I saw that I was up against
not only the superintendent but the Allis Company as well; and
I with no money, and six small children, gave in under protest.
He further explained that should I, on my own initiative,
outside of the company's service, invent any new and useful
improvement, it would assist me in obtaining the patent and
in its manufacture. I have thus given his explanations more
explicitly than I got them. Not long after this a machine
was wanted for sawing paving blocks, and I was directed
to design it. When completed, it was favorably commended
and accepted, with the suggestion that it ought to be patented
over my own name. I understood this to be merely a sop
to please me, as there would be but few sales and consequently
no value in the patent; so this Trout failed to bite, and nothing
became of it. A few after this, the first demand for a band
mill from the Pacific coast came to us from the Yesler Company of Seattle. The conditions were that we should design
a new mill for their needs, subject to their approval. The
superintendent regarded this as the specially opportune time
for him to distinguish himself in designing a band mill. Accordingly, he carefully sketched out a general plan, and instructed me as to various details, and while I was at work,
often came in and saw that I was embodying his ideas even
better than he expected. When after a few weeks the general
drawing was completely finished and blue printed, he felt
proud of it, and lavished his praise. Then turning to me,
said, "Now what do you think of it, Trout?" "Oh! it will
make a good mill." "You bet, a d - - d good one." "But,"
said I, "I can make a better one." "You can, eh?" "I
feel pretty sure of it." "Well," with several strong inter-
larded oaths, meant more for emphasis and challenge than
for displeasure, "If you think you can do better than that,
then let's see you do it." I at once began, and in less time
than I was on the other, had a simpler, much neater and

more stable mill than any previously put on the market. Blue prints of each were sent to the Yesler Company, so they might make a choice, and mine was selected. Mr. D. B. Hanson, our traveler, suggested two changes which were adopted. And for the second time the boss had the back seat, but not so in the patent application. He claimed all that was claimable. Along with the band mill was an order for a heavy carriage for logs, seven feet diameter by fifty feet long, to be operated by a double-manned, hand lever set works. While I was employed on this, Mr. Reynolds, our general superintendent, being interested in our big new carriage, came along to see what I was doing. I pointed out the heavy character of the job, for two men to set forward such an enormous log. He said, "It is too much to think of, you ought to have power, steam, or a belt, or running rope, something to set forward the log without loss of time. The running rope was regarded as the likeliest method of any for conveying power to the moving carriage. With this he left me, and in a couple of hours I showed him a good sketch plan for its accomplishment. He told me to go ahead, and see what I could make of it. I was glad to get such an order, and began at once. My superintendent came along. I told him of Mr. Reynold's suggestion and order; he evidently did not like it, and predicted failure. After I had been at work on this a few days, a Mr. Shaw, later head of the Shaw Electric Crane Company, a finely educated engineer, electrical and otherwise, who was designing the first electric crane for the Edward P. Allis Company, came around to see my big log proposition. He kindly looked over my calculation as to the weight of the log and the power to move it, and showed that my percentage of friction loss from the screws was not great enough. I laid before him my main problem, which was, that under all the varying conditions of small and immense logs, to automatically, or otherwise, stop the setting movement precisely at a given place. After some discussion, he advised the use of a worm and worm wheel, as the final member of the gear series; and while suggesting, as was his usual practice, he made a sketch in ink of his proposition, with name and date on it; then if it should prove valuable, as this did, he had the evidence of invention at a certain definite time and place.

I found that Mr. Shaw's suggestion was the best means for accomplishing my purpose, and when he came around again some days later, and saw his suggestion well embodied in the general plan, he commended the whole very finely; and said I was sure to have a good machine, and said further, "Your superintendent will endeavor to claim the whole thing. Now he will never claim that worm wheel scheme over me; and I advise you, Mr. Trout, to stand for yours, you are doing good work, and ought at least to have the credit for it." I told him I would gladly stand with him.

The drawings were finally finished, the power set works constructed, tested and approved, and a good price paid for them. As my superintendent had all along predicted failure, he had nothing to do with it but the formal work, as the order came through his office; but as expected he now began to make application for the patent.

I notified Mr. Shaw, and together we sent in a joint protest to the company. This came under the eye of Mr. Reynolds, who was cognizant of the whole matter, and who also had his name go in on it, as making the first suggestion, so that the patent was issued jointly to Reynolds, Trout and Shaw; and my superintendent had to nurse his wrath, except so far as he might vent it on Mr. Shaw, whom he regarded as the chief marauder on his domain.

This was the first time, and the only time, for a number of years that my name appeared in connection with Allis patents. The rule and usage of the company was that the inventor should assign a half interest in the patent to the company, and on his retained half-interest he received no royalty, while in the company's employment; should he leave, he was obliged to give the company the option of buying his interest, at such a price as it might determine. I signed no agreement, but in this case conformed to the usage. This has the appearance of value, but nothing more. To make a sale you had to leave the company's employment, then it would offer you a small nominal figure. You might refuse, but who would give you more, and thus face the entrenched opposition of the great Allis Company. My superintendent afterwards resumed his old role, but was more careful to have some show of reason for his claims.

PROVIDING FOR OLD AGE

If each yearly recurring birthday is a period for the reconsideration of the past, and renewing plans and resolutions for the future, certainly the decade birthdays ought to be much more so. On this account, in 1894, when leaving sixty years of life behind me, I was strongly led to consider how I could manage to weather out the stress to the end. Considering my pronounced dyspeptic tendencies, the end might not be very distant. Besides this, draughtsmen, like ministers, have an earlier dead line than in most other professions and occupations. It is not merely the slackening of mental activity, to which age is liable, but physical shortcomings, like failing eyesight and unsteady nerves. I judged that if my usefulness could be maintained for another decade it would be all I might reasonably expect. I had all along been in hopes that at some day I would be enabled to save some money. But at this period, though with good wages, my family expenses were at the greatest height. I saw that some extra outside effort must be made in order to get ahead. I took on work to do at my home—designed a small band mill and carriage for a Swedish firm, also a band mill and edger for my old Canadian employer, William Hamilton. The funds from the last job enabled me, after an absence of eleven years, to make my first return visit to Canada, occupying one month. Mrs. Trout had made her first visit two or three years previous. However, those home efforts were only transient advantages and small help. Mr. Albert Cunningham, my second Milwaukee friend, had succeeded well in the line of invention, and why not I? He got up a steam feed reversible engine for saw mill carriages, which I urged him to push forward, and obtained for him the consideration of William Hamilton, who was the first to test it and prove its excellence. Afterward the Filer & Stowell Company took it up, and Mr. Cunningham realized from it a handsome income. My efforts in his behalf were simply as a friend, but in consideration of what I had done, he gave me a half interest in the Canadian patent, which for seven or eight years gave nice little material help to my strained exchequer. When at the height of his machine's popularity, he wisely sold it out. Others butted in with somewhat similar machines, and divided the business, so that his purchasers never realized their price. That is one of the fates of good patents.

After designing two new styles of carriage offsets, one of which I looked upon as perfection in that line, but at best an offset is of small account, I gave my attention to applying power to our hand lever set works; or making a light power set works to take the place of the hand lever. In 1895 I made several drawings for this purpose, working at home or in extra hours at the office. In a short time I had my ideas embodied in a general drawing, showing a steam cylinder operated by a hand-opened but self-closing valve as the piston motion proceeded. This was connected up so as to accomplish the setting. Not having the money to spare to obtain the patent, or to begin the manufacture, I tried to enlist the attention of the company, showing the drawings and explaining their purpose to Mr. Hinkley. After a little examination, he replied, "There's nothing in it. Nobody is calling for the like of that." I replied, "That is true, but we may expect a call for the like of it any of these days." As he was not disposed to give it consideration, I laid away the drawings in my private drawer, where they remained for more than two years. About this same time the invention bee was buzzing in the bonnet of a young man in Marinette, in the north end of our state. He was in the employment of the Prescott Manufacturing Company, who also made saw mill machinery. His company, more wise than ours, backed the young man's efforts, enabling him to make tests and otherwise perfect his invention. In this way nearly two years elapsed till its merits were fairly well established, and he had obtained a patent, and was applying for a reissue. Not wishing to tie himself up wholly to his own company, he brought his patent to Milwaukee and offered it for sale or the right to manufacture, to our Company's President, William Allis, as Mr. Hinkley was absent at the time. Mr. Allis brought the patent in to me for my opinion. I said, "This looks fairly good, but I think I have a better one," and produced my drawings, the dates of which were nearly two years previous to the patent date. He was surprised; and still more so, when I related that I urged it upon Mr. Hinkley's attention at the time, who refused to consider it. He then ordered me to begin at once, and complete the necessary drawings, so that a patent application could be quickly made. This was a Saturday forenoon in August, 1897. I worked till late that night. On Sunday morning I arose early, and put in several hours before going to Sunday school at nine thirty in the morning. I remained to church meeting, went home, and had dinner by one o'clock; and was returning to the office on George's bicycle, when, on a rough piece of street, I ran over a tomato can which threw me violently, landing me on my right knee so forcefully as to break the neck of the femur. At the moment, I felt that it was the worst fall of my life, but was surprised that I could not get up. A young man who saw the fall, got me upon my good leg, and helped me to a seat, got a buggy and took me home. In seven weeks of too much activity for my condition, I was at work again, going on crutches with a loose joint and a short unmanageable leg, which improved somewhat for fifteen months, when I got very tired of going about as an old cripple on crutches. So I designed and had made a tricycle, on which I could make good speed, and enjoy myself going about. With this the cripple stage soon ended, and I could walk fairly well with a cane. The tricycle served me well for thirteen years, using it winter and summer.

Not being able to use it in my winter's sojourning in Texas, and for a few seasons being away from Milwaukee in summer; I got out of practice, and the machine out of condition; also diminished muscular strength, and greater street crowding with rapid power vehicles, made it advisable to let the old wheel lay aside. While this seemed to be an actual interruption of invention, it certainly has interrupted the story. The invention or rather the application for the patent of invention proceeded. My son Walter took up the drawings, and in a day or two had them ready, and the application for the patent was on its way to Washington. After examination in the Patent Office, an interference between myself and the Prescott Company's applicant for reissue was declared, and in the test our evidence of priority gained a decision in our behalf; but the Prescott Company set up a claim of error in their application, and petitioned for a rehearing, which was finally granted. Then they resurrected some old unpractical sketches, which were said to antedate our drawings; but with more reason and better effect, they urged their claim of continuous effort, and final success, with a demonstrated useful invention, whereas our company had let the matter lie in abeyance, till they had proved its usefulness. There was a long, expensive trial in which I, being the principal witness, was over two days under the grill of the attorneys. In the end it went against our firm, for the reason already indicated. However, as the Prescott Company were soon doing a fine business in their new steam set works, power set works became a matter for earnest consideration, and my prophecy to my superintendent was verified.

FURTHER BAND MILL PROGRESS

To those interested in mechanical progress, the evolution of the modern band mill, now so nearly universally used for sawing lumber from logs, whether they be jack pine poles from the rough mountain side or the great giant redwoods and other trees of the Pacific slope, which are sometimes twelve feet in diameter, this story to business men and mechanics should be a matter of interest. More than twenty years ago before this, progress reached its zenith. I wrote two articles for Cassier's Magazine on this topic, for which I received fifty dollars. Such would be out of place in a family history, and I feel that an apology is called for my already extended references to these subjects. My apology is that the story of struggle and progress is always interesting, but in this case it must be brief, with the disadvantage that the brevity may fail to enlist the deserving interest.

The essential feature of a band saw is that it is like a common endless belt or band running over two pulleys. The difference is that the belt may be of leather, rubber or cotton, while the belt that saws is of fine tempered steel, with the saw teeth usually only on one edge. The band wheels or pulleys, over which the saw runs, must be truly made, and held in an upright frame in absolutely correct line with each other; and be under stress away from each other, so as to strain and give stiffness to the saw, the sawing being done on the straight downward run of the saw between the two wheels. A log carriage is made to run back and forth along this side of the band mill; and the log to be sawn is mounted and secured on suitable blocks on the carriage. A set works, which may be operated by a hand lever or by power, is also mounted and connected with the blocks, so that the log may be set forward by it. When the log is thus set forward sidewise beyond the sawing line, the forward movement of the carriage brings the end of the log against the saw, and a slab is taken off the log; then after the backward motion of carriage takes place, the log is again set forward, and a board or plank sawed off; and this is continued till the log is all sawn. A further element, not yet mentioned, is the lower and upper saw guides to steady and hold the saw in its true position, one below where the log passes, the other above; the latter is mounted on an arm which may be raised or lowered, so that in the varying sizes it may be kept just above the log. These, with the necessary driving machinery, gives one a simple or fundamental idea of the essentials of an ordinary band mill.

About the year 1894, John Walton conceived the idea of raising and lowering the whole machine part of mill to suit various sized logs instead of raising and lowering the upper guide, the object being to do the sawing as near to the upper wheel as possible, which was the position of greatest resistance to the saw's displacement, the effect being faster sawing. With the help of E. E. Fitzgerald and some others, a small mill was built, which in a fairly satisfactory way proved the idea to be good. In 1897, Mr. E. E. Fitzgerald, traveller for the Allis Company, met a Minneapolis mill superintendent, who wanted to have his mill with teeth on both edges of the band saw, so as to saw off boards on both the forward and backward movements of carriage. Fitzgerald persuaded him to try along with it Walton's style of sliding mill, and a contract was made accordingly. When this was laid before me, it was suggested that I design the new mill on as cheap lines as would be at all practicable. This was done. It was a neat, light, nice mill, too light to do the best service; but it demonstrated the principle of its construction, and the value of double cutting. On the first day of trial it sawed twenty-two boards ten inches wide by sixteen feet long in one minute, and it made such a sensation among the lumbermen that many unsolicited inquiries came in regarding it. I am wearing a miniature of this as a watch charm. I was at once then called upon to redesign and improve this mill at greater cost, so as to have greater efficiency. This came to me when I was lying in bed recovering from the hip fracture previously told. As I could not go to the office, I studied up the band mill business in bed; so that when a few weeks after I sat up at the drawing board good progress was soon made on the improved telescopic double-cutting band mill. It is worthy of mention, that during my seven weeks' absence from work I had the sick benefit of our Allis Mutual Aid Society, which amounted to one dollar per day of absence; also I made a plea to our company for a consideration, as my accident occurred while in the course of service, and was awarded fifty dollars, so that I had something for my mental work while lying in bed.

The new, double-cutting band mill proved to be a great commercial success. It had one drawback, however, that it was liable to make thick and thin boards; and as the price of lumber increased, and the need for good sawing bcame greater, the sales of this double cutter have not been so well maintained.

The radical character of this double-cutting process required a great many other changes in the automatic handling of the lumber, all of them involving inventive ability and special design, one of which was getting up special new saw guides. Our superintendent saw that I had something that was quite new and likely to serve well its purpose. He had advanced beyond the idea that he could unblushingly capture what he had not in some way directed, accordingly he ordered a change. I endeavored to show him that the change was detrimental rather than helpful, and out of harmony with the general character of the job; but he insisted, and being the boss, the change had to be made. When the guides were completed, he told me to get the necessary blue prints, and make the specifications for a patent application. I did so, very fully defining the claims, and subscribing my name to the whole, as the inventor; and sent it down to his office. As usual, he examined all the prints and papers, and no doubt found them all satisfactory, till he came to the end and found my name. Though not present, it is not hard for myself, nor for the reader to imagine his emotions. I got a call to go down. I went, and took a chair near him. He turned, and rather savagely asked me, "What do you mean by putting your name to those papers?" My reply was, "Just what my signature signifies. I signed them because I was the inventor." In a boisterous, overbearing manner he attempted to show that he and not I was the inventor, but I met him promptly at every point. Then he jumped to his feet, and stamped on the floor, swearing at the top of his voice, and shaking his fist over me. The office men at their desks thought he might hit me. I sat still and looked him in the eye. In that manner he harangued away for some time, and when I could find a momentary chance plugged in some answers, that certainly were no help toward his equanimity. Finally the storm somewhat subsided, and I rose and was leaving, when he said, "See here, we can have a joint patent." "No," I said, "we won't." His wrath broke out again, and I left. One of his office men afterward said to me, "Trout, you beat all. For cool nerve, you take the cake. You sat there undisturbed when we thought he was going to strike you; and you answered back decently, but defiantly." It is not pleasant to write like this about a boss that one has been working with and under for more than

WILLIAM HENRY TROUT FAMILY 1895

twenty years. Of one thing he was guiltless, there was no duplicity. We always understood him. The worst side was out. Our chief superintendent, Mr. Edwin Reynolds, saw that the cause of our dispute was of some account to the firm; and regarding it easier to get me to accommodate myself to the situation than to get the superintendent, he pressed me to go in on a joint patent. But I positively refused, and continued to refuse for three or four months, during which the superintendent would not recognize or speak to me. Finally, to please and satisfy Mr. Reynolds, I told him that I would allow a joint patent, but my name should be first, being clearly entitled to that position; and so it was done. Thereafter the company employed its own special patent attorney, and one of the rules he laid down was that no one but the actual inventor or inventors, should sign the patent application papers; so Mr. Hinkley and I became again workable friends, not needing the intervention of a foreman.

FAMILY EVENTS—(Marriages).

The autumn of 1896 was to my immediate family a ripening time of more than ordinary interest; the lengthy acquaintanceship and engagement of our eldest son and daughter, Walter Charles, and Jennie Mabel, to their respective spouses, Miss Ellen Elizabeth Percy and Otto William Steindorf, culminated in their wedded union, the first marriage taking place at the home of the Percy family, September 3d, and the second at our own home five days later, September 8, 1896. They were both interesting social events, as were all our children's weddings. At Walter's wedding a large number of the Percy relatives and friends, of Milwaukee and vicinity, were the great majority of the guests, our relatives being too far away to be conveniently present. Of course there were friends common to both, as well as the new friends in the making. It was a heartily enjoyable time. This was the great affair of the Percy's, we only shared in it. Our daughter's wedding, five days later, was our special matter of interest, in which the Steindorf relatives and friends, as well as our own, might share.

Accordingly, in the afternoon of the fifth day from the previous wedding, our house was crowded with guests. It can easily be understood that the one most interested, and who carried the greatest burden of the event was mother; she was a royal good cook, everything for eating, decoration and comfort was well prepared. Our close adjoining neighbor and friend, Reynolds, gave us the use of his long, double room in which to have the wedding dinner; but after the wedding ceremony, conducted by Brother C. G. McNiel, was over, which deprived her of the help and companionship of her eldest daughter, she was really so much wearied and confused, that she was not mentally and physically in shape to carry out her own plans. There was abundance of help, but no cool directing head. Walter was about the first to see the situation and step into the breach. Mother was to keep her seat, and was consulted only when necessary. Walter quietly directed all the details of the big dinner, so that everything went smoothly on schedule time; this was so manifest as to be a subject of highly complimentary remark by many of those present, being mother's eldest child, and his native executive ability accounted for it.

Almost a year from these matrimonial events, on August 27, 1897, I fell from a bicycle when going to work, and fractured the neck of the right femur. This has already been twice briefly referred to, as it related to the course of my work. I now refer to it in relation to general body conditions, and the consequences that resulted from it. The weight of the fall came first on the knee, and second on the hip; the first caused fracture, and the second impacted it. It was technically an "impacted fracture," there was no separation or displacement of the bones; so though there was evidently a very great injury, there was no proof of fracture. Had our well-trained young doctor known of a previous case like mine, he would have assumed that the femur was fractured, as such a result, of such a fall, is almost certain to occur with old people. Then he would have put my hip in a solid plaster cast for a month or more, when the fracture would be mended, and I never would have known that my leg had been broken; but he left it alone, to await further developments. Though I could do nothing with my leg, except as I moved it with my hands, still I regarded it as only temporarily paralyzed; such was the case once on account of sciatica. Having gone through a fairly active risky life without serious mishap, I was not at all prepared to believe that my leg was broken. I got out of bed and in again as required. Two days after the accident, in getting into bed, the injured leg seemed to be hurt severely. I think at that time the bones separated, as I observed several days afterward that my leg seemed shorter, and so told the doctor. He led me to think that I was unconsciously pulling up that hip. I was willing to think of most anything but a broken leg. Our doctor one day told me he would like to have a consultation on that leg. I told him to get the best man he could. He came the next day with a good surgeon. He gave me a severely painful examination. The consultation, however, was in another room. The surgeon came and announced to me, as he left, that I would be better in a few weeks, would have to go on crutches for a while, and probably need a cane the rest of my life. This was poor comfort, but they thought it better than letting me know the nature of the injury. This, however, I determined to find out. I got the crutches, and began using them. I could get along well on the level; but it was dangerous to go up and down stairs without help. I could bend the knee or twist the leg, but could not put it forward. However, by daily exercise, I improved, so that in less than seven weeks I made my first street journey of seven blocks, to visit and welcome into this busy world our first dear little grandchild, Jennie Louise Steindorf, then just one day old. They say all infants look alike; that may seem true with careless half-observing people, but not with attentive sympathetic parents and grandparents. They can see not only variant features but also probable mental characteristics in the little infant face. Otto brought the baby to me. I told him there was a nice, quiet, intelligent spirit behind that beauitful little face, and I was right. The next day I made the journey to the drawing office, and began the drawings of the new telescopic band mill as previously noted.

An abundance of hard work awaited me, to which I gave myself most unreservedly, with the consequence that with the lessened exercise and depressing feeling, coming from being an old man on crutches, all three combined to cause the return of dyspeptic trouble with increased virulence. I was not what might be regarded as being sick, because I worked most all the time, with one or maybe two meals a day. There was a measure of comfort working with an empty stomach, but generally discomfort with a full one; but it became much worse, and at one period I ate nothing for eleven days. I then began with a teaspoonful of Philip's cocoa, three times a day, increasing gradually day by day till it became a teacupful. Then slowly began solid food, which, with constant watchfulness against overeating, finally brought on a slowly improving condition. After more than a year on the crutches, really carrying my lame leg without using it, or using it so little that it decreased in strength and size, I determined that I must ride something, so as to get off the crutches. A brief trial convinced me that I could work the pedals of a wheel all right, so I designed a tricycle, had it made for me, used it three months, sent the crutches to the garret, and used a cane for my walking of short distances. The improving effect of the use of the wheel was remarkable. The lame leg grew in size and strength, so that I could walk much better; and the dyspeptic condition also improved. I was proud of my wheel, and took good care of it. With it I passed the cripple stage, and became something like a young man again. Of course, in speed I was no match for the young men on bicycles, but with good favorable conditions I could make average street car time. I rode winter and summer, in snow, rain or shine. With the policemen who knew me, I was allowed the use of the sidewalks, and could mount the ordinary curb when required to; but I had several bad falls with it, three of which were caused by children running in my way. One fall dislocated a shoulder, and another kept me seven days in bed. But on the whole, the use of that wheel helped greatly to restore to me fair average healthy conditions for over thirteen years. As already noted, it was reluctantly given up, on account of spending my winters in Texas, and the crowded conditions of the streets with motor vehicles, along with the decreasing strength of age. The old wheel from disuse is now out of condition, but it could soon be made ready, and be turned over to anyone who might need it; and it could serve them well as it has served me.

LAST SICKNESS OF MRS. TROUT.

About the time of my accident, mother occasionally had troublesome and painful spells affecting her left arm and side. They were of a neuralgic character, often inflammatory, and sometimes causing depressing heart pain. She had for a long time regarded herself as having more or less heart weakness, but our physicians on examination could find no evidence of it. As most all the time her general conditions were good, I attributed this largely to imagination, but the manifest inflammatory turns were tangible and positive, and were not even by our doctor easily explained. However, being irregular, and sometimes months apart, with good conditions between times, they were more or less ignored, my frequent dyspeptic trouble engaging the greater attention. She looked much younger than I, her people had a better longevity record than mine, so that we might reasonably expect her to outlive me many years, and when she felt despondent on account of these troubles I used to tell her so. Those last two years, 1897 and 1898, were among the happier years of our married life. Our children had all grown up, the two eldest married and residing near by, so that we had their frequent company, as well as the dear little granddaughter that was so interesting to all of us. Besides this, lively young people attract others, so that our home was often the rendezvous for interesting young company, who with music, singing and interesting conversation would have a good time. Besides this a chance friendly visitor at our Sunday meetings was apt to be invited home with us to dinner. Added to this we had lengthy visits from her brother, sister and nieces. All this, though very enjoyable, was often rather hard upon mother. Still she continued much in the usual way till the winter of 1898, when a greatly aggravated instance of her trouble resulted in an extremely painful condition in and about the heart, which the doctor defined as "angina pectoris," a very serious malady, coming without warning or evidence of structural trouble, and with probable fatal results. We did not fully realize the seriousness of his statements, but with my usual optimism I regarded that as she had in the past, so she would then, overcome her physical disabilities, and in a day or two she recovered, but not to her usual condition. A few days after this we were to have our family Christmas at Otto Steindorf's. This was on account of mother's uncertain condition, and in the interest of our little fourteen month's grandchild, who was the recipient of so many presents. Christmas was on Sunday, but Monday was observed. Though the distance was short, mother was brought by a horse and cutter. Our dinner was about one o'clock, and the celebration with Christmas tree and the unwrapping of the presents, many of which were from Canada, took place in the evening. Walter and wife were present, also Uncle Henry (mother's brother) and his daughter Sybil. We had a rarely pleasant time, as my children can always have when they get together, mother enjoying it quite as much as any of us. It is memorable, because it was the last time parents and children were all together. That night, when we all left, we thought it best for mother to remain, and during the night her bad condition returned; so the doctor was again called, but could do but little to relieve her suffering, which continued more or less for several days. On Friday morning it seemed to have spent itself. The doctor gave us encouragement, that she would most likely recover; but the severe conditions returned on the Friday forenoon, there being a resumption of the violent heart pains, with hard breathing and great general stress. In the same week I had been in bed at home from the Monday night till Friday noon, having had a couple of visits by the doctor. At this noon I was apprised of mother's change for the worse, and went to see her. As I approached the bed, she said, "I never can live through this." I smiled at her, expressing by it, "Oh! you'll be better soon." The return look was one of half reproach, as if saying, "You never will understand me." I was sitting a few feet at one side, Lucretia sat nearer and facing her. After being there about twenty minutes, Lu called to me, "Look! Look! father." I turned my head, and saw her make three gasps for breath, and quit. I turned her slightly with a gentle shake, but there was no resumption of breathing. It was so hard to think she was dead. We sent for a doctor two blocks away to examine and report, he pronounced her dead; and a few minutes afterward our family physician came with another doctor for consultation on her case. They said it was all in accordance with the peculiar uncertain character of the disease. Suddenly thus did mother pass away from us, on December 30, 1898, in her fifty-seventh year. The funeral procession started from the church, where Brother F. N. Calvin preached a great sermon on immortality, making extended reference to her great kindliness, hearty hospitality, self-denying labors of love and continued work in behalf of the church. She was committed to her earthly rest on the Lord's day, January 1, 1899. When returning from the cemetery in the closed carriage alone with George, Nellie and Lucretia, I said, "Now there are just four of us left. It certainly behooves us to hold together in good spirit, working to each others' hands, while we may remain together; which, for me, may not be long. But, long or short, my efforts will be for your common good, and I want it to be the same in your relation to each other." Perhaps this advising request was not needed. Be that as it may, certainly a family more devoted to each other, and to their now more aged parent, will be very hard to find.

Mother's death was a distinctive epoch in our family life. It involved some direct changes. Walter came to the front as chief adviser in the council of the children. They concluded, that, as mother's chance for life seemed so much better than mine, yet she was so soon taken, and my health at the time being precarious, it was adjudged they ought to face the probabilities. The girls must cease attending high school. Nellie must be the homekeeper and Lucretia take a business course in stenography and typewriting. This, though greatly contrary to my inclinations, I could not oppose; and it was accordingly done. Lucretia soon mastered the practice and got into service, but at Nellie's marriage she abandoned that line of work and became the homekeeper. Though often poorly, I felt I was at least holding my own. A big sawmill was burned in Eastern New York; and our company had no spare travellers to get the new job, so I was sent to perform that, to me, new duty. I enjoyed the change it offered, and the proof of the company's confidence; but a lame man, on crutches, always more or less hungry, and every meal a problem and an experiment, offered a poor show for success. I had to face the opposition of other firms, but we succeeded in getting in the Corliss engine and boilers. On my return I crossed the great St. Lawrence river and came back by way of Toronto and Detroit, where short visits were made.

In the springtime of 1900 when the birds were nesting, George got the mating fever so seriously as to perpetrate matrimony. His necessary accomplice in the job being Miss Franke Kinzie, second daughter of Mr. Charles H. Kinzie, of Richland Center, Wisconsin, one of the old families of the West, if the West can really be said to have old families. Mr. Kinzie's father built the second log house on the flat prairie now known as Chicago, the Queen City of the Lakes and the second city in America. Myself, two daughters and a visiting niece, Miss Harriet Beach, accompanied George on this memorable journey, to witness and share in the ceremony, and enjoy the connected good time, which was extended to three days, and was quite an incident in that thriving country town.

Our family was now reduced to three, and a still further reduction came, when Nellie, who had always shown a decided inclination for art study and art appreciation, left us to take a course of study in the Chicago Art Institute. She made great proficiency for two terms, but the continued eye strain was too great, and she had to abandon the study for a time. Meanwhile, Irvin W. Davis, a clever young foreman in the E. P. Allis Company's works, had been trying to out-rival the art love, but with only moderate success; he now pressed his temporary advantage so adroitly as to win for matrimony the first consideration, and learning art for the second place. Accordingly, they were married January 7, 1902. Lucretia and I were thus left alone. Though I had only one child with me, our house was still the home. By this time I had gradually made marked improvement in health. Less watchfulness was allowable and there was more power for work and enjoyment. Though drawing near to seventy years I felt as if getting younger. With the children from under my care, and on their own account, I began little accumulations of cash, so I opened for the first time a bank account; and on Walter's advice invested a few hundred dollars in a Stock Lumber Company, which, at present and for some years past, has been yielding me a neat little dividend. Such inventions as I might make independent of our company I determined to finance them on my own account. I made drawings of new and very effective drawing instruments and had patterns made; but I found that even to start that small line of manufacture, and get trade in it, would require more time, and effort, and money than was possibly at my disposal. Instead of this I devoted more time, or rather all my spare time and energy to further projecting and perfecting the power set works that I had previously in some forms started in connection with our company.

Very near the beginning of 1902, January 7th, we had the Davis marriage, and very near its close, we had the first Davis grandchild, Dorothy, December 15, 1902. As the Steindorf family had removed to Wheeling, little Dorothy at once assumed the place of first interest. Shortly after this the Davis family found it desirable to change their residence. Lucretia and I were similarly disposed. We found a large suitable vacant steam heated flat and made a proposition to Davis and wife to become joint occupants with us; which was readily accepted. They said, "Dad wants to be near the baby," and they were not far wrong. While my claim on the grandchildren is small compared to the parents, my interest in them is undoubtedly great. We spent three pleasant years in this flat. The second Davis grandchild was born there. She was a beautiful, finely-formed, well-dispositioned baby. That summer, 1905, at the opening of one of our public parks, there was to be held a great baby show. While we all esteemed our

Margaret the finest little one we ever knew, Nellie was anxious to see how she would match up with other little beauties; accordingly she entered her for the show in the class under one year. At the park she found about three hundred babies. The judges discussed the merits and demerits of each child as if their mothers were a mile away. Finally they settled down to the conclusion that Margaret was upon the whole the most perfect baby. So the blue ribbon was tied on her dress, and when Nellie got her silver tea set, she triumphantly wheeled her prize baby home.

While Margaret, now over eleven years, is no striking beauty, yet for physical and mental goodness she still holds her place.

A SIGNIFICANT BIRTHDAY.

While in this flat my seventieth milestone on life's journey was attained. Our family is in the habit of remembering the birthdays, and as the seventieth is always a notable one, I regarded it quite probable that there might be some extra attention to this particular day, but was not ready for the surprises that came to me from morning till night. At the breakfast table on my plate lay a jeweler's box. On opening it there was displayed a handsome gold watch, from the boys, the sons and sons-in-law. This was thoughtfully chosen, as my good 35-year-old silver watch was often uncertain. That was a big beginning for the day. At noon, among other kind remembrance letters, was a specially good one from my old, much-prized friend, C. C. Smith; and after dinner upon leaving for the shop, a messenger boy brought in a long box for me, which being opened showed a great bouquet of magnificent Calla lilies. Think of Calla lilies in February. "See here!" I said, "I won't work this afternoon." "What!" says Lu, "ain't you going to work, father?" "No! It would be a shame to go to work after getting those flowers and gifts and letters. I'll go to my room and answer Brother Smith's letter and work on my own drawings." It struck me as a trifle strange that she should seem anxious about my going to work. I went to my room, and was there till near evening; when Lu came in saying, "Father, you remember Mrs. Perrigo invited you to tea with her on your birthday, so you better go early." "All right," said I, and started, and arrived back home before nine o'clock. I found our large double room full of friends, old and young. I thought first our church Young People's society were having a meeting of which I had not been apprised. But the presence of old friends not connected with the church, showed me it was no Endeavor meeting; and while trying to decipher it, the crowd, enjoying my evident perplexity, moved to the sides of the room, leaving Brother J. O. Klapp and myself prominent. He then drew from his pocket a paper and began reading a formal but very estimable address, beginning something like this: "On the momentous occasion of your seventieth birthday we, your friends," etc., and finishing with "We herewith, as a token of our high esteem, present you with this cane, which we hope may serve you as memento of our friendship, and a support in your declining years," etc. etc. At this time distance of twelve years, it now seems rather funny and almost farcical, but though in stereotyped, cane-presenting form, it was thoroughly genuine. I had suddenly to gather my wits to make a half suitable reply, which, however, seemed to be well received. In my wheel riding the cane was broken and other canes met the same fate; the declining years were slow in their march; in fact for a time were inclining. Yet there was nothing farcical. The cane was not the only present. There was a multitude of individual presents. Some that were well chosen, and are now valuable mementos. After a period of interesting general conversation, some entertainment and the service of refreshments, the friends dispersed, leaving a joyous imprint on memory's tablet that will not be effaced, while mentality remains with us.

TROUT POWER SET WORKS.

The residence period in this flat was a time of continuous and hard but pleasant work. The time when I worked out the power set works into their final successful form. My working hours were from seven thirty to ten in the evening, but often much later. While I always slept well, the Set Works problems were never far removed. I invariably awoke at five o'clock; from that hour to six, I could do the best thinking in the twenty-four. Then I would arise and embody the results of the hour's mental study, either in sketch, drawing or description so as to have it ready for the evening's further consideration, and final embodiment in the drawing. When my drawings were finally completed so as to be ready for the shop, I brought them down and got Mr. Hinkley's attention. He gave them a cursory examination, but was not disposed to do anything regarding them. He knew I was working independently of him and the company, and since there was neither credit nor profit for him in the matter, he was quite indifferent to the merits of the machine, or its advantages to the company. Unpleasant as it might be, I saw plainly that to get ahead with it I must go back of Mr. Hinkley, to the chief superintendent. After patient waiting for an opportunity, I obtained the consideration of Mr. Reynolds, who said, "I can't claim to be a good judge on this matter, but, I must say, the thing looks good to me, and I will see about it." Accordingly, a few weeks after, an expert on judging the probable costs and merits of new proposals, came to me, to examine the drawings and to compare them with what was then being manufactured for the same purpose. His report was, that the Trout set works were well designed, and would do excellent work, and the cost would probably not exceed the half of the one we had been manufacturing. The result was, that Mr. Hinkley was instructed to place the construction orders for my machine into the shop. Large bodies are said to move slowly; a big firm, where red tape must necessarily prevail, is a poor place to get new work quickly done, and when the one on which it mainly depends is unwilling, it is easy to see how very much slower it might be. In the course of regular procedure, the clerks had their work done, and turned the orders back to Mr. Hinkley for his final signature; which was duly appended, and then the papers were placed by him in one of his drawers, with the quiet statement that they would stay there till he was ready to send them out. This I did not fully learn till a long time afterwards. A week or two after this, I inquired of the pattern shop foreman if he had received an order for the new patterns for the Trout power set works. "No," he replied, "I have the drawings, but no orders. I can't make them without an order." "Well," I said, "the order must surely come soon." A month or two passed by with frequent inquiries, but no results. I finally went through all the small shop offices, making a search for them. Then through Miller's distributing office, and up again to the order clerks. One of them quietly told me to look in a certain drawer of Hinkley's and I would get them. I felt that I would almost need a search warrant to go to Hinkley's drawers. I went back to Mr. Miller and got him with me, and together we put the case to Mr. Hinkley—that as these orders were nowhere else, they still must be with him. He asserted they were not, and began pulling out drawers and looking. I pulled out the right drawer and of course found them. He expressed surprise. Miller carried them back with him, and they were soon at their destinations in the various shops.

But there was yet a standing hindrance to meet. Contract orders must always have precedence over new work, and at that time business was good, and contracts crowded the shops. Nothing could be done on the set works till the patterns were made, and pattern making required considerable time. It was months before they got started, and more months before completion.

The same hindrances were likely at every stage of the work. I tried to get a hurry up or rush order, but Mr. Hinkley would not grant it. At this juncture, my son Walter, who then had charge of the drafting room, said to me, "Father, you are not taking the best course, you can never get ahead, fighting Hinkley. If you would take him in with you, and give him a share in what you may get, there would be some prospect, and all will go smooth." I replied that I would have nothing to do with him. Win or lose, I would fight clear through. "Well, well!" said he, "it's your job, not mine." "Yes," I replied, "it will be mine to the end." When teaching drawing in the

Mechanics Institute classes in Peterboro, Canada, about 1880, I had a very promising pupil, a young millwright apprentice, Wallace Ludgate, the son of one of Canada's old lumbermen. He afterwards made his home in one of the rising lumber towns of the Pacific coast. He corresponded with me in the way of getting helpful information, that would advance him in his trade. He succeeded so well as to occasionally have charge of big mill contracts. I kept him apprised of my efforts in the set works line, and he kept me informed of the more or less futile efforts of other firms. When my final drawings were made, I sent him both general and detail prints, so that he could understand every part. He determined at the first opportunity, he would get the set works introduced. In 1904 he was employed to build a good large mill at Arrow Lake, British Columbia. Largely through his influence, the firm gave the contract to our company, which had then amalgamated with others and become the Allis-Chalmers Company. The sawmill carriage specifications of this proposed contract called for the Trout power set works. Regarding this, Mr. Hinkley wrote the mill firm that he supposed Mr. Ludgate and Mr. Trout understood each other in this matter; but he felt obliged to inform them, that while his company would make the set works it could not guarantee their successful working. Mr. Hinkley told me this. I said, "This firm guarantees the entire contract except this set works! Well! Well! that is surely the end of my chance at least as far as this firm is concerned." But to my great surprise about three weeks later came a letter stating "that if the set works are carefully constructed according to Mr. Trout's drawings, and under his directions, that we will accept the responsibility of their working." That was a tall feather in my cap. It was an expression of confidence that was certainly gratifying. The set works was no longer begging for construction. Now it had to be made in a short time; which was not fortunate, as new work should not be hurriedly made. In due time, however, the set works were completed and tested in the shop, as fully as our shop conditions would allow. The result being altogether satisfactory. Several months afterwards when the mill first started, Mr. Ludgate, in order to satisfy himself, for a brief time handled the set works, till he felt sure the machine was all right. He then placed a regular setter, a Swede, on the job, explaining to him the machine and showing its working. At the end of the day he inquired of the Swede how he liked the new machine. He replied, "Dem de best d - m set works on de whole coast." The rest of Mr. Ludgate's report to me could scarcely be more satisfactory.

As previously stated the use of power set works began with the massive logs of the Pacific coast, and besides, as already stated, the use was extended to the lighter logs of the eastern section of North America, in which steam set works were the first used. When inventing and designing my rope driven set works, I had the needs of both sections in contemplation. The different light character of the eastern log carriages, called for a different style of machine, which I had already designed, and now as the Pacific style had proved successful, I was ready and demanded the construction of the lighter eastern style. I readily obtained the construction orders, but was for a long time hindered by the pressure of contract work. After nearly a year, a machine was made and put on a testing frame with an electric motor, and the necessary rope and rope sheaves. The carriage frame was loaded to make a weight corresponding to the heaviest log. The trial manifested one defect, which, being soon remedied, the machine seemed to be perfect. But there was no Wallace Ludgate this side of the Rockies to give us the first order. Mr. Hinkley was only partly rid of his old indifference; but early in 1905 a southern mill superintendent called that was likely to leave us a good machinery order. Mr. Hinkley was steering him through the shops showing him sawmill machinery finished and in course of construction. I managed to meet them at the right time to head him toward the new set works. When arriving there I turned on the power and showed its working. Mr. Hinkley giving him explanations and favorable comments. The man was surprised and dumbfounded and in the end captured by it, ordering it to go on his carriage.

By this time, we had several orders from the Pacific for the larger size, and there were soon follow-up orders for the smaller. Also from the continuous service, weaknesses and faulty construction began to show. The quick start and stop of the machine was severe on itself. I had to make two long repair trips, one to Alabama and one to West Virginia; and as perfect satisfaction was guaranteed, in two instances our rope driven set works had to be replaced by steam set works. There was a period of reconstruction with better adaptation to the strenuous demands. This was costly to our company, but no royalties were paid me. I had not obtained full patents, and could exact nothing. I tried hard to get an agreement, but our worshipful president, Werner, of the new Allis-Chalmers Company, was too sacred to be seen. During his two years' term of office, I never saw him. He would come and go in a closed carriage, and keep the seclusion of his office with a guard in the ante-room, who would admit none without leave. I could not get my letters answered. It was a most discouraging time for me and a great change from the E. P. Allis regime. Many of the old employees left the service of the new company. I hung to it; so did Hinkley, though he was often under pressure to resign. A common fellow feeling had grown up between us, that continued. When Mr. Whiteside was given the presidency, prospects were better. And when I received my final patent, granted August 29, 1905, I immediately notified the company, that from and after that date, I must be paid a ten per cent royalty, on the sales of all Trout power set works. This brought attention. Mr. Babb, the general attorney for the company, inquired of Mr. Hinkley, if the parts of the Trout power set works covered by Mr. Trout's patent were necessary to its proper construction. Mr. Hinkley replied that they were necessary. Evidently then an arrangement must be made with me. Shortly after this, Mr. Hinkley asked me to go with him to the president's office. I found there a number of the superintendents and leading men. Mr. Whiteside began by saying that heretofore this company had been neglectful in the matter of patents. First, in not making applications on good inventions, and again, in neglect of the inventor. Hereafter, it would be the policy of this company to help the inventor by obtaining his patents for him, and in other ways giving him encouragement and consideration. Though his patronizing style was a great advance on the previous course, yet I, for one, did not approve of it. I politely told him that I expected to look after my own patents, without any favors, only a straight deal. There was more general talk on the subject, and when Mr. Hinkley and I were leaving, he said to me, "We will give you extra wages if that will suit you?" I replied, "I don't want higher wages. I only want fair royalties on the use of my patents."

Not long after this I was called to Mr. Babb's office, to confer with him and Mr. DeWein, the patent attorney, regarding the set works. They wanted my terms for transference of the patent to the company. I replied, "Ten thousand dollars for an outright sale." They regarded that as extravagant. I assured them it was quite moderate, but they would not entertain it. Then I said, "Give me a royalty of ten per cent." But they regarded that too high, and offered me five per cent; after some discussion we compromised on seven and one-half per cent on the selling price of each set works. Reports of sales to be made semi-annually, on the first of January and the first of July, when payment would also be made, and for the remaining four months of the then current year, as no account had been opened, I was to receive two hundred and fifty dollars when the agreement would be signed, which was done December 30, 1905. At this time also, an agreement was made that in consideration of my assigning to the company all inventions made while in its further service, I should receive as wages one dollar per hour. I accepted this, because I considered, that at seventy-two years a less strenuous life than formerly, would be altogether desirable, considering that "A bird in the hand is better than two in the bush."

Under this arrangement I continued with the company about one year and ten months. I was nearly all the time employed on new work. About fifteen patents were granted to the company over my signature, some of them quite valuable.

Besides this agreement, by which the company took over the different patents relating to power set works, and were paying me royalties thereon, I also gave the company an option of one year in which to begin the manufacture of three other patents, relating to sawmill carriages to be made and sold on the same terms as the set works. The company failed to use the option, and those improvements are still not made, the principal reason for this, being that sawmill machinery is now in a fairly well perfected state, and manufacturers are slow to meet the expenses of new construction, and the risks of successful introduction of new machines.

PACIFIC COAST JOURNEY

The working period under this agreement was the time of my greatest financial prosperity. With extra wages and rapidly increasing royalties, cash was easy; and since my whole life had been a pretty steady grind, I determined to have more leisure, and good pleasure during its brief remainder. Accordingly early in August, 1906, Lucretia and I started on a three-months' western journey; going north to Minneapolis through the wheat fields of Minnesota and Manitoba to Winnipeg. Thence west over the Canadian Pacific, making short stays in the mountains, to Vancouver. Then a delightful steamer voyage to Victoria, and among the islands to Seattle. Then to Portland and San Francisco, where we had two families of cousins. This was the year of the great earthquake and fire, so that we saw the great city in nearly its worst condition. From there we made a side trip for an eight-days' visit to my dear old friend, John Muir. Thence to Los Angeles and suburban towns, making a visit in Pasadena, where a brother-in-law, George Knowles, and part of his family resided. At all the places mentioned, from Minneapolis to Pasadena, we visited friends. The short ocean voyage to Catalina islands and back, with the natural wonder of that interesting place, made the most interesting sight-seeing day of our long journey. Leaving Los Angeles, on the Southern Pacific Railway, we had the change of the long, hot, dreary direct journey across the continent. Its strange, parched vegetation was the great interest. Our train made a brief restful stay at El Paso, where we took a walk over the Rio Grande bridge to see the Mexicans in their home country. Another good stay in San Antonio, enabled Lucretia, with other ladies, to visit places of interest. At Houston we took a one hundred and thirty-mile side trip to Lufkin, Texas, where my son Walter conducts a foundry and machine shop business. We spent eight days there with him and family, and other friends. Then southeast again to New Orleans for a pleasant stay of three days in that French-American city. From there we had a through train direct to Chicago. Then two hours landed us in our own Milwaukee home, after an absence of over two months, and a traveled distance of almost seven thousand miles. The longest continued railroad journey being on the Southern Pacific, which was seventy-seven hours, from Los Angeles to Lufkin. From entering the Rockies in Canada till we were half through Texas great mountains were always in view. Although it was a highly interesting and is now a pleasantly remembered journey, I have not the space to describe the details. Visiting relatives and friends was my main object. Sight-seeing was Lucretia's leading purpose. We were both well satisfied with our very enjoyable journey.

A great many people regard traveling as about the most enjoyable way of spending money. It is a great disturber of habits and is sometimes tiresome; we want to get to the end of our journey. But I seldom get wearied by it. On the whole, I rather like it. But there are other ways of spending money, that I like better. I like to help my children through hard places and trying times; and provide for them and my grandchildren, the means to enjoy lifelong pleasures, and the greater pleasures that reach beyond the common life. My appreciation of these things is expressed in a poem that has a place in my memory. The first of the stanzas runs like this:

I live for those who love me,
For those who know me true,
For the heaven that smiles above me,
And awaits my spirit too.

For the cause that lacks assistance,
For the wrong that needs resistance,
For the future in the distance,
And the good that I can do.

Consequently, it is a pleasure to see the Christian Church prosper; with all its directly connected, and remoter allied interests; such as the various missionary causes, philanthropic societies, Bible school, and other good educational work. Also temperance work, through real party Prohibition organizations, fighting against the monster "wrong that needs resistance," social and civic betterment, etc. All these need money; and being unable to work as heartily in these causes as I would like, I am the more anxious to see my money work. My small investments in these various lines being carefully made, I have not the least worry in regard to them. I see the work my dollars are doing, and lose no sleep about the proceeds. For a number of years I kept a nice little nest egg in the form of a savings account, which is all very good; but when I saw the greater needs of money outside of the bank than in, the money came out, and went into good service. It is probable I shall have little, or, may be, no legacy. These statements may look like self-adulation. I leave it to those who know me.

LUCRETIA'S MARRIAGE

One Lord's day in 1904, at the morning meeting of our church, a rather slight, boyish-looking young man came forward at the usual invitation for converts or new members, and presented a letter from the Metropolitan church in Chicago, and was duly received into membership. Of course, we scan the faces and general bearing of our new members, and right or wrong, we form our judgment. So I thought and afterwards remarked, that there is more in that modest boyish young fellow than we might be led to think. Nearly a year after this one Sunday eve he asked the privilege of conducting Lucretia home; which was granted. She being tall and he barely her equal in stature, she was inclined to look down on him. But with further acquaintance she found as Brother J. O. Shelburne had said, that the only thing small about him was his size. Of course, then he grew *up* in her estimation. A courtship began, and ran for several years in rather checkered fashion, in accordance with the old saying, that "the course of true love never runs smooth." However, it culminated all right on September 21, 1909. This wedding had some advantages over the four previous ones in that we had our own good combined home, or rather the home of the Irvin W. Davis family, in which Lucretia and I shared. We had good rooms and accommodation for our distant guests, nine grandchildren, having to be figured in this calculation. The Steindorf family forming five guests from West Virginia. Walter's five from Lufkin, Texas, and George and his wife from Lexington, Ohio. Also three cousins on mother's side of our house, from Wisconsin and Chicago. Like Nellie's wedding, this was held in the church; with the usual bride and groom processions converging in the central space in front of pulpit, to the wedding march of Lohengrin, with some of the little grandchildren as flower girls; the usual bridesmaids and groomsmen; and the "give away" by myself. All this, with the main marriage ceremony reverently performed and witnessed by a crowded congregation of interested people, constituted a social event of great importance; and an era in the family life, that should be, and is, long, lovingly and respectfully remembered. Lucretia's marriage was followed by an enjoyable reception of the wedded pair in the church parlors, along with the service of refreshments, the big old fashioned punch bowl was in use, but no alcoholic punch. No stimulation was needed for the exhilaration of that happy crowd. It would be like turning hell into heavenly places.

As this last family marriage event had brought us all together, and we might not soon be together again, it was thought best to have a large family group photograph taken;

which would be valuable in itself, and a worthy memento of this important family event. This was done, and the group picture immediately follows.

In the picture, directly behind the author, is the newly wedded pair, Peter M. Norgaard and Lucretia G. Trout. Next on the right is Irvin W. Davis, his wife, Nellie A., and two daughters and one son. On the extreme right is Otto W. Steindorf with his oldest daughter on his left, his wife, Jennie M., and one daughter and one son in front. On my left stands my son, George H., with his wife, Franke Kinzie Trout, in front, on the extreme left, stands my oldest son, Walter C., with his wife, Ellen E. Percy Trout, and three boys in front; in all twenty persons.

WALTER CHARLES TROUT

In following down this history from my great-grandfather, through the line of the oldest sons, I come to my children who are of the fifth generation. Already they have been extensively referred to in my own family story; yet as they are now men and women, on their own account in the active duties of life, it would seem proper that there should be some further brief notes in regard to each one. Dominant character traits in children are sometimes, but not always, easy to determine. In the mental make-up of my oldest son, Walter C. Trout, there was an early manifestation of an uncommon degree of enthusiasm in whatever he might be engaged in. It was shown in his childish play; and in his boyish enjoyments and voluntary work, there was such an intensity of effort, and obvious disregard of other matters, as to make some steady-going people think the boy was beside himself. An old friend once amused me immensely, by suggesting that I ought to have him examined, as to his mental soundness. Now at forty-one, this quality of mind has been well harnessed and disciplined as not to be so noticeable; but it is there all the same. Adverse health conditions interrupted the school period so much, that at the beginning of the working period he was behind in education. This, however, was in good part made up by self-study and watchfulness. Though never being apprenticed,

ADDITION TO THE W. H. TROUT FAMILY GROUP OF 1909.

he acquired an excellent, practical knowledge of machine shop work, and was a good draughtsman at twenty. I then obtained for him a place in the draughting room of the saw mill department of the Edward P. Allis Company, where he had my help and direction for more than two years. He was married about this time as previously told. His progress was so rapid that he soon began to relieve me of much responsibility; and when my leg was broken he had complete charge of the room, and when I returned I allowed him to retain it, and I received orders from him. It was characteristic of him that when he got near to his best in any line of work, he began to be dissatisfied with it and looked for something higher. So when he came to feel easy in the management of the draughting room, he determined to prepare for the work of a commercial traveler, designing and making mill plans and specifications, negotiating large contracts, sometimes with millionaires. This big work appealed to him, not alone for its public, masterful character, but also for its big pay, which with the E. P. Allis people and many others is the main basis of respect. He was getting ready for the chance, and if it did not come he would make one, but the chance soon came. The best traveler in the department, Ed. Fitzgerald, resigned; Walter applied, and stepped into his place. When up at Minneapolis, to take his first contract, a resident business employee of the company was requested to "keep an eye on the boy, as he was only a beginner." After Walter had the contract in hand, the man wrote back, "The boy needs no supervision, he can take care of himself." Walter continued in this line of work about six years, taking the largest and best line of saw mill contracts ever received by the company.

The next promotion Walter aspired to was the superintendency of the saw mill department. Mr. Hinkley used this expectation to keep him patient when he would be making his kicks for higher salary, telling him he was the only one to take his place when he would retire, which must be soon. For a time Walter waited, though keeping on in his field of work, which was principally in the South; and in order to have his wife and family more convenient to him, he made his residence in Shreveport, Louisiana. As Mr. Hinkley seemed to have no inclination either to resign or die, he determined in the course of his travels to keep an open eye for business chances. The South being known as the land of opportunity, he soon found what seemed likely to suit him. The small Town of Lufkin, a railroad center of some importance in the timber belt of east Texas, had in it a small foundry and machine shop, owned and financed by the saw mill proprietors of the neighborhood, for the main purpose of getting repairs on their mills promptly done. The management of this was unsatisfactory to the owners, and they gave Walter the offer of a good salary, with a good block of the stock, and chance of buying more, if he would take the management of the business. He saw the probable growth of this undertaking into a fairly prosperous business and accepted it; and while he has not realized his dreams and ambitions, he has not been disappointed. His standing among the business men and manufacturers is indicated by his having been for a number of years the president of the Manufacturers' Association of east Texas; and most all the mill men, if they contemplate new building projects, or additions or changes in their plants, will always call him into their consultation, pay him well for the plans he furnishes, and frequently give him the work without calling in opposing bids, being assured of a square deal. He has persistently refused public offices in the town, except that he saw the need of a new and aggressive school board, which was elected, and he became its president for five years. During this time Lufkin shook off its old southern conservatism, and is now a good progressive town with superior educational facilities, and other accompanying gains in civic improvement.

In one important respect Walter made no progress, rather he fell behind. The old home conditions, of church relationship and attendance on things divine, were not maintained. The commercial traveller's role was extremely unfavorable, if not positively in conflict. The business habits of the mill men were against it. Sunday was the time for special jobs. Repair work then received attention. The shop was sure to be

WALTER CHARLES TROUT

WILLIAM WALTER TROUT

busy on Sunday, and business in the office had also to be done. Consequently church services, duties and obligations, were in the background, and business in the front, and in command.

But now conditions have somewhat improved, but better still Walter's better determinations are ruling; he enjoys the fine help he gives in Bible school and church, and in other ways helping in the progress of the things that endure, and that are eternally worth while. His helpmate also heartily enters into his work with him, and is one of the leaders in the women's progressive societies of the town that are working toward the city's betterment. She is equally prominent in church, missionary and benevolent work; and their three fine, growing boys are following in their work, William Walter, Edward Percy and James Howard. As far as present prospects indicate, upon them will rest the good continuance of their grandfather's family line. I have no doubt regarding the reputable outcome.

This is the end of the direct line of the Trouts through the eldest sons, beginning with my great grandfather, George Trout, of London, England, then Henry George, then William, then William Henry, then Walter Charles, and lastly the eldest boy, William Walter Trout, of Lufkin, Texas, on whom the future reputation of the direct family line will certainly depend.

MRS. JENNIE MABEL TROUT STEINDORF

As has been already noted, our eldest daughter, Jennie, married Otto William Steindorf, a modest, retiring young man, but with evident good sense and good judgment. With outside people, family resemblances and common characteristics are the subject of attention and remark; but the parent, more than others, sees the differences. Jennie in her character-forming period was thoughtful and rather noncommittal, had a vein of dry humor in her mental composition, that belonged to none of the rest of us. She was an apt student, seldom asked help. She may be regarded as peculiar in the management of her children, for management it is; certainly it is not forceful control. Her children have a great deal of liberty while heading anywhere near the right way. If their inclinations seem to look wrongward, she diverts them before a purpose and determination becomes settled. She is careful to see that no ill will is aroused toward herself or toward each other. Her methods may not be what some would call good discipline, but the results on the whole are good. Her neighbors tell her, "Your children never quarrel," and it is true. All four of them seem to carry out the mother's method with each other. It is the rule of love, and the repression of ill nature, and along with this, high proficiency in study and general progress is maintained, with seemingly moderate effort.

Among the women of the large First Christian Church in Wheeling, Jenny holds a prominent place, as teacher of a teacher-training class in the Bible school, a leader in the Christian Woman's Board of Missions, and is helpful in the social betterment work of the city; and can write up a good paper on most of the subjects connected with these lines of Christian effort.

Otto Steindorf deserves more than passing notice. The name is clearly German, meaning stone village. But he is a native-born American, and nothing else. There is no German-American for him; if he has a soft side in his heart toward his ancestry it does not influence his judgment. He takes care to approach all subjects with an unbiased consideration.

In the spring of 1900, I received a letter from the super-intendent of the great steel tube works of Benwood, a suburb of Wheeling, West Virginia, requesting me to give him the names and addresses of three or four men who might be capable of taking charge of the machine shop of the tube works, asking also for some hints as to their character and fitness for the job, I gave him four names, describing the characteristics of each person, Otto being among them. I said of him, "His style is not the commanding forceful bluff and bluster manner often found in a boss, but he is quiet in de-meanor, uses few words, and uses them thoughtfully. Though red-headed he is not hot-headed, but has a most equable temper. He will respect the sense and judgment of the men under him. In his own practice he is a thorough mechanic, knows good work when done, and knows how to do it, and how much time it should take in the doing. He has an inventive streak, and can make new adaptations for new situations and new needs; and, finally, he will be found always truthful and entirely reliable." He wrote Otto, and made him an offer, which was accepted. Otto named the date and hour of his arrival; the superintendent met him at the train, drove him around to see the city of Wheeling, ending the journey in Benwood. He conducted him through the great steel works, arriving finally in the machine shop where Otto's future work lay. He briefly explained the nature of the new duties and left him, with the encouraging assurance that he (Otto) was the first man he ever employed for so responsible a position without before seeing him, but he was satisfied that he had made no mistake.

It is evident that the superintendent was correct. Otto is there still, now in 1915. During his fifteen years of service, he has received good advanced offers from other firms, of which he gave notice to his own steel company, who met the advance and kept him. He is a great home worker, making helpful conveniences for the family work, and for the amusement and progress of his children, all of whom form a very likely and most hopeful family. Otto's main round of interest comprise the shop, the home and the church; in the latter he is on the board as a deacon. In all of these he performs both intelligent, willing and very helpful service.

Accompanying the picture of my son George, is the portrait of Jennie Louise Steindorf, our eldest grandchild, who deserves mention for having finished the high school of Wheeling, with the second highest average in a class of seventy-five students. She is now taking a four years' literary and domestic science course in Bethany College, Bethany, West Virginia; but on account of credits obtained from a summer course at Kent Normal, Ohio, and at the Art School in Milwaukee, she expects to finish in three years.

GEORGE HENRY TROUT

My second son, but third child, now comes in for consideration. Beginning first with reference to native traits, as I have done with the former-mentioned children, I would say that George's most pronounced peculiarity was his unceasing good nature and unbounded playfulness. Everything seemed to be play to him. Study was play, if he was in company with studious boys. If he should be with the opposite class, then the best study-fun was how they best could torment the teacher. Of course, with that sort of play on hand there was poor progress in study; so that George as well as Walter was deficient in his common school education. Like Walter, he also made up for much of it afterwards and pushed on farther; but both know the loss of good elemental ground work in their school training. During childhood and youth, this playfulness predominated. When as a young boy he first started out to make the good confession, it seemed to be with the conception that a new and wider field of play was before him, and when its real seriousness broke in upon him he felt like backing down, but he did not. He and his two sisters, Nellie and Lucretia, were baptized by John McKee early in 1891. Walter was baptized by C. C. Smtih, 1890, and Jennie the same year by M. B. Ryan.

Since the Apostle Paul tells us, "For as many of you as were baptized into Christ have put on Christ"—Gal. 3, 27, so we should remember this beginning time, when being buried in the symbolic grave we arise to walk in the new life.

George's playfulness did not prevent his being a willing worker; particularly so if the work had the freshness of novelty. When nearly seventeen, I succeeded in getting him apprenticed to the Edward P. Allis Company, to become a mechanical engineer. It was a four years' service with very moderate pay, but the educative part was good. though the playful habit continued, so that, as the superintendent said, it seemed as if he never would quit being a kid. Though he did not seem to study, no one else made such good progress. When near the close of his apprenticeship, he was given the erection

GEORGE HENRY TROUT
DAYTON, OHIO

JENNIE LOUISE STEINDORF
WHEELING, WEST VIRGINIA

of a small Corliss engine in one of the shops of the city. This was so quickly and satisfactorily done that he was also given the placing of a large Corliss engine in the basement of a big store, a greater and much more troublesome job, that would test the good judgment of a veteran. Though it was good veteran service, it was done for an apprentice's pay, which in the last of the four years' term was about one dollar per day. This was the last work for the company. He took up the one hundred dollar bonus given at the finish of the apprenticed term, and left to get work in some other shop for at least one year. This was a compulsory regulation, so that the apprentice might get a wider knowledge of shop usage and wages paid; then, if he returned, he would more contentedly remain. Some of the head men wanted the rule suspended in George's case, but the shop superintendent said, "No, young Trout must be served the same as any other fish." He left in June, 1899.

George went to the office of the Filer & Stowell Company, met the superintendent, inquired for work; the superintendent looking him over doubtfully, replied, "I've got a good job for a good man." "Well, if you have a good job trot it out, and if I don't hold it down I will give you a week's work for nothing. What is your job?" "A big boring lathe." "What price goes with it?" "Twenty-seven and a half cents an hour; and you must work nights." "All right, I'll take it, and at the end of the week you can see how I come out." Of course, he held down the job, and exceeded the previous record work of the lathe, and after a month or two got a better job, and was steadily rising in the estimation of the superintendent, when at the end of the fourth month he was promoted to be foreman over the whole night gang of seventy men. He served in this good position about eighteen months. It had, however, one decided objection; it was always night work. A good offer came to him from Sarnia, Casada, to go and install there the steam, electric and hydraulic systems in a small and large saw mill then being commenced. This he accepted. It had the advantage of being a day job, with a varied character, and much of it new, furnishing more advanced experience.

Early in May, 1901, he removed to Sarnia, and once more became a Canadian. The construction work was carried on after the starting of the small mill, and was not all fully completed until 1903. Finally the work settled to the everyday routine work of running and keeping the power plant in good condition, which would be a good comfortable job for a much older man, but too monotonous and easy for George. So, late in 1903, when the mills were laid up for the winter, he and his wife returned to Milwaukee. He soon let his friends know that he was ready for a good shop job. His old shop superintendent, James Church, notified him that Mr. Edwin Reynolds, the chief superintendent, could direct him to a good position. He at once called on Mr. Reynolds, who told him a Marinette firm was undertaking the manufacture of gas engines, and wanted a good foreman; then with a smiling, quizzing look, he asked George, "What do *you* know about gas engines?" George replied, "Not much, but I am ready to try the job, and believe I can make good." "Oh, I guess you'll do all right. Now (continued Mr. Reynolds) you go up there and see about it, and I will send them a letter regarding you." George went up and secured the position. This was not because he knew so much about gas engine work, for, on account of its newness few were acquainted with it; but it was adjudged that he had a good knowledge of shop work, and the facile and adaptable mind that would soon understand and work out the best course in the situation. Accordingly, he and wife removed February 1, 1904, to this northern Wisconsin town with some prospect of permanency. There, in company with Mr. Walrath, the designer, and other fine leading mechanics and business men, George had enjoyable and helpful associations, and was enabled to contribute his full share to the common progress. In his fifth month he became shop superintendent. Mrs. Trout also found good pleasurable society acquaintances.

The gas engine business became so hopefully successful, that in a few months it was decided to reorganize the company, take in more capital, build a much larger new shop at Chicago Heights, a suburb of the big city, and remove their machinery and power plant, along with new additions, to the new situation. George had charge of the removal, and the new arrangement and resetting of the machines in the large new shop; and continued for several months in the superintendency, when owing to constant unpleasant friction between the new directors and the old management he resigned, December 1, 1904, only to become sales manager of Strong, Carlisle & Hammond Company, Cleveland. Here his knowledge of steam, gas and electrical engineering came into good service, and his work soon became specialized into selling and superintending the installation of all their power plants. In the course of this work he sold a gas engine to the Smith Gas Power Company of Lexington, Ohio, and made the acquaintance of Harry Smith, the inventor of his gas producer. He was a university graduate, specializing on chemistry. George saw that his producer had distinctive merits, and so reported to his company, who instructed him to make a more critical examination and report. He did so, and his company arranged for its exclusive sale in northern Ohio. Several producers were, soon after, sold, which brought George in closer contact with Smith and his new company. The latter began to feel greatly the need of a sales manager, and one to take care of the business end of the work. Favorable overtures were made to George, which he accepted, on condition that after one years' service he should, if mutually agreeable, become a member of the firm. Accordingly, on January 1, 1906, he began with the Smith Gas Power Company, and his itinerating career, though a good one, ended; "The rolling stone" settled, and began to "gather moss." Ten years have elapsed; George still retains this connection. The Smith Gas Power Company is now, in 1916, doing an immensely increased business; and has lately been reorganized under the changed name of the Smith Engineering Company, with a capital stock of four hundred and fifty thousand dollars, and will remove this coming winter to Dayton, Ohio, into new and greatly enlarged shops, where a good, successful future seems to be awaiting this enterprising business firm.

George's progress in study and business has been quite equal to the progress of the firm, in fact it must lead it. There seems to be nothing in the range of steam, or gas, or electricity, that he does not clearly understand, and can readily lead others to his clear apprehension of the subject. In this respect he was once highly complimented by our Milwaukee city engineer.

He is the respected spokesman of the Smith Gas Engineering Company. His steady activity in church and Bible school has been already noted, and his persistent good nature is made subservient to every good movement.

George's home is now in Lexington, Ohio, but will soon be in Dayton, Ohio; it is mine too, when I choose to use it, the same as all my children's homes; but I am less frequently at George's home than any of the others. Unfortunately I have no grandchildren there. Certainly more unfortunate it is for George than for myself, as no one among us enjoys the presence and company of children better than he does. And the feeling is reciprocated, all the children enjoy Uncle George. If he should hold out his hands, and with his assuring smile say, "Come," even a strange baby will most likely leave his mother's arms and go to him. But if no childish chat is heard in his house, or playthings litter their well-kept rooms, still they are seldom lonesome. Mrs. Trout entertains very nicely. Her skilful playing on her good piano is always interesting; and George, in his evenings at home, particularly if "company" is present, contributes his quota of song. He is a baritone of no mean ability, with a fairly good repertoire, and sings very expressively in sympathy with his subject. All this, coupled with good conversational ability, makes an interesting social evening. The same talents come in most serviceably in the work and worship of the church, where he, when at home from his business tours, leads the singing, with Mrs. Trout at the organ, and often a solo by George as part of the program. Added to all this, at times, in the absence of the Bible school superintendent, he fills the place; or, in the absence of the pastor, he is called upon for the more serious work of conducting the meeting and doing the preaching. It is a great pleasure to see progress of this kind backed up by square dealing, and the unsullied reputation springing from a good life. If, as England's immortal bard has said, "The evil men do lives after them," though he does not affirm it, yet the same is true of the good; so we look for a prolonged effective life for George that will not be forgotten at the end of its term. But it would be all much more to our pleasure, could we be assured that such a life would have its natural successors as well as its influence.

MRS. NELLIE AMELIA TROUT DAVIS.

In my own family story, referring to Nellie's courtship by Irvin W. Davis and her marriage, there comes in also her distinctive bent toward the study and practice of art. This was so manifest as to warrant me in the expenditure of the needed funds for an extended course in the Art Institute of Chicago, where she made progress in both drawing and color. Her second effort in oil received honorable mention. The eye strain resulting from this work demanded an extended relief from study and the use of the pencil and brush. This was cupid's opportunity, and he made good use of it. She surrendered, on condition that she might afterwards resume the study and continue her art practice. Of course, Irvin consented; as it depended mostly upon herself, he was quite safe in doing it; and he really was proud of her progress, and anxious that she should have the leisure and the means to proceed. But the greater and more pressing considerations of a new home, and the needs of three lively babies in the course of six years, shelved the art pursuit for more favorable periods, which seem to be still in the future. However, her efforts in this line have neither been lost nor laid aside. They can be found in the atmosphere of her home, in the aptitude of her children in sketching and drawing, particularly Margaret, the second daughter, who seems to have inherited all of her mother's natural bent plus her directive help, having at the age of eleven just been awarded a scholarship in the Milwaukee Art Institute. This is the first prize baby of former mention, who will undoubtedly hold her first place in drawing and art design, and possibly other lines as well, as she is a most cheerful, diligent student.

Nature study is another line of interest to which Nellie has devoted attention. While art study and practice has been reluctantly left in the background, nature study came to the front, not for her own consideration, but that of her children, whose attention, from their earliest showing of interested observation, has been directed to this end. As the immensity of this universal subject is too great for ordinary minds even to think about, let alone study, so she devoted her attention and that of her children to the birds, with some little passing attention to the flowers and seeds. One of the large, finely wooded parks of the city is only three blocks distant from her home, and as many of the migrants in their northern journey make a resting place of the park, she determined to make it her main place of observation. Accordingly, at the beginning, and through the migration periods, she and the children were down into the park by sunrise, when the city was still measurably quiet, and the song birds in their liveliest ecstatic grand concert. I am referring to this as Nellie and her children appreciated it, not as I regard it, for the best wild bird singing I hear in these degenerate bird days seems like weak attempts at bird music, compared to the great overwhelming chorus that began with the early dawn in the Canadian spring time of sixty years ago. The continued harmonious melody pervaded the woods and seemed as steady as the rippling of the water in the rapid running stream. It began with the first light of the morning, in the long bright days of late May and early leafy June, and the sunrise period seemed to be the zenith of its melody, which slowly diminished as the day wore on. One sentimental songster reserved his half melancholy lay for the quiet evening twilight, when from the highest tree top he poured forth his strong, but pensive and prolonged notes, that might be heard for half a mile. This was long before the days of the plume hunter for ladies' hats; and the advent of the English sparrows—"The rats of the air" the great disturbers of the equilibrium of American bird life. Pardon this digression, which forcibly springs up from memory's depths and seeks expression.

On account of ill health last winter, 1914 and 1915, she sojourned with me in southern Texas, having with us also her youngest child "Billy" to share and contribute to our interest. There she renewed the acquaintance of her former bird friends in their southern winter quarters, and also gained an introduction to many of the settled denizens of that particular region. The vegetation was also a matter demanding attention, as the rocky hills and rich valleys furnished such a variety, from the cactus and mesquite of the desert, and flowers of the tropics, along with luxuriant growths of more northern trees and crops, all forming a matter of continued interest. The pleasant drives we had about San Marcos, San Antonio and Austin, will not soon be forgotten.

Besides the art and nature study there is another characteristic in Nellie's make-up that deserves respectful notice; that is her economic ability. I should hardly say disposition. Though disposition and ability should necessarily accord, there is undoubtedly a disposition to save money, but not for money's sake, but for the necessities and needs as well as the comforts and pleasures, that money could buy; and economic ability comes in, in making a limited number of dollars supply the largest possible limits of real service. She has all the food values in figures, knows what growing children should have, as well as the best for old folks; and gets it all down into terms of dollars and cents, so that it may match the income whether small or great.

There is another kindly peculiarity that deserves a reference, which is, that Nellie is the custodian of all the confidences of her friends. She has a sympathetic ear to their troubles, and a kindly advisory tongue to help them out. On this account she is generally pretty well loaded up; greater often than she cares to carry. Being the wife of the chairman of the church board, and the daughter of the senior elder, helps her to a great deal of this, which though hard on Nellie is helpful to the church and community; whose respect and love to her is so readily accorded.

She is the mistress of the creditable and convenient Irvin
Davis home on the South Side of Milwaukee, the result of
their industry and economy, with help from father, who shares
the home with them a great part of the time; and who must
be excused if there seems to be too much appreciation manifested.

IRVIN WILBUR DAVIS.

It is no disrespect to Mr. Davis that his wife precedes him
in this family history. Blood relation takes the lead; other
connections follow. The Davis courtship and marriage story
formerly given, introduces him to the reader as a young man
of cheerful, lively disposition, wide-awake turn, and active
manner. One who always seemed ready for whatever might
turn up. A quick reply to jolly repartee, the placing a locomotive back on the track were all one to him. He never
seemed to study about anything; he was ready. This was
shown in other matters as well as mechanics. He could see
through a shop trouble among his men and quickly adjust it;
or could suggest a good practical solution of a church problem.
He seldom reached or tried to reach the remote or underlying
causes of anything; but soon would compass all the surface
reasons, and could advise or act on them to good purpose.
His frank, outspoken, jolly, bantering manner kept his men
in pleasant humor, while much good work was being done.
But his patience was short with incompetent, inefficient, un-
truthful, beer soaking, or careless men, and his invectives
against them were severe. He knew what each man could do
in his ordinary gait in a given time, and what he could accomplish when keyed up to his best efforts; so that he could plan
and promise the completion of a job by a given date, and
make his promise good. He knew the value of minutes and
noted their passage, seeing that each was loaded with its com-
plement of work. He could employ his own time, and that
of his men, to get the best economic results against a specified
time. That he could make as judicious use of money as Mrs.
Davis, may be doubted, certainly it has not yet been demonstrated. We know him to be ready to spend when there is

manifest need, and to be always considerate and helpful to others. He sees the interest of others as well as his own, which would all be very good, if the others would do the same. While he gives good value in the shape of good work, he has fallen behind in working up good wages. I understand this defect, because it was one of my own shortcomings. It is a man's duty to get good pay for good work; but it is not always easy of accomplishment. The wage question is the tug of war between employer and employee. It is rare to find a man so efficient in so many lines of effort as is Irvin W. Davis; he will make his own working drawings of such machines and parts as may be required, studying out new forms and combinations, on some of which, patents have been obtained. He will also make his own patterns, machine and finish the castings and assemble them into the final machine. In the Davis Manufacturing Company's shop he may be assigned to supply the place of any absent foreman, or go out on the road to fix broken down machines or troublesome engines, or become salesman. He seems to be the handy man in any required place. At home, furnace mending, plumbing, or almost any manner of house fixing is a matter of course with him.

In the church work he turns aside from nothing except preaching and baptizing. He has been repeatedly elected chairman of the board. Serves also as assistant Bible school superintendent, and leads the singing in the Bible school. Besides the pastor, C. L. Milton, he is said to be the best liked brother in the whole congregation. Such is the genial, forceful Irvin Davis. His family of three fine, intelligent children do now and will continue to reflect credit on their parents.

LUCRETIA GARFIELD TROUT NORGAARD

She is the youngest of my children living. As previously told, a younger cherub than she, Clara, at four years winged her way from us through an accidental burning. Lucretia was born on my birthday, therefore, I claimed the right of naming her. Though we discussed names together for the other children, yet Mrs. Trout had the final decision. President James A. Garfield had died by the shot of the assassin,

Gitteau, a short time before this; when, not the United States alone, but the world was shocked by the occurrence, and was interested in his family. Though I had never met him, I felt that I knew him, having heard so much about him, through my former student acquaintances made in Hiram in 1855. One of these students was Miss Lucretia Rudolph who afterwards became Mrs. Garfield. With all this knowledge, and the fact that by religious association he was Brother Garfield, my exceptional interest in him may be judged; and the honored name which this dear baby received was quite as much a remembrance of him, as of the worthy lady who also bore it.

I have never been away from home at the birth of any of my children. Of course, I was allowed to be only a good general outside helper, and if not at liberty to see, I could not be prevented from listening. When I judged sufficient time had elapsed, following the main episode, I presented myself in the open door. The old nurse said, "You're in too big a hurry, Mr. Trout. Wait." "No," said our old doctor friend, "Come along and see your latest good gift." Of course a loving acknowledgment to the bearer had first to be presented; then I turned to the little one as she lay ready to be dressed, and remarked to the doctor regarding her fine plump muscular form. "Yes," said he, "a fine fully developed infant like every other one of Mrs. Trout's children." While this was a well-deserved compliment to mother, I felt it was no detraction from the other parent.

I have given the distinctive peculiarities of my other children, but it is hard to find one for Lucretia. I judge we will have to regard her greatest peculiarity as the complete absence of anything peculiar. A plain, even-tempered disposition seems to be her portion, without any strong mental bias in any given direction. As previously stated, on account of my poor health in 1900, she gave up the high school and took business studies, and for a number of months did office work, till Nellie was married and she became my housekeeper. Fortunately my health was then improving so she was kept at home, and for several years gave special attention to music in which she became decidedly proficient.

If Lucretia had to be cut short in the matter of general education, it was more than made up in the advantages of fairly extensive travel. Her long journey with me around by the Pacific has been briefly described; she also had several shorter journeys with me, and a summer visit to Manitoba and Winnipeg on her own account, besides her long trip to Europe with her husband after marriage, in which the old parental home in Schleswig was visited, and in Bavaria they witnessed the last passion play in Oberammergau in 1910.

I regard good motherhood as about the highest attainment of womanhood. It is usually not regarded as a great ambition, but rather as a common natural endowment, coming in the usual course of things. Most of mothers think they are all right, and that they have done the best under their peculiar conditions. Few give the subject serious prolonged observation and study, and adapt their management to the needs and nature of the child. The few that do this find a subject of interest that scarcely has an equal, and when successfully worked out affords a steady satisfaction, that is seldom achieved in any other line of effort. The ability of my daughters in this respect has been already stated, or clearly intimated. But were we to select the one who has given the most attention, and made the most progress in the shortest time, it would be to Lucretia. She had the advantage of marrying later in life, and seeing and profiting by the experience of her sisters; add to this a real earnest study of the family question from good books on the subject, of which in this present decade there is an abundance, while thirty or forty years ago, they were nearly unknown. The researches of modern science have reached their highest and most useful service, when directed as they now are to the rearing and the culture of young humanity. Physically and psychologically the child is studied; or, in less grandiloquent but much plainer terms, the child is studied in relation to the various growing conditions of the body, and the continually unfolding progressive states of the mind. Psychology is a modern term, much used in these days, its briefest definition being, mind study. You can get a program for child life and training, from birth to young manhood or womanhood, when he is supposed to be an intelligent, loving and lovable worshipful being. Lucretia works the scientific program. Old folks like myself that were not regulated by the clock nor fed on precise percentages, were inclined to smile at such an application of numbers and time; but jolly laughing babies turned the laugh against us. When you see active little tots placed in their crib to go to sleep at their leisure, as they do without a whimper, and wake up about the expected time and go to playing till their mamma comes to take them, you may then judge there has been some good care and training somewhere in the background. This relegates nursing, cradle rocking and hymn singing, to the misty memories of the laborious past.

Good family rearing calls for a good family home, not necessarily a luxurious one, where idleness may languish into imbecility, or wanton mischief go unchecked; but a good, self-dependent home, run solely by the family whenever practicable, is the ideal. A home that can be run independent of the servant problem, if need be. Such are the homes of my children, where not only the family needs and comforts and means of educative recreation are supplied, but also where the children are partners in the home business; and, as every business requires a suitable housing, so the best home is the best center of family culture and uplifting associations. In this respect, Lucretia has been favored with the latest and perhaps the best of any. It is finely situated, overlooking the largest and best park in Milwaukee, and in it a generous hospitality is extended, not alone to friends and relatives, but is also one of the social centers for our missionary and other helpful societies of the church and community. But this home with its matronly mistress and interesting little children must be dismissed for a brief reference to the head of the house.

PETER MATHIESEN NORGAARD.

P. M. Norgaard was born March 24, 1881, in the province of Schleswig, Germany. This is one of the provinces wrested from Denmark in 1864, when Germany first entered upon her aggressive Bismarckian policy of grabbing all she could get, so the Norgaards are really Danes and belong to the great Scandinavian family of nations, of whom no better foreign people come to our shores. The Norgaards have their racial characteristics and were Germans only by compulsion. Now however, the greater part of the family are in this country, and are Americans without any hyphen.

Peter left his Denmark home when seventeen years of age, took passage to the east coast of England, thence across the country to Liverpool. From there he shipped on a British line steamer to Quebec, Canada; where he arrived a complete stranger, speaking only Danish and German. He found his way to Chicago, Illinois, to which an older brother had by a few years preceded him. After a brotherly visit, he went northward to Owatanna, Minnesota, near where lived an uncle whom he visited. In the town he engaged with a Scotch Canadian tailor, at two dollars per week, with board and lodging. There he felt he had to learn the English language in the shortest possible time, so with the help of a few books and evening classes, he soon succeeded in mastering everyday English. His first accumulation of twenty-four dollars was sent to his father, and the next bought a bicycle. By this time he began to get beyond the two-dollar-a-week wage, and in the course of a year gravitated back to Chicago. Here he entered the great Marshall Field store and for three years he served a practical apprenticeship working under instructions in the ladies' tailoring department. This experience and teaching was a great advantage, by which he greatly profited. Here also he left his German nationality and the Lutheran religion behind him, and became an American citizen, and a citizen of Christ's Kingdom, under the name Christian, leaving off the Lutheran hyphen. He and his younger brother, Arthur, who followed him to this country, joined the Union church of Christ or Metropolitan Christian church in 1901. Then under the pastorate of the well and favorably known J. H. O. Smith.

The four Norgaard brothers were all tailors; it was the family trade, and might almost be regarded as inherited; as the father and grandfather were tailors and the sons grew up in it, so, if not inherited, it was at least like second nature, and certainly well rooted, as three good ladies' tailoring establishments in as many American cities, now testify. The best being in Milwaukee. But I am anticipating. After several years in Chicago, Peter found employment in Milwaukee, and united with our first Christian church, formed the acquaintance, and intimate connection with the Trout family, already noted. He became the head of the ladies' tailoring branch of one of our large department stores. After a year or two of service with this firm, he saw that their increasing business was very largely dependent upon his reputation, and for which the wages paid, though regarded good, were but a moderate recompence. Accordingly, in the early winter of 1910 he gave them notice to quit at the end of the year. Peter at once went into business and soon entirely outrivaled his former employers. He now has the best business of the kind in the city.

The Norgaard boys, in common with most of the European people, have a decided instinct toward the soil. They want to call some of it their own. It is a close second to the savings instinct, so generally manifest among them.

Peter's characteristics are not readily discernible, but when one gets up against his real personality, he meets a clear, careful thinker, who never commits himself to hasty plans, a serene, kindly nature, and a man of inflexible integrity; and the last superlative feature can be affirmed of all my sons-in-law. And it is also a great continued source of pleasure to see their twelve, lively, bright children growing up under such good conditions and right influence, that *augur* possibly even greater and better prospects for the future.

This concludes my family line, which ends the line of the eldest sons, and we now will briefly follow with the record of my brothers and sisters, which will complete my father's line.

MARY TROUT JAY.

This dear half-sister of mine has already been frequently noticed in the course of the general histroy. Her association with grandfather and grandmother and some of my aunts until her fourteenth year enabled her to be a fine link in the

MRS. MARY TROUT JAY

JOHN JAY
MEAFORD, ONTARIO, CANADA

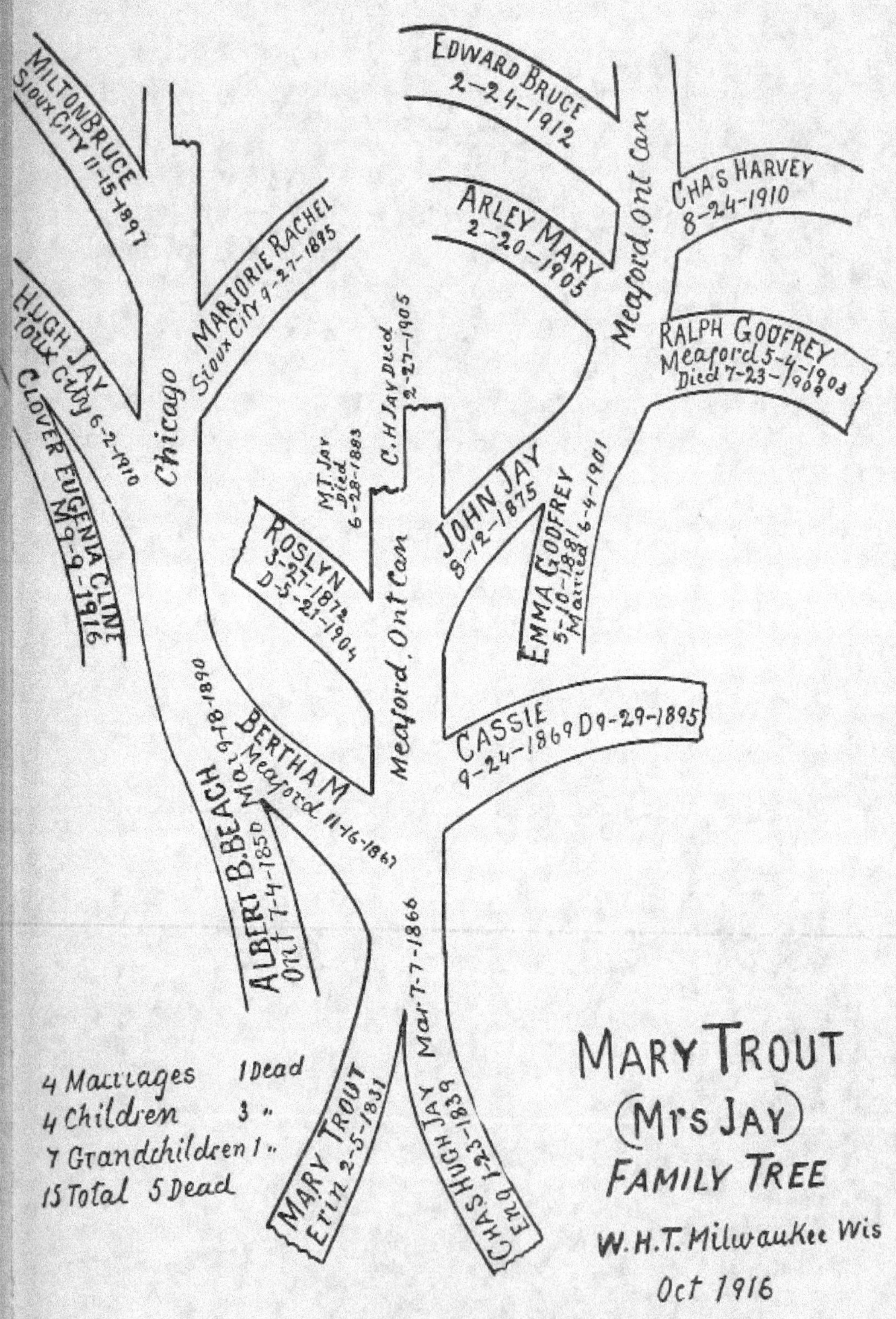

MILTON BRUCE
Sioux City 11-15-1897
HUGH JAY
Sioux City 6-2-1910
CLOVER EUGENIA CLINE
9-9-1916
Chicago
MARJORIE RACHEL
Sioux City 9-27-1895
EDWARD BRUCE
2-24-1912
ARLEY MARY
2-20-1905
Meaford. Ont Can
CHAS HARVEY
8-24-1910
RALPH GODFREY
Meaford 5-4-1908
Died 7-23-1909
C.H. Jay Died 2-27-1905
M.T. Jay Died 6-28-1883
ROSLYN
3-27-1872
D 5-21-1904
JOHN JAY
8-12-1875
EMMA GODFREY
5-10-1881 Married 6-4-1901
Meaford. Ont Can
CASSIE
9-24-1869 D 9-29-1895
BERTHA M
Meaford 11-16-1867
ALBERT B. BEACH Mar 9-18-1890
Ont 7-4-1850
Meaford. Ont Can
Mar 7-7-1866
4 Marriages   1 Dead
4 Children   3 "
7 Grandchildren 1 "
15 Total 5 Dead
MARY TROUT
Erin 2-5-1831
CHAS HUGH JAY
Erin 1-23-1839
MARY TROUT
(Mrs JAY)
FAMILY TREE
W. H. T. Milwaukee Wis
Oct 1916

traditional line. Being the oldest of my mother's family, I was next to her in age, and was her most companionable brother, so her family knowledge was added to mine. As already mentioned, she married my business partner, Charles Hugh Jay, to whom also frequent reference has been made. The union was a happy one, trial and suffering from ill health near the close of her life in 1883 being the drawbacks. As already mentioned, on account of father living with them, her home was regarded as the family center, and place for reunions of our scattered members. She had four children, three daughters and one son. Bertha, the eldest, became the second wife of Albert Beach, as shown in family tree. They had two sons and one daughter, all now reside in Chicago except Mrs. Beach, who died in 1914 on account of a violent fall. She was a lovable and loving woman, which I have some right to know, as she and her brother regarded me as the nearest in kinship and sympathy after their mother passed away. Her three, grown-up children are a fine testimonial to her goodness and motherly care. Mary's other two daughters died unmarried.

John Jay, the youngest, is now living in the beautiful town of Meaford, on the shore of Georgian bay, the place of his birth, and the former headquarters of the William Trout family; but now himself and family are the only descendants to represent us. He is the active manager in a good hardware store in the town.

He knows all the people in the town and surrounding country; and they know him to be a fine, agreeable, dependable business man, that looks to their interest as well as his own. His fine comfortable home is presided over by a sweet-spirited mother, who with her three fine children, can furnish a place for rest and enjoyment that is seldom equaled. I have reason to know this, being the recipient of its hospitality and pleasant company in the summer of 1913 for a whole week. I feel like lingering here and referring to the renewing of the few old acquaintances, and the interesting old scenery and associations; all of course changed more or less, which only adds to their interest, but I forbear.

CHARLES HUGH JAY

But I can not leave the Jay family and Meaford without a final reference to Mr. C. H. Jay, boyhood acquaintance, brother-in-law, brother in the church and business partner for a few years. In all these relations there was a cordiality and agreeableness that is seldom surpassed between real brothers, and though our lives diverged, yet friendly relations continued throughout life. When we separated at Beaverton, I to go forward in a mechanical career, and he to go back to Meaford, and into business with my brother James, amid the old associations of business and church relations, our lives and views of life's great interests then began to diverge. I went to a larger town where I was nearly a total stranger, starting in lines of work that were new to me. I had to study the principles of mechanics more fully, and keep in touch with its rapid progress, and if possible anticipate it. Naturally, this habit of mind would be turned to other fields of thought and study, particularly our great religion. I could see that while our brethren had better defined and more correct views of New Testament teaching and practice, still we did not compass the whole of it. For that matter no one does, nor does any body of people; but our brethren of the Meaford church seemed to think they had it down fine. In the meaning of a passage, or combination of passages, they regarded their conclusions as the absolute truth in the case, from which there could be no appeal, and I shared largely in their views with them. But in Peterboro, where I met other good people with their different points of view, and with my New Testament and myself alone to compare and consider, I gradually began to see, that the teaching and example of Christ, the records of the Acts and the Apostolic letters, were not a finely drawn legalized system like the Mosaic law, for one nation, and one period, but a book with a message to all nations, in all periods of time. A message of love to the heart of man; on which heart, according to the new covenant, the law is to be written, and the statutes upon the mind; so that obedience springs from implanted motives quite as much as from formal declarations or specific examples; both of the latter limit our action and field of view, and may be applicable to similar times and conditions to those in which they were given, while principles are eternal, and are adaptable to the changing conditions of all ages. Such is the breadth and comprehensiveness of "God's purpose, which he purposed in Christ Jesus our Lord," or as expressed by the sublime hymn:

> There's a *wideness* in God's mercy,
> Like the *wideness* of the sea;
> There is *kindness* in His justice,
> Which is more than liberty.
>
> For the love of God is *broader*
> Than the *measure* of man's mind,
> And the heart of the Eternal
> Is most wonderfully kind.

Had Charlie and I changed places, perhaps I might have been something like he, and he like I. As it was he receded into the old, still more narrowed position, and, right or wrong, I expanded into the wider one. About the only unpleasant talk we ever had was in relation to those differences. He was as conscientious and sincere in his views as it is possible for me to be in mine. He is not forgotten. He was an elder in the Meaford church of Christ, and a much respected citizen of the town. He passed away February 27, 1905.

EDWARD TROUT.

Edward is the second son in father's family. See the Wm. Trout Family Tree. He is fourteen months younger than I. When children and boys together, I led in the work or whatever was to be done, while he led me in talking. With the next brother, John, we formed a trio in work or play, and Edward was our spokesman. This leadership in speech was not retained in his fully adult life. He was careful, tidy, and attentive in regard to his person. When a child, I have heard mother say, that he kept his clothes cleaner than would the rest of us, and they were not so quickly worn out. That innate characteristic remains to the present. The bent of his inclinations was toward business. Though he worked with father

EDWARD TROUT

and me with the tools, which experience he afterwards found useful, yet that was not his purposeful employment. Fine writing, good bookkeeping, and business interested him. He acquired excellent proficiency in these lines, in the Bryant & Stratton Commercial College of Buffalo, New York. They were the pioneers in business teaching. His first independently earned money came from teaching winter writing classes in a number of the towns and villages of Ontario, Canada. The several prosperous years of business agency in behalf of the Leader Printing Company which began in 1861 and continued through 1867 have already been referred to. About this time, 1862, Edward married Jenny Kidd Gowanlock, of Stratford, Ontario, Canada, who will later receive attention. His first independent business venture was the purchase of a half interest in the British American Business College of Toronto. Two or three years later, he became sole owner. This was a prosperous undertaking and was favorably sold out about nine years afterwards. While Edward was at the head of the advertising department, John was also on the staff of the Toronto Leader as market reporter. He and Edward, without detracting from their Leader service, put their wits and their funds together and published a Market Bulletin. This continued for a while, and the proprietor, James Beaty, kicked up such a row about their building up their business ambitions on his basis, that they left the old man's service to seek out a new venture. The little Market Bulletin suggested something more ambitious. So John projected the Monetary Times, and enlisted the help of W. E. Foster, a rising young lawyer, who agreed to write the editorials; John to conduct the general business of the paper. They published a commendable journal, but were slow in getting subscriptions, and the relation with Foster was not at all satisfactory. John was carrying the main load, and felt that there was poor progress. He employed Edward, as an expert bookkeeper, to examine and report on the whole result of nearly three years' business. The report showed expenses greater than income by several hundred dollars, though neither partners had drawn salaries. Pressure was brought to bear on Foster to sell, and Edward to buy; but Edward would not purchase, regarding Foster's claim too high. It appears, however, that John bought out Foster, and continued the paper alone. In the summer business college vacation, John, knowing Edward's ability as a canvasser, had him go down to Montreal in the general interests of the paper; and in the course of ten days such an advance was made, that John gave Edward no peace till he arranged his college business, so as to give his whole attention to the finances of the Monetary Times, which he accordingly did; and at the end of a year bought a third interest for three thousand dollars; when a year previous he refused Foster's half-interest at one thousand dollars. Under this good combined management, with John as chief editor, determining the character of the paper, and Edward looking after the subscriptions and general business, it grew amazingly, absorbing two Journals of Commerce, the Trade Review and Insurance Chronicle; attaining the high respect of the great bankers and business men of the various provinces, some of whom were contributors; Sir Francis Hincks, a former premier of the Dominion, being an occasional writer on government finances. It was educative in the direction of good business management, and critical, when giving the lists of failures, exposing fraud and commending honorable effort. This critical course made it liable at times to suits for damages; but so circumspect was the course of the paper regarding its facts, that in its thirty-five years under the Trout control, only one hundred and fifty dollars were so paid. There were a number of suits; one adventurer, after being pretty fully exposed, instituted suit for fifty thousand dollars. This hung along in an uncertain way for three years; at one time seven hundred dollars costs were assessed against the Monetary Times. Two directors, that were actively connected with the company, insisted on paying these costs and closing the case. Edward replied, "You know he is a scoundrel, yet you are willing to give in to him. I will fight him to the end." Then they replied, "You should use your own money, not the company's." Edward accepted their challenge, made his appeal, demanded bonds from the plaintiff, to cover probable costs; and at the final trial non-suited him, recovering fifteen hundred dollars' costs, which his bondsmen paid, and which Edward turned into the treasury of the company without protest from the former cringing directors. This is only one instance out of many, showing the moral stamina that stood behind the paper, and which resulted in the wholesome respect of would-be crooks and speculating grafters. No matter how specious the plea, and strong the inducements, the Monetary Times stood like a rock for the right and the public good. At John's death, Edward purchased his interest, and continued, as he had done for more than a year previously, the full charge of the paper. He did not write much. His steady dependence for this work was on Mr. Lindsay, the veteran former editor of The Leader, a son-in-law of William Lyon MacKenzie, who once was looked upon as Canada's arch rebel, but now occupies a high niche as one of her noted worthies. Mr. Headly was the man in the business editor's office. A prosperous adjunct was the Monetary Times Printing Company, of which Edward was the president, and Mr. Todd the successful manager.

On the first of July, 1902, the Times was sold out to the present proprietors, who seem to maintain its good standing. Edward had also a good interest in The Toronto Paper Manufacturing Company, and was until 1908 its secretary-treasurer. In 1903 he bought a small tract of land in Florida, and built a winter residence there, returning to Toronto in the summer time. About 1907 this southern property was sold, and a visit to the Bahamas made and a sojourn in California.

Edward was always considerate of his poorer relatives. He would give rising, struggling, young folks a chance. A good number received free tuition in his college. Those that were struck with hard luck, received more than sympathy; this I have a right to know. No children were born to him, but two young fatherless relatives of Mrs. Trout were adopted, and taught and trained to be of great service to themselves, their parents and society.

In the year 1889, the year of the great Paris Exposition, Edward and Mrs. Trout spent the greater part of the summer at Paris, and in visits and excursions in England and Scotland; both having relatives in the last highly interesting country. During their absence the Monetary Times business and work was conducted so successfully, that at the end of the year, when profits were declared, a big slice went back to those whose management and faithfulness contributed to the result. The typos were not left out. He rightly regarded it all as their extra earnings while relieving him of care and worry.

In the summer of 1903 Edward made another trip to Europe, taking with him his daughter Nellie, and niece Mary Stirling. The Rhine provinces, Switzerland, Italy and France, as well as Great Britain, were visited. This was more for the benefit of the young folks than for his own pleasure.

The winter of 1907 and 1908 was spent in Los Angeles, California, and a decision was reached in the spring to sell most all his remaining property in Canada, and remove to a permanent home in Hollywood, California. This was done in the early autumn of 1908. The beautiful home they have there is the present family residence.

In the same summer the Canadian owners of the Los Casados Silver Mine in Northern Mexico, persuaded him to make it a visit, which he did. As Edward could not claim any knowledge of mining, my brother Peter, who is an expert, just then from Nome, Alaska, was taken along, the mine owners paying the cost of the journey. Peter made a careful examination of the property below and above ground, and reported abundance of accessible ore for a great many years to come. Edward bought a good block of stock. The money to be used to install a steam plant and modern mining machinery. The Diaz regime was then in power, Mexican investments were generally regarded as good, though there were mutterings of the coming storm but it was not thought to be serious. Fortunately the new plant was not installed, as there would be then something to tax or seize or destroy. The mine has been working in a moderate way by manual labor entirely, paying its own expenses. Their immunity from trouble, no doubt, coming from the fact that there was little or nothing to steal, the ore was too heavy to carry away and there was nothing

DR. JENNY KIDD GOWANLOCK TROUT

that was readily convertible into cash. If a dependable stable government becomes established in Mexico, there is a possibility that Edward's heirs may reap some benefit. Poor Mexico! Other suffering countries have some hope, but there is poor prospect in Mexico.

We regard Edward as the best physically preserved member of our family. He early learned how to take care of himself, and he had a good doctor wife to help him. He kept up a moderate system of health exercises, which he and sister Jenny urged upon me. The value of gymnastics to young people I could readily understand, but had doubts about its needs to old age, though I well know that a moderate amount of muscular effort each day is essential to the maintenance of strength. Edward has certainly well maintained his. A year and a half ago, in the beginning of his eightieth year, he and his daughter walked from Hollywood to Pasadena, seven miles, and made the return journey the same day. Of course, I am handicapped by my loose hip joint, but my strength now would not allow me to make one-tenth of that journey. This fall of 1915 we much regret to learn that Edward's health is failing very much, so that he does not feel at liberty to make long journeys alone. While my strength and activity is much less than his, yet the general uniformity of my condition I think warrants me in making my usual Texas fall journey, soon to take place. Our remaining three brothers and one sister are all, as John Muir has said, near sundown; so it would be idle to speculate as to probabilities. It is satisfying to know that all are ready.

We must now leave Edward and make some extended reference to his life partner.

DR. JENNY KIDD GOWANLOCK TROUT.

Whatever may be the advantages of wide choice in the selection of a wife Edward had them over his brothers. Being the general agent of the Toronto Leader, his business brought him to all parts of the country, renewing old acquaintance and forming new ones. Good attention to business never left the young ladies out of consideration: and a young chap,

with the poise and dash for a successful news agent, was
bound to receive their attention. What seeming chance conditions resulted in a first acquaintance with the chosen one is
not to me at present known. When she taught a good, large
country school near Stratford, Ontario, he would keep a sharp
lookout after business in that section, and come around Friday
afternoons with the fine fleet steed and good riding rig his
employer furnished, and would take her home. Of course,
that was a nice journey for her, and nice for him, too, to ride
alongside of a graduate of the Ontario Normal school, who as
teachers outranked all others; but the real interest was not in
the teacher, that was only incidental, it was in the girl.
There was sure to be needed business for Saturday, and on
Monday another happy journey to the school.

Miss Gowanlock was born in Kelso, Scotland, April 21,
1841, and came to Canada with her parents in 1847. She was
educated in the schools of Stratford, Canada. She was baptized, and took upon herself the Christian name and profession in Toronto in 1860. She graduated from the Ontario
Normal school in the same city in 1861, and continued teaching in the neighborhood of Stratford, till in 1865, through
marriage with my brother Edward, she became Mrs. Trout;
and all her earlier married life was lived in Toronto. Having
no children, and occasionally subject to troublesome nervous
bodily ailments, and also with her studious disposition and
time on her hands, it is easy to see that health matters should
have first consideration; and be studied not only for her
own sake, but for the help she might give others. Accordingly, she took a course of study in the Pennsylvania Women's
Medical College in Philadelphia, and in due time graduated;
but as that gave her no legal standing in Canada, she entered
the College of Physicians and Surgeons in Toronto, and after
three years passed her final examination in 1875, and became
the first woman member of the medical and surgical fraternity of Canada, and first lady licensed practitioner in the
Dominion. Edward in relating this to me shortly afterward,
said that when calling at the office to take her home, he was
roundly complimented by the examiners on behalf of his

talented wife who had so creditably passed the trying examination. Being the wife of the Monetary Times man, the press of the country took up her story, and gave it the widest circulation. As a consequence she was soon deluged with letters from women in all parts of the country, seeking relief from their physical ailments. Being of a highly sympathetic nature, this disconcerted her immensely. She could not possibly meet the calls and had in self-defense either to limit her work to her moderate strength and endurance, or take on help. The latter course was chosen, and a large sanatarium was the final outcome, which though accomplishing much, was, as stated previously, a losing investment, and too severe a strain on Dr. Trout; accordingly she retired from medical practice in 1882, but did not loose her interest in it. She advocated the advisability of a Woman's Medical College in Toronto, and offered ten thousand dollars to help start it. Other wealthy ladies backed it. Disagreements as to its control delayed it for a number of years. Finally, however, with Dr. Trout's assistance a good college was started, and is now of significant interest in that great educational center. Our missionary cousin, Dr. Martha Smith, of India, being one of its graduates in 1902.

With Dr. Trout, however, the interest in medical matters was gradually eclipsed by her increasing interest in Bible study and missions. She never had any interest in "Society," was always disposed to retirement and seclusion.

She is the grandaunt of their adopted children, Helen Huntsman Trout, and Edward Huntsman Trout. Both are well educated, the latter having taken his B. S. degree at the University of California in 1913, and is now completing an extended course in Harvard.

In answer to my request regarding her ancestry, I received the following: "About the middle of the 18th century the first man of our name (Gowanlock) reached Scotland, he and his family having to flee from southern Switzerland in consequence of persecution. He was a minister and preached his first sermon, in Scotland, standing on a flat tombstone in the cemetery of *Judburg* Abbey. On my mother's side we came from the Danes. My grandmother, Elizabeth Haldane, being born in Haldane Hall.

My father was born in 1790 and died in 1874. He married my mother in Coldstream, Scotland, in 1817."

As stated at the beginning of this now lengthy family story, the Trouts claim no high pedigree, illustrious names, or long ancestry; but sister Jenny Kidd Gowanlock Trout has a decided lead on us in this respect. To be a part of the progeny of a persecuted Swiss preacher is a family credit well worth all the traditional remembrance that has handed it down. Humble he no doubt was, but he had seen fiery trials, and was of God's nobility. Besides this to have a Haldane for a grandmother the illustrious name that has for its crown the present Lord High Chancellor of England who lately visited the United States and received the homage and respect of the leading lawyers of the American bar. And back at the beginning of the last century two Haldane brothers, Robert and James, preachers of reform, called the people of Glasgow and Scotland back to the clear New Testament teachings, and the Apostolic church; and sought to embody it in the lives and conduct of their congregations. Alexander Campbell, when a student in Glasgow, had the advantage of their acquaintance, and the benefit of their teaching. Which no doubt gave the initiative for his work of restoration. But, after all, the oft quoted old couplet still holds good—"Honor and fame from no condition rise; act well your part, there all the honor lies." While Mrs. Trout has good ancestry behind her, she has also acted well her part and like more of us, the record is nearly made up.

JOHN MALCOLM TROUT

In the course of father's family account brief mention is made of John's marriage and Toronto residence. Unlike Edward, who had traveled so much and selected his girl, John might be said to have grown up with her, and they simply coalesced or grew together. It was the first and only love of both, and an unbroken one till the great Reaper made the separation, and then it was only an apparent or bodily separa-

JOHN MALCOLM TROUT
Founder of the Monetary Times, Toronto, Canada

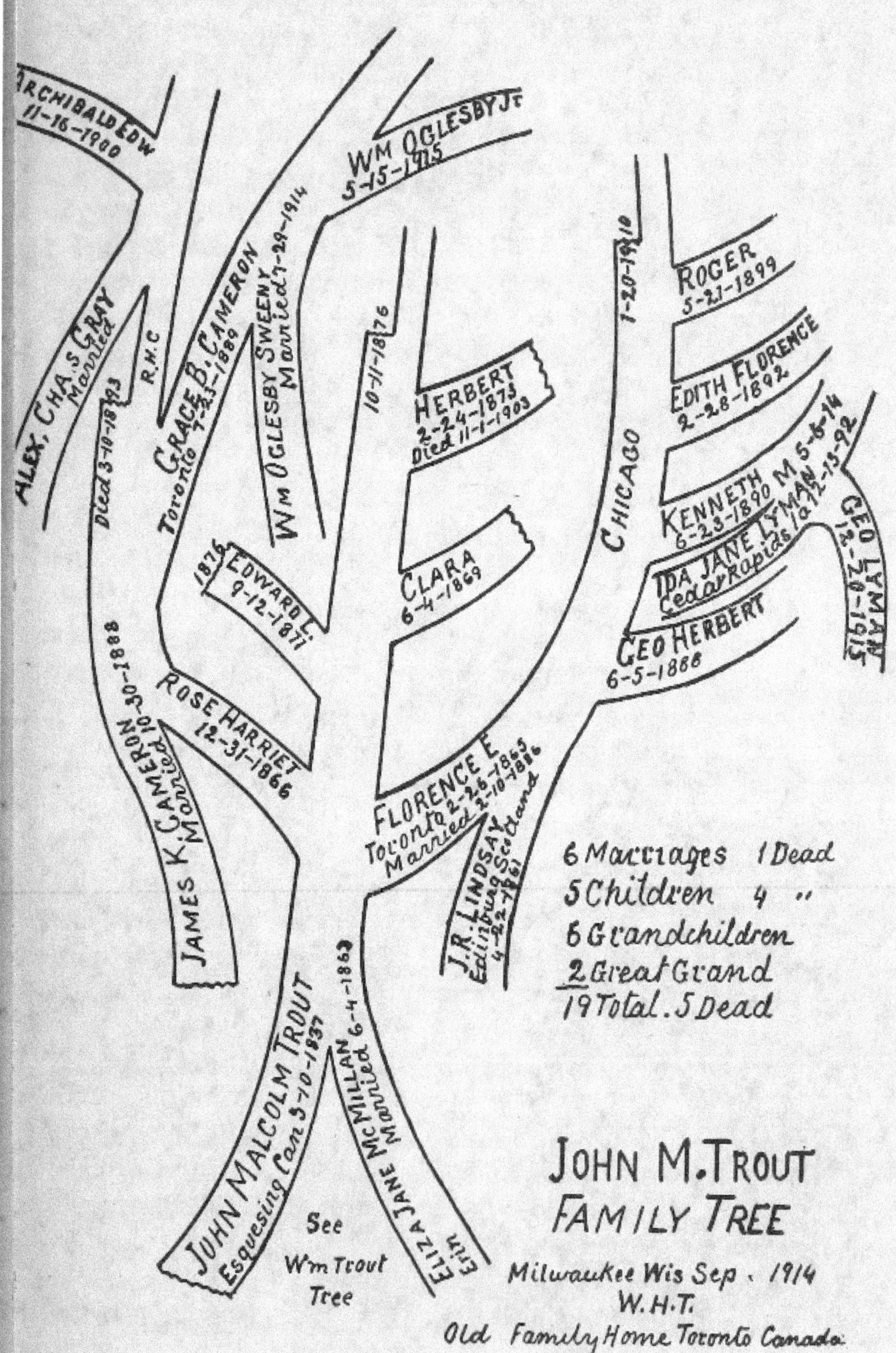
ARCHIBALD EDW
11-16-1900
WM OGLESBY Jr
5-15-1915
ROGER
5-21-1899
ALEX. CHAS GRAY
Married
Died 3-10-1893
R.H.C.
GRACE B. CAMERON
4-23-1869
Toronto
WM OGLESBY SWEENY
Married 1-29-1914
10-1-1876
HERBERT
2-4-1875
Died 11-1-1903
EDITH FLORENCE
2-28-1892
CHICAGO
1-20-1910
KENNETH M 5-6-14
6-23-1890
IDA JANE LYMAN
Cedar Rapids Ia
LYMAN 12-15-92
GEO LYMAN
12-20-1915
1876
EDWARD L.
9-12-1871
CLARA
6-4-1869
GEO HERBERT
6-5-1888
JAMES K. CAMERON 10-30-1888
Married
ROSE HARRIET
12-31-1866
FLORENCE E
Toronto 2-28-1865
Married 2-10-1886
J.R. LINDSAY
Edinburgh Scotland
4-22-1761
JOHN MALCOLM TROUT
Esquesing Can 3-10-1837
ELIZA JANE McMILLAN Married 6-4-1863
See
Wm Trout
Tree
6 Marriages   1 Dead
5 Children   4 "
6 Grandchildren
2 Great Grand
19 Total. 5 Dead
JOHN M. TROUT
FAMILY TREE
Milwaukee Wis Sep . 1914
W. H. T.
Old Family Home Toronto Canada

tion, for there is no evidence that Mrs. Trout ever entertained the possibility of any other union.

The residence of Edward McMillan was less than half a mile from our home. Father built it as well as his barn. I was his helper, and a few years ago was on a visit to the old neighborhood, and inspected the work done over sixty years previous. Among the jobs was the chopping and fitting, or in the parlance of the times, the "carrying up of the corner" of a good log stable which was regarded as the expert young bushman's job. The work was well done and is still all right, and we would have to travel far to find men who could do the same today. Along with father and D. L. Layton, Edward McMillan was also a leader in the Meaford church, and a cheerful, ready-witted conversationalist; this with Mrs. McMillan's kindly welcome, along with two handsome interesting daughters, the influence and attractions of the McMillan home can readily be understood. So that it seemed the most natural thing in the world that my ardent, ambitious younger brother John should lay his claim and win the heart and hand of the eldest daughter, Eliza Jane, and in due time when ready to begin their united life to marry her, as was done at her parental home on June 4, 1863, in the presence of assembled friends and relatives, father officiating. This was an important event, being the first breakaway from our large family of six boys and four girls, all but two being grown up; and it was more sensibly felt in the McMillan home because it deprived it of half the family. The wedded pair soon left us, and set up their new humble home in Toronto, in the modest manner befitting a young law student. He engaged as a helper in the law offices of James Beaty, Jr., et al., for which a moderate recompense was paid, which with the help of savings from the former school teaching was to carry him forward until sufficient advance in salary would be given to meet current expenses. He kept up his studies, and regularly passed the examinations; but the expected salary advance was postponed. Family responsibilities were increasing; a daughter was born to them. As a temporary arrangement, he took up market reporting for the Toronto Leader, where Edward was employed. By the time he expected to return to law study he found his work so congenial, and the pay and prospects so good, that he kept on, though still postponing his law purposes; but a further continuance, and progress in newspaper work, as related in Edward's story, led him to abandon the study of law, and give himself wholly to his new venture, the editing and publishing of the Monetary Times. At the same time he was assistant editor on the Toronto Evening Telegraph. The onerous character of his varied and exhaustive duties led him to induce Edward to leave his college business in other hands, and turn in and help him, which Edward did to the great advantage of both. The publishing undertaking brought them into public notice, and fine extensive and valuable business friendships were formed, all more or less willing to throw good chances in the way of the rising young men, yet equally anxious to receive their help and use them when they could, which is the usual good business game, that is, help the other fellow and have him help you. Professor Goodwin Smith and a Mr. Robertson (G. B., I think) and John got their heads in a close triangle and projected a new paper, to be independent in politics, and characteristically Canadian, to be called The Nation, to be published weekly, printed and issued by the Monetary Times Printing Company. It is easy to see that the great burden of the work fell upon the managing head and shoulders of the Monetary Times Company, and for a few years it was well carried; but when John's health failed The Nation began to fail, and he regretfully saw it die before he passed away. He remarked to me, "This never would have happened could I have kept behind it."

From the short but active business career so briefly told, the cause of his broken health may be easily guessed. He knew how to work, but never learned how to rest. His energy no doubt pushed him through the first stage of tuberculosis without a suspicion of the trouble. When it became manifest, so slow but steady was the progress of the disease, that his mental activity continued till near the last. Had we all known what is now so generally known regarding this malady, it is highly probable his valuable life might have been at least very greatly prolonged. The old idea of "hereditary taint" is exploded, still that notion lingers, else why do people want to hide this, when it causes the death of their relatives. The microbe is more or less prevalent everywhere. It is weakened resisting powers that allows it to get a good start, so that it becomes difficult or impossible to overcome. It is similar with pneumonia and many other diseases; but consumption or tuberculosis, without manifest reason, seems to be about the most unpopular malady to die by that we have. The bubonic plague, typhoid and other filth diseases are deservedly so, but not tuberculosis. However, it is fortunate that its ravages are diminishing.

It used to be a subject of remark that consumption usually carried off the pick of the family. It certainly seemed like that in John's case, he undoubtedly had more good, strong, alert and effective characteristics in his mental and physical makeup than had any of the rest of us. Beyond the cheerful, good, humorous manner in which friends were met, and in which the details of ordinary business was done, there was a decisive positive manner of treating all the greater questions in most every line of thought. He seemed to have preconsidered everything that came to his attention, and could quickly express himself regarding it. He had a masterful way of planning and disposing of his business, like as if it were an off-hand job. Like every member of the fourth estate, he had to be watchful and tactful, but when sure of being on the right ground he was bold and unflinching. His range of thinking and of study ran through the religious, political and business interests of the times in all of which he was at home. He was a good writer. A brief essay on "The Good Fight of Faith," published in the Bible Index of 1876, of which he was associate editor, will bear a comparison with much of the excellent literary work in our language. A reprint of this now follows:

THE GOOD FIGHT OF FAITH

(I Timothy 6, 12.)

There is peace which hell approves, and a war that heaven sanctions. One is the brush of the vampire's wing, humming the lullaby of death; the other, like the anguish pains of travail, eventuates in life and joy and beauty. (John 16, 21.) Since Satan usurped the world and the heart, he is for peace—peaceable possession. The strong man armed, having gained the palace, would keep his goods in peace. So the wolf in the fold craves freedom from hindrance while destroying the flock. "Let us alone, what have we to do with thee, thou Jesus of Nazareth," (Luke 4, 34), is the abject, base, cowardly, deprecatory, let-us-have-peace policy of demons. "The empire is peace," is the deceptive watchword along the lines of darkness. But there is, there can be, no peace. An irrepressible conflict has been inaugurated. The "enmity" has been divinely put (Genesis 3, 15). The presence of sin in the mortal alembic excites to their intensest activity the expelling energies of holiness. Truth waits not to be attacked, but marshals her hosts for aggressive war. She neither sends nor receives truce, but fights to the death. The horsemen of Israel are rough riders, the chariots thereof rush furiously along the steeps of sin. God's heroes have ever been troublers of the world. Enoch, the seventh from Adam, reproving an ungodly race; Noah, a preacher of righteousness, condemning all the world except his own little family (how very uncharitable in that old-fashioned saint); Moses in the Egyptian court with his hated refrain, "Thus saith the Lord, let my people go, that they may serve me"; with Elijah and Micah (I Kings 18, 17), whose names come to us across the ages as the troublers of wicked kings and idolatrous priests; these only anticipate the captain of our salvation, who came, not to send peace, but a sword (Matthew 10, 34), to kindle a fire (Luke 12, 49), to produce division, and set mankind at variance. In righteousness doth he make war. The stronger than the strong man (Luke 11, 12) hath taken from him his armour wherein he trusted. Satan trusted in words to destroy, and lo, the gospel is the word of salvation. A lie spoken, heard, believed, and obeyed, makes us servants of him. The truth spoken, heard, believed and obeyed, makes us servants of righteousness (Rom. 6). Driven from the citadel of the Spirit, Satan entrenches himself in the flesh, and risks all upon his ability to hold captive the body in the grave. Death is the very gate of his power. Vain boast! The stronger than the strong will not permit him in peace to retain the human body. He goes down into the pit. Now is the judgment (Greek, crisis) of this world (John 12, 31); now shall the prince of this world be cast out. The crisis battle was fought in the grave, since which the complete subjection of all opposing influences is only a question of time. The struggle in the death pass was short; crushing the defeat. The prisoners of hope are released. (Zech. 9-12.) The weapon in which the strong man trusted is taken away from him. Death is destroyed, captivity led captive. The Lord is a man of war. The Lord has triumphed gloriously. The Lord, strong and mighty in battle, hath all our foes o'ercome; and now by death we shall be saved from death, and life eternal gain.

> "See truth, love, and mercy in triumph descending,
> And nature all smiling in Eden's first bloom;
> On the cold cheek of death smiles and roses are blending,
> And beauty immortal awakes from the tomb."

Tremble not, soldier of the cross, at the trumpet blast of strife. It is the stern necessity of our fallen state. The storm cloud, the thunder crash, and the lightning's vivid glare are followed by the beautiful blue of the atmosphere, the music of birds, the fragrance of flowers. The evening as well as the morning make the moral, as they do the physical, day. Bliss is the child of contrast. The rest that remaineth for the people of God is a rest for the weary. Suffering precedes glory; the cross, the crown. The healing virtue imparted to Siloam's waters must be diffused from the troubling angel's wing. Liberty blooms in the track of revolution. Religion is not the frail, sickly sentimentalism that many paint it. Its baby clothes were sprinkled with the blood of Bethlehem's slaughtered innocents. The good fight of faith is a great fight of affliction. Christianity is a nursling of the storm; was rocked into vigor upon the purple crest of opposition. The apostles, as they sped along the highways of earth with the message of salvation, were hailed as the troublers of cities, and the upside-down turners of the world. Princes trembled in their presence; the faces of priests gathered blackness. Hated of all men for his name's sake, they ceased not from aggressive war till judgment was brought forth unto victory; rested not, but resisted unto blood, striving against sin, and now await the victor's crown beneath the altar. Shall we be worthy of the society of those who attained heaven through much tribulation? Of some it is said, "They shall walk in white, for they are worthy." What is it to be worthy of the world to come? The soldier who endures with his leader the toil of the weary march and the dangers of battle, is accounted worthy to share with him the wealth of victory and the glory of the triumph. Jesus says, "He that taketh not up his cross and followeth after Me, is not worthy of Me." To be worthy of Christ is to be worthy of the world to come—of white robes, of the palm and the victor's wreath. If we suffer with Him we shall also reign with Him. Again, "Where I am, there also shall my servant be." What is it to be with Jesus? Where upon the sands of time shall we search for the footprints of this sublime life? Evermore would the young convert linger with Him upon the flowery banks of the baptismal scene, while the sweet voice of a new found Father is sounding in his ears, and the dove of peace is nestling at his heart. But it may not be, for the Jordan and the heavenly recognition give place to the wilderness and the temptation. We must be wet with the midnight dews that fall upon the Mount of Supplication, if we would stand with Him beneath the overshadowing glory of the holy Mount of Transfiguration. In the cottage of the poor, sitting at the bedside of the sick, binding up the broken heart, going about doing good—here is where we shall find the blessed Saviour.

(The following piling up of gloomy, trying conditions can be better understood by referring to John's peculiar situation. A few years previous he had lost a little daughter, Clara, and about the time of this writing, a son, five years old—Edward, died of diphtheria; while himself was well started in the last stage of tuberculosis; how easily, then, discouraging thoughts could be gathered into those fine sentences; but the sunlight of hope shines in at the last. —W. H. T.)

And when the hour is come, when the crisis sorrow of life is upon us and the soul is exceeding sorrowful even unto death, when those upon whom we leaned for support fail us; when churches whose prosperity we prize as we do life, are swept to ruin before the dreadful sin tempest; when death sits at the hearthstone, and none shall wait and watch with us in our Gethsemane; when the trial comes and all deny us; when the dearest hopes and loves of our being expire amid the darkness and the earthquake, and the

DR. HERBERT TROUT

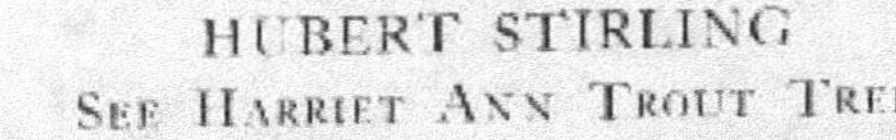

HUBERT STIRLING
See Harriet Ann Trout Tree

terrified spirit driven from anchorage in the heavens, shrieks her despairing wail, "My God, why hast Thou forsaken me." O, then is the time to remember that "God hath said that He would dwell in the thick darkness"—that this, after all, is being with Jesus; that the pathway of worthiness lies across the burning marl of tribulation, and just beyond the agony and Calvary is the garden of the resurrection, beautiful with the sunlight of immortality. Yes, the good fight is a great fight of affliction. They loved not their lives unto death. We may not die for Christ, but much weariness and painfulness attend upon the march heavenward. We war against spiritual wickedness in high places, and what is more difficult, to subdue the promptings of our own heart, more than the pope and all his cardinals. The conflict between the law in our members (Rom. 7) and the law of the spirit will end with life. Let us put on the whole armour, and praying with all prayer, and watching thereunto, gird ourselves anew for the fight. The old year has gone with those beyond the flood. A new year takes its place. Shall we in the "storms that sweep our wintry sky," hear "the sound of a going" and arouse us to smite the hosts of the enemy (2 Sam. 5, 24). The "conflict of ages" was never more sanguine than now. Never was sin more impudent in its mien, nor potent in its sway. Inadequate views of the malignant nature and tendency of sin, coupled with a chilling indifference, is the bane of the present generation. O, that the "enmity" between us and the serpent were quickened anew. All intelligences, supernal and infernal, are actively engaged. Shall men, on account of whom this strife is waged, remain neutral?

> "This soul of thine, God's wondrous breath,
> It keeps two worlds in strife;
> Hell moves from beneath to work its death,
> Heaven stoops to give its life."

John seemed to prosper financially in every undertaking except The Nation. The Monetary Times became a business journal of wide influence and good profit; and the Monetary Times Printing Company under the able submanagement of Mr. Todd gave steady and profitable returns. In this way he was not only enabled to build a good home, costing near six thousand dollars but also to have provided at his decease a good permanent fund for the support and education of his family. As previously told Edward succeeded to the business and was the principal administrator of his estate.

His was a brief but rather brilliant career. Cut off at forty when good progressive men, such as he, have hardly attained the height of their powers. We looked forward to a magnificent life of high service. So did he. Such a life was needed, and he more than anyone saw its need. We were all disappointed. We saw the aspiring masterful soul struggling to find its expression through a declining, wasted, emaciated body, till it finally was of no possible further use; and like the worn out garment, had to be thrown away. The triumphant spirit was there still, but the bodily expression was cut off. The influence of the life is still with us, but the life itself has gone on, and has taken on the "the manifestation of the sons of God." It becomes "clothed upon with the house from heaven," has "a spiritual body," "like His glorious body" when "we shall see him as he is." Disappointments here and the failures of the flesh must be a part of our reckoning, but the triumphant spirit led by the conqueror of death meets no disappointment, sees no defect, or possible despair. That even the good purposes and plans of this earthly life go forward in the life to come can hardly be entertained, because they are cut off from their necessary material manifestations. But the resulting character continues, and it is quite admissible that character-growth and progress may continue, if "we shall be like Him." Why may we not be *more* like Him?

This is getting to be a disquisition on immortality, which was not our intention; but was manifestly suggested by the gradually failing bodily powers of a great life.

The accompanying family tree, page 283, shows that five children were born to them, a son and a daughter dying in childhood. Two daughters and a son reached manhood and womanhood. All had the advantages of the great educational facilities afforded in Toronto. Herbert, the youngest, had a complete university education, and besides graduated in medicine and surgery, and was licensed to practice. He held for a year or two a position under the Ontario government, where he had the care and oversight of the Indians and half-breeds on the islands and north shore of Georgian bay. While engaged in this duty he contracted tuberculosis, and died at the age of thirty. This was the second sore disappointment for his mother, who had so long been his companion and helper in the attainment of his education and general oversight of his needs. Her two daughters had been for a long time married, and in charge of their own homes; he alone was her charge, and at the beginning of his usefulness was taken from her, leaving her in her sorrowing loneliness.

JAMES TROUT   DONALD TROUT
GRANDSON   WILLIAM E. TROUT
SON

Florence, the eldest daughter, married a young Canadian lawyer, J. R. Lindsay, formerly of our old home township, St. Vincent, afterward of Duluth, Iowa, but finally of Chicago, Illinois, where a fine family of three boys and one girl has been reared, Mrs. Lindsay, however, passing away in Chicago a few years ago. The second daughter, Rose Harriet, married Mr. James Cameron of Toronto to whom a daughter, Grace, was born. She is now the wife of Wm. O. Sweeney, and the French professor in Transylvania university. They have a son, William Oglesby, Jr. Mr. Cameron died and Mrs. Cameron married Alexander Charles Gray, a young minister in the Christian church at Toronto; afterward he was minister at Cincinnati, Ohio, and for a time professor and president at Eureka College, where he now resides. One son, Archibald Edward, was born to them. Mr. Gray lately took post-graduate studies in Yale, passing with high credit, and adding to his title degrees. Mrs. John Trout now (January, 1916) resides with her daughter and family in Eureka, Illinois.

JAMES TROUT

(See William Trout Tree, page 53.)

James is our fourth brother. He was the farmer boy that stayed at home. The only one that farmed with any real farming purpose; and even that did not last very long. The only farming feature in which he made any distinction was in his breed of pigs, and that was only on a moderate scale; but he always carried off first prizes at the township shows, and sold his pigs at fancy prices.

In 1869 he married Mary Williams, daughter of John Williams, one of the old respected pioneers, magistrate, clerk of the division court, township clerk, and treasurer. The farm was their home for only three or four years. James sold it and they moved into the town of Meaford, and engaged in money lending, insurance and real estate business, with C. H. Jay as partner.

On the door of their large office safe they had a well-painted significant picture. It was a water scene—a fine big trout was making his leap out of the water to catch a big fly; and above the fly was a jay perched on a limb ready to pounce down on the fly should the trout miss him. Indicating that they were sure to catch and serve their customer; whether to his benefit or their own, or both, might only be afterwards determined. I know that James regarded his business as a useful public service; and I think had a right to so regard it. He had the quality of mind in a high degree of readily understanding people; and not only adapting himself and what he might have to sell them to their benefit; but also to adapt people to one another. Sometimes, among family connections, there would be a property row hard to understand and still harder to settle; but he would soon see through it and what could be done with it, to the general satisfaction of all and some profit to himself. Or, in the winding up of a heavily involved, complicated estate, his genius was in seeing at once all the possible solutions of the problems and working them out to the interest of those concerned. His abounding good nature, tact, and agreeableness, helped him through everything.

Like all father's children the welfare of the church and the cause of Christ were matters of chief concern. He was never associated with any other than the Meaford congregation of the Disciples of Christ. Like many more of those brethren, his beliefs in the New Testament teaching were exceedingly well defined and there seemed to them no possible logical basis for any difference of view. However, he was never harsh in judgment on those who might not agree with him. He was too kind for that. About a month previous to his death, I made him a last special visit. He had been fighting against a slow, but fatal, kidney disease for a good number of years. Its final strangle grip was then upon him. His feet and legs were so greatly swelled as to be of little service. During that winter, 1905, he had been confined to his room; his heart weakness did not allow him much lying down. His mind was clear, and his resignation and cheerfulness constant. Toward his helpful, loving wife he had that cordial easy, kindly manner that cuts out trouble, and leaves no place for pain. When she would be helping him, I have

PETER LAIRD TROUT

known him to remark to me "Mary and I have been having the time of our life this winter. We had some of our courting over again, and we are having a second honeymoon too." But the honeymoon did not last long, for, less than a month after that, his spirit took its place among the immortals. The date being February 16, 1906.

Mrs. Trout still retains her home in Meaford, looks after the property left her, which is ample for her needs and the help she may give to others. They had only one son and one daughter; the latter dying of diphtheria in childhood. See William Trout tree, James Trout branch, page 53. The son, William E. Trout, married Emily W. Lewis in 1894. Their first homekeeping and business venture being in Detroit. Afterwards they removed to Toronto, where he held, for a good number of years, a leading place in a manufacturing plant for business office conveniences and supplies. Of late years he has followed his father's pursuit; hoping, if possible, to rival his dad in the handling of real estate. William E. Trout is a good singer. This was undoubtedly his mother's share in his heredity, she being a good singer and James the only one of us who did not sing. William taught singing and led a good choir at the Toronto Bathurst street Church of Christ. He enjoyed immensely the service of a fine speedy horse to which he would willingly give his personal attention, and the horse would most sympathetically respond to his master's wish. He would spring at a hint, and slacken as required. A ride with William behind one of his favorites was a spell of fine mental exhilaration. William and Emily have a fine growing up family of four lively children, two girls and two boys, besides one little boy that died in childhood. We look to those to ultimately carry forward their share of the good reputation that has come down to them in father's family line.

PETER LAIRD TROUT

Mother used to tell her friends that she had the three-select apostles in her family—Peter, James and John, but she had them in their inverse order, John, James and Peter. Of the five brothers in succession the first three, Edward, John and myself were a group by ourselves; when we were grown up, the other two were boys, and so they continued to be regarded, though they became much bigger men than we were, being over six feet tall and much heavier. In 1908 when Peter returned from Nome, he, Edward and I were weighed. He weighed two hundred and seventy pounds which was ten pounds heavier than both Edward and I together. He was not "incorporated" either. The youngest was the biggest, still they were always "the boys." They seemed like a well-mated pair, yet there were natural marked characteristic differences between them, which became more apparent as they grew older. Peter was studious and quiet and an omnivorous reader. James read very little, but was talkative and observing. Peter had the newspaper news all down fine, and he remembered it; he seemed to have an unlimited capacity of memory. Compared to what he read and retained, the little everyday family and social happenings were of small account, and were not always noted or considered. Though James had the least educational advantages of any of us, yet they were sufficient for his business needs, and were of the everyday practical character for which his natural abilities seemed so well fitted. He could readily see the others point of view and tactfuly act with regard to it. Peter was the recluse, the quiet reader and thinker, who dealt with ideas as well as facts, and drew his own settled conclusions without consulting others, and held to them. He had the same heritage of good principles inwrought and ingrained by the teaching and example of our parents, which was common to all of us. With this, and his exceptional memory powers, studious, concentrated thinking, and persistence, it is easy now to see that with such teaching and training as would bring to use his more latent powers, there was the promise and possibility of a rare, clever, useful man in the lines of his natural talent. But we did not see it. Father did not see it. The educators might have missed it. Scientific pedagogy and psychology were then little known. Peter, when grown up, went for one winter to the Grammar school in Owen Sound, which was the last of his school education, and the most at the time that we could do for him. This was small indeed, but when each was contributing to the common family good, we had to make the best with the attainable. Peter taught school for one school year in a Quaker settlement in the township of Sydenham. Old style Quaker peculiarities and solemnity amused him greatly. He could recite some of their solemn sonorous sermons in their awe-inspiring manner.

He understood saw-mill work better than most any other, having learned it with me. When our mill was burned we all separated, each for himself. Peter spent one summer at saw-mill work on the Christian island. Afterwards bought a small water power site on a beautiful mountain stream in Collingwood township; built a small circular mill and dwelling house, and married Elizabeth Hewgill, a thrifty farmer's daughter, and a good practical style of a girl of that neighborhood. They made their home at the mill, where one daughter and two sons were born to them. After six years' residence there, this mill property was sold and the family removed to Toronto, where after a temporary residence of several months they removed to Hamilton, where a large house was rented, and a combined sanitarium and boarding place was instituted and conducted for a few years. Here, though both were anxiously active for the general family welfare, yet the differences, in modes of thought and matters of judgment, culminated in a personal separation, at least, until such time as he hoped to be able to accumulate the means to make life at home less strenuous. But in this there was only very moderate success.

Not long after this Chicago became the family home. Mrs. Trout entered a good medical school, and in due time graduated, and obtained a good medical practice. Their children went through their common and high school courses with further educational preparation for their special pursuits.

While all this mainly depended on each one's effort, and their mutual help, yet well-deserved credit is due to willing relatives for substantial help, advice and interest, all through the hard places in this good family progress.

Cathrine Jane, the eldest, prepared herself well for the teaching profession, and has been teaching for many years in Chicago, holding a principal's certificate, though not the position. Charles Eliphalet took a civil engineering course, and graduated from the Massachusetts Institute of Technology, and now holds an important position on the engineering staff of New York City. He is married and has four children. (See Wm. Trout tree, page 53.) Edgar William had the misfortune in his boyhood to lose his foot, the leg being severed between knee and ankle, by a railway car, and though having an artificial substitute, is still deprived of much of his natural activity. He also became a teacher, and, besides, took up a course of law study, and became a recognized member of the Chicago bar; but he never hung out his shingle. There were too many impecunious shingles begging for business out already. As a teacher he was doing well, and his star was rising. He was for a few years principal of one of the penal institutions of Chicago, the House of Correction, where by his suggestion some useful reforms were effected. Though a good position, yet by his own choice it was given up, and he is now principal of one of the city elementary schools.

He was married to Miss Mabel Gerlach of Chicago, December 26, 1914, and now resides in this big Western metropolis, where his mother, Dr. Elizabeth Trout, and her daughter, Cathrine Jane, also reside. Charles Edward has his home in Westerleigh, Staten Island, which is a part of greater New York city.

Peter, after his long peregrinations on the Pacific coast and far north to the Arctic sea, has come back among his relatives where, in several instances his mining experience and judgment has been drawn upon to some advantage, the last being in the summer of 1915, when he was requested to visit and report on some new prospects near Hudson bay. As much of the journey had to be made through the woods on foot, and up the small rivers in canoes, and he being an old man, with enough of that kind of experience, he wisely gave up the job. While I am now writing this tame story about him and others in my prosy family history, he may be writing some of his tales of "hairbreadth escapes and thrilling incidents in flood and field," which will appear in his proposed forthcoming book "Memoires of Alaska."

CHARLES EDWARD TROUT   CATHRINE JANE TROUT   EDGAR WILLIAM TROUT

See William Trout Tree

However, in these stirring times, when bloody, barbarous and inhuman war is the overshadowing concern of all humanity, it is not at all unlikely that family and personal considerations might be for the time of small account. Still, the family is the God given foundational unit of society, and it will live and retain its interest, when, as we assuredly believe, "men shall learn war no more."

"When the war drum throbs no longer, and the battle flags are
        furled;
In the parliament of man, the federation of the world."

MRS. HARRIET ANN TROUT STIRLING

Harriet was mother's eldest daughter. After five successive boys held the innings, she led the girls to the bat, and she truly was a leader, not from any particular disposition to control but from her natural capabilities and energies. As a girl she was always the liveliest and merriest of any group. In a party of young folks, with a lively mate, there would be no possible chance for dullness. Sprightly thinking and clear, rapid speaking was her regular style, with always a quick sense of the humorous, which would soon be brought to others' notice and enjoyment. When about twenty-one years of age (though in memory she seemed much younger), it was decided that Harriet be educated and trained to be a good thorough teacher, with a life certificate, and the specially designed place to obtain this was the Normal School of Toronto. But first it was considered advisable that a preparatory course be taken in the Model School, which was connected with the Normal. I had some business that brought me to Toronto, and she came with me. I introduced myself and sister to Mrs. Clark, the principal of the Model School, explaining our purpose. She replied that the school was absolutely full, and she had been refusing pupils for a month past.

But good teachers know how to estimate pupils at sight, so she decided that Harriet should not be turned down, and replied, that having come so far, with the Normal course as the outcome, she must find room for her. Mrs. Clark was like

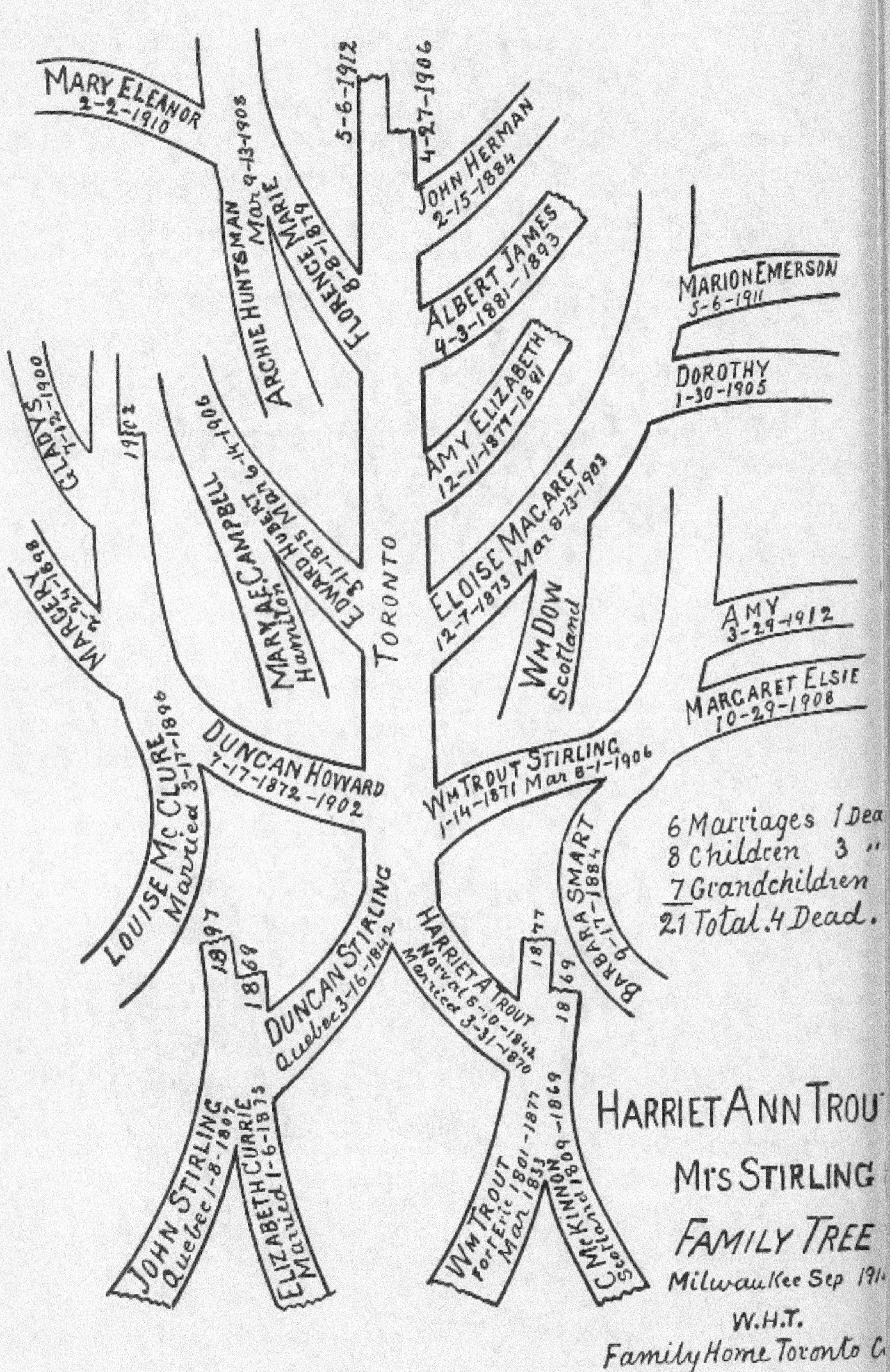
MARY ELEANOR
2-2-1910
ARCHIE HUNTSMAN Mar 4-13-1905
FLORENCE MARIE 8-8-1879
5-6-1912
4-27-1906
JOHN HERMAN
2-15-1884
ALBERT JAMES
4-3-1881-1893
MARION EMERSON
5-6-1911
AMY ELIZABETH
12-11-1877-1891
DOROTHY
1-30-1905
GLADYS 7-12-1900
1903
EDWARD HUBERT 3-11-1875 Hamilton
MARY A. F. CAMPBELL 6-14-1906
ELOISE MACARET
12-7-1873 Mar 8-13-1903
MARGERY 2-24-1868
WM DOW
Scotland
AMY
3-29-1912
TORONTO
MARGARET ELSIE
10-29-1908
LOUISE McCLURE Married 3-17-1896
DUNCAN HOWARD
7-17-1872-1902
WM TROUT STIRLING
1-14-1871 Mar 8-1-1906
6 Marriages 1 Dea
8 Children 3 "
7 Grandchildren
21 Total. 4 Dead.
1897
1869
DUNCAN STIRLING
Quebec 3-16-1842
HARRIET A TROUT
Norval 6-10-1844
Married 3-31-1870
BARBARA SMART 6-11-1884
1877
1869
JOHN STIRLING
Quebec 1-8-1807
ELIZABETH CURRIE 1-6-1815
Married
WM TROUT
Norfolk 1801-1877
Mar 1833
1877
1869
C McKINNON 1809-1869
Scotland
HARRIET ANN TROU
Mrs STIRLING
FAMILY TREE
Milwaukee Sep 191
W.H.T.
Family Home Toronto C

HARRIET ANN TROUT STIRLING

DUNCAN STIRLING

a great mother in the school. Scarce any discipline was needed. It was a rule of love. This school life and city life, residing with my brother John, was a most valuable experience to Harriet. When nearly two years had passed, and she had obtained her first-class Normal School certificate, and was ready to return home, it was arranged that she should come to a big June meeting in Erin, and a number of us would meet her there, and bring her home with us. When the big concourse was assembling, I was watching the door for Harriet; when she entered, I rose up and signaled, she came, and room was made for her between James and I. Finding herself after such a long absence between her two big brothers was too great for her gravity, which her countenance showed; she just wanted to pinch us both, and have a squabble right there in meeting. Harriet's natural and acquired teaching ability gave her the best places. Meaford was her stamping ground for a number of years, where as a teacher she was respected and loved.

In 1870 Harriet married Duncan Stirling, son of John Stirling of St. Vincent, formerly of Quebec province. The Stirling family and our Trout family were close friends, which partly accounts for the double root parentage of the Harriet Ann family as shown by the tree. This departure also shows the fine old age attained by the head of the Stirling family. He lived the full term of ninety years, and they were ninety years of good health and bodily activity. He told me he never had a headache and scarcely the tinge of a toothache. But this physical characteristic did not descend to his children, they had much more than the average sickness and fatality. Even Duncan, though he lived the period allotted by the psalmist of seventy years, they were generally years of uncertain health and sometimes severe sickness. While Harriet, on account of her good health record, carried the heavier end of the burden, yet she laid it down six years sooner than he did. According to Harriet the happiest part of their family life were the few years in the earlier portion that was devoted to preaching in the vicinity of Owen Sound and Meaford. While Duncan often followed other occupations, he was still regarded as a good preacher. Five sons and three daughters were born to them. One son and daughter died in childhood; and the young smart preacher of the family, Duncan Howard, died at thirty, leaving a wife and two children. The other members of the family all live in Toronto, and except Herman, the youngest, all are married. In all there are eight grandchildren, all being girls. William Trout Stirling, the eldest, has been the main help of the family. In his boyhood, Edward gave him a business college training, as well as others of our young relatives, and he fortunately soon obtained good employment and became a good helper in meeting the family expense. Good business opportunities increased, so also did the ability to use them, until now he holds a high place in the ranks of Toronto business men. Still his father and mother, brothers and sisters, shared the best he had till the parents passed away, and each could care for himself. Not until then did he marry and set up his own family establishment, which we are happy to say is on a scale of comfort and style commensurate with one so worthy, one who continues to see the need of others and appreciates the specially divine truth "that it is more blessed to give than to receive." Mrs. Stirling is in accord with her husband in all he does, is a most gracious hostess, and with their three beautiful children form an interesting and charming group.

I had hoped to be able to present Wm. T. Stirling's picture, as deservedly worthy a place along with those of his father and mother. However, he modestly but decidedly objects, suggesting that his parents sufficiently represent the Stirlings.

William Dow, the older son-in-law, is engaged with Will Stirling, as he is familiarly called, in the wholesale bakery and confectionery business. Hubert Stirling also fills important duties in the office.

Deserved reference should also here be made to the second son-in-law, Archibald Huntsman; a brother of the adopted children of my brother Edward. He married Mary, the second sister of the Stirlings, and they have now two children.

Professor Huntsman is a graduate of Toronto University. He was a very diligent and successful student, closing with honors in most every department. Also has taken more extended studies; specializing in biology, giving particular attention to marine life.

The last time I saw this dear sister, Harriet, was when I last visited James. I bid him my final goodbye; but not so with her. I left her cheerful and happy on account of my visit. On a rare beautiful January day in 1906 we drove around the city for two or three hours, enjoying not the sights particularly but each other's company, but this was final as she lived only a few months longer. Her active, helpful life will long be remembered.

RACHEL EMERSON TROUT BEACH.

One beautiful little daughter, Janet, preceded Rachel, and in her fourth year died of pneumonia, or as it was then called, inflammation of the lungs. While she deserves mention, we have practically left her out of the account.

Rachel was named after her grandmother. I believe there were characteristic resemblances, of course, these were not the cause of the name, it was simply incidental. Rachel did not have the vivacity and snap peculiar to Harriet, but was quieter and more reflective, yet equally as good a student. She began her general reading early, and remembered it well. While still in short clothes and attending the common school, she surprised us one autumn day by saying that she would go before the examining board next winter and take a third-class certificate. We laughed at her childish presumption, but she insisted, saying the teacher says I can do it, and I *will* do it. And she did it very creditably. Some of the teachers regarded this as a reflection on themselves, that a slip of a growing girl should rank with them. I think Rachel never taught on that certificate, but continued studying, and next winter went before the board again, and took a second-class; upon that she taught for several years, then went again and took a first-class. Rachel's great peculiarity was her constant steady nerve and quiet self-control, she never dreaded examinations; her faculties and memory seemed to be at command, and she went through with the tests with apparent ease. In the reading tests

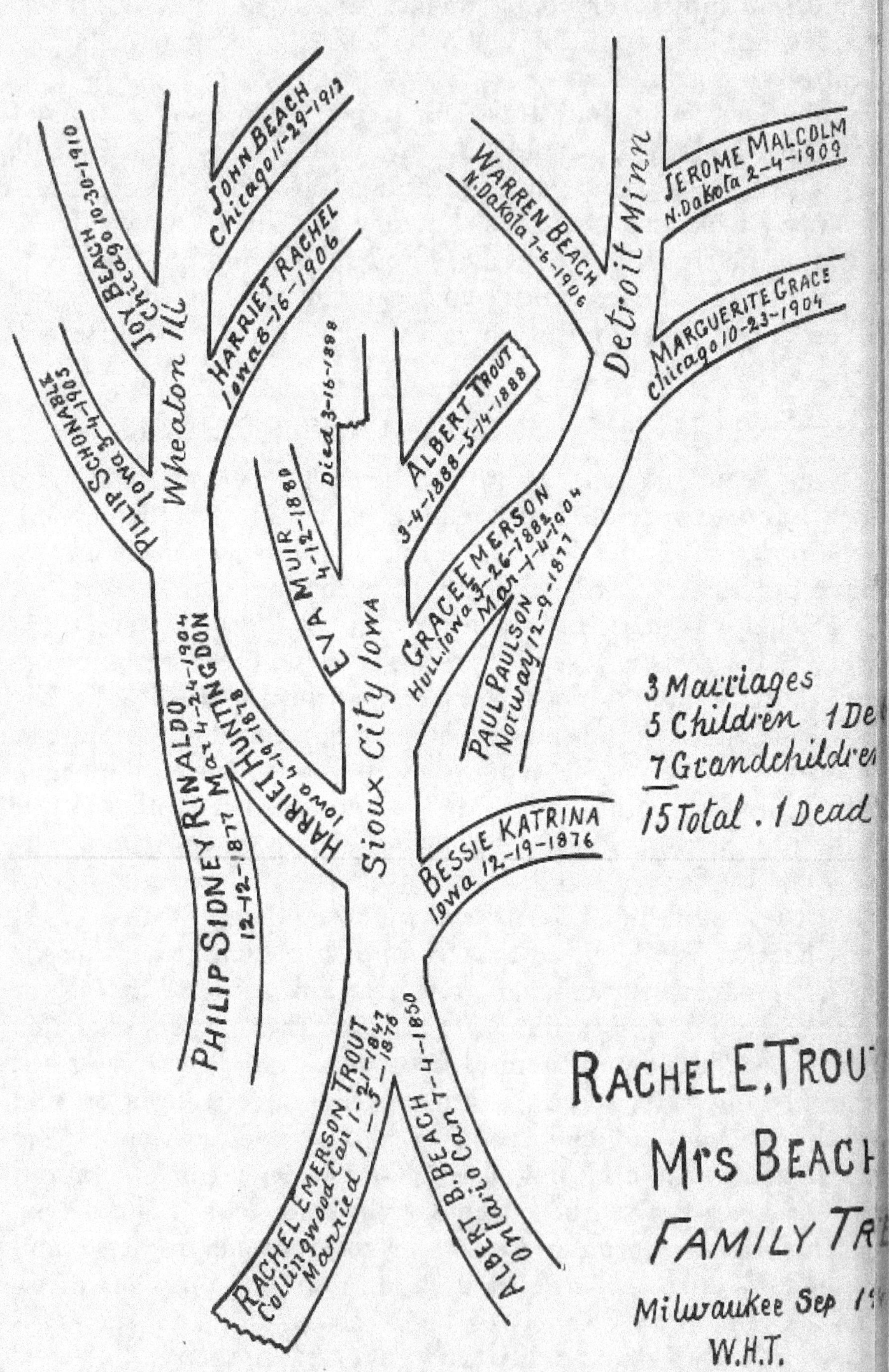
JOY BEACH Chicago 10-30-1910
JOHN BEACH Chicago 11-29-1912
HARRIET RACHEL Iowa 8-16-1906
PHILIP SCHONABLE Iowa 3-4-1905
Wheaton Ill
EVA MUIR 1880
Died 3-16-1898
ALBERT TROUT 3-4-1888-5-14-1888
WARREN BEACH N.Dakota 7-6-1906
Detroit Minn
JEROME MALCOLM N.Dakota 2-4-1909
MARGUERITE GRACE Chicago 10-23-1904
GRACE EMERSON Hull Iowa 3-26-1882 Mar 7-4-1904
PHILIP SIDNEY RINALDO Mar 4-24-1904 12-12-1877
HARRIET HUNTINGDON Iowa 4-19-1878
Sioux City Iowa
PAUL PAULSON Norway 12-9-1877
BESSIE KATRINA Iowa 12-19-1876
3 Marriages
5 Children 1 De
7 Grandchildre
15 Total . 1 Dead
RACHEL EMERSON TROUT Collingwood Can 1-3-1847 Married 1-5-1876
ALBERT B. BEACH 7-4-1850 Ontario Can
RACHEL E. TROUT
Mrs BEACH
FAMILY TR
Milwaukee Sep 19
W.H.T.

she excelled the whole class, as was noted by the examiners at the time. I think it was in the summer vacation period of 1873 that Rachel, when attending the British American Commercial College, taking a course in bookkeeping, met Mr. Albert B. Beach; and the acquaintance and friendship was formed that afterwards ripened into a matrimonial union on January 5, 1876. They made us a visit at our Peterboro home before leaving for Sioux City, Iowa, where they lived about twelve years, and four daughters were born to them. After my three months' stay in Milwaukee with the Filer & Stowell Company in 1880, just before leaving, Mr. Beach called on me, and I accompanied him to Chicago, and was his guest at the hotel for a day or two before returning to Canada. In June, 1884, when for the second time I was in the service of the Filer & Stowell Company, I met Rachel and her four little girls while the train halted that was carrying them back to the old Canadian home for a visit. It was a snatched interview after an absence of eight long years, when I was finding her the wearied mother of four small, train-tired children, with their long journey hardly half completed. And that brief twenty minutes in her company was the last I saw of her.

On March 4, 1888, a welcome son was born, Albert Trout Beach, but his young life lasted only two months and twelve days later the mother's life had to be surrendered. We need no details of the anguish that entered that home. The youngest four years, the eldest over eleven, all felt the need, and could appreciate such mother love and care as fell to the lot of few other children, and think too of the father's situation. The press notice of her death was furnished by the Congregationalist minister, of whose church she was a most helpful member, there being no congregation of Disciples in the place. I transcribed the closing sentences in my notebook, and now give them, "Hers was an exceptional life; she seemed to have grasped the genius of Christianity as all should, but few do, and realized that it is a life, and not simply a theory. Her place cannot be filled."

I have heard and remember good stories of her kindness and good judgment in that far Western town that are too long to reproduce; but they are on the eternal record, along with those where meat was given to the hungry, and water to the thirsty, and where the welcome "come, ye blessed" awaits them.

Mr. Beach still continued his relation to our family by afterwards marrying my niece Bertha Jay, as is recorded and shown by the Mary Trout Jay tree.

MARGARET TROUT WHITELAW.
(See William Trout Tree, page 53.)

This is our youngest sister, the least in stature and physical proportions of any of us; but we must not judge the owner of the body on that basis. However, a fine purposeful spirit is, of necessity, limited by the strength and endurance of the human organism through which it finds expression; she could not stand the strain that her older sisters did, though she has greatly outlived them. From childhood she had to be careful, and the necessity for carefulness has increased with the accumulation of the years. But she has now quite fully learned all her limitations, and is still ready to cheerfully undertake the moderate tasks that she may feel pretty sure of accomplishing. The necessity for economy in effort begets economy in other lines—time, money, and opportunities—all of which Margaret had to learn without a teaching helper, as we shall see.

Margaret married Joseph C. Whitelaw in 1877. William Whitelaw, father of Joseph, was one of the most respected men of the township, and was able to provide a good start for his many sons and daughters. Joe was a rare, good man, well prepared for a great and useful life. If not known as a preacher, he certainly preached, and did it with profit to his hearers. Their happy married life was brief, lasting only ten years, during which time four children were born to them, the youngest dying in infancy. Shortly after the death of her husband she transferred her residence from Meaford to Toronto, and as the city was growing fast, and real estate rapidly rising, it was thought best to invest her little wealth in city

MARGARET TROUT WHITELAW

ALEXANDER LINN WHITELAW

property. But in a year or two with a reversion in business the bottom of the boom fell out, or the gas exploded and the balloon came to earth, and for ten or more years could not be again inflated. Rents fell, good property failed to be kept rented. In the meantime taxes and insurance and interest had to be paid; Margaret held on till near the last, when she had to sell at a sacrifice a year or two before the resumption of good prices. Her boys and girl were being educated, and soon afterward began to help in the care and needs of the family. There was a rare compactness of sympathy and purpose between that mother and her three children; and they kept together much longer than most families do. Headley, the eldest, the fatherly boy, married Miss Campbell of Winnipeg, when about thirty years of age, in 1908, and now has four children. When he left, the apex of the triangle was gone, but Linn was good and ready for the leading place, which he now holds to the comfort of his mother and all concerned. Katrina has lately taken on matrimonial responsibilities with Arthur Kennedy of Toronto in a style that might be expected from a pair so well prepared for their common life purpose. Katrina was mistress of the home, and Linn and his mother contributing helpers. Now since this arrangement is broken up, what the outcome may be is Linn's remaining life problem. The factors in the solution are certainly extensive, as he teaches a Bible class of over fifty girls. Like all our Toronto relatives he is intensely active in good, effective church work. He teaches a large girls' Bible class there; some will surely have more than a scholar's interest in him, and he has a fine chance for a choice. Linn has made splendid success in selling the Burrough's adding machine, and now holds the Canadian agency for the Ellis Adding-Typewriter Company.

Linn Whitelaw, with his office help and adding machines, is much used by the public. The election returns come in to him and are quickly compiled and sent out. He was also called upon to handle the accounting, in the great campaign of February, 1916, when Toronto raised $2,000,000, for the dependents of soldiers, who have gone to the front. And just lately, in October, two weeks' time is spent on the accounting work of Toronto's $700,000 contribution to the fund of the British Red Cross Association. This not merely records Linn's willing public service, but the grand loyal liberality of his home city as well.

Margaret is my only sister whose life story is not ended; it goes on, and in the Bathurst Street and Fern Avenue Churches of Christ she commands the influence of a real mother in Israel.

ALEXANDER ANDERSON TROUT.

(See also William Trout Family Tree, page 53.)

He was named after father's warm-hearted friend who for a time was his fellow preacher and a true companion, and who wrote father's obituary previously copied in this record. He was the youngest of the family, and, like Margaret, lacked the measure of robustness that characterized the rest of us. Also like her, he had fine good sense that measured well, and matched his work with his powers. Having a fine, clear-working intellect, study was easy, and what he gained was well retained. He had but little to do with manual labor; between his school days, business college course, and teaching and preaching years, and the business period of his life in Detroit, there was no call for the more laborious life experiences that were met by his older brothers. In his young man's preaching time he went entirely beyond the rest of our attempts, in that he held several good successful evangelistic meetings. This was when he was about twenty-two years of age. He modestly felt that he was a very young man to play so important a role. I remember well the glow of satisfaction his countenance and speech showed when telling me afterwards about these fine meetings. This feeling was not pride but a sense of high privilege and power, that he was thus enabled to win souls for Christ and extend His kingdom. At Detroit he was the leader of a number of young men who made it their special religious work to plant missions in the city and suburbs wherever they could.

At Detroit he early made the acquaintance and friendship of the family of Alexander Linn, the senior elder in the Plum

ALEXANDER LINN TROUT

ALEXANDER ANDERSON TROUT

DETROIT, MICHIGAN

Street Church of Christ. Between the youngest daughter, Caroline, and Alexander there quickly grew up that strong mutual attachment that culminated in their marriage in 1881. Their brief married life of seven years is a rich heritage of memory to the surviving widow. And, as a further living link of affectionate remembrance, there is left one son, who greatly resembles his father, but he is really a Linn-Trout combination, as his name, Alexander Linn Trout, manifestly indicates. He has the names of both grandfathers, who were both highly esteemed and greatly respected men; and so far Linn Trout, as he is usually known, follows their example, as well as his fathers, and reflects nothing but credit on their revered names. With regard to attainments in education and knowledge he has gone away beyond them, as the advanced conditions of our time has enabled him to do. He has taken a complete literary course and a full mechanical engineering course in the University of Michigan. This is also backed up by good shop practice. Though hardly thirty years of age at this writing, January 1, 1916, yet he has now been for two years an architect and engineer, designing modern steel and concrete buildings on his own account with good prospects. Detroit has already some good monuments of his work. Linn has been a pet boy among all his friends and relatives, but he is not a spoiled one. He and his good persistent mother had no sort of a soft time in reaching their present good standing. Continued laborious struggle attended their steady upward course. The broken health of the mother, on account of this, is greatly to be regretted. We look forward to a fine career for Linn, if he keeps his health. He certainly has the good will and wishes of a host of friends. The continuance of the Trout family name and credit, so far as father's line is concerned, depends on the successors of four of us—James, Peter, Alexander and myself. Linn, the latter's only son, is father's youngest grandchild, and though still alone, we are hopeful, not only for his own useful life, but that he may add a significant quota to the onward swim of the Trouts. This concludes William Trout's family line. We will now follow the line of the next oldest of grandfather's children.

MRS. ANN TROUT LEE BLANCHARD.

Through the good care and kindness of Mrs. C. W. Smith of San Francisco, a granddaughter of Aunt Ann, I am enabled to show the oldest portraits in my history, Mrs. Ann Trout Lee Blanchard and Lot Blanchard.

Whatever may be the judgment of relatives and friends regarding this history I think it will appear that I have tried to be brief. If the stories told are by some regarded as trivial, they have not been unduly spun out. Still with all my effort at brevity, I have already written a mass of manuscript about twice as great as first calculated. And now after going down father's line so fully, it would seem hardly fair to cut short my uncles' and aunts' lines because of this manifest need; but such will have to be done. There are no doubt matters of interest connected with every family line, but I do not know them all, and what I do know there is not the space in a reasonably sized book to give them all suitable record; so that brevity is a necessity which I must endeavor to meet.

Aunt Ann was the third of grandfather's children, she was next to father, and was the eldest daughter, the one who in the household comes next to the mother; in those days of early marriages, she remained with her mother a reasonable time, marrying Captain James W. Lee at twenty-three years of age, in 1826, the first marriage date of the family. He was then or afterwards the proprietor of a schooner, and sailed Lakes Erie, Huron and Michigan. He was an intrepid fellow that would undertake the severest tasks; father related to me that one fall he came into Detroit after all the other vessels had laid up. A contractor, who had to deliver certain winter stores to the government lighthouses in the upper lakes, could not get any vessel to go out and deliver his goods; but one of the vessel captains, seeing Lee's schooner coming in, pointing the contractor to the incoming vessel, said, "There is your only chance." Lee made good terms, took on the goods and one or two extra men, and was soon on his way to the North. It was near the first of December, for two weeks he had good weather. He delivered the supplies to the lighthouses, took

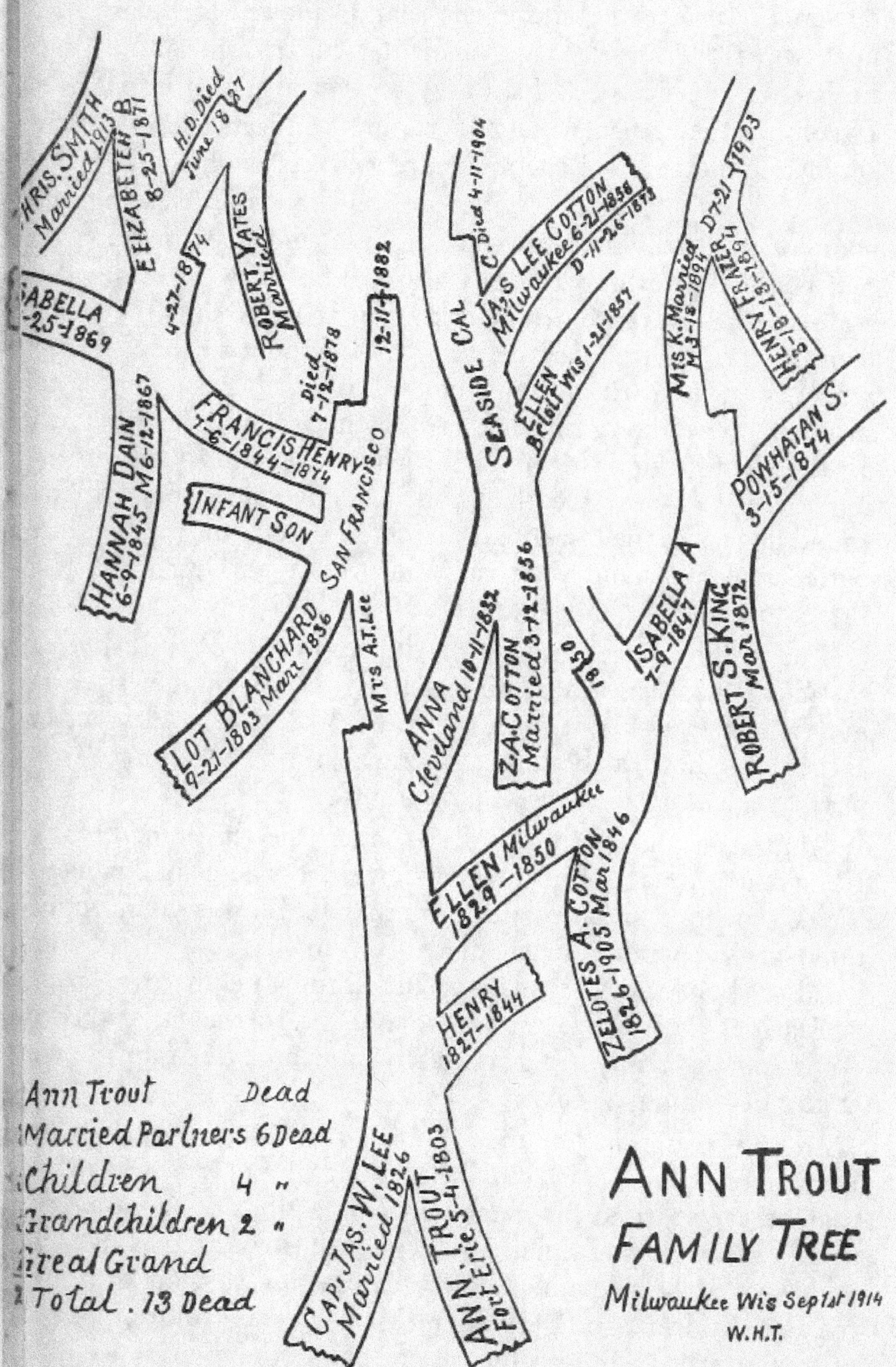
CHRIS. SMITH Married 1913
E. ELIZABETH B. 8-25-1871
H.D. Died June 18 97
4-27-1874
ROBERT YATES Married
Died 7-12-1878
12-17-1882
ISABELLA 1-25-1869
HANNAH DAIN 6-9-1845 M 6-12-1867
FRANCIS HENRY 7-6-1844-1874
INFANT SON
LOT BLANCHARD 9-21-1803 Mar. 1836
San Francisco
Mrs A.T. Lee
ANNA Cleveland 10-11-1852
Z.A. COTTON Married 3-12-1856
ELLEN Milwaukee 1829-1850
HENRY 1827-1844
ZELOTES A. COTTON 1826-1905 Mar 1846
1850
SEASIDE CAL
C. Died 4-11-1904
JA'S LEE COTTON Milwaukee 6-21-1858
D-11-26-1873
ELLEN B.Calif Wis 1-21-1857
Mrs K. Married M3-18-1894
D 7-21-1903
HENRY FRAZER 1-18-1894
POWHATAN S. 3-15-1874
ISABELLA A 7-9-1847
ROBERT S. KING Mar 1872
Ann Trout   Dead
Married Partners 6 Dead
Children   4 "
Grandchildren 2 "
Great Grand
Total . 13 Dead
CAPT. JAS. W. LEE Married 1826
ANN TROUT 5-4-1803 Fort Erie
ANN TROUT FAMILY TREE
Milwaukee Wis Sep 1st 1914
W. H. T.

on some return cargo, and in the islands about Mackinaw and northward purchased large quantities of frozen fish so that he had to carry a deck load. After getting well into Lake Huron on the return voyage, a raging wind and snow storm set in, and increased to such violence as to carry off some of the sails. Occasional great waves swept the deck, clearing off some of its load. Lee saw one of his men swept overboard, and could do nothing to help him. The spray froze in the rigging, and prevented the working of the few sails that they could carry. Three days and nights Lee held to the steering wheel, wet, cold, tired, and hungry, giving his commands to his men, all realizing that it was a desparate fight for life with all the chances against them. However, on the fourth morning there was clear weather and a calmer situation, and he found he was in the lower end of Lake Huron, not far from its outlet at Sarnia, and soon came into dock at Detroit with a vessel looking like an iceberg.

The freight money and big profits on the sale of the fish near the Christmas season was nearly equal to the summer's work, but he never risked another voyage like that. His active career was short, as he died a young man of about thirty-four years; regarding the cause I am not informed.

Aunt Ann and James W. Lee had three children, Henry, Ellen and Anna. The first two were born in Milwaukee. Anna was born in Cleveland. Henry died in his young manhood at seventeen. Ellen died after marriage and motherhood at twenty-one. Anna is in her eighty-fourth year, living at Seaside, California. All these and the further relations of Aunt Anna's family are graphically shown by her family tree, at the beginning of this reference.

In 1834 Captain Lee died, and in 1836 Aunt married Lot Blanchard. We know but little about him, I am not aware that he ever visited his Canadian connections. From all accounts he was a good man and a good husband to Aunt. He and Aunt always retained a close connection to their own and the Lee children. In 1839 Aunt and her three children visited at grandfather's, my sister Mary being there at that time.

LOT BLANCHARD

MRS. ANN TROUT LEE BLANCHARD

She told me afterward what a fine time she had with her three American cousins. Henry, the oldest, and the only boy in the group, was Mary's admiration, a kindly youth of twelve years, while Mary was eight. She told how helpful he was—carried them all across a creek.

Aunt's married life was almost wholly spent in the cities, such as Milwaukee, Cleveland, possibly Detroit, Honolulu, and San Francisco. This, with the easy circumstances that seemed to be her lot, gave her opportunities for information and culture in advance of her sisters, and she evidently used them with good profit. My acquaintance with her was made during her visit to Canada in 1854, accompanied by Anna Lee and six-year-old Isabella Cotton, her granddaughter. They came to Creemore to visit Aunt Harriet and the most of her family who were then residing there. Father, cousin Samuel Orr, Edward and myself, were five miles from there, building a sawmill in the great pine woods. Uncle John and family were also with us. We made Sunday visits to Creemore to see our American relatives. Two Sundays and one brief week-day visit was their extent. In the presence of my city-bred, silk-dressed cousin Anna I felt all the possible awkwardness of my country style. She was a year and a half older than I, and a true democrat, so without being at all condescending she led me into conversation which was easily and pleasantly maintained. We had a few enjoyable walks together. She remembers the Creemore visit as well as I do, and Isabella, now Mrs. Frazer, remembers the forest scenery most clearly. Father and Aunt Ann and Aunt Harriet had their interesting times together. I shared in some of it. Mr. Cotton, Aunt's son-in-law, came to conduct them back to the states, from whence they all shortly afterwards made the long, tiresome, overland journey to California. After a brief stay, they added to this the long sea voyage to Honolulu, on the Sandwich islands. After a few years' residence there, they returned to California. Mr. Cotton was for a considerable time engaged in business, but in the later years of his long life he and family resided on a small fruit ranch about a hundred miles from San Francisco. He was a typical, active, bustling

Western business man, kindly and considerate, not alone to his immediate family and Aunt Ann, to whom he was twice a son-in-law, but also to Uncle Blanchard. They kept their fortunes together till after the return from Honolulu to San Francisco, where Aunt and Uncle finished out their earthly term as keepers of the lighthouse at the Golden Gate. Isabella Cotton, daughter of Ellen Lee, married Robert S. King, having by him one son. After the brief married life and death of Mr. King, she married Henry Frazer, a mechanical superintendent of railway work; she also had become a good business woman, in connection with one of the railway offices, which was continued after Mr. Frazer's death, in 1900. Now she is retired on a moderate pension, and is living with her unmarried son, Powhattan King. He seems to be about the only possible chance for the further extension of Aunt Ann's family line. This responsibility does not appear to bear very hard on him; the chances are that this line may be extinct in thirty years, and it is the only one of which this is likely. Aunt Rachel's is immensely in great contrast to this. Adverse circumstances, about the time of Mr. Cotton's death, deprived the family of the fruit ranch, so Mrs. Cotton and her daughter Ellen came in to San Francisco and joined housekeeping with Mrs. Frazer. This was in 1904; in 1911 they again separated, and Ellen Cotton and her mother are now living at Seaside, California, running a large pigeon loft or rookery, and making a scant living from the proceeds, the daughter, resolute and strong in her fifty-ninth year, and the mother somewhat feeble in her eighty-fourth year. The latest news is that they all four are together again in San Francisco.

Two sons were born to Aunt Ann and Uncle Blanchard, one dying in infancy, the other at thirty years of age; he had two daughters, the younger of which is married with no children, and is now forty-five years of age. There are five living descendants of Aunt Ann, the youngest forty-two, the eldest, eighty-four, while her younger sister, Rachel, Mrs. Dan McDonald, has nearly three hundred. Here is a problem for the experts in eugenics to solve.

In this line story the absence of any reference to the religious question may be noted, simply because it was not particularly manifest. It accords with San Francisco.

This is a long story for a short family, but by no means an unimportant one.

HENRY TROUT.

This was grandfather's third son and fourth child. I have no recollection of ever seeing him. Father described him as the tallest of the family, being about six feet high, and in every respect fine looking. His marriage at twenty-two was the earliest of any of the boys. Though he was apportioned two hundred acres of land, the same as the other boys, he never farmed any. According to father, he was too decidedly mechanical to entertain it. He assisted father in some of his first building ventures in Erin village, as already mentioned. No doubt his married life began there, Margaret Kirkwood of Caledon being his life partner. But no backwoods village would hold him, he made a strike for more room. At the port of Oakville, which was then quite a town, a steam dredge was being built by a contractor named Lawton. Henry applied to him for work, and frankly told him of his inexperience. Lawton found that to be common, but he rightly judged that he had a man before him who would learn fast, and one to be depended on. So he quietly instructed him, gave him good work, and put him forward. Henry used his good opportunities so well, that before the dredge was completed he had mastered the details and was given full charge of the work. When finished, Mr. Lawton had to leave to look after other jobs. Uncle Henry was left to employ a tug or a steamer to tow the dredge to Hamilton, and set it at work. The machine was brought to its destination and started. Very properly he was cautious, and determined to avoid a breakdown. In the course of the first week the contractor for the harbor work came around to inspect and said to Uncle "everything seems to be working nicely, but I would like to see more work turned out." Uncle replied that the machine was new, and the men new on the job; but he would soon get to good

ROB. FRANKLIN 12-2-1909
HENRY FRANKLIN 9-2-1882
GRACE ELIZ. H. BALL Married 12-12-08
MARY GENEVIEVE 3-28-1889
King Iron Works Buffalo N.Y.
LILLIAN MAY 1898
WILLARD HENRY 1895
R.J. Trout Co. or King Iron Works
D 2-9-1892
9-14-1891
Hamilton Ont Can
HENRY E 1879-1882
JESSIE T. 1876-1879
CLARA MAY 1870-1884
GERTRUDE N 1864-1883
Twins ELLEN Y 12-4-1862-1863
JOHN TROUT 1872-1873
HELEN MARR 1867-1891
ANNA LEE 1879
JANET M 1860-1892
Accidental 5-11-1853
1850
WM B 4-19-1850
Married 12-12-1876
ESTELLE EASTMAN 2-24-1854
D 1880 1943
Ed HENRY 7-10-1874
H.C. Trout Co.
BERTHA WRIGHT Married 2-8-1894
D 7-22-1911
JESSIE Hastings 1836 Married 12-8-1869 READING London Eng 1845
HENRY N. READING
Buffalo N.Y.
LILLIAN GOLLAN Married 6-19-1892
MARGARET Caledon 6-12-1854
JOHN MONTEITH Married 1857 Scotland
HENRY GEORGE Erin 11-29-1829
FANNY WILLS Coburg Can Married 1853
HENRY TROUT Fort Erie April 4-1805
MARGARET KIRKWOOD Married 1827
1 Henry Trout
8 Married Partners 4D
4 Children   3 Dead
12 Grand 9 Dead
3 Great Grand
28 Total : 16 Dead.
HENRY TROUT
FAMILY TREE
Milwaukee Wis Aug 191
W.H.T.

regular working condition, which proved to be the case. Excepting greater brevity I am giving this story as father told it. He regarded Uncle's natural mechanical abilities as superior to his own.

Uncle Henry lived a year or two in Hamilton, and moved eastward to Crook's Rapids, now known as Hastings, on the river Trent, where a great dam was built. Here he purchased a site and built mills. After a good number of years' residence there, he disposed of his property and went back to Hamilton, built a dredge for himself, and worked it for some time. This venture seemed not to have been a business success; also about this time, 1850, Mrs. Trout died, not very long after the birth of their youngest son. After he had arranged for the proper care of his young family, and settled up Hamilton business, he engaged with the contractors of the Grand Trunk railway as superintendent of bridge construction. While in their service out in the pine woods near Georgetown, Ontario, he was sitting on a stick of newly hewn timber, stooping over, writing in a notebook, when a small pine bough, its weight scarcely two pounds, having on its tip one brush of pine needles, which had been broken by the falling trees, now became loosened, and falling arrow-like, struck Uncle on the back of the head, breaking in the skull. He became at once insensible and remained so for two days and died. Thus was a fine good man laid low, in an astonishingly simple, accidental manner, at the age of forty-eight years.

HENRY GEORGE TROUT

In sketching the career of Uncle Henry Trout, as is done above, I claim no more than general correctness. The one on whom I depended for more definite information, his son, H. G. Trout, the present subject, suddenly passed to his reward on July 22, 1911. An intended visit by me about that time was thus cut short. It forcibly reminded me of a conversation we had a few years previous. He asked me, "When are you going to finish your history?" I replied, "I will take it up again very soon." He said, "You better get busy, none of us have very much time." The hunch was for me, and rightly so, as I considered he would outlive me; but he put himself in with it, and was the first to go, and I am cut off from the company of a cousin that was like a brother, and also from the large fund of family information that he alone had. However, I must not anticipate, but begin his story at the proper end.

Henry G. Trout was born in Erin, November 29, 1829. His boyhood education was evidently the best the new country afforded. This was mostly at Hastings. His father apprenticed him to be a mechanical engineer in, what might be adjudged at that time, as the best engineering works in America, Shepherd's of Buffalo, New York. Mr. Perry, the superintendent, was abreast, if not ahead, of his time in the improvements for using steam expansively. Buffalo was then a great ship building port, and Buffalo Creek, with its vessel building and boilermaking, was a noisy, busy part of the great waterfront. That was the kind of atmosphere and environment to raise great engineers. His apprenticeship must have begun not later than 1848, when about nineteen years of age. He would refer to his beginnings only when the conversation led that way. Generally his work and interests were in the foreground, and himself out of sight, so he told little about himself; but I learned that as an apprentice he had special consideration, and when it was completed he was placed as foreman over a gang of workers. I also know that early in his Buffalo life he attended and soon united with Dr. Lord's church (Presbyterian); in this church connection he continued throughout his whole life, entering as a Sunday school pupil, he went through all the grades of church promotion below that of the minister.

About the last thirty years of his life he was senior elder, minister's adviser, and general helper for the needy. The fine old church building met the fate of all down-town churches, in that it was deserted by the rich, who built it, and came to be occupied by the poor, to whom it was most accessible. Henry, being a "father to the poor," stuck with the old church, and for a long time was its main financial stay, and not till near the time of his death was the fine old property

FORMER PROPRIETOR OF KING IRON WORKS, BUFFALO, NEW YORK

surrendered to business uses. And it was his generous sub-scription and legacy that was the main support of the new building project in the northern suburbs. His widowed part-ner looked carefully after this investment. I saw the beauti-ful, old, solid walnut pews of the old church being transferred and adapted to their new situation.

In the early fifties of last century the old business was reor-ganized, retaining the name of Shepherd's Iron Works, and Henry became shop foreman. Several years of varying busi-ness success followed, until 1870, when on account of several large contracts, which proved disastrous, a new company was formed, with a Mr. King at the head, who gave it the name of the King Iron Works, which has been retained ever since. Mr. King also failed in his enterprise about 1872. For a time the fine old works went a begging for a buyer or a boss. As neither of these offered themselves, the creditors, in order to keep the estate from decay, and at least help in the interest payments, and seeing Henry to be the one continuously reliable man that hung to its varying forlorn fortunes, they offered him a favorable lease for several years, which he accepted. He saw that the shop, though once the best, was now old, that new well-planned shops, particularly in the rival city of Cleve-land, with tools and appliances of new design, could outbid him on high-class work and retain a profit, while a possible loss might be his portion. That was the kind of work that had been the pride of the shop, and the work he enjoyed, but it had to be given up, or else the entire shop be reconstructed; so he confined himself to the smaller contracts, that offered surer prospects of profit, and these were gradually diminished for the sake of devoting more attention to his best exclusive specialty—propeller wheels. He operated this property under lease for nearly forty years; during this time the "Trout Wheels" were the most important line of manufacture.

In my perambulations about this country, when voyaging on the lakes or west coast, as I have done to a moderate extent, I like to see the style and class of the marine engines and boilers—the power plant that sends the great vessel forward through storm or calm. The acquaintance and the permission of the engineers are the first steps. In such cases I have found the name Trout an honorable introduction to begin with. Out of several instances I will refer to one or two.

In 1893, in Chicago one afternoon, I had an hour or more at my disposal, so I devoted it to seeing the then new steamer Virginia, not the largest, but the most finely equipped on the lakes. Coming on board I inquired for the engineer, and explained my wish; he was sorry, men were ashore, he had no time, etc. I said, "Could I not look around on my own account?" "Oh, we could not allow you to do that! Where are you from?" "Milwaukee." "What is your occupation?" "Engineering and machinery draughtsman." "What's your name?" "W. H. Trout." "Any connection to Trout of Buffalo?" "Yes, sir. He's my first cousin." He dropped what he was carrying, and gave me the heartiest kind of a handshake. He said, "My name is Walker, I was an apprentice in Henry's shop." I said, "Henry had a particular friend by the name of Walker that I knew when he was a young man, William Walker." "Yes, William Walker is my father's brother," he said. "He spent several evenings with us when at Milwaukee, fitting the engine in one of Fitzgerald's vessels about nine years ago." After such interchange of greeting, and our mutual friendly standing disposed of, he said, "Well, Mr. Trout, I am at your service for all the time you want, or for any other close relative or friend of Henry Trout's that may come along." I went through, and in the depths with him; he accompanied me to the gangway, where our parting was prolonged to the last minute. I had a similar good time on the Princess Victoria, en route from Seattle to Vancouver in 1911. In that instance there was the more powerful standard Glasglow built marine engine in the performance of its heavy duty. A Canadian engineer was in charge. We had a good number of common friends in Canada to talk about. He knew the Trout Wheel by using it, and its maker by reputation.

An old lake engineer, who had served on many boats during twenty-five years, said the captains never asked a guaranty from Henry, his plain statement of what he would likely do, was all they required. His interest was in the job, as well as the price. The young university experts of the time would take size and model of vessel boiler and engine power, and after elaborate calculations determine the character and dimension of the wheel to suit. He would make the wheel to their specifications and if it failed, as such often did, he would look the subject over and make his guess, which would generally be a hit, gaining a few miles on the hour with the same expenditure of steam. If he was not satisfied that the best was attained, he would say so, and get another chance. He had the unlimited confidence of the lake captains, vessel owners and engineers, not only with regard to his judgment and skill, but his uniform square dealing in all transactions. In person, Henry was rather above the medium height, solidly built, the face generally indicating qiuet repose. He was always quiet and unobtrusive in manner, his feelings seldom rising higher than pleasant animation. He had a calm reasoning method, that generally brought complicated matters down to simple issues, where they might be acted upon. If the matter seemed to be irresolvable, he would follow it down to the last tangible idea, then say, "Now I give it up." With him it came either to a blind alley or an absurdity, and he would let it remain there till at least he would learn more about it. He never could be betrayed into boisterous noisy talk, his sentences, particularly in business talk, were brief, clear, and decided. He seldom talked on trivial subjects, in that line he was never more than a careless listener. His parlor talks regarded the welfare of friends or relations, for these were always a matter of interest, or the shopworkers or the city's welfare, or matters of the state, nation or church, were discussed in a tentative way, to gain the views of others before settling to a manifest conclusion. Old-fashioned Canadian hospitality continued with him to the last. The year 1901 of the Buffalo World Exposition made heavy demands on him and his partner, but they were all graciously met. They kept open house to all friends who came to the great exposition. His summer holiday term was an extended visiting time for himself and Mrs. Trout, spending it mostly among relatives. He could find them east, west or north, and devote a season in either direction. These visits were all well remembered. He was a Republican in politics, yet he was the veriest kind of a democrat; he was of the people, and with the people, regarding himself to be no more privileged than anybody else.

He liked a good horse, and such was to him a helpful companion, not merely a beast of burden. His horses, like his friends, were well chosen, and "for keeps." When brother Edward left Canada for California he had no further use for the fine horse that so long and faithfully served him. The horse Royal George, had won many good prizes at public fairs, had speed and high mettle. Though he would bring a good price on the market, Edward would not sell him, for fear the noble animal might be ill used; so he shipped him to Buffalo to Henry, assured that both horse and new owner would enjoy the relation, which they certainly did. Henry's appreciation was such that he insisted on sending back a good check. In his younger days the horse was liable to some nervous foolishness that once was nearly serious to Edward; but now he had experience, and horse sense along with his aged dignity, all of which was greatly needed in the busy city of Buffalo. I rode behind him with both owners, and the sense exercised was noticeable, as at a crowded place he would halt for the word and direction that he no doubt expected.

In driving, Henry used no whip, that would be a surprise if not an insult to George; but he gave him horse talk in plenty, which George evidently understood, although greatly intermixed with our mutual conversation, for he seemed to distinguish his part of it all right. Equines grow old like humans; this horse outlived his master. I saw him last in the fall of 1912; his step, though still stately, was minus its former vigor. He was a pensioner, putting in time, like some of the rest of us. The difference is that with him there was no future and no responsibility. His good horse sense was built on his horse experience, with no possible thought of immortality. Then what about us humans? Is there not sometimes a similarity? That great question deserves its own special time and space.

Until well in his eightieth year there seemed no marked

diminution of either bodily or mental power with Henry. Then gradually there came a shortening of his business hours; that was quite noticeable in his eightysecond year. In that midsummer, when he and Mrs. Trout were making their usual summer visits, and were to see friends in Brooklyn, on the short journey of a block or more from the cars to his friend's house, he became suddenly weakened, and had to sit down on the steps of a grocery store; soon, however, he rallied, and safely reached his destination. As his normal condition seemed to quite fully return, anxiety was greatly lessened. He enjoyed an afternoon at the parks with the friends and their children; but late in the evening the weakness returned much more depressingly, so that he could speak but little. Though a physician was soon at hand, no help could be given; and Henry passed to the eternal mansions. Friends without stint were left behind to mourn his passing, but though twice married, there were no children to take up his work and carry forward his honorable name.

His business affairs were all kept well in hand, and a considerable portion of his assets quietly descended to the new H. G. Trout Company, which now carries the work forward. (See William B. Trout.)

MARGARET TROUT MONTEITH
(See Henry Trout Tree, page 314.)

She was Uncle Henry's eldest daughter. Born in Caledon, Ontario, Canada, June 12, 1834. She was sixteen years old when her mother died. From my hazy recollections I conclude that Uncle Henry broke up housekeeping not long afterwards, and before working on the Grand Trunk railroad, I think one of the Kirkwood uncles in Caledon took the two daughters to his home until after H. G. Trout was married, when they resided with him, until they were married. It was at the brother's home where I first met them. Margaret had from childhood often suffered from attacks of asthma, which, along with the responsible interest she felt in her younger sister, gave her an air of soberness, that was a contrast to the lively style of the younger one. In 1857 she was married to John Monteith, a young Scotch molder. Their family life was mostly in Hamilton, Ontario. They had seven girls in succession and two boys. The whole family died at various ages from infancy to thirty-two years, this being the eldest daughter, who outlived her mother three years, and died the same year as her father, in 1892, he being about fifty-eight years. The cause of most of the deaths was tuberculosis or other lung affections. I visited the family several times. They were a fairly well-educated, religiously trained, cheerful, happy lot, struggling with seeming fair success in life's battles; but this was the only cousin's faimly of children in the whole record that has come to complete extinction. It is in the greatest contrast to cousin John McDonald's, which will receive attention farther on.

John Monteith deserves much more than mere mention. The iron molders of fifty or sixty years ago were very much a class by themselves. To do good, skillful work, and receive good pay, seemed generally to be their thought and their only ambition, the pay being necessary to their enjoyment, which was not always of the elevating kind. Their well systematized unions kept their wages up, and they could readily send out their young men where work was most needed. This gave them a care-free, jolly, independent style, that was not so manifest in other trades. Such was John Monteith; he early prided himself in his good work, and was interested in the unions. He soon became an officer in them, and in the way of recreation he had a violin, that gave fine expression to his jolly, musical soul, and helped others to have a good time. He would not accept a foremanship in a foundry, as that would take him out of the union, and out of association with his fellow molders, whom he desired to help. In Hamilton he and other helpful ones started a co-operation store with prices slightly above cost, but each year showed a loss on account of bad debts, made by dishonorable union men; these had to be made good by John and the other substantial men behind the undertaking. Like the leaders in every line of progress, they had the care and push of the job, and the deficit to make up, and no thanks for their pains. Naturally they got tired and quit it. But long before this he took up a larger scheme for humanity—the great world-wide cause of Christ. He had united with a Presbyterian church, and now became one of its human pillars. The fiddle had long rests, and the molders' unions were left behind. He took a shop superintendency where the interests of others besides himself and the unions came into play; and, above all, was the interest and the hope of a union with the redeemed of the earth, as his great aspiration, which by faith we are satisfied his spirit attained in his fifty-ninth year.

MRS. JESSIE TROUT READING
(See Henry Trout Tree, page 314.)

This is the second and only remaining daughter of Uncle Henry, and has been previously noticed. In 1869 she married a young Englishman, Henry N. Reading, a good competent machinist and railroad engineer. Their home was in St. Thomas, Ontario, Canada. They had only one son, Edward Henry, who followed his father's occupation; he is now married, has a son and daughter, and is an active member of the H. G. Trout Company of Buffalo, New York.

My acquaintance with Mr. and Mrs. Reading in their marriage relation, was limited to two visits in 1879 at their home in St. Thomas. Mr. Reading was an enthusiastic railroad engineer; his locomotive was his pet; and well it might be, as he was continually putting his best study and skill into it. The management gave him the liberty to do this if there would be no interference with duty. The ordinary locomotive boiler, in good condition, with proper supply of good fuel, will furnish a given amount of steam. The economic effective use of that steam, in train pulling, depends on the engine proper, but, more especially, on the valves and their action. It was to this that Reading gave his attention, changing and testing until it was well understood that he had the best locomotive on the line. He soon had a chance to demonstrate this. A trainload of priests, three cars, returning from some big conclave at Rome, was due in Detroit at seven-thirty p. m. It came into St. Thomas behind time; but it was turned over to Reading, with the notice that he had a clear track and was to do his best. He had to make one or two stops for water, but if my memory serves me correctly, he made the run of one hundred and fourteen miles in one hundred eight minutes, getting in ahead of time, making the highest speed record up to that time in America, if not in the world; and several years elapsed before this was beaten. I read the brief statement in the papers, and Mr. Reading gave me the story in detail.

WILLIAM B. TROUT

(See Henry Trout Tree, page 314.)

William B. Trout was the youngest of Uncle Henry's family. He was over twenty years younger than his oldest brother, Henry G. William never knew his mother, she died a short time after his birth. Aunt Harriet mothered him in the tender years of his infancy. Her picture no doubt will be on the first page of his memory's album, along with scenes of Creemore village. Henry G. came to Creemore in 1854 and took his little brother back with him. I know Henry regarded himself as his child brother's natural guardian through his school days and apprenticeship up to manhood. This guidance was faithfully and judiciously given. William probably had better school advantages and training than Henry. If my memory is right William worked for a year or two after his apprenticeship in one of the other large Buffalo shops before working permanently with Henry. Shop work and work on vessels in dry dock and at other ports, were William's first working experiences. Afterward he had the leading place in the draughting room, and the designing of new work. Near the close of the year 1876, Miss Estelle Eastman and he were married, and not long afterwards located and made a nice home in North Buffalo. I say, made the home, because so much of it was the result of the good economical plans and industry of Mrs. Trout. A son and daughter were born to them. The son, Henry Franklin, married Miss M. E. Ball,

W. B. Trout.

and they now have a son, Robert Franklin, so that Uncle Henry Trout's line has a fair prospect of continuance. William B. Trout regards himself as having been remiss in the cultivation of acquaintanceship with his Trout relatives. He may have regarded cousin Henry's considerateness in that respect as good for both. We ought to be more in touch with each other than we are, and one of my hopes in writing this history, is that I may introduce to each other a good many relatives that are total strangers. This Trout home, like most all the others, has a place for Christ in it, which greatly helps to cement the common bond.

With his usual wisdom and foresight, cousin Henry organized his business from the individual to the corporation form, shortly before he died, under the title, H. G. Trout Company, King Iron Works, Buffalo, New York.

William B. Trout, who had been second to Henry, was now made president; the surviving wife, Mrs. Lillian G. Trout, was made vice-president; Herbert G. Walker, secretary and treasurer. Edward H. Reading, William H. G. Walker, Frank C. Waldow, and William Mummery, were made directors. Marine engineering and Trout propeller wheels were to be their main lines of manufacture.

It will be seen that the new corporation is composed of the good dependable relatives and friends, who had been employed under H. G. Trout, each interested in the common good; and no doubt their combined good judgment will carry forward the business with the steady success that has heretofore attended it.

HARRIET TROUT ORR

This second daughter in grandfather's family has already been introduced and given frequent reference. She has been very much more closely associated with father's family than any other aunt or uncle. On this account her story to us, at least, has greater interest.

Her marriage to Hugh Orr, a native of Vermont of Scotch parentage, took place at grandfather's, January 2, 1827, when a few months under nineteen years of age. Aunt was always

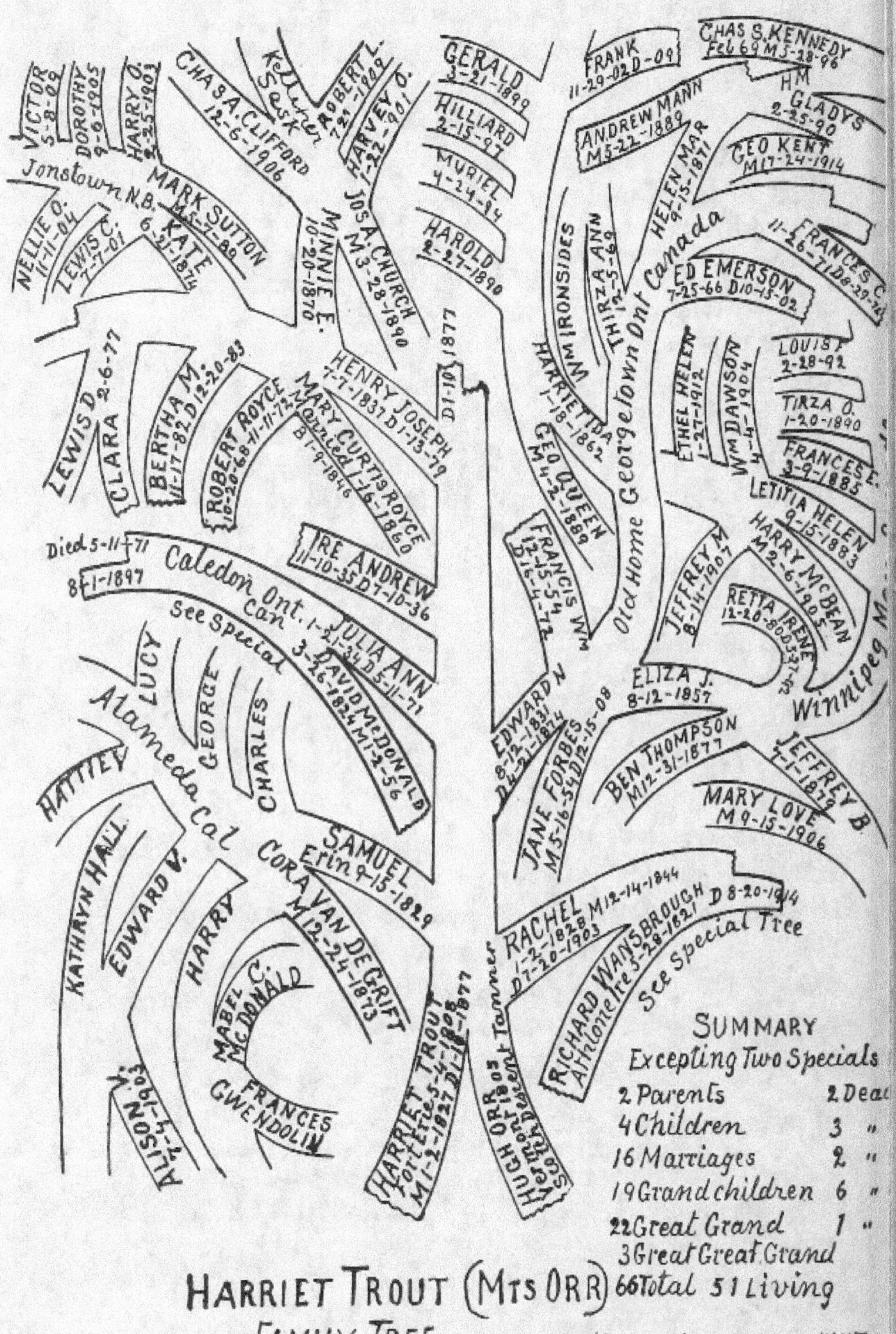

HARRIET TROUT (Mrs ORR) FAMILY TREE

Wheeling West Va June 1916 W.H.T

HARRIET TROUT ORR

a fine attractive looking woman, though not alone in this respect, she undoubtedly led her sisters; so that her appearance as a blushing bride can well be imagined. Though there are no pictures left, she unquestionably had a good looking mate. It was conceded by those who knew, that her son Edward, in features, style and general manner closely resembled his father, so there was about an equally good looking man alongside of her, when her troth was plighted; and those good looks were deservedly claimed as a family inheritance. By occupation Uncle Orr was a tanner. He also had the style and standing of a good business man, as well as his trade. Just where they resided and where he carried on his business in their early family life I am not fully informed, most likely it was Erin village.

A family of five fine small children were growing up around them when in the year 1838 he departed. Henceforward aunt comes to the front as the main provider and family manager.

This unexpected situation, with its added responsibilities, to which she had to address herself, brought out the fine courage, faithfulness, patience and good judgment, that seemed so natural to her, and became manifested as ordinarily they would not have been. New family arrangements had to be made: the two older little boys were placed in the care of good, dependable farmer friends, who agreed to treat them as their own, giving proper training and schooling till they came to man's estate. I think Edward was released before that time, in order to learn at Stewarttown the tanning trade, and shoe business, his father's pursuit, which he afterwards followed at Creemore as already mentioned.

The old home of grandfather's now became aunt's home center and that of her children, Rachel the eldest being about eleven years of age, would be soon increasingly helpful, the two youngest, Julia and Henry, being constantly with her. The weaving room connected with the house was her workshop, which furnished at least the main reserve employment for the living of herself and children. This work was never wholly given up, while she was able to carry it on. The last time I saw her at her home at grandfather's old place she was thus engaged.

After Henry had passed his babyhood, she took him and Julia, who then with myself was about six years of age, and came to Norval, and occupied a room in our large McNab house, and also used another large room that opened on the street, as a schoolroom, where small children were taught the rudimentary studies, and larger girls were taught needlework. In this village and well-settled country, with good convenient church relations, there were greater means of culture and enjoyment than could be had in Erin, and she used them; and in that respect she could give as well as receive. Her company was sought for, and in any group she could bear a good part in the conversation. She had a strong but sweet and expressive voice for singing, often leading the singing in the meetings. I well remember she and father practicing together from the same note book. It was then the old-style fa, sol, la, mi; the present style came into vogue some time afterwards.

Married women in those days wore muslin caps with a frilled or otherwise ornamented border; were it not for the cap wearing, as I remember her then, she might have been regarded as a fairly handsome girl, though at that time in her thirty-second year, and having been the mother of six children, one of whom died in early childhood. Always, at work or at leisure, she was neat in her person, had an uncommon fine poise of manner, and could express herself thoughtfully and well on most all ordinary subjects; one who was ready with good advice and practical help on all needed occasions, and held the esteem and respect of all those who knew her.

RICHARD WANSBROUGH
MINISTER OF M. E. CHURCH SOUTH

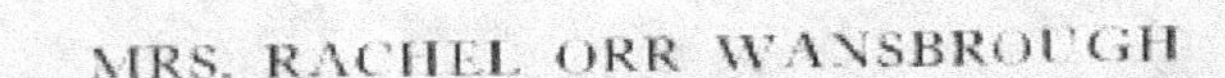

MRS. RACHEL ORR WANSBROUGH

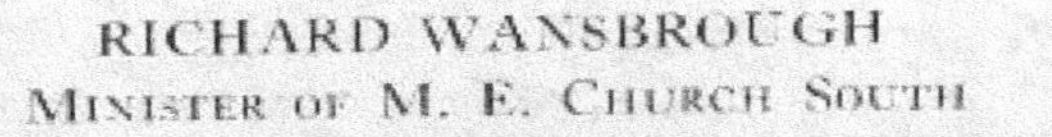

RACHEL ORR WANSBROUGH.

Her eldest daughter, Rachel, was the first grandchild and made the earliest marriage in this record. For this and other reasons, religious differences being likely the most prominent, Aunt was against her match with Richard Wansbrough or "Dick" as he was then known. He was not then a reverend, but a farmer's boy, then a school teacher, afterwards a Methodist minister, in which respected calling he continued throughout his long, active, useful life. However, in this matter of marriage, as usual, the young folks get their way, and if there is any little unwisdom, or want of foresight, they fix it up, or fit themselves to it. Old folks, too, have to make their accommodations, I know Aunt spoke respectfully of her preacher son-in-law.

Cousin Rachel began her wedded life early and continued it long, as she passed away at seventy-five and one-half years, leaving a long line of descendants, as the Wansbrough tree of sixty-seven in number will clearly testify. Her preacher partner outlived her fully eleven years, dying at the advanced age of ninety-three; and saw or might have seen his children's children to the fifth generation, for beginning with Aunt and Hugh Orr there are six generations in this line. In this respect it is ahead of all the rest, and Richard Wansbrough has the greatest age in all this record. This longevity belongs to his line, as his father and mother died at greatly advanced ages.

Samuel Orr, Aunt's eldest son, now living in Alameda, California, is our oldest cousin; he is in his eighty-seventh year, and the oldest in all our direct Trout connection. In contrast with his older sister, Sam married late in life. His partner, Miss Cora Van de Grift, had a sister that became the wife of Robert Louis Stevenson. Samuel's fine family of four sons and two daughters seem to be following his example, as only two of the six have so far undertaken matrimony. As there are only two grandchildren, Samuel's branch number is easily counted. (See Orr Tree.)

Edward, the second son, who had married Jane Forbes of Stewarttown, Ontario, Canada, had seven children, his branch

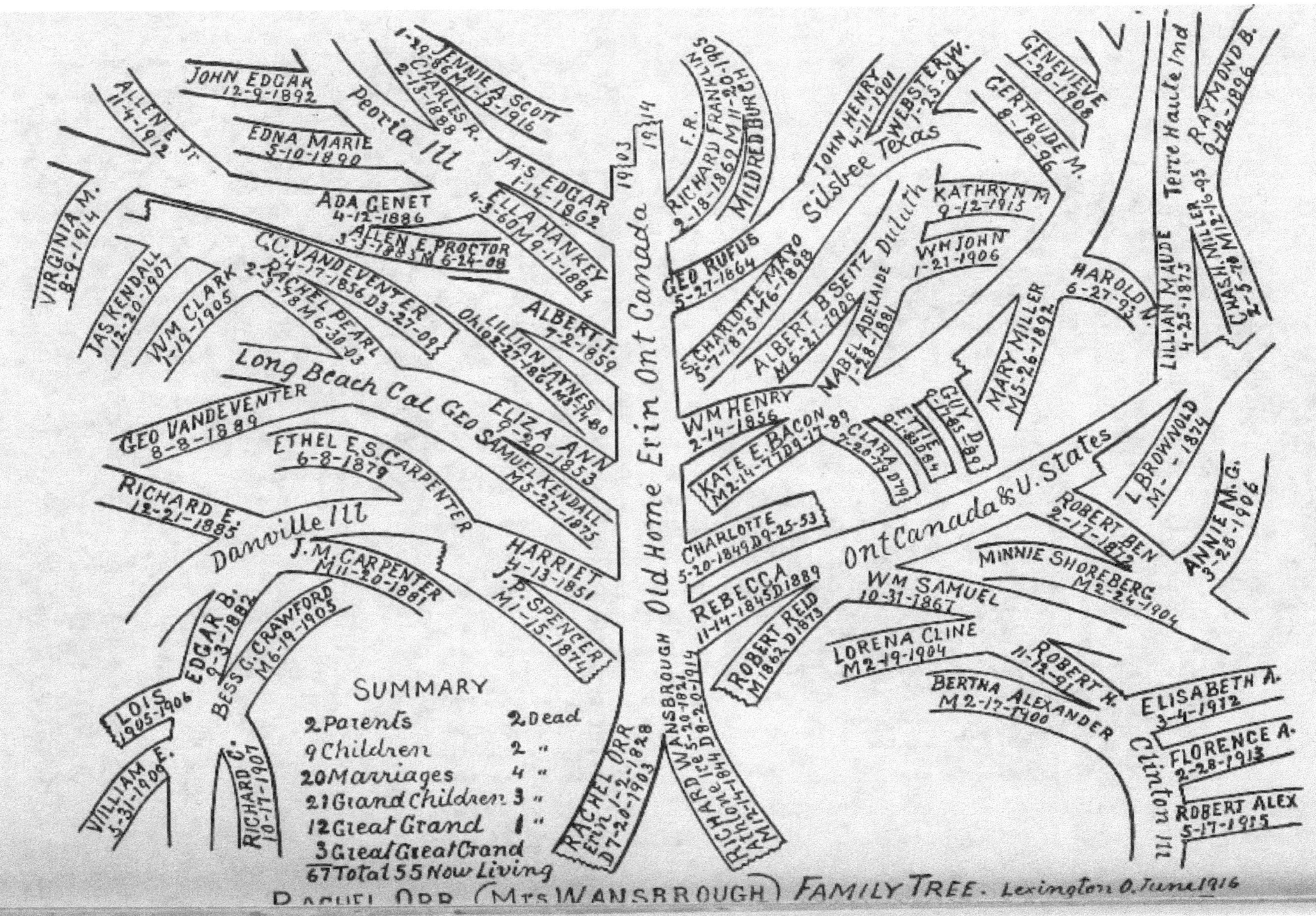

Old Home Erin Ont Canada
1903 1914
Ont Canada & U. States
Silsbee Texas
Adelaide Duluth
Clinton Ill
Peoria Ill
Long Beach Cal
Danville Ill
Terre Haute Ind

JENNIE A SCOTT 1-29-86 M1-15-1916
CHARLES R. 2-13-1888
JOHN EDGAR 12-9-1892
EDNA MARIE 5-10-1890
ALLEN E. Jr 11-4-1912
VIRGINIA M. 8-9-1914
JAS KENDALL 12-20-1907
WM CLARK 1-19-1905
ADA GENET 4-12-1886
JA'S EDGAR 1-14-1862
ELLA HANKEY 3-60 M9-17-1884
ALLEN E PROCTOR 3-78 M 6-24-08
C. C. VANDEVENTER 4-17-1856 D3-27-09
RACHEL PEARL 3-78 M 6-30-03
ALBERT T. 7-2-1859
LILLIAN JAYNES Ohio 2-27-1864 M8-14-80
ELIZA ANN 9-20-1853
GEO VANDEVENTER 8-8-1889
ETHEL E. S. CARPENTER 6-8-1879
GEO SAMUEL KENDALL M5-27-1875
RICHARD E. 12-21-1885
J. M. CARPENTER M11-20-1861
HARRIET 4-13-1851
J. S. SPENCER M1-15-1874
EDGAR B. 9-3-1882
BESS G. CRAWFORD M6-19-1905
LOIS 1905-1906
WILLIAM E. 5-31-1909
RICHARD C. 10-17-1907

F. R.
RICHARD FRANKLIN 9-18-1862 M11-20-05
MILDRED BURCH
GEO RUFUS 5-27-1864
SCHARLOTTE MAYO 5-7-1875 M6-1898
JOHN HENRY 4-11-1901
W. WEBSTER 1-25-01
ALBERT B SEITZ Duluth M6-31-1929
MABEL ADELAIDE 1-28-1881
WM JOHN 1-21-1906
KATHRYN M. 9-12-1915
GENEVIEVE 1-20-1908
GERTRUDE M. 8-18-96
HAROLD N. 6-27-93
LILLIAN MAUDE 4-25-1873
RAYMOND B. 9-12-1896
C. H. ASH. MILLER 2-5-78 M12-16-95
WM HENRY 2-14-1856
KATE E. BACON M2-14-77 D9-17-89
CLARA 7-20-79 D79
GUY D. 6-1785-89
ETTIE 9-1-80 D84
MARY MILLER M5-26-1892
CHARLOTTE 5-20-1849 D9-25-53
REBECCA 11-14-1845 D1889
ROBERT REID M1862 D1873
L. BROWNOLD M: - 1874
ROBERT BEN 2-17-1872
ANNIE M. G. 3-28-1906
WM SAMUEL 10-31-1867
MINNIE SHOREBERG M2-24-1904
LORENA CLINE M2-19-1904
BERTHA ALEXANDER M2-17-1900
ROBERT H. 11-12-91
ELISABETH A. 3-4-1912
FLORENCE A. 2-28-1913
ROBERT ALEX 5-17-1915
RICHARD WANSBROUGH Arthone Ire 5-20-1821 M12-14-1844 D8-20-1914
RACHEL ORR Erin 1-2-1848 D7-20-1903

SUMMARY
2 Parents
9 Children
20 Marriages
21 Grand Children
12 Great Grand
3 Great Great Grand
67 Total 55 Now Living
2 Dead
2 "
4 "
3 "
1 "

RACHEL ORR (Mrs WANSBROUGH) FAMILY TREE. Lexington O. June 1916

MRS. HARRIET WANSBROUGH CARPENTER
ELDEST LIVING OF RICHARD WANSBROUGH FAMILY

CHILDREN OF ROBERT H. REED
THE EIGHTH GENERATION FROM GRANDFATHER HENRY GEORGE TROUT

in all numbering twenty-two, quite a number of whom are still unmarried. As mentioned, Edward started in his father's line of business in Creemore, but afterwards undertook and carried on, for about fifteen years, a stone-cutting and monument business in Georgetown, Ontario; but with failing health came also business difficulties, and, finally, his death in 1874.

Henry, the youngest brother, married Mary Curtis Royce, by whom there were six children, three of whom are living, and two are married, with eight grandchildren. Henry had been with Edward in his Georgetown business, and sought to re-establish it, but did not succeed, and died in 1879.

Henry's youngest child, the only living son, Lewis D. Orr, felt the urgent call of his country, and became one of Canada's half-million enlisted men. He is now with the Canadian contingent at Salonika, is a first lieutenant, and, being a pharmacist, he was given charge of the medical stores in Hospital No. 5. He is not married, but has been making a home for his mother, and she has been its keeper for him. In a letter to me, she said, "He felt that he *must* go, but hated to leave me alone. Of course, I felt it was a great sacrifice for me to *see* him go, but I felt I ought to be as brave as he was, and 'do my bit' at home when he had gone to the front." He writes regularly to his mother; and in a recent letter gives a vivid description of the shooting down of a great German Zeppelin, that had begun its second destructive raid over Salonika. It would be interesting to give this lively eye-witness story, could we spare the space.

The daughters' side of the Orr line makes much the largest showing; Julia Ann, the second and youngest daughter, married David McDonald, with a resulting family of eight children, with eight marriages and grandchildren and great-grandchildren numbering in all thirty persons, who are still largely Canadians. (See special tree on accompanying page.)

The Orrs and connections, as a whole, number one hundred and sixty-three, of whom one hundred and thirty-three are living. They are scattered from Canada to the Gulf of Mexico, and from Alaska to Southern California, on account of which the extent of my correspondence may be judged.

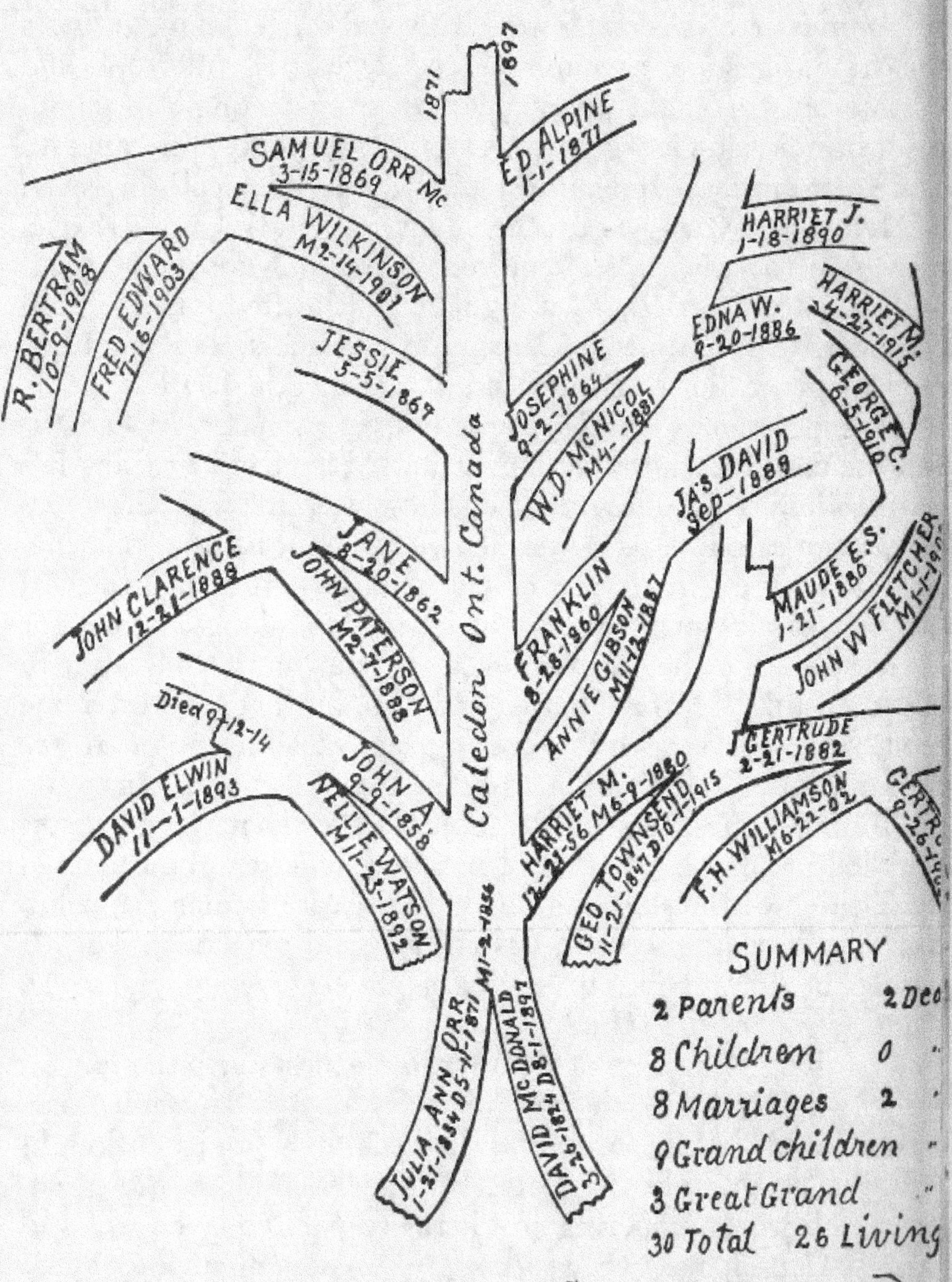

JULIA ANN ORR (Mrs DAVID McDONALD)
FAMILY TREE

JULIA ANN ORR McDONALD

HENRY ORR

From my limited acquaintance with the great body of these relatives, I judge them to be largely a fine, whole-hearted style of people, actively filling good useful places in our common American life.

My correspondents among them have, with a very few exceptions, been total strangers to me, but there has been nearly always a helpful, kindly response to every request for information. I would like to know more about them, which is not by any means likely. While this record introduces me to them, as well as to others, I hope it will have the effect of introducing the separate groups of Orrs, Wansbroughs and McDonalds, and their various subconnections to one another, and to the larger fraternity of the general Trout connection. For this purpose I have given residences as well as I could. We all converge in Aunt Harriet. She is great enough, good and lovable enough, to be the common center of esteem and affection for all of us. The father in this case is largely unknown; but the remembrance of Aunt continues, as both a pride and a pleasure to all that have known or heard about her. Her name is the most popular in the whole connection. There are twelve Harriets. We feel that these brief references are but scant justice to one we so highly esteem and to so large and worthy a line of relatives, but space forbids more attention. We must go forward with the next in order.

RACHEL TROUT McDONALD.

The marrying season in grandfather's family began in 1826, when in the common parlance of old times, Aunt Ann "jumped the broomstick" at the good age of twenty-three. Then on the second day of January, 1827, Aunt Harriet followed suit, at nearly nineteen and one-half years. Then on March twenty-first, the subject of our present notice tied the nuptial knot. Father and Uncle Henry were also married the same year. Aunt Rachel was the youngest in entering the married state, being scarcely seventeen and one-half, and her boy spouse, though just three years older, was more than six months short of man's estate. How much we all would have liked to have been at that wedding. It was thirty-five years

Old Family Home Caledon Ont Can

Winnifred Alta Can

WILLIAM 8-14-1855

ANNA S. THOMPSON M 2-6-89

Wm ALEX 12-24-1890

RACHEL 5-15-1850

SAMUEL 6-3-1852

Home Unknown US

UNKNOWN

JAMES About 1882

Port Huron Mich

DANIEL 4-16-1848

MARTHA VERNON 11-9-1848 M 2-20-1887

D 11-4-95   See Special

David 7-31-1845   Port Huron Mich   Died 1-12-19..

MATILDA BEATY 2-29-1848 M 7-26-1865   See Special

D 3-19-1913 Niagara Falls NY

ALEXANDER 8-17-1843

MARGARET E. McARTHUR 5-6-1845 M 7-4-1868

Died 1861   See Special

HARRIET 8-6-1838 M 12-26-1855

Arthur Ont Can   D 9-19-1..   D 4-30-18..

ISAAC NUNN 3-30-1833   See Special

Died 10-2-1910

Hawley Minn   HENRY 6-6-1841

ELIZABETH BREEZE M 1871   See Special

MARIA HYAT M 1869 D 1870

GEORGE Rockside Ont 2-15-1835   D 11-23-19..   6 Sons 7 Daughters

FRANCIS A. HARRIS 7-12-39 M 1-26-39   See Special

Drowned 7-20-1853

WILLIAM 7-15-1832

JAMES Caledon 8-3-1830   2 Sons 2 Daughters   Died 8-5-190.

MARY A BEATTY 8-__-1833 M 7-12-1859   7-25-1905   See Special Tree

Died 10-24-1901   9-13-1906

JOHN Caledon 8-27-1828

SARAH ANN TURKINGTON 8-25-1830 M 1-31-1850   See Special Tree

RACHEL TROUT Fort Erie 10-1-1809 M 3-21-1827

DANIEL McDONALD 10-20-1806 Scotland 10-10-1890 Died 12-10-189.

RACHEL TROUT (Mrs McDONALD)
FAMILY TREE   Lupkin Texas June 19
W.H.T.

RACHEL TROUT McDONALD, AND DANIEL McDONALD
OF CALEDON, ONTARIO, CANADA

before the days of photography, but we may presume to imagine the scene. It was in grandfather's large living-room, which was about the best in that whole country.

It was full of guests, and the rooms adjoining would hold an extra portion. They were plain people. Home-spun and home-made garments were the standard style. Tailors made most of the men's clothes; but the women generally made their own, after having made the fabric both for themselves and the men. There would be some store goods and ribbons, but not much. The best would be on the bride, and the next best on the groom, still we would regard them plain people. The girlish bride of seventeen and one-half years was no willowy, slender, reed-like form, but a good, hearty, redcheeked, bright-eyed buxom lass that manifestly was good for great accomplishments. The groom was boyish appearing, but a sturdy and athletic figure, about medium size. His usual smile was mixed up with his bashfulness, so that it would be hard to determine whether good humor or modesty prevailed. They both looked young, and some might say "green," but that would be a great mistake, it would never be a safe thing to intimate to Daniel McDonald. There would be a gleam of hostile mischief in his eye right away that called for apologies, or trouble would quickly come. Though he may not have looked it, yet that boy under twenty-one was every inch a manly man. Those two minors standing together, in that solemn assembly of relatives and friends, promising to live helpfully to each other while life should last, truly lived out their pledge. The happy wedding party separated, and these two youngsters went to their small home "in a hole of the woods" (as we usually called the beginning small clearing) on a two-hundred acre bush farm to carve out a competence and make a family home; a place where strength, prolonged labor, with continued persistent good management were required to clear off the immense trees, fence the fields, and bring the results that I saw fourteen years afterwards, in the fine large stretch of a cleared-up farm, then with good log buildings. Equal to this was the family progress in their log house, five, hearty, fine-looking boys and one little daughter graced the family table;

and this progress continued until the farm was largely cleared, with frame buildings in place, and ten sons and two daughters as the occupants of the enlarged home. What think you of that, you miserly, selfish, ease-loving, pleasure-seeking, married folks, who say and determine, "we will not have any children, but just have a good time by ourselves and quit"? This dodging-duty, lazy, cowardly policy never yields what is expected. A good time? Not by any means, but a dull time, that grows duller still, as the long wearisome years go by. I recall a visit made by Uncle Dan and Aunt Rachel to father and mother, when the children of both pairs were nearly all away from their old home shelter. They had traveled by cars and steamboat one hundred and forty miles, and spent several weeks at our old place. Did those aged people have a dull time? Why, the rich memories of well-filled lives was enough to keep them happy. At that time I saw Uncle play the young lover with his aged mate just for the pure fun of the performance.

In those old Canadian days, while the winter time had its share of hard work in chopping down the forest, rail-splitting, etc., it was also the business time, play time, and traveling time of the year. There being no railroads, the public road travel was large. Farmers might sell their grain or pork at the nearest big village, or drive fifty or a hundred miles to the nearest lake port, where they were sure of better prices, so that in winter time the principal main roads of the country were extensively travelled. The snow would be beaten down and hardened the full breadth of the turnpike. By common consent the loaded teams had the choice, and best right of way, and were driven slowly; but after sales were made, dinner and social drinks disposed of, and the home journey begun, it was different. "Whoop her up, boys," was then the style of the time; though the horses had no share in the stimulant, they knew the role to be played, and entered into it in the same spirit as the men. They would all spring off at a high brisk trot, but some excited Jehu would determine that he would run his fine team past everything on the road, so with a few cuts of the whip his team was off on the keen gallop; those ahead knew by the changed sound of the bells what was coming, and the horses knew it, too, and were instantly off at the same gait. Those drivers ahead that might not choose to run, had to run, or else get entirely out of the way, or they might choose to give the Jehu a good fair run, letting him win if he could; but some, rather than allow him to pass, would crowd him into the ditch, where he must either hold up or risk a broken sleigh and runaway horses. The presence of women in a sleigh generally insured fair play; but, anyway, the home-run was sure to be an exciting journey.

In the winter of 1852 and 1853 Mary and I made a journey to Erin and Caledon, remaining at Uncle Dan's several days. His boys generally had their own young horses for their riding or driving, there was also a light sleigh for riding only. George, then like myself a well, grown-up boy, came in from Cheltenham one evening, with his team dripping perspiration and with spreading, panting nostrils and fiery eyes. Uncle saw their condition, and scolded George severely. He made no reply, but remarked to myself and others afterwards, "It's all very well for Dad to scold us, but he never let a team pass him on the road." It certainly took Uncle Dan a long time to become an old man.

I have frequently referred to the drinking habits of the times; there was very little decided temperance sentiments. Liquor had many advocates as a good thing. Scotch whiskey to a Scotchman seemed to fit all right. Paul tells us, "Every creature of God is good, if a man use it lawfully," so that whiskey was surely lawful, if you did not take too much. Father told a story of two Highlanders travelling on foot together; they could eat their lunch by the side of a spring or a sparkling brook, and drink the purest heaven distilled liquid that might be found in that pure water country, but to them the real refreshment could only be had at the taverns, and, of course, they stopped to get it. One was quite pious in his ways, and the other rather waggish. When the drinks were set down to them, the first put up his hands and closed his eyes, and was thanking God for the gift, while the other swiped his tumbler and drank it, and his own, too. When

LEOLA H. ADOPTED 8-21-1908
ALLEN R 4-15-1900
HENRY L 8-16-1896
JAMES S 7-29-1892
DANIEL W 10-19-1889
LEIGHTON 8-5-1911
ROBERT H 5-21-1909
Hawley

ELIZABETH E. 8-23-1908
ALICE MAE 6-5-1906
ANNA ADA 1-12-1904
DONALD 1-16-1902
SADIE A 6-1-18
FRANCIS K. 10-5-1914
HELEN REYDD M-12-27 Hawley
THOMAS 4-25-1890
6-9-1890 1913
Died 10-24-1890

ROBERT 1905
RUSSELL 10-3-1907
IRVING ARCHER 8-5-1931
GERTRUDE 12-14-1910
GEO M 88 BURT 4-4 1885
ELIZA 10-28-1886
RAYMOND WHALEY 1-18-1881 M-13-1911
Hawley
Minneapolis

JOHN T 1-18-1896
RACHEL McG 3-11-1804 Died
RACHEL 1-11-1892 Died
MARY 2-18-1890
BLANCHE E. 7-18-1889
GEORGE A 1859 M 12-12-1888
ANNIE HSILL 2-20-1869
Chicago
6-9-1904
Hawley

SARAH ANN 11-19-1859 Died 4-14-1871 Scottish Fever
D 9-13-1906
Died 10-24-1901
LAURA JOHNSON 4-6-1887
ROBERT H 1-24-1888 M 9-2-1908
HERMAN R BURRILL 9-19-1858 M 4-19-1885
HARRIET 2-26-1865

ANNIE 1-5-1867
ISAAC REED Married 6-26-1892
Hamilton Can
SADIE 6-15-1893
E.GLADYS 10-26-1898
CLARA 10-11-1900
JEAN 3-20-1895
ROBERT R. 1902
GLADYS 11-23-1897
STANLY JOHN 3-27-1899

DAVID J 5-26-1863
M BLANCHE JOHNSON 1-1-1890 Born 2-5-1862
Muscoda
ANNA P. 10-31-1893
WILLIAM H 2-17-1891
Hawley
AMOS ROLFE 8-24-1892
ANNIE ETHEL 9-5-1885

ELIZABETH 9-2-1881
WESLY R TAINTER 1-7-1862 M 12-3-1884
DOUGLAS
MARY A 1895
H.GROVER 1892
JOHN W 1887
Winnifred Alta

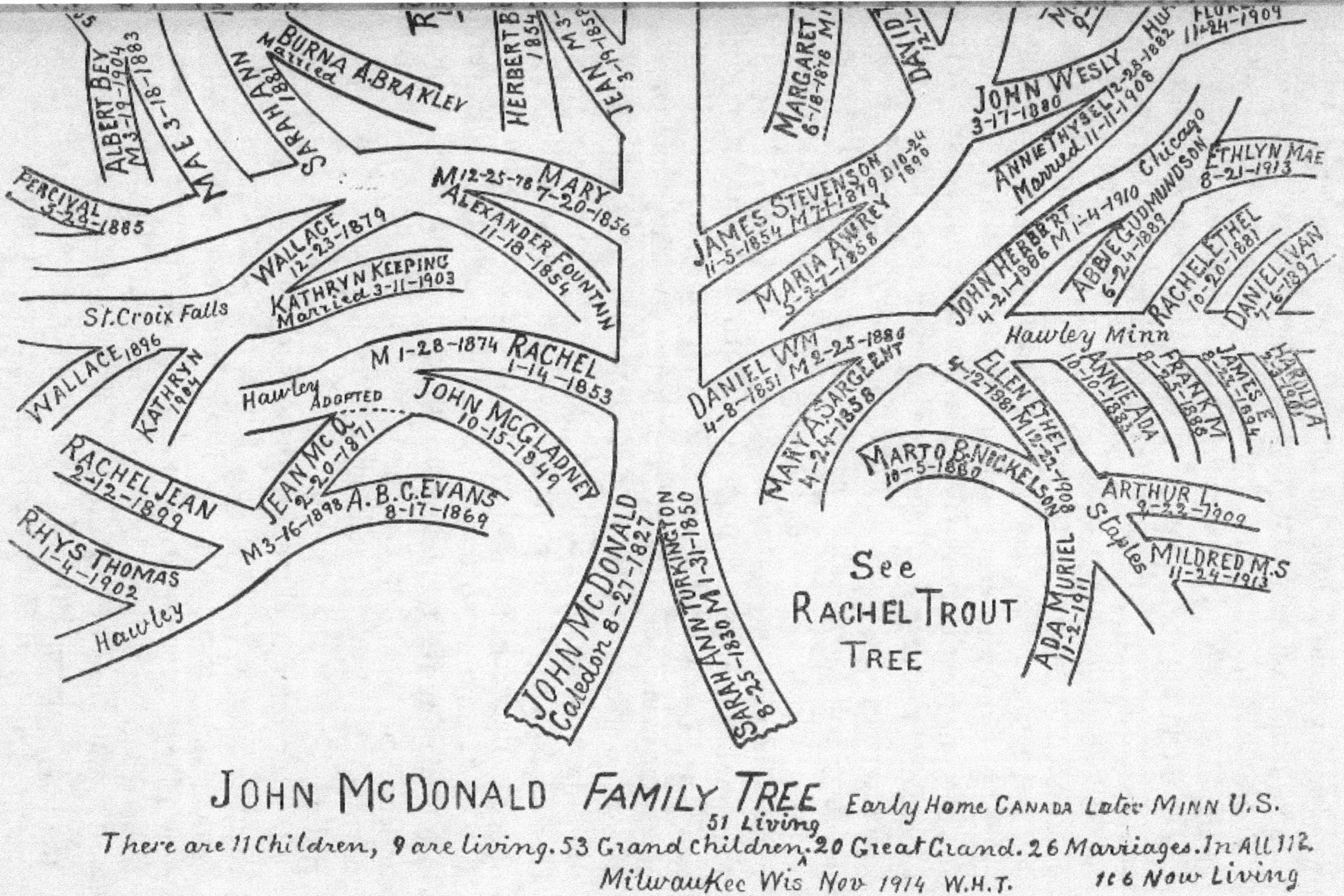

JOHN McDONALD FAMILY TREE   Early Home CANADA Later MINN U.S.
51 Living
There are 11 Children, 9 are living. 53 Grand children. 20 Great Grand. 26 Marriages. In All 112.
Milwaukee Wis Nov 1914 W.H.T.   116 Now Living

the thanking was done, seeing the empty glass before him, he turned a reproachful look on his mate, who responded with, "Maun, don't you naw that you must *watch* as well as pray."

There were few habitual drinkers, and the occasional ones are the most likely to get drunk, as it takes less to do it, and they don't know their gauge. One of the great troubles of the social drinking, at taverns or logging bees or barn raisings, was that the little squabbles that were not worth settling when sober, generally came up for settlement when liquor fired the blood; then there was chance for a fight and a worse estrangement. A fight was easily started, some of the young men would go in for the fun of it. Uncle would not seek to turn aside, and his eldest son John would never back out of a row no matter how big it was. There is a story told of his cleaning out a bar room full of roughs after several had pitched on him. When I saw him last, early in 1853, at hard work in his smith's shop by the roadside at Rockside, and at his home in the evening with his wife and little baby boy, it seemed as if "the Fighting John" was far away, and so he was. These times and conditions did not last long, and the McDonalds, though so strong and capable, were the best natured boys you could meet anywhere. The McDonald clan is Highland, but Uncle was raised in the Scotch Lowlands, and spoke the broad dialect. Between him and Aunt and the children they had a modified form that softened and euphonized the English very nicely, making their good nature the more expressive. These dialects soon wear out, and the Canadians are known to speak very pure English. (See Double Tree and portrait of himself and wife.)

Cousin John McDonald, along with George and Henry, early became citizens of the United States, by moving to Hawley and its neighborhood in Minnesota, where there is now a large colony of McDonalds and connections, who seem to be reflecting nothing but credit on the good name.

Through one of Cousin John's daughters, Mrs. Tainter, and her daughter Ethel, I received quite promptly the fullest, most orderly, and complete family returns of those three families, that have come to me in all my correspondence. How-

JOHN McDONALD AND SARAH ANN T. McDONALD

JAMES McDONALD AND MARY A. B. McDONALD

ever, there is an error in the birth date of John on his Family Tree; he was born in 1828 instead of 1827. It involved considerable patient labor, but it was cheerfully performed. As a life and health record it is quite extraordinary, surpassing all the other family lines in this history. (See the family trees.) Of the six parents four are dead, at an average age of seventy-five. In John's family, numbering in all one hundred and twelve, besides the two parents, there are three infants under three years and a son at forty-six, the only deaths since 1852. George's record is about as good. There are two infantile deaths and one son at thirty-seven. George lived to near the close of his seventy-ninth year, and the widowed mother still lives at seventy-eight, four deaths out of sixty-six persons since 1839. Henry's, though much more limited, is also good. Two infants and the first wife are dead, also himself at seventy-seven. The mother of the family still lives. Four deaths out of twenty-eight persons. In all three families there were two hundred and five people, of whom one hundred and ninety-one are now living; counting out marriages, the actual living progeny is one hundred and forty, the net life result of six parents who began their lives at an average of eighty-one years ago. That is the kind of family progress that would please our ex-president Roosevelt; and they are all native Americans, for a Canadian is an American, though not an American citizen, which is the final result in this instance.

James McDonald, the second son, has been passed by. He was the home boy, while all the others, though not prodigals, "went to the far country." There were five boys in the household before the first girl, Harriet, was born; evidently the mother must have some dependable help, so James was assigned to her. He was to be her special helping boy. I have heard Uncle Dan refer to him as the mother's boy. As far as my limited observation went, it seemed to be agreeable. Certainly James remained by the old people to the last, and succeeded to the fine, old farm, which his eldest son, Daniel Robert, now owns and occupies, and has named Maple Hill Farm. James also bought another good farm in the neighbor-

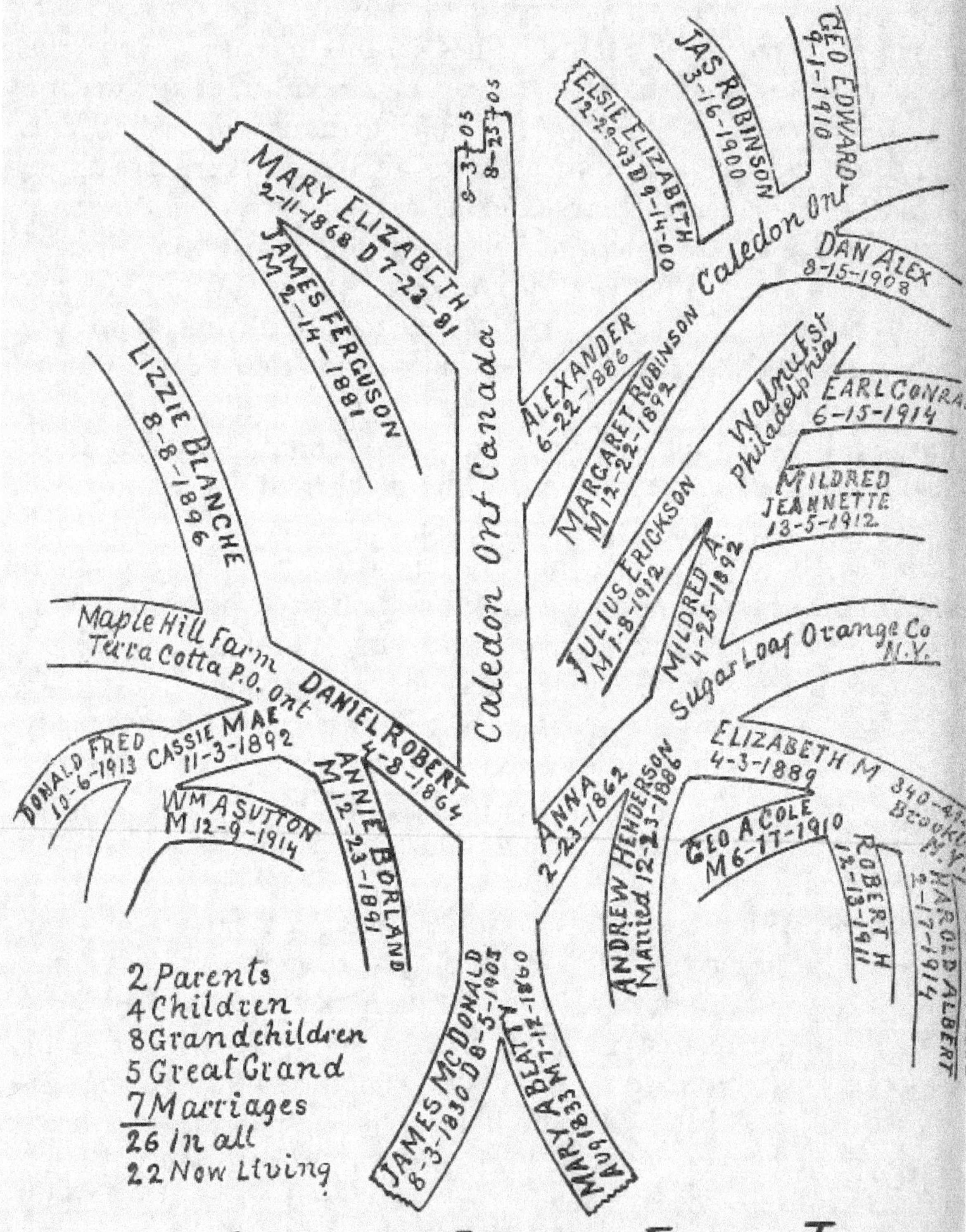

JAMES McDONALD FAMILY TREE

Lufkin Texas   April 1916 W H.T.

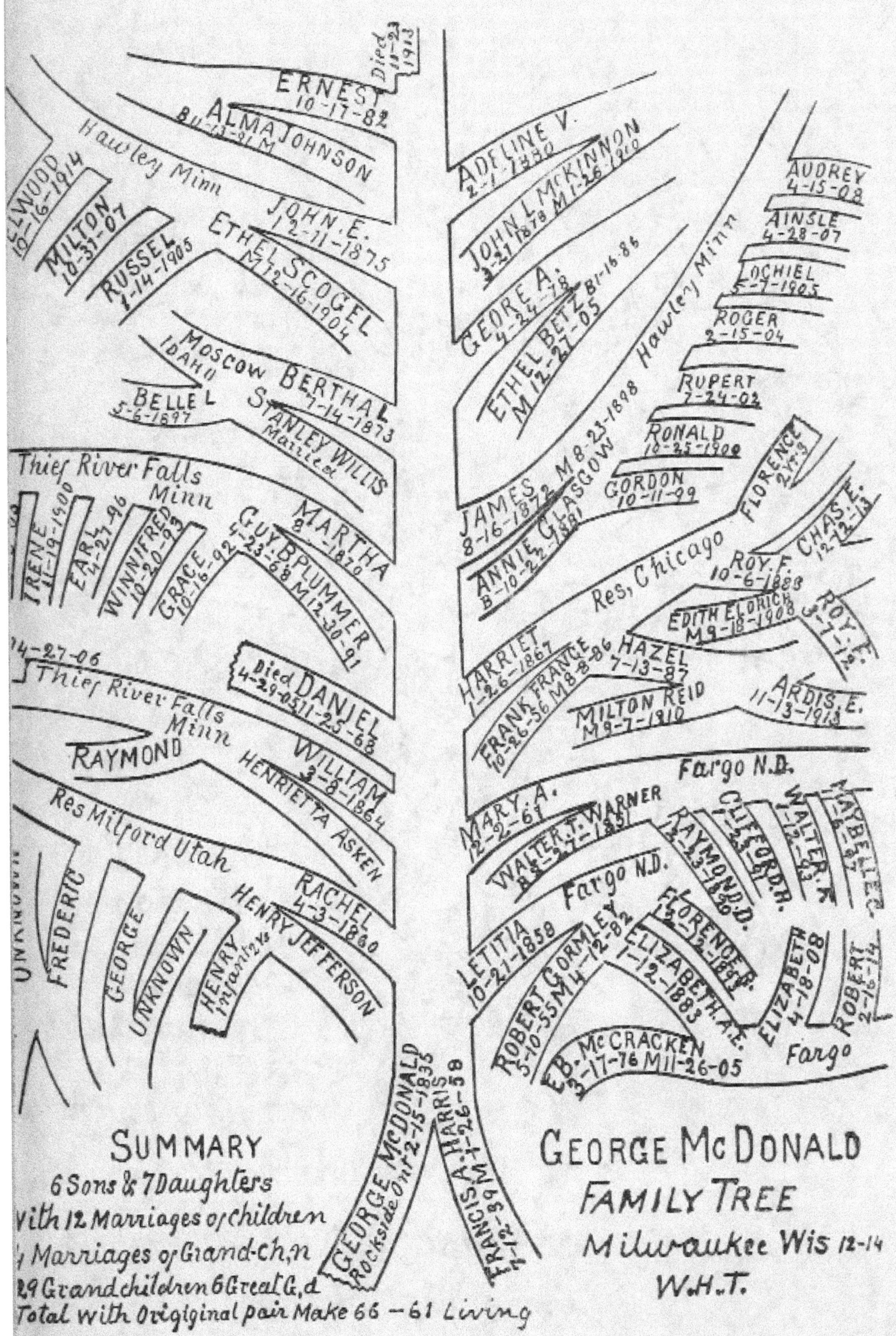
ERNEST
10-17-82
Died 10-23 1913
ALMA JOHNSON
8-13-81 M
Hawley Minn
ELLWOOD
10-16-1914
MILTON
10-31-07
RUSSEL
1-14-1905
JOHN E.
12-11-1875
ETHEL SCOGEL
M 7-16-1904
Moscow BERTHA L
IDAHO 7-14-1873
BELLE L
5-6-1897
STANLEY WILLIS
Married
Thief River Falls
Minn
IRENE
11-19-1900
EARL
4-27-96
WINNIFRED
10-20-93
GRACE
10-16-92
MARTHA
8-1870
GUY B PLUMMER
4-23-68 M 12-30-91
4-27-06
Thief River Falls
Minn
Died DANIEL
4-29-05 11-25-68
RAYMOND
WILLIAM
3-8-1864
HENRIETTA ASKEN
Res Milford Utah
UNKNOWN
FREDERIC
GEORGE
UNKNOWN
HENRY Infant 2 ys
RACHEL
4-3-1860
HENRY JEFFERSON
GEORGE McDONALD
Rockside Ont 2-15-1835
FRANCIS A HARRIS
M 1-26-58

ADELINE V.
2-1-1880
JOHN L McKINNON
3-21-1879 M 11-26-1910
GEORE A.
4-24-78
ETHEL BETZ
M 12-27-05 Br 16-86
JAMES 8-16-1872 M 8-23-1898
ANNIE GLASGOW
B 10-22-1881
Res, Chicago
HARRIET
1-26-1867
FRANK FRANCE
10-26-56 M 8-8-86
MILTON REID
M 9-7-1910
Hawley Minn
AUDREY
4-15-08
AINSLE
4-28-07
LOCHIEL
5-7-1905
ROGER
3-15-04
RUPERT
7-24-02
RONALD
10-25-1900
GORDON
10-11-99
FLORENCE
2 yr 9
ROY F.
10-6-1883
EDITH ELDRICH
M 9-18-1908
CHAS E.
12-22-13
HAZEL
7-13-87
ROY
5-7-12
ARDIS E.
11-13-1913
MARY A.
12-2-61
WALTER T WARNER
B 5-27-1851
Fargo N.D.
LETITIA
10-21-1858
ROBERT GORMLEY
5-10-55 M 4-72-82
Fargo N.D.
E B. McCRACKEN
3-17-76 M 11-26-05
RAYMOND D.
CLIFFORD R.
FLORENCE
13-3-1899
ELIZABETH A E.
7-12-1883
WALTER K.
1-13-11
MAYBELLE C.
3-97
ELIZABETH
4-18-08
ROBERT
2-16-14
Fargo
Fargo N.D.
SUMMARY
6 Sons & 7 Daughters
with 12 Marriages of children
4 Marriages of Grand-ch,n
29 Grandchildren 6 Great G,d
Total with Original pair Make 66 — 61 Living
GEORGE McDONALD
FAMILY TREE
Milwaukee Wis 12-14
W.H.T.

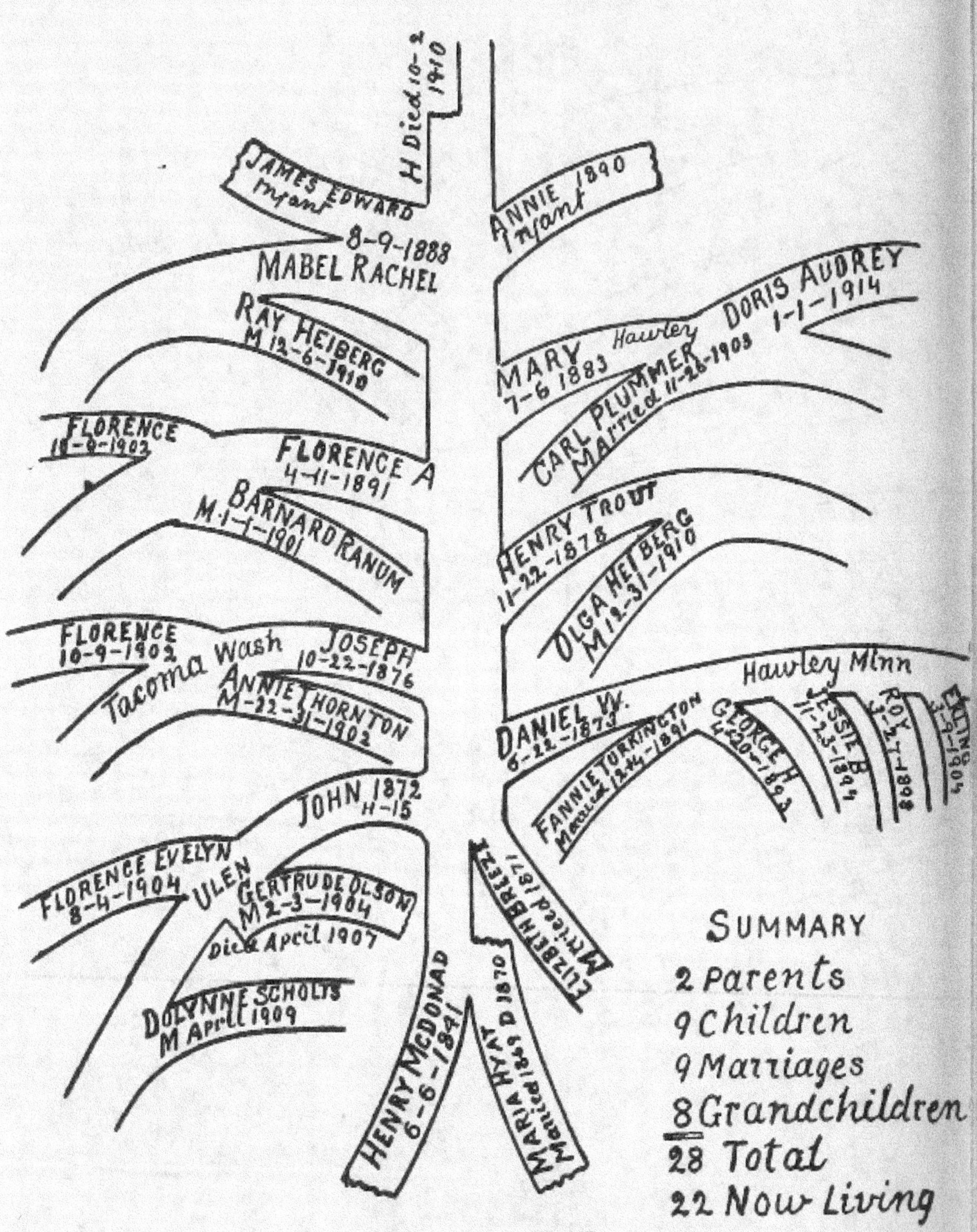

HENRY McDONALD

FAMILY TREE

FAMILY HOME MINN. U.S.

Milwaukee, Wis. Nov, 1914.

W. H. T.

hood, which was given to the second son, Alexander, who, evidently providing for the future of his own three boys, purchased two other good, large pieces of farm property in the vicinity. In this case, at least, home loyalty has paid. If those who left the homeland have done as well, the McDonalds must be regarded as decidedly thrifty people. James filled several important offices in connection with the township and county. His sons no doubt are following in that line as well as the others. These Canadian Mac's are active Presbyterians, the church body that prevails in the McDonald line.

William, the third son, was a fine, big, manly fellow about six feet, the tallest of the family. He left the old home early, and became a sailor on the northern lakes. About the year 1853, he met his death, by descending as a diver into a sunken schooner in Lake Erie to recover some valuables. My remembrance of the event, as I heard about it shortly afterwards, was that the air pipes, connecting his head armour to the air pumps above, got fouled, and he was said to be drowned, though strictly he was smothered to death.

Harriet, the only daughter that had a family, deserves extra notice. As I knew her, when a girl and a young married woman, she was a person of rare, modest beauty and fine good sense and kindly spirit, though I have known little about her since that early time; and the good man of her choice, Isaac Nunn, was in every way deserving such a prize. They made us a good, sleighride visit to our old home in St. Vincent, when they had their first baby.

October 28, 1916. I have had great difficulty in getting in touch, or rather in getting responses with names and dates, with this large Nunn family. They seem to be mainly farmers, scattered widely over their broad Canadian country. Only lately have I had even half-way success.

Isaac Nunn and Harriet McDonald had six boys and three girls, all living, except one daughter, Margery. One son, Bowman, never married. There are eight marriages, all having children; and there are a good number of subfamilies, which, though my returns are yet very incomplete, I would

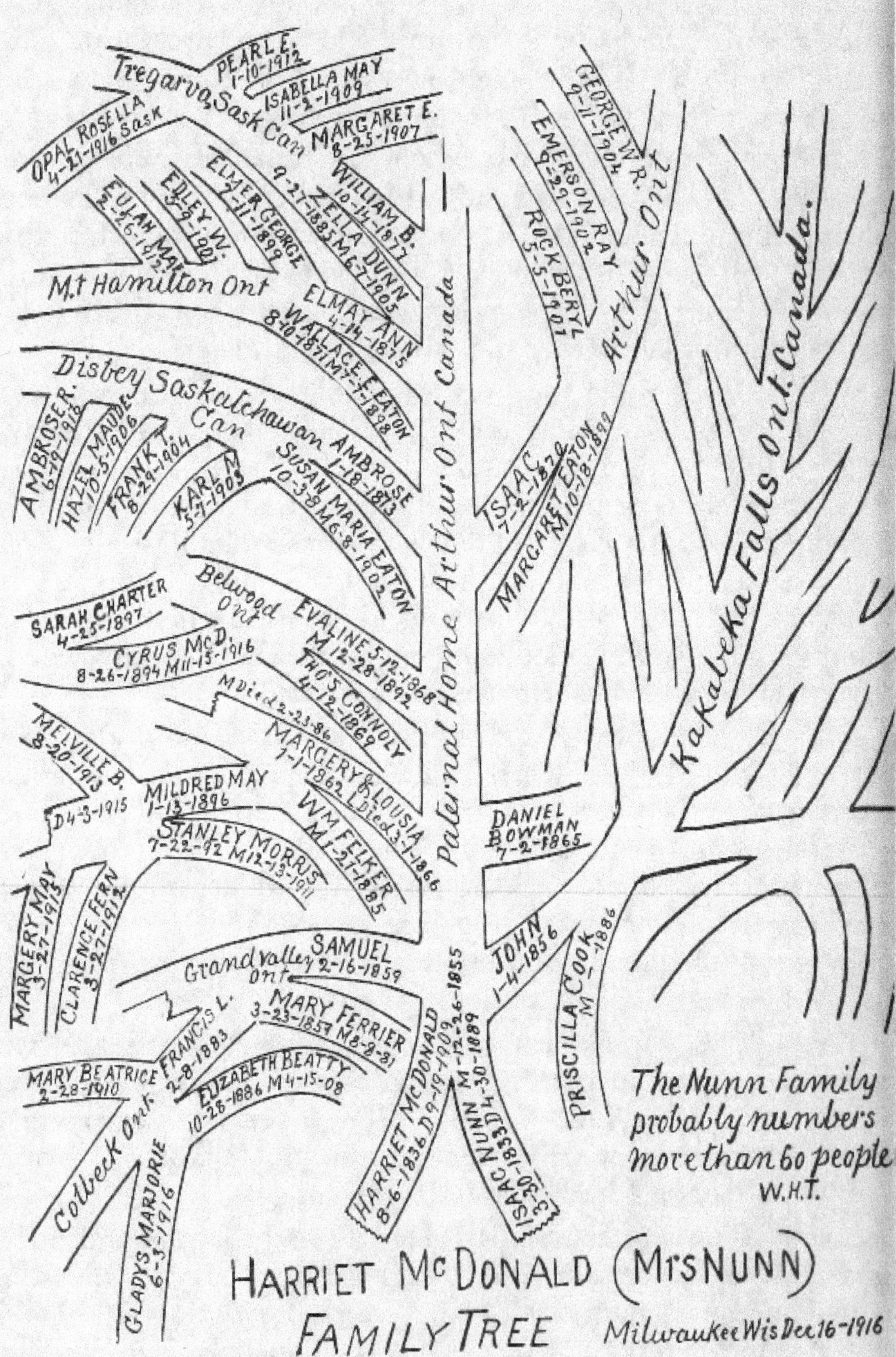
PEARL E.
1-10-1912
Tregarva Sask Can
ISABELLA MAY
11-3-1909
OPAL ROSELLA
4-21-1916 Sask
MARGARET E.
8-25-1907
WILLIAM B.
10-14-1877
EULAH MALTON
3-26-1932
EDLEY W.
3-8-1901
ELMER GEORGE
7-11-1899
ZELLA DUNN
9-27-1885 M 6-7-1905
M.t Hamilton Ont
ELMA Y ANN
4-14-1875
WALLACE E. EATON
8-10-1871 M 7-1-1898
Disbey Saskatchawan Ambrose
1-18-1873
AMBROSE R.
6-12-1912
HAZEL MAUDE
10-5-1906
FRANK T.
8-29-1904
KARL N.
5-7-1903
SUSAN MARIA EATON
10-3-39 M 6-8-1902
Can
SARAH CHARTER
4-25-1897
Belwood Ont
EVALINE 5-12-1868
M 12-28-1892
CYRUS McD.
8-26-1894 M 11-15-1916
THO'S CONNOLY
4-12-1869
M Died 2-23-86
MARGERY & LOUSIA
1-1-1862 L Died 3-1-1866
MELVILLE B.
8-20-1913
D 4-3-1915
MILDRED MAY
1-13-1896
STANLEY MORRIS
7-22-72 M 12-13-1911
WM FELKER
M 1-27-1885
MARGERY MAY
3-27-1915
CLARENCE FERN
3-27-1912
Grand valley
Ont
SAMUEL
2-16-1859
FRANCIS L.
2-8-1883
MARY FERRIER
3-23-1857 M 8-8-81
MARY BEATRICE
2-28-1910
ELIZABETH BEATTY
10-28-1886 M 4-15-08
Colbeck Ont
GLADYS MARJORIE
6-3-1916
HARRIET McDONALD
8-6-1836, D 9-19-1909
M-12-26-1855
ISAAC NUNN D 4-30-1889
1853 D 1-30-1913
GEORGE W R.
2-11-1904
EMERSON RAY
EQ-29-1902
ROCK BERYL
5-5-1901
Arthur Ont
ISAAC
7-2-1876
MARGARET EATON
M 10-18-1899
Paternal Home Arthur Ont Canada
Kakabeka Falls Ont. Canada.
DANIEL
BOWMAN
7-2-1865
JOHN
1-4-1856
PRISCILLA COOK
M 1886
The Nunn Family
probably numbers
more than 60 people
W.H.T.
HARRIET McDONALD (MrsNUNN)
FAMILY TREE
Milwaukee Wis Dec 16-1916

MRS. HARRIET McDONALD NUNN

DANIEL McDONALD AND GRANDSON
PORT HURON, MICHIGAN

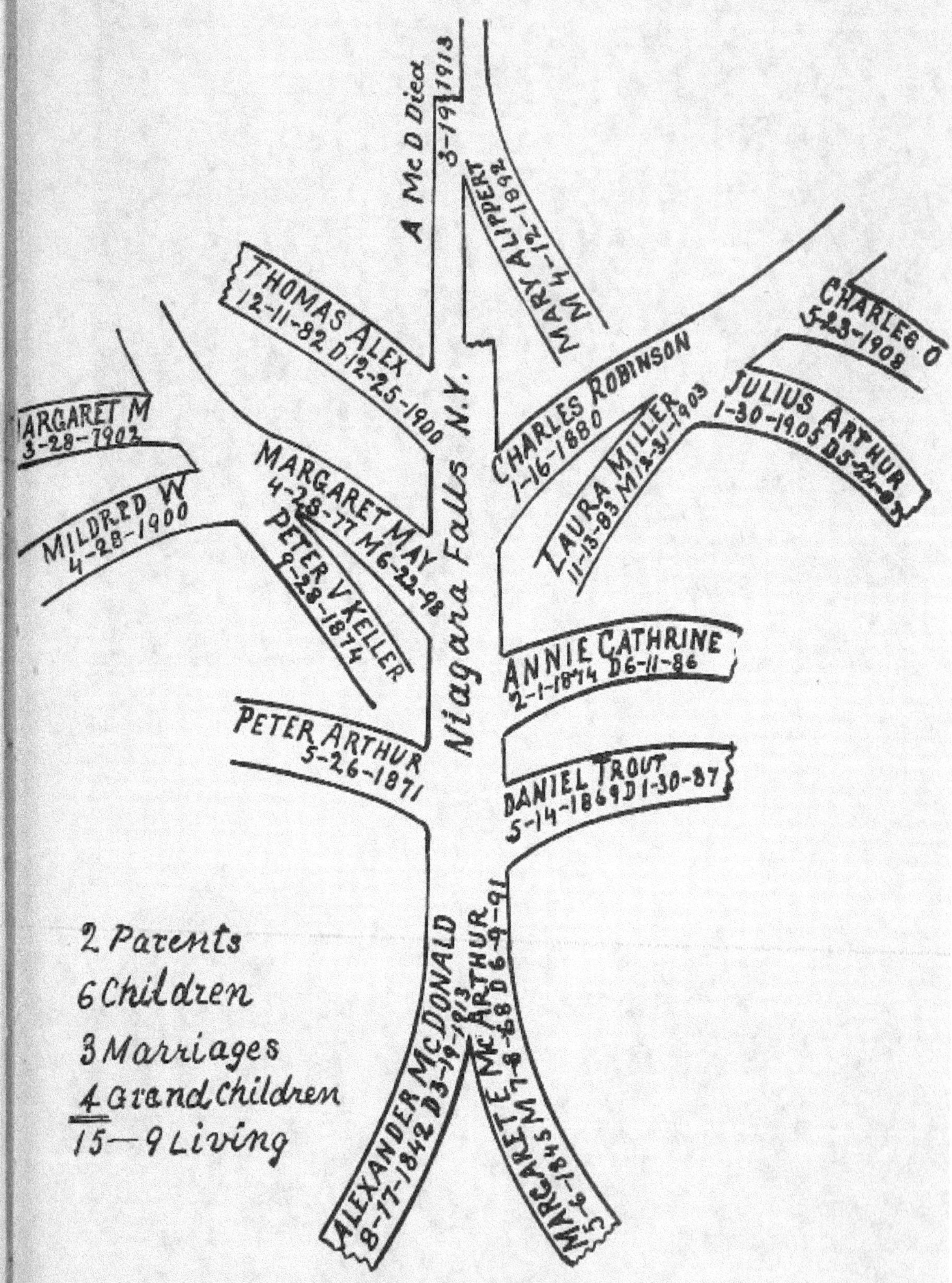

A McD Died 3-19-1913
MARY A LIPPERT 4-12-1892
THOMAS ALEX 12-11-82 D 12-25-1900
CHARLES ROBINSON 1-16-1880
CHARLES O 5-23-1908
MARGARET M 3-28-7902
LAURA MILLER 11-13-83 M 12-31-1903
JULIUS ARTHUR 1-30-1905 D 5-22-07
MILDRED W 4-28-1900
MARGARET MAY 4-28-77 M 6-22-98
PETER V KELLER 9-28-1874
Niagara Falls N.Y.
ANNIE CATHRINE 2-1-1874 D 6-11-86
PETER ARTHUR 5-26-1871
DANIEL TROUT 5-14-1869 D 1-30-87
ARTHUR McARTHUR 7-8-68 D 6-9-91
ALEXANDER McDONALD D 3-19-1913
8-17-1842
MARGARET M 7-8-45 M 1-7-61
2 Parents
6 Children
3 Marriages
4 Grandchildren
15 — 9 Living
ALEXANDER McDONALD
FAMILY TREE Lufkin Texas
April 1916 W.H.T.

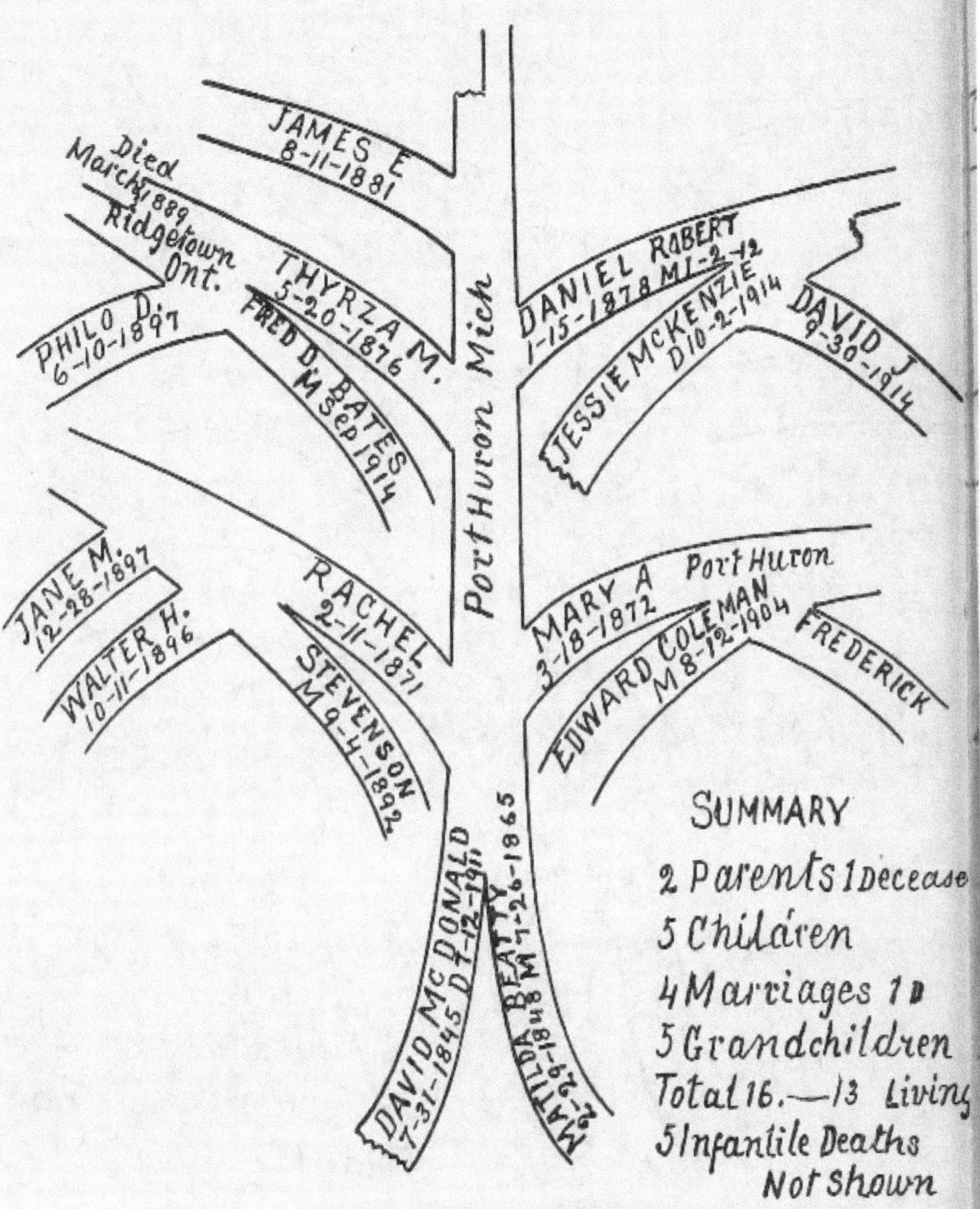

DAVID McDONALD
FAMILY TREE
Lufkin Texas June 1916 W.H.T.

SUMMARY

DANIEL McDONALD
FAMILY TREE
Lufkin Texas June 1916 W.H.T.

fairly judge there would be about sixty people. I regret very much that I must present to them, and their friends, their incomplete family tree; but all will readily know, that it has not been for want of effort on my part. All that may yet come in before the final printing will be embodied in the tree.

CHARLOTTE TROUT McKEE

This was grandfather's seventh child and fourth daughter, and since we have no picture to present we must give a brief description. She was a little less in stature than her sisters, rather slightly built, had dark hair, and eyes that were moderately deep set, aquiline nose and distinctive chin, a good, strong but pleasant face. My acquaintance with her was more limited than with some others of my aunts, but their common characteristics were her's without any very marked distinction. Samuel McKee, a son of one of the old pioneers in the great Queen's bush which extended northward from Garafraxa, made her acquaintance, and she united with him in marriage. She began life's responsibilities at the then ripe age of twenty-three. She accompanied her husband into the woods far beyond the Erin settlements into the township of Garafraxa. They were beyond and out of touch with all of us. More than ten years were spent in this seclusion. But after grandmother's death, grandfather, no doubt, invited them to come with him, and take care of himself and the farm. Aunt Harriet, as usual, was in the needed place when grandmother died, and was caring for grandfather. But the place needed a farmer as well as care for the household. I have not been informed as to the arrangements regarding this; the result was that at grandfather's death Uncle Sam owned the farm, Aunt Charlotte having grandfather under her kindly care for about seven years. Uncle Sam cleared more of the land, and enlarged the cultivated portion, and built a large barn capable of holding his entire crop, with a substory of stone, of which a small part formed a cellar for his root crops, the remainder being a great stable and shed for all his live stock; through this there flowed in conduits pure spring water that did not freeze in winter.

MRS. CHARLOTTE TROUT McKEE AND HER THREE SONS,
JOHN W., WILLIAM AND SAMUEL.

To Mrs. William Davidson, Sr., formerly Mrs. Wm. McKee, who has preserved so many mementos of grandfather and his family, we are indebted for this good picture of this aunt and her boys. Made from a small photo taken probably in the late seventies of last century.—W. H. T.

4. Teresa Smith   7. Henry Frederick Smith   5. A. Ethleen Smith   8. Samuel Edmund Smith

9. N. Howard Smith

3. Martha Smith   1. Matthew Thompson Smith   2. Rachel McKee Smith   6. Thirza Smith

The numbers correspond with the order of ages.

MATTHEW THOMPSON SMITH FAMILY, 1894

Uncle was a large, tall man, heavy boned and thin in flesh, had light complexion and sandy hair, was steady and industrious, helpful in the church and community; and with his good helpmeet, their children were well trained, and followed their parental Christian example. Uncle died at the comparative early age of fifty-four. Aunt survived him thirteen years, passing away at the age of sixty-five, being the shortest term in my aunts' lives, which averaged seventy-two years.

This McKee family had one great advantage over our other relatives, it occupied the home of our grandparents; and for a long time after they had passed, it retained much of its old influence. It was Trout headquarters. The McKee family seemed on this account to be a little closer than other cousins, so that with the young folks there was a good degree of friendly contact. Susan, the eldest, who remained at home until her twenty-fifth year, was one of those radiant, kindly spirits that awaken and sustain true friendship in others. She was twice married, the second time to Hugh Milloy, by whom she had two sons, David and Spence, who have been so much out of our connection as to be but little known to us. However, we find them to be like the rest, bearing well their part in life's great activities. David's home is in the Canadian Northwest at Cereal, Alta. He is married and has two grown-up sons. Spence has a good lumber business in Erie, Pennsylvania, is married and has two sons and two daughters.

Eleanor, the second daughter, was much like her older sister, only a little more lively. At twenty years she married John U. McClellan, a prosperous farmer of Caledon. Their fine family consisted of four sons and three daughters, all of whom married and have children, and some of them grandchildren. The whole progeny, with the married partners, number forty at the present time, and is much the largest branch on the McKee tree. They are widely scattered, mostly in the great Canadian Northwest, so that we have not been in close touch with them. We present a picture from a snapshot of this old McClellan home.

With Rachel, the third daughter, we were much more intimate, she being with Aunt Harriet and us when we were on

JOHN EMERSON 12-16-1904
SARAH ELSIE 3-19-1900
WM ORMISTON 1-20-1896
SAMUE... 7-11-18..
SARAH L... M 4-2..

SylvanLake, Alberta. Can.

LILA IRENE 2-18-1906
SAM ELMER 2-21-1903
PAUL T. 8-26-1907
RICH B. HAWKIN... M 4-11-190..
CLARICE M. 4-12-95

EVELYN 4-9-1902
JONATHAN K Winnipeg
IDA M. SMITH 7-25-1876 D 11-14-1914
M 3-7-04
H. ROSS 10-24-1902

Vermillion Alberta
NORMAN 1-6-1872
MINNIE WALKER M 5-23-09

PETER V. LEMON M 9-13-1908
Alton, Ont, Can.

OLIVE RAE 4-21-16
GRACE HILL 1-24-1914
RUTH 10-24-1912
MARTIN Mc... M 12-13-82 D 4..
HAR... 5-184..

ANDREW GEO 4-15-98 D 8-1-06
J. HAROLD 6-10-96

Alton R.R.2, Ont. Can.

ROY EGERTON 3-18-1883
CHESTER Winnipeg 6-15-1885
KATE E. HILL M 12-27-1911
Orangeville Ont

CHARLOTTE 7-11-67
GEO CAMERON 2-14-94
HENRY 10-26-1860
SARAH J. MURCH M 2-16-83

Died 4-17-92
MARGA... 7-10..
D 9-15-41
JA... 7-2..

Bowen Ill
ERNEST C. 2-12-1911 D 12-7-1915
EMELINE 7-17-69
JOHN McC. 9-24-1909
JOHN PORTER M 10-17-03

MARY G. 4-30-1914
HARRY J. BUCHANAN M 6-11-1913
RHEA 4-15-1890

Old Home Alton Ont.

D 11-14-95
ELEAN... 2-5-1..
JOHN U McCLELLAN 12-5-1828 M 6-11-1857 D 11-14-1908

Winnipeg Man
CHESTER 5-25-1862
MARY ALGIE 9-21-68 M 5-22-89
ANNIE S. 3-28-1858
JAS A. McCLELLAN M 6-11-1879

E. JEAN 1-24-98
OPAL 7-21-93

Candiac Sask Can

ELEANOR 6-17-95
EMERSON 4-28-93
REGINALD 8-31-1883
MABLE IRENE 7-26-1880
DANIEL PRETTY M 1-15-1908
NORMAN L. 4-26-1911
HOWARD 12-29-1912
REGINALD C. 2-15-1915

CHARLO... For...

2 Parents   2 D
10 Children   6 D
33 Marriages   5 D
29 Grand Children   2 D
39 Great Grand   2 D
7 Great Great Grand.

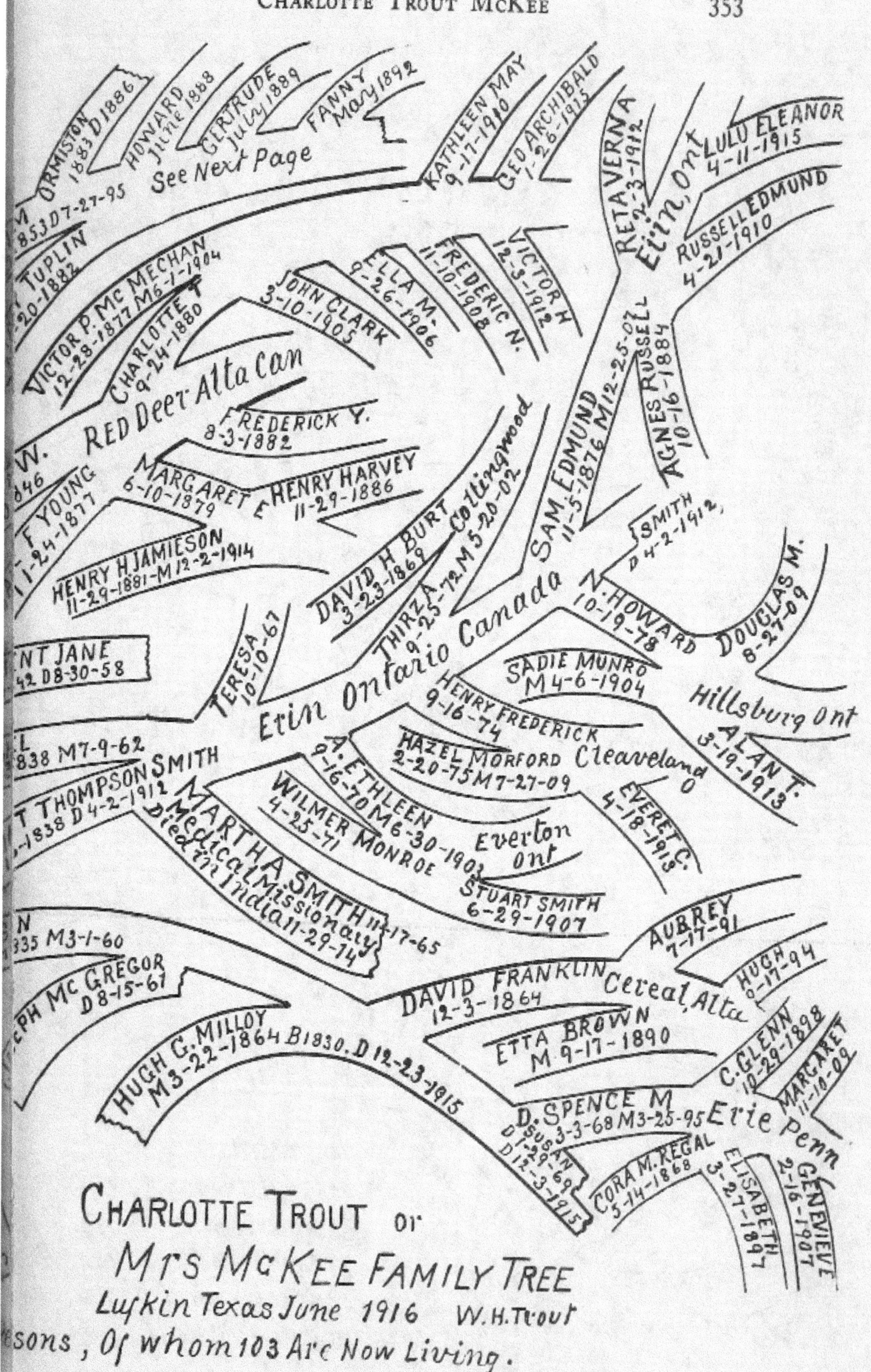
M. ORMISTON 1883 D1886
HOWARD June 1888
GERTRUDE July 1889
FANNY May 1892
See Next Page
KATHLEEN MAY 9-17-1910
GEO ARCHIBALD 1-26-1915
RETA VERNA 2-3-1912
Erin, Ont
LULU ELEANOR 4-11-1915
RUSSELL EDMUND 4-21-1910
853 D 7-27-95
T TUPLIN 20-1882
VICTOR P. McMECHAN 12-28-1877 M 6-1-1904
CHARLOTTE T 9-24-1880
JOHN CLARK 3-10-1905
ELLA M. 9-26-1906
FREDERIC N. 11-10-1908
VICTOR H 12-3-1912
SAM EDMUND 11-5-1876 M 12-25-07
AGNES RUSSELL 10-16-1884
SMITH D 4-2-1912
DOUGLAS M. 8-27-09
W. Red Deer Alta Can
FREDERICK Y. 8-3-1882
846
T YOUNG 1-24-1877
MARGARET E 6-10-1879
HENRY HARVEY 11-29-1886
DAVID H BURT 3-23-1869 Collingwood M 5-20-02
N. HOWARD 10-19-78
HENRY H JAMIESON 11-29-1881 M 12-2-1914
THIRZA 9-25-72
Erin Ontario Canada
SADIE MUNRO M 4-6-1904
ALAN T. 3-19-1913
NT JANE 42 D 8-30-58
TERESA 10-10-67
Etin Ontario Canada
HENRY FREDERICK 9-16-74
HAZEL MORFORD 2-20-75 M 7-27-09
Cleaveland O
Hillsburg Ont
838 M 7-9-62
T THOMPSON SMITH 1838 D 4-2-1912
A. ETHLEEN 9-16-70 M 6-30-1901
WILMER MONROE 4-25-71
MARTHA SMITH 11-17-65
Medical Missionary Died in India 11-29-14
Everton Ont
EVERET C. 4-18-1913
STUART SMITH 6-29-1907
AUBREY 7-17-91
N 835 M 3-1-60
ph McGREGOR D 8-15-67
DAVID FRANKLIN 12-3-1864 Cereal, Alta
HUGH 9-17-94
HUGH G. MILLOY M 3-22-1864 B 1830. D 12-23-1915
ETTA BROWN M 9-17-1890
C. GLENN 10-29-1898
MARGARET 11-10-02
D. SPENCE M 3-3-68 M 3-25-95
Erie Penn
CORA M. REGAL 5-14-1868
D Susan D 7-29-61 D 12-3-1915
ELISABETH 3-27-1897
GENEVIEVE 2-16-1907
CHARLOTTE TROUT or
Mrs McKEE FAMILY TREE
Lufkin Texas June 1916   W. H. Trout
esons, Of whom 103 Are Now Living.

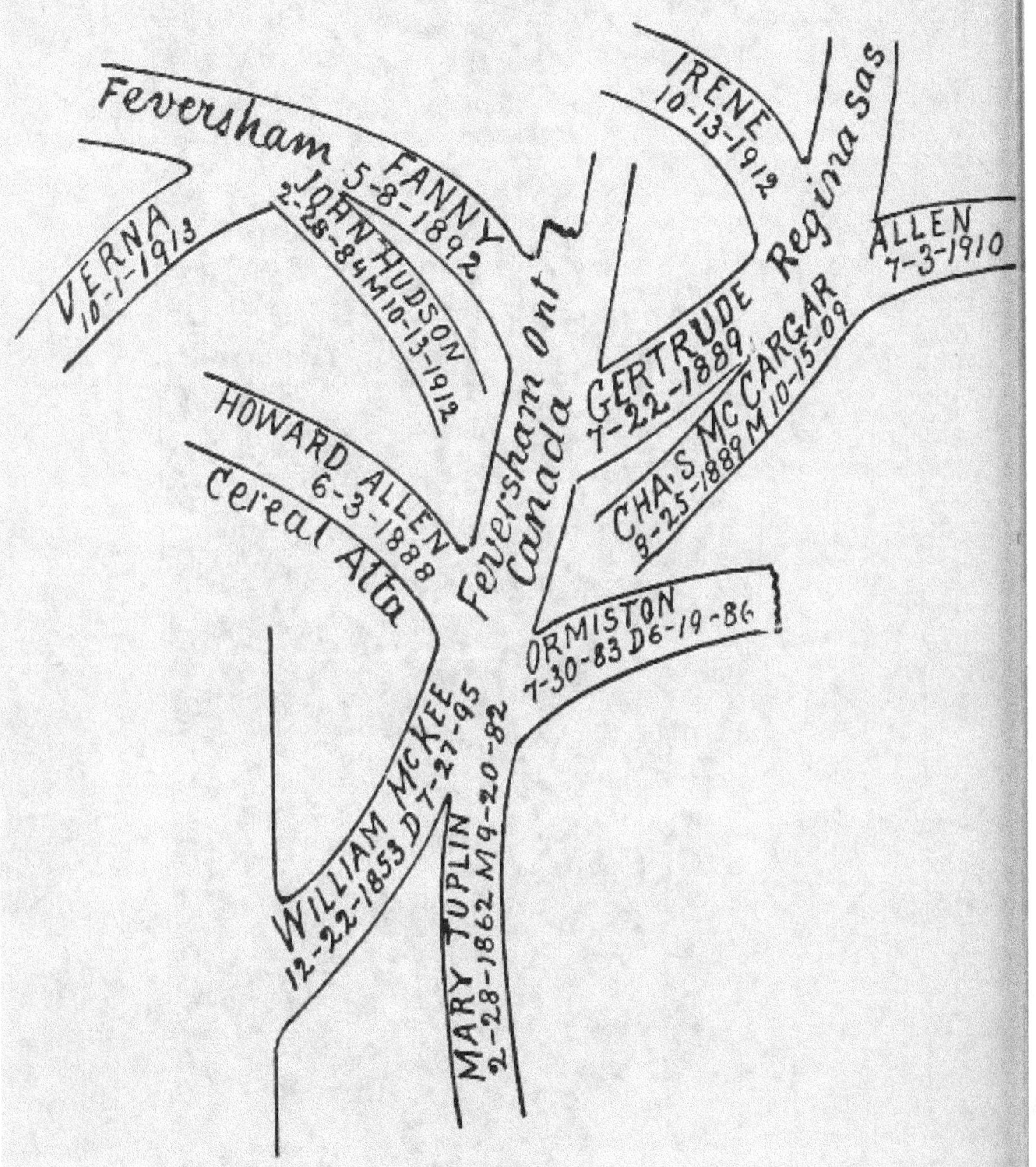

MC KEE EXTENDED BRANCH

See preceeding page

JOHN U. McCLELLAN'S HOME

the large Creemore mill job, which, as previously related, occupied the greater part of a year. We also had a good acquaintance with Margaret and John, who had been with us more than others, except Rachel. John had a store and the post office at Balinafad, about nine miles south from the old home. With the two youngest we were not so much in touch, I had one good visit with Samuel in 1895, shortly after the death of his next older brother, William. He and Samuel were joint owners of the old place. After William's sudden death in his forty-second year, Samuel arranged with the widow regarding her rights, and not long afterwards sold the old paternal home, and removed to the new province of Alta in the Northwest; and in a few years, John with his family followed him, and now resides in the town of Red Deer, Alta, Canada, where, according to their letters, they all have succeeded finely. From Winnipeg to the Rockies, in all that great prairie country, our relatives are scattered, and many don't know each other's location.

The only ones of our first cousins, now near the old home center, is Harriet McKee, now Mrs. Lemon. Though one of the younger members, she knows a great deal of the old associations. She is nearing the sixty-sixth milestone, but she neither looks nor acts it. She has the characteristic life and vivacity of all our Harriets, and there is usually one in every large family. Her residence is in Alton, not far from the old home of the McClellans, Eleanor's children and grandchildren.

The families of the sons, John, William and Samuel, are moderate or small, but there are seven boys to carry forward the McKee name, and three girls to make the connections with other family lines.

The Thompson Smith or Rachel McKee branch is the second largest in the McKee tree, but in some respects it might be regarded as first in influence. Thompson Smith was a plain, steady-going farmer, making barely noticeable progress year by year, but never going back. Was also an elder in the Erin church of Christ, and a much respected member of his community. His life partner was abreast with him in all his labors and progress. They had a fine substantial farm home, into which worry and discomfort never seemed to enter. Thompson Smith's seventy years of good useful life were closed April 2, 1912. Their family was the sacred number seven, four girls and three boys, in the order I have given.

Martha, the eldest, deserves a much extended notice, on account of her splendid service in India missions. As a student she was diligent and thorough, liking the mastering of hard problems. In her early womanhood she didn't hold back, waiting for some matrimonial chance to turn up, but struck out for a useful life. Following her school days was a systematic course in Bible study at her home. And the next important move was to Rhode Island, where she entered the State Training School for Nurses in 1889, and graduated in 1891. She became matron of Springfield, Massachusetts, hospital, where she did good service for over two years, and came home for a much needed rest. It was then I had my brief personal acquaintance with her. Her interest in medical matters, and her much greater interest in missions, led her to see that by combining the two she could be of great service as a foreign missionary. Accordingly, in 1897, she entered the Toronto Woman's Medical College, graduating in 1902; and was happy in being sent to India by the Christian Woman's Board of Missions in 1903. The extensive preparation for such a great service made heavy calls on her purposeful energy and persistent determination, but she met all without flagging.

Her complete education as nurse, physician, gospel teacher and singer, was such that her services in these lines were in constant demand. For a long time she had the charge of the medical work at four stations several miles apart, where the journeys were made on a bullock's cart. For a change or rest from exhaustive work she would relieve the tension by going and playing with the children, teaching them games and songs.

Dr. Martha Smith spent eleven happy years in India, in the work of the Christian Woman's Board of Missions, besides being home one year on furlough, which is more of a change than a rest, as returned missionaries are called on for addresses all over our country, and they cheerfully respond.

At the office of the Christian Woman's Board of Missions, Indianapolis, Indiana, on December 4, 1914, the following cablegram was received, "Dr. Martha Smith died Sunday. Pneumonia. Advise her Mother." This is quoted from the Missionary Tidings, January 15, 1915. The remarks of the editor follow: "What a few words it takes to express so great a loss and so much sorrow. We grieve for ourselves, but most of all for the suffering ones of India, who were helped in body and soul by our good doctor." She died November 29, 1914, with just twelve days entry into her fiftieth year. Pneumonia generally comes to us like an accident. It was so in her case. Her God-surrendered, effective life was suddenly cut off at the height of its greatest accomplishments.

Smith is a very common name; but not all the Smiths are common, so this Smith family must have further attention. All of the three remaining daughters seemed to have copied more or less from Martha. Teresa, the second, after her school days and a few years at home, also went to Massachusetts for a two years' period of educational nursing. Returning home and carrying for years her full share of the cares of the family, she now has become its kindly "old maid," or more fittingly, its "angel of mercy," as, according to the old saying, in every large family some one must be the old maid; but that term does not carry the discredit it used to hold. When it is known that the women are slightly in the majority, and so many men shirk their manly responsibilities, there must of necessity be single ladies, who make more creditable use of their lives than do most of the single men, whom we call, "old bachelors," and when we want to soften and dignify them a little, we call them "benedicts," and similarly their unmated mates are often truly spoken of as, "angels of mercy," and such our Teresa undoubtedly is.

Ethleen's course after high school was that of a nurse, graduating from the Rhode Island Training Hospital in 1893. Her nursing service of over three years in Massachusetts was cut short by making the acquaintance and afterwards marrying Wilmer Monroe, an all-round good man and Christian minister of fine ability and high ideals. Drake University of Des Moines, Iowa, was his Alma Mater.

He came to New England in 1895 where he served churches in Massachusetts, Connecticut and New York states. In 1904 he resigned his pastorate in Watertown, New York, and engaged with the Christian Woman's Board of Missions to be a Missionary in India. Of course, Cousin Ethel, as she is familiarly called, accompanied him, and shared in this as well as every other work he was engaged in, always creditably bearing her part, but the trying climate was so greatly against her, that they were obliged to return after a five years' service. I think their little boy, Stuart, was born in India. Since returning, brother and cousin Monroe has had charge of a church in Keele Street, Toronto, and now is minister at Everton, Ontario, close by the old Trout stamping ground in Erin, and Ethel's own old home.

Similarly to the others, Thirza, the fourth daughter, entered the training school for nurses in the Springfield hospital, Springfield, Massachusetts, in 1894, and graduated in 1896. Did private nursing there till 1902, when she married David Burt, a fine Christian man, previously well-known to the family. Their residence is Collingwood, where he is employed in the great ship yard as pattern maker.

Henry Frederick took a course in a Guelph Business College. Afterwards a four years' course in Hiram College, where I had been about forty-five years ahead of him. We both had the ministry in view, but both went back on it. My reasons were good, perhaps his were better. He certainly was better prepared than I was. I think much of old Hiram, the memory of old academy days in 1855 is fresh and pleasant. His memory must be much richer than mine. He was there so much longer, and besides, there he found his life partner. Hiram is a likely place to find a good girl, and I judge the young ladies regard it as a good place to find a young man. Hazel Morford and Fred Smith evidently found each other. So after he had finished his Hiram course, and taken a complete course in dentistry, and made good preparation for the important event, he and Miss Morford were married, July

27, 1909. They set up their home in the big city of Cleveland, where he has now a large dental practice, and is rapidly rising in the estimation of his wide acquaintanceship. So far there is one son, Everet C., to continue the line of the everlasting Smiths.

It was my good fortune to visit Cousin Fred at his home in July, 1916, thus renewing my very slender acquaintance, and extending it to his worthy wife and fine little son. The short visit fully bears me out in all the statements previously made regarding them.

Samuel Edmund undertook the study of pharmacy, but wisely gave it up and returned to work with his father on the farm. To which, on the death of his father, he finally succeeded. He met Miss Agnes Russell, a dressmaker, and they became partners, not in dressmaking but in the farm and family business. The dressmaking being only a convenient adjunct.

They were married on Christmas Day, 1907. One son and two daughters grace the family table, so far this is the largest among the young Smiths. The farm is a fine place to raise a family. This fine old two hundred-acre farm has been in the Smith line for a hundred years back, and evidently will so continue, as Samuel Edmund has his heir, Russell Edmund, to follow in his place. Sam is succeeding not alone to the farm, but to the position of respect and influence held by his father in that fine, well-settled community.

Nelson Howard, the youngest of the Thompson Smith family, learned the miller trade, and also took a business course in Chatham, Ontario, and for a time served as a miller, but gave it up for business on his own account.

In Hillsburg, Ontario where the well-known James. E. Hill, the great railway king, began his career, and left his name with the town, was a large stone flouring mill, built about sixty years ago, and had gone through all the improved changes of construction that have attended the flouring mill business; on account of adverse trade and other conditions it became unprofitable. On good easy terms Howard either purchased or leased this, and turned it into such a good general purpose use for farmers' service as to make it pay. If a farmer brought in a saw-log he had a little mill in a connected shed where he could turn on the water power and saw it for him. If he brought a load of grain to chop for feed a pair of old burrs would quickly grind it. If he wanted fencing or flooring or most any old thing, Howard would have it or make it. This was a most interesting place for me, it seemed like going back to primitive manufacture. Like Edmund, he found his wife in college; and like Agnes, Sadie Munro was a teacher. They were married in 1909 and live in a neat house, close alongside the mill, as if it were a part of it. So far, two fine little boys constitute their family. Hillsburg town with its beautiful natural surroundings is a good place to visit, and Howard with his old mill should not be left out.

SUSAN TROUT NISBET

When making my first attempts at this history writing Aunt Susan was living at her own Nisbet family home, she was for a long time the only surviving member of grandfather's family. I could appeal to her memory in regard to events of the earlier times, and I have her letters regarding them, which have given much help. Our occasional visits together, when I lived at Peterboro, which was ten miles from her home, were also helpful, though at that time I had not contemplated the history.

Her marriage to Alexander Nisbet, formerly of Scotland, but then and till his death a resident of the township of Otanabee, Hastings County, Ontario, Canada, has been referred to, also the stay over night with us at Norval on their wedding journey homeward—a sleigh ride of nearly two hundred miles on the roundabout roads they would have to travel. I was then eight years old, but memory serves me well. Mr. Nisbet was not fleshy, but a big, broad-shouldered man about six feet tall; Aunt Susan was fully medium size, fresh, handsome, and girlish looking, with her fully twenty-five years behind her. The long sleighride journey ended at a small log house on a hundred acre lot in an immense woods. Aunt was used to log houses and great tracts of bush, but this must have been much more lonesome than the situation she had left behind. Grandfather's house, on account of his business, was quite a public place, but this, so far away from her own friends, and with no near neighbors, must have been really lonely. It had this offset, however, that she had three children to care for, the offspring of a former wife of Mr. Nisbet's, which would furnish both company and continued employment, both of these militating against loneliness, at the same time making a pretty sudden jump into family responsibility, which carries with it its own worries.

While Mr. Nisbet had a farm he was strictly not a farmer; he learned the cutter's and stone mason's trade in Scotland, and worked at it quite extensively in Canada. He built one of the first, if not the first church, that was built in Peterboro. On this account the farm had a poor chance for improvement. Stone houses were built for other people, but none for himself. It was similar to the blacksmith's horse and the shoemaker's wife unshod. Log houses and log barns were of necessity the first buildings; and we used to say that if the frame house preceded the frame barn, the woman was the boss in that situation. Generally it was the other way, as the barn had the best claim to be a money saver. But in this case you could not tell, as both kinds of log buildings remained for a long time. In behalf of Uncle Nisbet it must be said that in the middle and latter part of his life he was a frequent sufferer from asthma, which immensely crippled his energies, making him for long periods an invalid; so that not until his two sons grew up to near their manly strength did the place show much signs of improvement. Alexander, Jr., then became the real farmer, and progress began to be manifest.

Aunt Susan had six daughters and two sons, which, with the former family of three, made eleven children under her care, not that many at one time, as the first family were no doubt married, and on their own account, before her youngest was born; but there was a large number of them, with very often the father and husband absent, or if at home, an invalid. Seeing all of this, with the inconvenience and necessary hardships of a bush life, then we can judge of the heavy part

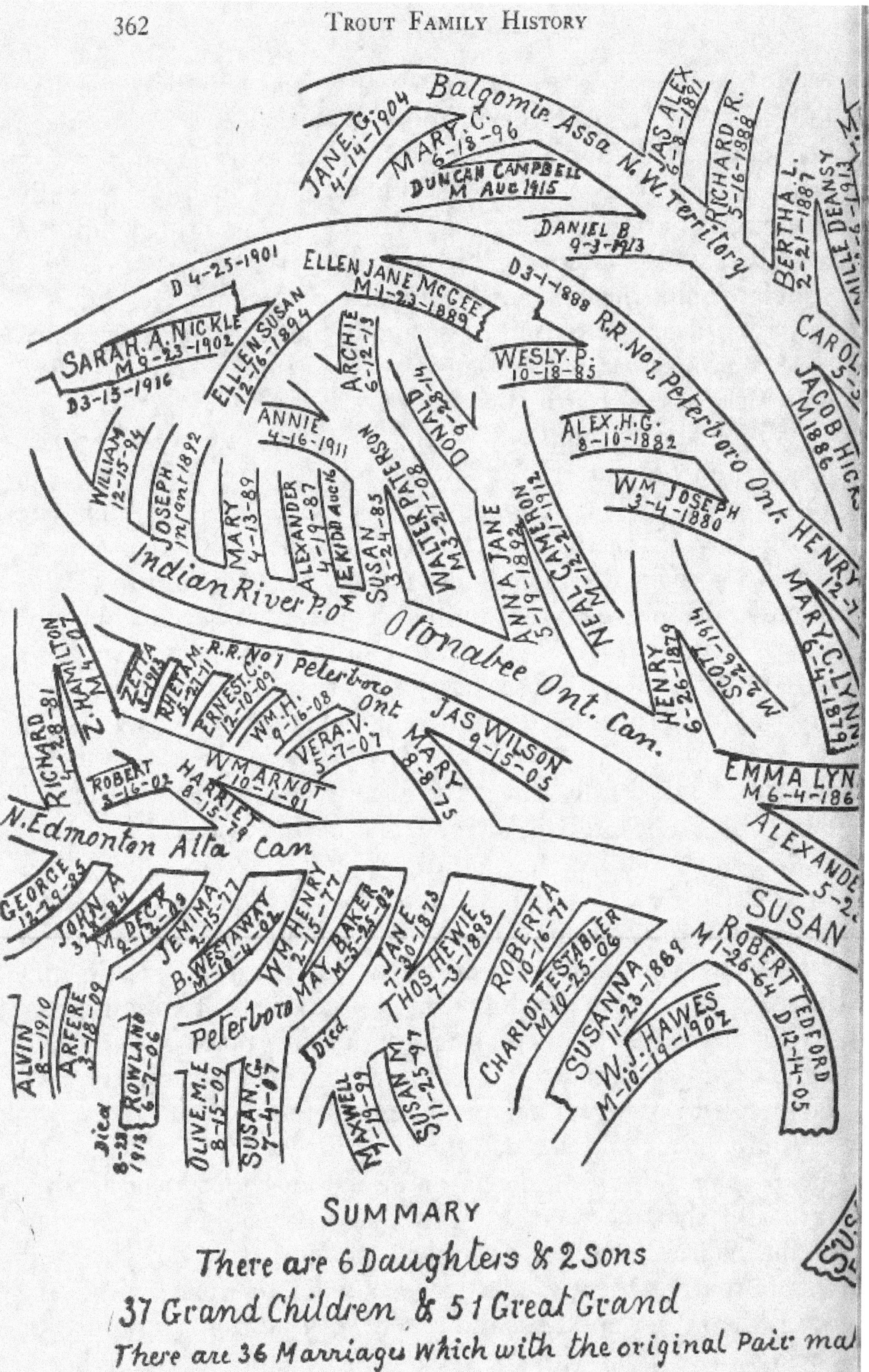

SUMMARY

There are 6 Daughters & 2 Sons

37 Grand Children & 51 Great Grand

There are 36 Marriages which with the original Pair mak

Penetanguishene

2-9-1914
HERMAN A.
RACHEL 10-19-06
CLIFFORD 1-17-04
JEMIMA 6-12-1881
WALTER VAN ALLEN M 1903
18/79
Peter V. ELSWORTH 2-1-06
ISABEL 3-1904
WILFRED H. 3-22-03
GORDON 9-19-06

Penetanguishene

HERBERT S 1-29-1913
ISABELLA K. M. 12-12-1910
LESLIE IRWIN 1-30-1903
WM GEORGE 4-23-1900
WILFRED 5-8-08
JOHN ROBERT 11-28-05
MARY A.S. 9-11-99
D-6-22 1911
ETTA 4-4-1878
SAM DEVEL M 1903
GEO. EDWARD 10-13-1873
ARTHUR H.E. 2-21-08
MARY W. SHAFFER M 1887
GLADYS M. 3-9-1899
RACHEL MARY 9-27-1895
CLARENCE M 10-6-1900
FRANCISE 4-18-1910
GEO. HENRY 8-3-01
HARRIET 3-6-1876
JOHN DOWNER M 1898
1912
Peterboro

SAM. HERBERT 6-29-1870
KATHLEEN M 1893
GEO STANLEY 5-13-1829
HERBERT O 7-5-1897
KATHLEEN M 1892
ERNEST M 8-21-04
D 8-20-05
Rochester N.Y.

GEORGE FLACK M 1869
1866
ISABELLA SUSAN 7-28-1866
JAS H McCARROLL M-1886
PERCY M 4-19-1887 Peterboro
MABEL M. MOORE 1-1-1913
D6-1898

LY LEWIS 11-22-1888
WILFRED T. 12-24-1900
1858
1855
HAMILTON 4-30-03
D 12-24-1909
1900
HARRIET D11-3-1900
MARTIN 9-15-1880
SUSAN. V. 8-27-83
NOBLE PERRIN 4-18-1906

WM SAMUEL 5-29-1864
AGNES MOORE M 1889
HERBERT W.M. 9-11-1890
EDITH 11-22-1891
DONALD L. 6-11-1897

4-16-1843 ce 4-16-1843 D 1868
SAMUEL FLACK M 3-4-1862 D 1868
ALEXANDER 11-19-1862
20 Hutchinson St Montreal
HAZEL MAY 11-19-1898
JOHN S. 11-4-1903
KATHLEEN I. 6-20-1906
ALEX VICTOR 2-26-1891
MAY MOORE M 1890

SUSAN TROUT (MRS NISBET)

FAMILY TREE   OLD HOME OTANABE ONT CAN

Trout 118 Living April 1916

W.H.T. Milwaukee Wis Dec 1914

borne by Aunt; and I feel sure there was never a complaint. Her aged face, as I last saw it, was the perfect expression of quiet endurance and patient trust. The husband was an elder in the old Scotch kirk. I question if there was a Sunday school in that neighborhood, but I am certain there was a family religion in that home. The head teacher was not always present; but the assistant, the one with the earnest kindly influence, was always on the job, so that if fine farming was not the result, there was certainly fine extensive family raising, on a noticeable and deservedly worthy scale. The farmer, who raises fine stock, and takes prizes at the great exhibition, and becomes wealthy thereby, is known throughout the country, and regarded as great in behalf of the interest of his community. How ought we then to regard the pair who rear and train eleven children for the responsibilities of life, all sound in mind and limb, and strong in morals, living out their steady, plain lives for their own and the common good? Such parents ought to take rank above the cattle raisers, but they don't. May be that big families were too common; if so then, it is not so now; so the old style deserves the greater commendation.

The Nisbets were plain people, the kind that Lincoln said, "God was so gracious towards, because he made so many of them." Like their parents they were pioneers, nearly all went into the newer parts of the country, the township of Harvey, about sixty miles north of the old home, which the oldest son still retains. This new township was for a time quite a gathering place, but some of them pushed on into the far Northwest. The farming occupation leads, but most others are represented. Presbyterianism, the religion of the parents, prevails among the children and grandchildren. A good number are Baptists. Other denominations are also represented. There is one lone Mormon, or Latter Day Saint, as he no doubt calls himself, who is connected with this line, the only one in our whole fraternity. For a long time there has been one or two representatives of the family living in Peterboro, where I formerly lived. Mary Nisbet, now Mrs. William Hamilton, lives there still, in a good comfortable manner. I visited her and her sister (Mrs. Lewis), Jemima, in 1911.

It was an enjoyable visit with two good cousins; but when I returned in 1913, Jemima had passed away, and Mary being a widow felt her loneliness. I am obliged to her more than any-one else for helpful information in making up the Nisbet family tree, not alone what she contributed but what she got others to give. On this account Aunt Susan's tree is the most complete of the larger trees, except cousin John McDonalds. An examination of the tree shows a good degree of virility, the deaths coming in mostly through the married partners. There were only two boys, but they have seven to carry forward the Nisbet name.

In the latest years of his life Alexander Nisbet was much relieved of his troublesome asthma, and had a comparatively restful period; though bodily strength gradually failed, mental activity was fairly well retained. He spent much time in reading, and in consideration of matters connected with his church, and its teachings, and obviously also, the things of the world to come. While his mind retained much of its usual strength, the body dwindled; it seemed to contrast and gather to its center. When seeing him sitting in his easy chair, it was difficult to think that he had ever been the stalwart man I once knew him to be. His eldest son told me afterwards that before his death he could take up his father with both hands as he would a child, and set him in the seat of the wagon, a good example of the "outward man perishing" and the "in-ward man renewing." His life period was seventy-five years, three months and nine days.

Aunt Susan too had her restful period in her later years. She was much younger than Uncle, and survived him nearly eleven years. After her long term of motherhood and active leadership, she became rather more like a guest in the homes of her children, not only relieved of her cares but cared for, as all such mothers deserve to be, interested in the growth and prospects of a third, and in two instances of a fourth, genera-tion. Her steady health continued until her seventy-seventh year, when she met with an accident that no doubt hastened her departure. On retiring to her bedroom one night her toe caught in the edge of the carpet, and she fell heavily on one

knee, breaking the neck of the femur, a fracture to which old people are very liable, and which at the best is difficult to reunite. I know all this from the experience, but I was about fifteen years younger than she when I had mine. I have a false joint and a short leg as the result, but walk fairly well with a cane. She never got on her feet again. Her life term was finished in 1894, aged seventy-seven years old, six months and twelve days. The only one of grandfather's children with a longer life record was Aunt Ann, whose life term was seventy-nine years, seven months and seven days. It is not pleasant to record untimely deaths, but well-rounded-out careers, like those thus briefly given, make an easy story to tell. (See double page family tree and photos.)

JOHN EMERSON TROUT

He was the youngest of grandfather's large family. Four daughters had preceded him, the youngest, Susan, being over three and a half years old when he came into the family. Being the youngest and a boy, and having four older sisters to care for him, there was a fair chance of the care being overdone; and the handsome baby boy, with jet black eyes and ruddy cheeks, was very likely somewhat of a spoiled child. This was not manifest by any babyish or dependent manners, for I am sure he must have been always robust and manly, but by his care-free, happy-go-lucky, irresponsible style. I have not much memory of his young manhood days, it really begins with his married life. The responsibilities of the married state generally have a sobering effect on young men, but not much with Uncle John. Miss Francis Amelia Hunter, from Caledon township, where all grandfather's sons went for their wives, was much younger than he, who was under twenty-four at the time, so there was little help to soberness. Sisters are apt to be critical of their brothers' wives; it was so in Uncle John's case; but as far as she could see it, I am sure Aunt Francis never failed to do her best. Like his brothers Uncle John sold out his patrimony of a two hundred acre farm; but unlike his brothers he did not replace it with a good steady occupation or regular business. He had not learned a trade.

JOHN EMERSON TROUT

Through my cousin, James Hunter Trout, we can add the above good picture of my uncle John.

The most flagrant omissions and errors, in this record book, have occurred in this uncle's first family tree and record.

In the family of James H. Trout, as shown on the tree, Elizabeth Alice was born in 1885; it should have been 1875; and she is not single, but was married to Dougald M. Couch, June 12, 1906; and they have four children—Cordelia M., November 4, 1907; Kenneth D., June 14, 1909; and Stewart J., and Ewart G., twins, January 27, 1917.

—W. H. T.

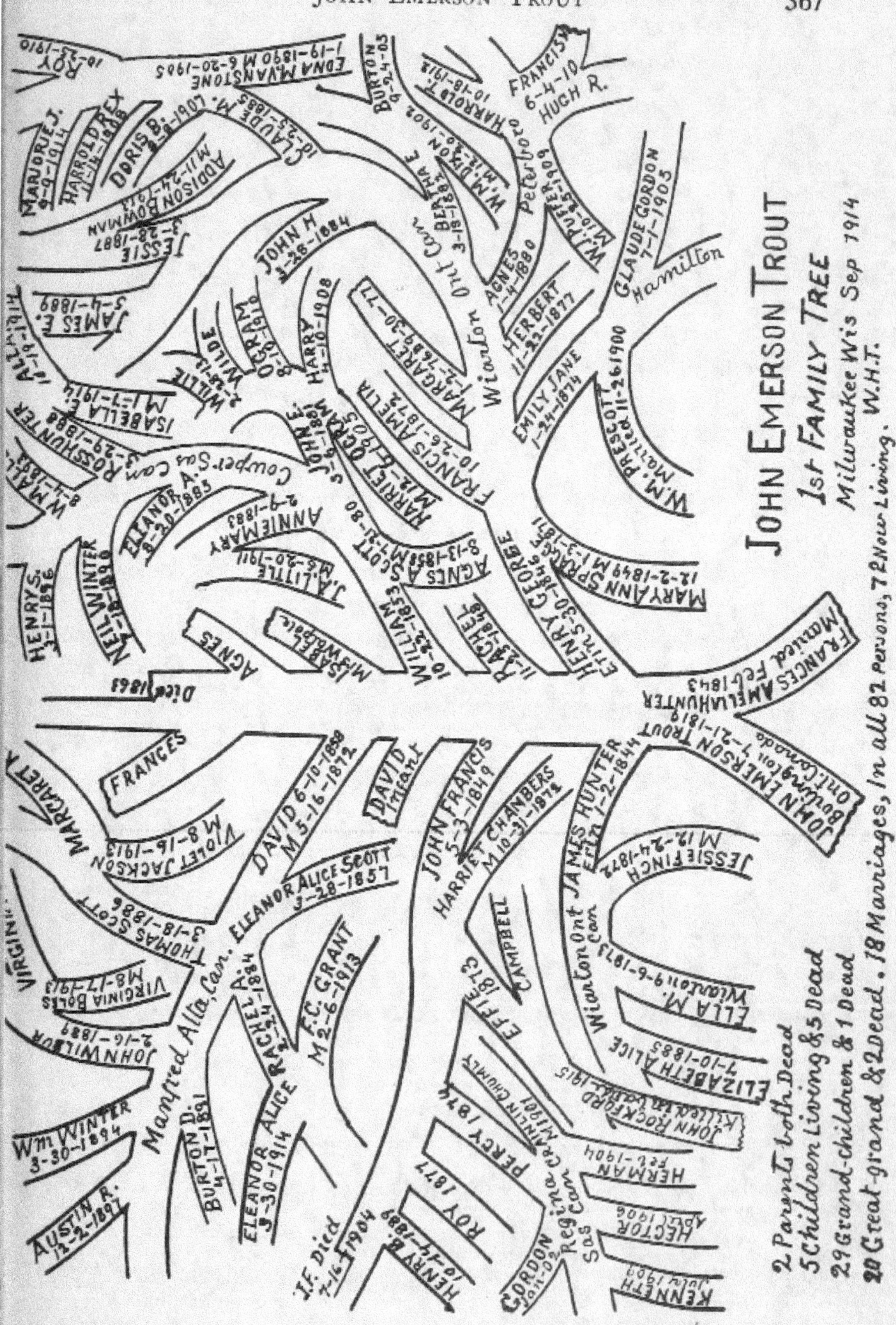

JOHN EMERSON TROUT
1st FAMILY TREE
Milwaukee Wis Sep 1914
W.H.T.
ROY 10-25-1910
EDNA M VANSTONE 1-19-1890 M 6-20-1905
MARJORIE J. 8-9-1914
HAROLD REX 4-17-1878
DORIS B. M-1907
CLAUDE M. 12-25-1885
ADDISON BOWMAN M 11-24-1913
JESSIE 3-28-1887
BURTON 9-2-4-05
HAROLD E. 10-18-1912
FRANCIS 6-9-10
HUGH R.
PETER 9-6-1909
W.L. PUFFER 1905
CLAUDE GORDON 7-1-1905
Hamilton
JAMES E. 5-4-1889
JOHN H 1-28-1884
WILLIE
ORA M 8-10-1906
HARRY 4-10-1908
ALBERT 3-18-
AGNES 1-4-1880
HERBERT 1-23-1877
W.M. PRESCOTT 11-26-1900
ALBERT M 1-19-1911
ISABELLA E. 3-4-1888
ROSS HUNTER 3-29-1888
MARGARET 7-1889-30-77
FRANCIS AMELIA M 18-6-1905
MARRIETT 10-26-1872
Wiarton Ont Can
EMILY JANE 1-24-1874
WM MARR 8-11-1881
NELL WINTER 11-10-
ELEANOR CLARA 8-30-1885
ANNIE MARY 2-9-1883
Couper Sas Can
J.A. LITTLE M 5-20-1911
AGNES A. SCOTT 8-13-1858 M-1-31-80
WILLIAM 10-22-1853
HENRY GEORGE M-5-30-
RACHEL 11-
MARY ANN SPRINGS 12-2-1849 M-1-3-1871
HENRY S. 3-1-1856
AGNES
ISABEL M 5 W Ebb etc
Died 1863
FRANCES
DAVID Infant
DAVID 6-10-1858 M 5-16-1872
FRANCIS AMELIA HUNTER
Married Feb 1843
JOHN EMERSON TROUT Bowmanton 7-21-1819 Ont Canada
VIOLET JACKSON M 8-16-1913
JOHN FRANCIS 5-3-1849
HARRIET CHAMBERS M 10-31-1872
JAMES HUNTER Erin 1-2-1844
JESSIE FINCH M 12-24-1872
MARGARET
VIRGINIA
THOMAS SCOTT 3-18-1886
ELEANOR ALICE SCOTT 3-28-1857
VIRGINIA BOLLS M 8-17-1913
JOHN WILSON 2-16-1889
RACHEL 2-24-1884
F.C. GRANT M 2-6-1913
Manfred Alta Can
EFF 1873
CAMPBELL
ELLA M. Wiarton 9-6-1913
Wiarton Ont Can
WM WINTER 3-30-1894
BURTON D. 4-17-1891
ELEANOR ALICE 3-30-1914
AUSTIN R. 12-2-1891
PERCY 1874
ELIZABETH ALICE 7-10-1885
JOHN ROCKFORD Killed in War 1915
Regina Can
GORDON 1-01-02
Regina Can
HENRY R. 10-15-1889
J.F. Died 7-16-1904
ROY 1877
HERMAN Feb-1904
HECTOR Aug 1906
KENNETH July 1908
2 Parents both Dead
5 Children Living & 5 Dead
29 Grand-children & 1 Dead
20 Great-grand & 2 Dead. 18 Marriages, In all 82 Persons, 72 Now Living.

Father was regularly apprenticed, and had a good start in millwright and carpenter work before they moved into the bush; so that father was the leader in skilled work, and Uncle Henry his principal assistant, who with his great natural bent acquired a good use of tools. But there was a gap of eighteen years between father and Uncle John, and when the latter was old enough to be helpful, the skilled work was mainly done; there was nothing left for him but to clear and farm his two hundred acres, which, according to the ideas of the times, needed no special training or particular good sense or judgment. Muscular strength and steady endurance were regarded as the essential requisites. Uncle John had the strength, but did not farm very much; he was evidently disinclined, so that he sold his farm, and took the most promising job that lay before him, and followed it until it gave out or he found something better. In this way a good many shifts were made, while an increasing family of fine, little boys were growing up around them and school facilities needed, which were obtained when he moved to Erin village and took charge of a sawmill, running it for a certain sum per thousand feet of lumber sawn. Through grandfather's influence, I judge, he was made bailiff of the division court and constable for that district. In both these capacities he did good service.

In the winter of 1853 and 1854, father made a brief visit to the old parental home in Erin, and induced Uncle John to migrate with his family north into the great pine woods, at Hogback in Tossoronto, now known as Glencairn. He assisted us in the building of a sawmill there, and ran the mill, sawing by the thousand, as he had done in Erin. When the property was sold to the Stephens' Brothers, he continued with them through the winter of 1854 and 1855, and came in the early spring with his family to St. Vincent, where he also helped father in building and afterwards running the sawmill on the property purchased from Laycock. Uncle John's children had for more than a year missed the advantages of the schools, but after coming to St. Vincent they were able to resume. Once in conversation about children, Uncle maintained it was quite possible to be too careful of them. He said, "Our children in their early school days frequently had squabbles and little fights with neighbor's children, when coming from school, and we punished them for it; but that did not abate it, it simply gave the other children an advantage over ours, so I told them finally to look out for themselves, which they undoubtedly did, and we had no more trouble." But it was only a short step from their expert little defensive warfare to the offensive, just for the fun of it. When they came to our St. Vincent small country school, the three eldest boys, James, Henry and John, respectively about twelve and ten and eight years, took the first day to size up the situation, and on the second day, as the teacher was absent during the noon hour, the two younger boys determined to lick the whole school. James was not so pugnacious, so he took the place of the reserve corps, to serve if needed, but he was not called upon. By one o'clock every one of the dozen or more boys was licked or had run away. I got the story direct from one of the nearest neighbors who had one of the licked boys. He said that little John, though not then eight years old, would fight like a young tiger. I was talking with Henry and his wife in 1913; he with his abundant snow-white hair and hearty looking face, and she a good mate for him. We were laughingly enjoying the stories of these old time childish scraps, when she breaks out with, "Yes and they have scarcely got over it yet." "Ah, come now, mother," was his reply, it is not unlikely that her statements might in some manner apply to Henry, as, like his father, he was an officer of the law, and would have to deal sometimes with ugly characters. Henry told me that up to the time that John was eighteen years of age a good scrap was just the liveliest kind of excitement to him, something that seldom went by him; but after that time no one could have been more peaceable. It was not long after this, that the boys took on the Christian relation, which leaves these, "works of the flesh" behind them. Henry had a high regard for his brother John, who passed away rather prematurely. He spoke of his cleverness, his considerate patience under severe trial, and fine self-control.

HENRY GEORGE TROUT
WIARTON, ONTARIO, CANADA

DAVID TROUT AND WIFE
MANFRED, ALBERTA, CANADA

Uncle John remained in St. Vincent but little more than a year, when, after an investigation of the newly settling portion of Elderslie township, he entered on some government land there, and moved his family once more into the woods. I was told that Aunt Fanny, as she was familiarly called, looked upon this as their best and hoped-for last move, and so it proved to be as far as she was concerned. As she had grown up on a farm, she wished to end her days on one. The soil was good, others were prospering. Why not they? And though the family needs were great, yet with all this the boys were growing up and becoming helpful, and there was a good measure of progress. Aunt Fanny died in 1863 and in 1864 uncle married Mary McNeil. The two older boys purchased rights to one hundred acre lots and improved them. But for reasons not fully known by me, the property rights were all sold, and the family in 1868 moved to the little village of Oxenden, and the rising little town of Wiarton, where James and Henry afterwards purchased lots and built their homes, and John and David later purchased farms near by. Uncle, for a year or two, resumed his sawmill work, and following that, his old bailiff and constable work. In the meantime his first family had grown up and were leaving him and a younger bunch of husky black-eyed Trouts were taking their places.

There were five sons and two daughters; Rachel was the third child, and Isabel, Mrs. Walpole, the seventh. She died shortly after her marriage. Three other children died in infancy. Rachel deserves more than passing notice. She had her hearing very much injured by the measles in early childhood, and along with this were the greatly interrupted periods of school education, that were a great handicap to all of Uncle John's first family. These two drawbacks narrowed her circle of interest very much, but did not prevent her being greatly useful in that circle. She was and is still the old maid of the family, and the angel of mercy to all her relatives and neighbors who might be in need. She resides now mainly with her brother William on his farm at Cowper, Saskatchewan. She has been one of my most dependable helpers in getting dates and other family information of what she remembered or could gather. The youngest brother David, is also a farmer near Manfred, Alberta. Percy, the eldest son of John F. Trout, is a grocer at Regina, Saskatchewan, who, with his family of four boys, will help to make the Trouts known in that region of the great Northwest, where they are all prospering, in that prosperous country. I regret much that this family has not furnished me with more complete dates and other information.

It is deserving of particular notice, that those boys of Uncle John all married good, hearty, clever women; the partner of John F. might possibly be regarded as an exception. In this case, at least, there was not a very happy wedded life. Another remarkable feature of this first family is the great preponderance of the masculine element. Of the sixty descendants thirty-nine are males. Thirty-three of these are Trouts; so the name is not likely to perish in that line. There are only twenty-one female descendants; and the three married granddaughters of uncle, that have children, have five boys and only one girl. The other four married granddaughters have yet to begin their family record.

When on a visit to Wiarton, over ten years ago, my daughter Lucretia being with me, one of Uncle's little grandsons was telling her about his good standing in the public school, and finished up by saying, "I tell you when we Trout boys grow big we are going to run this old town." Which was all very well for a boy's ambition; but their fathers, William and David, wisely left the narrow, rocky, picturesque peninsula between the two lakes, for the broad fertile plains of the great Saskatchewan, where there is limitless prospect for their ambitious endeavor. Evidently these Trouts are a virile lot and will ultimately give a good account of themselves. Though scattered as they now are, and ought to be, I feel sure their influence will be felt for good wherever they go. (See John Emerson Trout's family tree.)

A change of mothers in a large family is a momentous event, particularly so in such a family as Uncle's at that time. Aunt Fanny died in 1863, the eldest son was nineteen, the youngest child was close to babyhood; the eldest and only

SUMMARY

5 Children.
11 Grandchildren.
5 Marriages, 1 Dead.
With former Family = 92 Live
Total 103 Persons

JOHN E. TROUT

2d FAMILY TREE

Milwaukee Sep 1914

W.H.T.

ARCHIBALD EDWARD TROUT
OWEN SOUND, ONTARIO

capable daughter, Rachel, was only fifteen, though ever so willing, as I feel sure she was, the demands that would come upon her would be vastly too great for her strength and ability. Mary McNeil, a good, reliable Scotch girl, at that time thirty-three years of age, had been an occasional helper for Aunt. Manifestly she was the one to turn to in their family need, and the acquaintance and mutual confidence thus formed resulted in her marriage to Uncle one year later; and in the full course of another year the propitious beginning of another Trout family was ushered in by the birth of two, hearty, twin babies, a boy and a girl, on June the 24th, 1865. In the course of nearly eight years two other sons were born and one daughter, making a family of five. These all grew up together with the former family, except that the older ones were leaving for the marriage state, while the younger were arriving by the state of babyhood. But under all the conditions, Aunt Mary performed her motherly part in a good, capable manner, that made her a strong influence for good with Uncle and the entire family. She survived Uncle just eleven days short of twenty-nine years. In the first ten or fifteen years of her widowed life she had the father's labors and duties to carry as well as the mothers, but with the courage and trust that becomes a good, true, Christian woman, she faced her added responsibiliites, and served in the double capacity, both faithfully and well. And when her children became self-dependent, and had households of their own, they not only relieved her of her care for them, but gracefully requited her with their kind attention to her comforts and pleasure. In this way she enjoyed a long term of mutually helpful years with her children, and without any serious disease or struggle, at the good, old age of eighty-one, her kindly spirit quietly glided into the realms and the rewards of the unseen and eternal.

While there was and is a good common bond of brotherly regard between those two families, still there is quite a marked distinctness; David, the youngest living of the older family, is seven years older than the eldest of the second family. This alone makes a decided gap. The older children were pure Canadians, which is good blood all right. The younger were half Scotch, which is a fine mixture and often an improvement. The older family was handicapped by rather inferior school facilities and long interruptions, while the younger had fairly good continuous instruction and the associations of a good, thriving, small town in the formation period of their lives, thus enabling the three boys to assume and retain leading positions in their several chosen callings. Archibald, while still a boy, began in the Owen Sound post office, where his faithfulness, promptness and discretion, brought him forward till he became the assistant, and was recognized by the general public as the actual postmaster. For about twenty-five years he held this position, being about the best known and one of the much respected citizens of that important town. In 1913 he took up benevolent work for the county, looking after the orphan children and the waifs, and finding homes for them. Possibly some could take such work and make money out of it, but not so with Archie. His kindness of heart and the pressure of Christian people drew him into it, and though he must live by it, yet not for the living, but for the greater reward of Him who said, "Whoso receiveth one such little child in my name receiveth me," and also, "See that ye despise not one of these little ones." He enjoys his Christ-like job, and I have no doubt but that he will feel himself bound to it for life, though it takes him from home a great deal, and is often troublesome and perplexing. He early gave himself to Christ, and while "growing in grace and in the knowledge of God" he was always helping others to grow in the same high line of heavenward progress. He is an elder in the Owen Sound Christian Church, one that can rule kindly and well, and can occasionally "labor in word and doctrine." As a citizen he is in the front rank of civic and social progress. In the first family we have referred to Rachel as the generally helpful one, the old maid of the family. Mary Ann, the twin sister of Archibald, seems to have taken a similar position in the second family. Sharing with him the eldest position, she was quite naturally the mother's main helper in the family care. That interest seems to have continued, and finally merged into the care of her mother until she passed away in 1911. A year or more after that she went to Toronto, and with another lady runs a small millinery and dressmaking business. While the married relation is properly regarded as the natural goal for normal girlhood, still the time has passed when disrespect attaches to those who fail or decide not to win. In most of the world's countries the females are the majority, so that all can't have mates, and, besides, there is always a good sprinkling of selfish predetermined bachelors with corresponding willing or unwilling old maids, and there is a large and increasing class of young ladies who will not lower their high ideals of what their husband shall be, and are on this account apt to remain single. And among the unfortunate results of this great war will be a greatly increased crop of "maiden ladies," who must of necessity become helpful to themselves and society. Along with this, greater self-dependence of the sex will most likely follow; and the manifest outcome is equal voting franchise with the men.

Neil, the second son, is the mechanic of this family. He learned the molder's trade with William Kennedy & Sons of Owen Sound, and is still working with the same firm as one of their leading and most dependable men. He has been married a good number of years, but has no children, and resides in his own good home, as all these Trout first cousins do, though differing more or less in their moderate wealth.

Harriet Susan, named after two of her Aunts, is the only remaining daughter, and is now the wife of Richard Crane, a good farmer near Wiarton, and the mother of three fine daughters and one son.

Robert Emerson, the youngest of this second family, is the only Trout merchant, unless the grocery and feed business directed by his cousin, Percy Trout, of Regina, Saskatchewan, may be regarded as a mercantile pursuit. Robert conducts a good general store in Wiarton, the place of his birth and education, and where he climbed to his moderate eminence by the usual ladder rounds, first the handy boy, then a clerkship, then a partnership, then finally full ownership. It is a fairly well-beaten route, and a pretty sure one. He also has three daughters and one son. This would be the second family standard, had not Archie's son so far failed in appearing. As it is there are nine girls and only two boys. We noticed in the first family the preponderance of males; here in the second, though on a much smaller scale, the reverse occurs, and, in a much greater ratio. Dare we look for a cause for this, or must we content ourselves with the declarations of the biologists that the sex chances are always even? According to accounts lately received Robert E. Trout, the last mentioned and my youngest cousin, though forty-eight years of age, has enlisted, and also six of my second cousins in Uncle John's line; and at least one of these has already given his life for his country, and not alone for that, but the world cause of liberty, justice and peace among the nations. No doubt there are many relatives in other lines, who have also contributed to the half million contingent, that Canada is furnishing for this great world conflict. Canada, like her neighbor, the United States, might have acted like a neutral, and withheld her help from the mother country and the Entente Allies; but she evidently regarded the ultimate question, "Shall emperors rule, or shall the people rule? Shall the best prepared and greatest military power in the world dominate and dictate the policy of the nations? Shall emperors, who claim the God-given right to direct, protect and rule their subjects, plunge them and the world into war at their nod?" That this shall not be, is the determination of the Entente Allies, and to them a conquered peace is a necessity; and Canada seemingly determines to have her share in the work in behalf of the regenerated outcome.

With the youngest son of Uncle John his story closes; and with it also ends the present Trout Family History, excepting a few subsequent considerations.

CONCLUDING SUMMARY.

Beginning with grandfather, Henry George Trout, and his marriage to Rachel Emerson, in 1798, we find in our final reckoning, October, 1916, the total number of individuals

Tabulated Family Report

	Totals	Dead	Married Partners	Dead
Henry George Trout AND Rachel Emerson 1798	2	2		
CHILDREN				
George Trout and Hannah Trout	2	2		
William Trout	148	35	38	8
Ann Trout Lee Blanchard	20	13	8	6
Henry Trout	28	17	8	4
Harriet Trout Orr	163	30	45	8
Rachel Trout McDonald	350	50	93	13
Charlotte Trout McKee	120	17	33	6
Susan Trout Nisbet	134	16	36	6
John E. Trout	103	21	24	2
Total Descendants and Connections	1070	203	285	53
	285		53	
	785 Total Descendants		232 Living	

1070—203=867 Total Living.

232

635 Actual Descendants 1916, Living.

in all the family trees amounts to 1,070 persons. This is not the entire number—Samuel McDonald, one of Aunt Rachels ten sons, left his Canadian home country for the United States, and returned once for a visit, with his wife and child, but has not since been heard from. There may be anywhere from fifteen to fifty people of whom we know nothing. Two or three others of the younger generations have left without giving their location. Of the whole number known, 285 have come in by the marriage relation, and when deducted, there are left 785, as actual descendants of grandfather. The 285 married relatives have a record of 53 deaths, leaving 232; which taken from the whole living number, 877, leaves 645 actual living descendants in 1916—the final and narrowest result of one hundred and eighteen years of family life. I am not a sufficient statistician to properly adjudge the vital standing of such a showing; but it looks to me pretty good.

To give the characteristic estimate of the whole, as has been done with the different families, is not so easy: manifestly we are a plain people; scarcely any falling low, and a few with enough prominence to place us perhaps a little above the average. In this we cannot be impartial judges; but there are some facts that we might like to remember. We are all Protestants, connected almost wholly with what is known as the Evangelical churches. I have not known, or been enabled to discover, one single jail commitment in the whole fraternity. There is, unfortunately, one victim of booze; but total abstinence quite uniformly prevails. There is also one divorce case. The Trouts, particularly, as well as many of the other relatives, have kept quite free from the use of tobacco. In regard to abnormal mental or natal bodily conditions, we can say there is not one lunatic, or one idiot. There was one girl somewhat feeble-minded. Most singularly, this occurred in the largest family of all; one having a good mental, and the finest physical record of the whole. There are two children with rather serious bodily defects.

In regard to vital productivity, Aunt Rachel, who married Daniel McDonald, greatly exceeds any other one of grandfather's children. Of her sons, one (William) met his death by accident. The death of five others who have gone, was at the average age of seventy-five years and five months. The whole number of her progeny with the married relatives so far as we have account is now 350. Her eldest son, John, leads with 112 all told. His married life began 66½ years ago; since that time the only deaths in that large number of people, are the original pair, one adult son, and three small children, leaving the living members, 106. Deducting 26 wedded mates, who came into the family, we have 80 living descendants. In contrast with this, his youngest brother at fifty-six years has only one son, a young bachelor of twenty-eight years. And a further contrast is that of another cousin, Margaret Trout, who married John Monteith, in which almost the whole family of nine children died nine years before the death of parents who died at fifty-eight years. And in contrast to Aunt Rachel's prolific family, is that of Aunt Ann, who though living to the advanced age of seventy-nine years, being married twice, and having children by both husbands, yet her whole family number was only 21, of whom only seven are living, and there is no prospect of extension.

Biologists tell us that the sexes have exactly equal chances at birth. In the case of father's family this has proved true, there were 46 males and 46 females. Statistics usually show that more males than females are born, but a less number of males arrive at maturity. In Uncle John Trout's first family line there are 40 males to 18 females. In the second family, the scale is smaller, but the ratio is greater, and is reversed; there being eleven females to four males. While in the main the biologists may be correct, yet there would seem to be some sort of modifying influence. The value of good hearty mothers is manifest in Uncle John's children's families; they married well, and the grandchildren and great-grandchildren show a characteristic vigor and buoyancy that will increasingly be of benefit to themselves and to others.

Looking over this long family story, I can see where it has been defective in plan, and often too elaborate in details, some subjects getting more attention than they might deserve, making the book larger than was intended. Still to undertake the cutting out and rewriting is more than I feel disposed to do. My limited strength and uncertain tenure of life might not allow me to see its publication. I want to see it in the hands of all those who have a natural interest in it; and since it is the result of prolonged, patient, and persistent effort, without any idea of remuneration, except the chance of getting back the direct cash outlay, it is hoped that many will make it a prized possession; and will thereby acquire a greater interest in their own past, present, and future. And in order to enable each one to conveniently continue his own family history there is appended ten prepared blank forms ready to be filled in as the family events may occur. If this easy work is done, the future general historian will have a much easier job than has fallen to my lot.

A cursory reconsideration of the leading characters in this history will emphasize the well-settled fact, that *moral stamina*, based as it most always is, on profound religious *Christian conviction*, is the force that makes lives *good* and *great*. The characters whose "works do follow them," these are the ones who are best and longest remembered. So the value of such lives cannot be too highly estimated.

May this volume contribute to this end, and be of lasting benefit to all concerned; which is the highest wish of the author.

W. H. TROUT.

322 24th Avenue,
Milwaukee, Wis.
December 12, 1916.

APPENDIX

An Added Subject of Interest

As a relic a sword takes precedence above most other things; and among the questions, revived by the publication of this book, is the identity of grandfather's sword. There are two swords in the possession of different branches of the family, each claiming to have grandfather's sword. If he had two, both parties might be right; but this matter has not been clearly determined.

My brother Peter, when in Seattle about 25 years ago, met a Mr. Thompson, who said he was born and grew up in grandfather's neighborhood; and gave proof of his statements by his manifest knowledge regarding grandfather, my father, and my sister Mary, with whom he had been a schoolmate. Near the end of a long conversation on old memories, he asked Peter if he knew where his grandfather's sword was. Peter replied that he did not know, nor was he aware that he had a sword. "Well," he said, "I can tell you where it is: You can find it sticking up between the rafters of my brother Joseph Thompson's granary, near Salmonville." As an explanation of how it came into the possession of the Thompson family, he stated that his father and a few leading old pioneers concluded that they would contribute relics for a local museum, and among the things borrowed was what his father referred to as Major Trout's sword, which he judged was obtained about a year after grandfather's death. In the course of a few years most of those pioneers died, and the museum was neglected. Owners came and took back their things, and as no one came for the sword, the Thompson's retained it. He said that when a boy at his father's home he used it cutting down thistles and burrs, and in doing so at one time he broke off the point. It was also said to be used in the degrading work of slicing turnips to feed the cattle.

Peter promptly wrote my brother Edward, relating the story. Edward went directly to Salmonville and found the sword in the place described, which, with its broken point, satisfied him regarding its identity. He then, as a Trout grandson, claimed it; and leaving a small money gift, carried it back to his home in Toronto. When he removed to Hollywood, California, he left it with William T. Stirling, who along with others advise that it should pass on into the keeping of my oldest son Walter C. Trout, of Lufkin, Texas. There is enough interest in it, though doubtful, to make it a relic well worth preserving. The doubt remains because there is no positive testimony regarding the transfer of the sword from grandfather, or anyone who could act for him to the Thompsons. Those who could have testified are dead, and though admittedly possible, there is no record, and no remembered statement, that might refer to two swords.

On the other hand there is a well-proven fine sword, with scabbard and all intact in every particular, carefully kept, and now in good condition. It is in the possession of John W. McKee of Red Deer, Alberta, Canada, who, in answer to my recent inquiry, describes the sword as having a blade 33 inches long, averaging about 1¼ inches wide, with handle 5 inches long, made in the form of a horse's neck and head, the guards to protect the hand springing up from the mouth and head to the hilt and crossbar. It has an iron scabbard, which is perfect, except a few small dents. Mrs. William Davidson, Sr., gives similar testimony. It is known to have been continuously in grandfather's keeping, and that of the McKee family, who occupied the home after he left it, so its identity is unquestioned; while the sword with the broken point has only probabilities in its favor. However, at least its partly true story lends it an air of interest; and as an old-timer it will receive due care and consideration.

Cousin John McKee also tells me, that he has grandfather's old Connecticut clock, with its musical strike, as referred to in the History, and that it is regularly performing its time-keeping duty, which has been continued for upwards of 90 years.

[FROM THE WISCONSIN CHRISTIAN MONTHLY, MILWAUKEE, WISCONSIN]

William Henry Trout

LAST Saturday afternoon, October 13th, W. H. Trout went to sleep never to awake here below. He passed away at 10 o'clock that night and the next day was his first Lord's day in heaven. Near two o'clock he sent for his son who had just arrived from Ohio, to come to his room and tell him the war news. After relating the latest reports his son described an aviation meet he had recently witnessed. When he had finished telling of the machines, the flyers and their flights, the father said, "Well, George, I will dismiss you now. You can go downstairs and I will go to sleep," and when the son had left the room he said to his nurse, "In a little while now I'll fly higher and broader than any of them ever flew." He went to sleep about 3 o'clock and when the end came, without a tremble in the body or the twitch of a muscle, his spirit took its flight.

W. H. Trout was born in Erin, Ontario, Canada, and lived in that section of the country till the year 1884 when he brought his family to Milwaukee.

Brother Trout was one of the most remarkable men the writer ever met. His natural ability qualified him for success in any realm. He was a genius, a mechanic of no mean ability, a draughtsman among the best, an inventor of recognized worth by millers throughout the country. With an indominitable will bent on the highest purpose of life he used up every ounce of his physical strength. For several years he was gathering material for a family history and after he was eighty years of age he prepared and published the "Trout Family History," a book of 330 pages, written in the very choicest language.

But—above all and better than everything else was his Christian life. A life and death so beautiful and so complete the writer never saw outside of the church. He grew old beautiful. His character was the finished product of the Christian religion, and his loved ones have in that life an inheritance richer than if he had left them silver and gold, houses and lands. He knew what he believed, he believed what he believed and knew why he believed it. At one time he had fully decided in his own mind to dedicate his life to the preaching of the gospel but conditions changed his plans. Throughout his long life, however, by life and lip he was a mighty minister of the word. He was never at any time a slacker, that word is used surmising that there can be slackers in the church as well as in the nation, in the service of his Master. He was faithful in his attendance at Sunday school, church services and prayer meetings. When a young man, instead of exercising his gifts as a speaker in the home church where there were others capable of edifying the congregation, he would walk eleven miles after supper of Saturday nights that he might the next day tell the gospel story to the people of a neglected district, and throughout his long career as elder of the First Church, Milwaukee, he would, in the absence of his pastor, be called on frequently to speak to the congregation at the hour of their worship which he did invariably to their satisfaction. He was liberal in his offerings to his church and to all of its interests, was interested in every effort put forth to advance the Kingdom of his Lord, and no man, with a like amount of means ever entered the acquaintance of the writer who responded to so many what seemed to him worthy appeals.

Brother Trout leaves five children and all of them are active workers in the Church of Christ, and his grandchildren are falling in line as they reach that age. His two sons, Walter, of Lufkin, Texas and George, of Dayton, Ohio, and his three sons-in-law, O. W. Steindorf, Wheeling, West Virginia, I. W. Davis, and P. M. Norgaard, of Milwaukee, are all officers in the church. The father of W. H. Trout was a preacher but worked at the millwright trade to pay expenses. He had ten children, and every one of them, with their married partners, and their children are identified with the Christian Church, and now the great-grandchildren are following in the same path, and so far not one of the number has decided to be anything else than simply Christian.

Brother Trout's funeral was held at the First Church, October 15th, conducted by his pastor, assisted by Judge J. H. Stover and his frail body was laid to rest in Forest Home cemetery, to await the call of the resurrection.

C. L. MILTON, *Pastor*,
First Christian Church,
Milwaukee.

[FROM THE CHRISTIAN STANDARD, CINCINNATI, OHIO]

William Henry Trout

ON receiving a telegram from his daughter, telling me of the death, on October the 13th, of William Henry Trout of Milwaukee, Wisconsin, I sent a brief notice of the same to The Christian Standard. It is evident, however, that his life and character and his relations to the Church merit a more extended notice. William Henry Trout was born in Erin, Canada, of English and Scotch parentage, in the year 1834, hence he was 83 years old at the time of his death. His boyhood home was near Meaford, Canada.

In a book he wrote, and published only last year, entitled, "Trout Family History" he gives an interesting account of his school days in Hiram, Ohio. He attended there when Professor Thomas Munnell was the principal, and was there associated with my own brother William. He also gives an account of attending school at Williamsville, New York, when Professor Munnell was the principal and Joseph King and wife were his assistants.

In the book above alluded to Brother Trout speaks thus of his marriage: "In the early part of November, 1867, came the pre-arranged time for my marriage to the handsome, buoyant, good girl I had courted for nearly three years, Miss Jane Barclay Knowles." To this union eight children were given, five of whom are now living. A friend of many years' standing, of both Brother Trout and myself, writing me since his death says: "He was a man that took much satisfaction in his children, as was reasonable and just in his case, and no children could be more loyal to a father than were his." His wife preceded him to the Heavenly home many years, passing away at the close of December, 1898.

Brother Trout was a resident of Milwaukee for about a quarter of a century, and during many years of this time served the E. P. Allis Company as mechanical engineer and machinery designer, receiving the highest wages paid to any laborer, as his work required the very highest mechanical skill. Machinery now in use in the E. P. Allis works was not only drawn but designed by him. For many years he worked with intense zeal in this work of designing new forms of machinery. This might indicate that his time and thought were absorbed in this activity, but not so for his chief love and devotion were to his Church. In 1885 I was sent to Milwaukee to establish our Church in that city. We organized with nineteen members among whom were Brother Trout and his wife. At this organization he was elected an Elder, and in this capacity served the Church there until the close of his life.

In our struggle to establish the cause in Milwaukee the members were brought very close to each other, so that during all the intervening years we have continued the intimate friendships thus formed. Among these Brother Trout held a high place. To all our deliberations he not only brought wisdom of the highest order but cheer and encouragement. While charitable to all, he firmly believed in "Our Plea" and stood ready for its defense at all times, and used his wide influence for its advancement. It was a great joy to him to see our feeble beginning in the city of Milwaukee grow into two Churches, each with a fine house of worship, and an aggregate membership of nearly one thousand.

How I wish I had the power to paint his character in words so that all might know it as I do! The friend already quoted also wrote:

"You knew him well in the past. There was a steadiness in his character that left little room for change from year to year. Something seemed a little out of gear if he were not in his place at every service." How true this was for the two years when I served the Church, and how I prized his presence when I was preaching! Before I commenced a sermon I glanced to see if he were in his accustomed place. He seemed to listen with all his mind and soul. Brother Trout was always welcome, he was welcome in all meetings of worship, for he was always devout, he was welcome in Church Board meetings, for he was wise; he was welcome among the young people, for he was always young in spirit; he was welcome to those in sorrow, for he was truly sympathetic.

He was so kindly in spirit that even those who differed with him admired him. He had a very large circle of friends. One of these friendships, extending from early days until the close of life, was with a man of note—the late John Muir, naturalist, explorer and author. And many other friends he had will miss him from now on along earth's ways.

The love I had for him, when so closely associated with him, has not been dimmed by the years which have come and gone since that time. He so impressed himself upon my life that he will endure until the close.

Who can measure the power for good, for the Church of Christ, for righteousness, of such a life as his?

C. C. SMITH.

Melrose Avenue,
Cincinnati, Ohio.

From the AMERICAN LUMBERMAN]

William Henry Trout

THE death was announced late last week of W. H. Trout, of Milwaukee, Wisconsin, October 13th. Mr. Trout was born in 1834 in Canada and was reared in that country. He went to Milwaukee in 1884 and entered the employ of the Edward P. Allis Co., later the Allis-Chalmers Co., and was the head designer of the sawmill department until seven years ago, when he retired. Mr. Trout had always been associated with the sawmill business, getting his start in Canada, and was in the milling business himself at one time. He began the designing of sawmill machinery in the early seventies. At one time John Muir, the naturalist, was associated with him in the sawmill business in lower Canada.

Mr. Trout was the owner of a number of patents on sawmill machinery, many of which are now in use in the larger and best mills of the country. One of his important inventions was the Trout power set works, extensively used now practically everywhere where sawmills are built. Within the last few years he sold many of his patents, devoting the proceeds from the sales largely to the Christian Church and its societies of which he was a member. He was an active and constant church worker.

Five children survive the deceased. They are: Walter C. Trout, Lufkin, Texas; George H. Trout, Dayton, Ohio; Mrs. I. W. Davis, Milwaukee, Wisconsin; Mrs. P. N. Norgaard, Milwaukee, Wisconsin; and Mrs. O. W. Steindorf, Wheeling, West Virginia. Mr. Trout's funeral took place Monday, October 15th.

ALEXANDER NISBET

SUSAN TROUT NISBET

ALEXANDER NISBET, JR., AND EMMA L. NISBET

MRS. MARY NISBET HAMILTON

CONTINUOUS
FAMILY RECORDS

MAN'S NAME

Born_____________Died_____________

Marriage Date_____________

MAIDEN'S NAME

Born_____________Died_____________

Special Family Events or Notes_____________

NAMES OF CHILDREN	BIRTH	DEATH

NOTE: One of the children on this page may be a married partner on the next page.